Justice, Ideology, and Education

An Introduction to the Social Foundations of Education

Justice, Ideology, and Education

An Introduction to the Social Foundations of Education

SECOND EDITION

Edward Stevens, Jr.
Ohio University

George H. Wood
Ohio University

McGRAW-HILL, INC.
New York   St. Louis   San Francisco   Auckland   Bogotá
Caracas   Lisbon   London   Madrid   Mexico   Milan
Montreal   New Delhi   Paris   San Juan
Singapore   Sydney   Tokyo   Toronto

This book was developed by Lane Akers, Inc.

Justice, Ideology, and Education:
An Introduction to the Social Foundations of Education

3 4 5 6 7 8 9 0 DOC DOC 9 0 9 8 7 6 5 4 3 2

ISBN 0-07-061267-6

This book was set in Palatino by General Graphic
Services, Inc.
The editor was Lane Akers;
the production supervisor was Annette Mayeski.
Cover design was done by Caliber/Phoenix Color Corp.
Project supervision was done by The Total Book.
R. R. Donnelley & Sons Company was printer and binder.

Library of Congress Cataloging-in-Publication Data

Justice, ideology, and education: an introduction to the social
foundations of education / [compiled by] Edward Stevens, Jr., George
H. Wood. — 2nd ed.
    p.   cm.
  Includes bibliographical references and index.
  ISBN 0-07-061267-6
  1. Educational sociology—United States.   2. Education—Social
aspects—United States.   3. Educational equalization—United States.
4. Education—United States—Aims and objectives.   I. Stevens,
Edward, (date).   II. Wood, George H. (George Harrison).
LC191.4.J87   1992
370.19'0973—dc20   91-30419

For our children

Contents

Chapter 4

PART THREE
Schooling and Ideology

Chapter 5

Chapter 6

Chapter 7

Chapter 12

Chapter 13

Foreword

Justice, ideology, and education are provocative words in the English language. Volumes have been written on each of these terms, and we still argue vehemently about what each of them means.

Who should decide the purposes of schools? Does it make a difference what kinds of schools exist for different students? How is justice a dominant consideration in providing schooling? What ideologies lie behind our efforts at mass education, and which ideologies are to be taught? How do the current reforms in education fit with our traditions—most particularly, our traditional ideology of democracy and its attendant concern for justice? Why does the pressure for "excellence" in school reform literature pose serious justice problems for a democracy?

Democracy is hard work. It can be time consuming; decisions can be difficult and may not be wise; and it can certainly be frustrating and imperfect. Yet the major political documents in societies of the modern world proclaim democracy as the best available way to operate a government. Even highly authoritarian national governments publicly support the concept of democracy, although they fall far short in the practice.

The point here is that belief in the idea, the ideology, of democracy is widely accepted. It is predicated on the concept that people are capable of self-governance. This powerful concept has two extremely important features that this book addresses: justice and education. Justice is basic to the idea of democracy: Can one imagine real democracy without respect for the rights of others? There is a presumption that fair treatment in some form is necessary, although there are many disputes over what justice is and how it should operate. Education, like justice, is fundamental to the idea of democracy. Self-governance requires knowledgeable people; ignorance is inconsistent with democracy. Justice, ideology, and education are intertwined, and they are individually and jointly debatable concepts.

Not only are the concepts of justice, ideology, and education of concern to societies, they are also reflected in individual viewpoints. I like to think that justice is on my side in a debate on social policy; income tax, affirmative action, and abortion policies raise such debates. I like to believe that the ideologies that undergird my views in a dispute about politics are clearly superior to those of my opponent. And, of course, I expect my ideas about a proper education to have wide support among those who have been properly educated. It is often a surprise to me to discover that strongly held opposing arguments can also find their roots in justice, high-minded ideologies, and excellent education. That internal confrontation is the essence of education, including education about schooling. This book poses many schooling issues in this context.

Professors Stevens and Wood provide a challenge here, in original essays and in the words of significant writers over a long period of time, to consider the state of our schools in terms of justice, ideology, and education.

Jack Nelson
RUTGERS UNIVERSITY

Preface

The beliefs that underlie the theory and practice of American education are deeply ingrained in our culture. They affect our expectations for students, the way we organize curriculum and instruction, the decisions we make about school funding, and our judgments about the contributions of education to the national welfare. In addition, they shape our views on how people should be treated, how the rewards and benefits of education should be distributed, and who should make decisions about education.

When a system of beliefs functions to shape people's behaviors, to give them direction, and effectively acts to exclude other beliefs, we call that system an ideology. In American education the concepts of merit, opportunity, and equality together form an ideology that has helped to shape virtually every dimension of public schooling. Our beliefs about fairness and social justice in American democracy are organized around the concepts of merit, opportunity, and equality. These same concepts also determine much of what we think about how schools should be organized and how the outcomes of education should be evaluated. In this book we examine both the beliefs that make up an ideology of American education and how that ideology helps to determine the outcomes of education.

Two questions have guided our thinking about the educational issues presented in this book. The first is, Who makes decisions about schools and about how children are treated when in school? The second question is, Are the processes and outcomes of these decisions fair or just? Responses to the first question have to do with authority and power and how they are distributed in the decision-making process. The second question has to do with our ideals of individual and social justice.

The concepts of justice, authority, and power must be understood in some social context. They are, moreover, closely linked in practice. The principles of justice in a society help define the rights and obligations of people relative to each other and to the social institutions of which they are a part. These same principles define to whom and for what society's rewards ought to be distributed.

Fairness, itself, is often considered a part of justice. A situation is usually considered fair when no one feels exploited by participating in it or denied some legitimate claim.[1] Fairness, then, is very much a matter of common expectations as to how people will be treated. People feel unfairly or unjustly treated when agreed-upon expectations are not fulfilled or when those in authority deny them their due. Quite clearly, then, injustice may occur through delinquent or abusive authority. It may also occur when those in authority are not recognized as having a right to that authority or when their decisions are out of keeping with the rules most people accept.

In education, as in other social institutions, authority and justice are closely linked. Parents, children, and political leaders have certain expectations for what schools should accomplish and implicitly recognize certain legitimate means for achieving these. Virtually everyone recognizes schools as institutions that dispense credits that can be redeemed later for economic and social rewards. Everyone recognizes also that the public school serves a larger public interest as well as the interests of individuals. Because public schools are called upon to serve so many individual, group, and public interests, questions of individual fairness and social justice often arise.

Each of the sections in this book relates selected educational issues to the broader themes of individual and social justice. Thus issues having to do with equal opportunity, evaluation, student classification, curriculum, the politics of schooling, and democracy in schooling are all seen in the light of a broader concern with justice.

Part One (Chapters 1 and 2) focuses on the concept and practice of equal opportunity, including its relationship to the ideals of meritocracy and social utility and its application to minority groups in American culture. A historical overview is provided that introduces the students to issues of justice and fairness and how these have been played out in the legal system and legislative action.

Part Two (Chapters 3 and 4) addresses the ways in which American public schooling has dealt with human diversity. Race, ethnicity, socioeconomic strati-fication, sex-role socialization, and gender are dealt with in the contexts of literacy and language acquisition and tracking. The readings provide a close-up and sometimes personal view of these issues.

In Part Three (Chapters 5 through 7) the concept of ideology is examined in detail as are its implications for the curriculum of the public schools. These chapters deal at length with citizenship and the quest for efficiency in the management of public schooling. The shaping of behavior through the structure of the school and curriculum is foremost in our concerns as we look at the school as a culture within which students' expectations for themselves and others are formed.

Our concerns in Part Four (Chapters 8 through 10) cut across the ways in which the bureaucratic structure of schools has influenced educational decision making and the dilemmas this raises for those interested in local control, more "choice," and democratic decision making. Here we deal broadly with the problems of whom should the public schools serve.

---

[1]John Rawls, "Symposium: Justice as Fairness," *Journal of Philosophy* 54 (Oct. 1957): 657.

The final section of the book (Chapters 11 through 13) focuses on proposals for reform in the 1980s. Like previous sections, it begins with a historical overview: a summary view of reforms from the 1890s, the Progressive Era, and the 1950s. The common element of reforms in these watershed periods—debate over the role of schooling in the civic and economic welfare of the nation—is then traced through to proposals of the 1980s. Issues of efficiency, quality, equity, and elitism are examined critically, and alternatives to present dominant trends are considered. Our discussion of current issues in education concludes by asking students to reconsider the historic conceptions of schooling in the United States and how they might aid in the resolution of current issues. We ask, also, that students critically reexamine the ideological foundations of American education to see how they converge with—and diverge from—democratic ideals.

McGraw-Hill and the authors would like to thank Denise Davis, John Carroll University; Robert Fenske, Arizona State University; and Max Kopilman, Hunter College, for their reviews of this manuscript.

Edward Stevens, Jr.
George H. Wood

Justice, Ideology, and Education

An Introduction to the Social Foundations of Education

PART ONE

Schooling and Justice

1

Equality, Opportunity, and Justice

The central purpose of this chapter is to show the ways in which debates about education are related to concerns about social justice and equality. In considering how fairness, social justice, and education are related, we must deal with the purposes of schooling and education, how people expect to be treated, and how they actually are treated. Many issues, even when they appear to be limited to instruction, curriculum, and testing, actually involve questions of justice and fairness. Thus, for example, measures of achievement and aptitude, methods of instruction, and the grouping and classification of students are often based on particular conceptions of what is right or what is fair. Issues directly related to equal opportunity, the rights of the handicapped, bilingualism, and sex equity are more obviously related to the problem of achieving social justice in society.

Many of the ways in which we think about the problem of fairness and justice today were formulated by Aristotle in his treatise on ethics written in the fourth century B.C. The end of justice, said Aristotle, is to "produce and preserve the happiness of the social and political community."[1] It is the good of others, he pointed out, that is sought through justice.

Aristotle claimed there were two basic standards of reference for justice. The first, he said, was justice in relation to law. In the United States, for example, parties to a legal case are treated as equals, and the law must determine if someone has been wronged and how to rectify the situation. Justice, understood in this way, is the correct application of law so that arbitrariness and favoritism will be avoided.

The second standard of reference of which Aristotle spoke was justice in the sense of having one's fair share. Aristotle explained the idea of a fair distribution in terms of proportion. He argued that there should be the same equality between what is distributed, such as material goods, as there is between persons themselves. Equal persons receive equal shares, and unequal persons receive unequal shares. In other words, "to each according to his deserts." The relationships between the idea of equality and the idea of justice is thus a close one historically and remains so today.

The principles laid down are very straightforward, but as Aristotle realized, not everyone agrees on how we decide who and what *deserves* to be rewarded. This, of course, is still the problem today when we attempt to determine what shall be rewarded. What knowledge, skills, or personal characteristics will count the most in determining who will get the scarce resources of a society? Will it be IQ, achievement, productivity? And how, for example, will a person's need be considered when distributing rewards or benefits?

In the case of education we have to ask, At what levels are educational needs to be provided for by a society? If education is considered necessary to good social order and political survival, for instance, then at what level and at what cost should it be offered? If education, on the other hand, is an item for consumption like other consumption items, such as cars or TVs, then there may be no obligation to offer it at all, or it may be appropriate simply to offer it to the highest bidder. It is easy to see that we are faced with a series of issues related to the level of education desirable in a society and the fairness with which it is distributed. To address these issues, we will next look at three basic concepts that have guided our thinking about education and justice in the United States: merit, equality, and opportunity.

MERIT, EQUALITY, AND OPPORTUNITY

Merit

In the United States the relationship between education and the problem of justice has usually been seen in terms of the concepts of merit, equality, and opportunity. Merit is important because it is often used as a criterion for determining one's "just deserts." It is often assumed that just rewards are made proportional to merit.

The concept of a society based on merit (a *meritocracy*) evolved historically as a reaction to aristocratic theories and practices, which assumed that rewards should be based on inherited social status and wealth. The idea of merit, on the other hand, rested on the assumption that the individual is free and capable of making decisions in his or her best interests. That is, the individual is free to choose and is morally responsible for that choice. In a meritocratic society it is effort and achievement that should be rewarded, providing the purposes and outcomes of the choices are worthy of reward.

The analogy most often used to illustrate the concept of meritocracy is that of a foot race. The assumption is that life is like a race with winners and losers, but with certain guarantees that the race will be run fairly. As in a race, it is performance that counts. The runners have talent and they work hard at what they do, but it is the combination of the two (talent and effort) that produces a winner. *Why* some finish and some win while others drop out and lose is not crucial to the idea of merit, although it is important to making a judgment about whether the race was won fairly.

Even though the analogy of a race is simplistic and does not begin to describe the complex situation we call life, let us assume that in the race for status, wealth, and honor there are winners and losers and that merit has something to do with the outcome of the race. If we assume that fair play is important and that the rewards for performance are "just" rewards, then we must ask questions about the *sources* of effort and talent and possible obstacles to a fair race. For example, is talent mostly a matter of genetics or environment, and if so, should an individual be rewarded when, in fact, the race was stacked in his favor at the outset? Are discrimination, favoritism, or poverty practically unsurmountable obstacles to the winning of the race? These questions will receive greater attention in the pages that follow.

Equal Opportunity

Proponents of meritocracy insist that some approximation of equal opportunity to win the race should exist. They see equal educational opportunity as a precondition for equal opportunity in general. They have a tremendous faith in the efficacy of education to break down barriers to equal opportunity and to create an environment that will stimulate talent and shape attitudes necessary to putting forth maximum effort. Can education, and more specifically the school, really do this? In a society in which cultural backgrounds are diverse, in which there is a tremendous range in wealth, in which the means for discovering and assessing talent are imperfect, and in which all may not agree that life is a race, to what extent can the school really help guarantee that the race is fair, that justice will be done, and that the rewards will go to the most deserving? These are questions that should receive a great deal of attention, especially when educational reform is on national and state political agendas.

Our current way of thinking about equal opportunity and equal educational opportunity is of recent origin. Its modern foundation, however, lies in seventeenth- and eighteenth-century liberalism. The liberal ideal emerged as a challenge to inherited wealth and status and the seemingly arbitrary authority that accompanied them. Thus one of the enduring concerns of the liberal ideal of equality has been that historical inequalities not be perpetuated from generation to generation. There is, in effect, an assumption that talent and ability are widely distributed and do not belong only to a privileged class.

Equal opportunity is a term now commonly associated with economic opportunity rather than political opportunity. Prior to the late eighteenth century it was rare to find educators speaking in terms of the economic benefits of schooling. The coming of the industrial revolution and the decline in importance of the family as the primary economic (production) unit, however, set the stage for greater concern about opportunity. Greater occupational mobility and the emergence of major economic (employing) institutions—corporations and large manufacturing concerns—beyond the family brought to the fore the importance of education to the national economic interest.

Nineteenth-century educational reformers in the United States were aware of the disadvantages under which children of the poor labored. Part of their intent was to offer such children greater opportunity for upward economic mobility. This concern was motivated both by humanitarian reasons and by a commitment to basic capitalist values and a capitalist system of production. The availability of education was the main concern in this early concept of equal educational opportunity. In the early nineteenth century, parents were not required to send their children to school. The role of the school was relatively passive, and the burden for taking advantage of the opportunity for schooling was on the family and the child. The coming of mass elementary schooling followed by compulsory attendance laws activated the school's role in offering equal educational opportunity.[2]

With the rapid expansion of education at the secondary level in the early twentieth century, it became evident that the common curriculum was out of step with the realities of the occupational futures for most children. Most children were not college-bound, and the traditional liberal arts and language-oriented curriculum of nineteenth-century secondary schools lacked relevancy for large numbers of children. Different "children had different occupational futures and equality of opportunity required providing different curricula for each type of student."[3] In other words, equal educational opportunity for an individual did not mean the *same* opportunity but opportunity that was fair relative to the type of student. Whether or not this was fair is highly questionable. As we shall see in Chapter 4, methods for classifying students and tracking them toward certain occupations were highly suspect.

Most thinking about equal educational opportunity in the first half of the twentieth century focused on providing students with educational opportunities that related to their future occupations. The development of the comprehensive high school with its differentiated curriculum (tracks and homogeneous groups) was seen by many as a way of bringing students of different ethnic and socioeconomic backgrounds together while at the same time differentiating among them for purposes of instruction.

It was not until the issue of racial equality was raised and the *Brown* decision was handed down by the United States Supreme Court in 1954 that Americans were forced toward some basic reconsiderations of what it means to have equal educational opportunity. It was in this case that the "separate but equal doctrine" (different but comparable schools for different races) was declared unconstitutional. The *Brown* decision represented a fundamental shift in thinking about equality of educational opportunity. Prior to *Brown,* the emphasis had been on the "inputs" or resources of schooling. Gradually, emphasis shifted to the effects ("outputs") of schooling. Inputs such as teacher and program quality and facilities have remained important concerns for assuring equality of educational opportunity, but the gradual ascendency of the output view has created a new agenda for educators—for example, competency testing—and has given the problem of educational accountability new prominence.

Rethinking the Ideas of Opportunity and Merit

The concepts of merit and equality of opportunity just described were generally accepted by the American public. This is still the case. Their prominence, however, should not lead us to accept them uncritically. Since the era of civil rights and equity legislation beginning in the early 1960s, there has been renewed debate over the time-honored concepts of merit and equal opportunity and about liberalism as a theory of social justice. We begin our reexamination by looking at the work of American philosopher John Rawls, which expresses the rethinking of basic liberal ideals without abandoning them.

Rawls argued that an *un*just society is not worth having. Justice, he said, does not depend on particular social norms or particular social purposes established by groups in a society. Even the general welfare of the society cannot override the individual's right to justice. When speaking of Rawls's theory, Michael Sandel observes that the rules of social cooperation must be established in such a way that "each person will have the fullest liberty to realize his aims and purposes compatible with an equal liberty for others."[4]

Even though Rawls's own thinking was very much indebted to the liberal tradition, he made a strong challenge to our usual way of thinking about meritocracy. In his major work entitled *A Theory of Justice* (1971), Rawls contended that to allow a "natural" system of rewards to emerge on the basis of individual talent and effort is morally *in*defensible. Even if equal opportunity is present in the sense of formal (legal) defenses against cheating or discrimination, the reward system is unfair, said Rawls. This is so because rewards are made on the basis of talents, characteristics, attitudes, and so forth that are controlled by factors (genetic and environmental) unrelated to an individual's choices. In other words, we do not deserve to be rewarded for characteristics that were an accident of birth. Thus, said Rawls, we must move beyond equal opportunity to a system that compensates or corrects for at least social and cultural disadvantages.

Rawls advocated a concept of sharing talent which assumed that there is a diversity of talents (assets) in the population. The benefits of these ought to be shared, he argued, in the pursuit of common purposes. Strangely, Rawls observed, there is no real basis for a person's deserving something at all. Instead, he said, social institutions set up expectations so that people receive benefits if they fulfill them. The real point of distributing society's benefits is *not* to reward deserving individuals for the characteristics or talents they possess; rather the system used to distribute the benefits is intended to facilitate the development of talents or resources that will serve the common interest.[5]

Rawls's theory of justice has come under attack by critics who claim that his idea of sharing would result in the exploitation of individuals having talents by those who do not have them. According to Robert Nozick there is another, less literal, way of thinking about talent and ability. Nozick argues that even though an individual may not *deserve* his or her talents, he or she nonetheless *has* them and is certainly entitled to benefit from them, at least more than anyone else. This is referred to as an "entitlement" theory of benefits. Talents and abilities cannot really be separated from the individual who has them. What is most important, explains Nozick, is the way the benefits came about—the way in which the individual was involved in their acquisition. If the way was just, then the individual deserves the benefits.

Nozick's position is a conservative apology for basing the distribution and worth of rewards and benefits in a society on the value of talents and skills in the free market. What he wishes to preserve is individual choice, and he wishes to make the distribution of benefits come from choices, not from some pattern imposed by government, for instance.[6] The benefits that come from an individual's talents and abilities, says Nozick, should go to that individual.

A third way of thinking about rewards and benefits is from the utilitarian position. It is different from both Rawls's and Nozick's positions, but it has much in common with the latter because it focuses on free choice and the benefits coming from the value of talents in the market place. The utilitarian ideal sees individual choice in terms of pleasure and pain so that the measure of what is best or good for the individual is that which leads to the most pleasure. When we judge the goodness of a society in general, we ask whether there is more pleasure or more pain in it.

In determining the goodness (justice) of a society, it is the average "utility" (happiness) that counts. From this point of view, a just society is one that distributes rewards and benefits so that the result will be the highest average utility. Following the example of Kenneth Strike, Table 1 gives an example of the great inequalities that could be present even when the average happiness is maximized. In a three-person society, one individual might have 2 units of happiness, another 3 units and another 10 units. In this situation, the third person is a lot happier than the first or second person. The table contrasts this hypothetical society with another in which the individuals have 5, 5, and 4 units of happiness respectively.

Though there are large inequalities in Society I (Person C has five times as much happiness as Person A), the average utility (5) exceeds that of Society II (4.7). Therefore, from the standpoint of average utility, Society I is the better choice. This is the society, however, in which both inequality and maximum utility are greater.[7]

For the utilitarian, the best outcome is achieved in the free market where the most valuable talents, labor, or products are rewarded. Thus the utilitarian argues that equal opportunity in a free market will result in the best possible

TABLE 1   An Illustration of Average Utility

	Units of Happiness	
	Society I	Society II
Person A	2	5
Person B	3	5
Person C	10	4
Average Utility	5	4.7

(optimal) distribution of rewards. Though some individuals may get very little out of the system of rewards, the *average* utility will be higher.

Because the ideal of merit is central to many educational issues, we should view our commitment to it critically. Some strong objections may be made to the meritocratic ideal in general and the concept of justice and fairness to which it is linked. These might begin with the challenge that there is no such thing as a free individual who, despite all obstacles, ultimately makes his or her own choices. The challenge here would be that individuality and the supposed freedom accompanying it always arise within some environment.

The argument would continue by pointing out that we are products of a set of circumstances, events, and influences. What we think of as freedom may be only the influence of a particular environment, such as wealthy parents and elite schools. Perhaps we are free only to the extent that the experiences and social and material conditions of our existence allow us to be free. We have only what our environment allows us to have. Under these conditions, the way we behave (our performances, successes, and failures) is very much the product of our environment. Thus children who grow up in an environment of poverty have severe limitations on their freedom of choice compared to those who grow up in an environment of abundance. To claim that we have really accomplished anything on our own is simply an illusion. Most of the credit ought to go to the people and circumstances that made us what we are.

This type of argument is a very basic challenge to the ideal of justice and meritocracy that is commonplace to us. Yet it must be seriously considered, for it shakes the foundations of our educational ideals and policy. There is a basic tension in the ideal of justice when it is understood as part of the tradition of liberalism. The tension may be expressed by the following question: In considerations of justice, which is to take priority, equality or the larger social good? This is a philosophic not a legal question, for it is assumed that equality before the law (fair administration of justice) exists. It is a question every educational institution and system of government must face.

RESPONSES TO EDUCATIONAL INEQUALITIES

Having set forth some of the basic dilemmas we must face when dealing with questions of individual fairness and social justice, we can now view the problem historically to see how American society has worked out these matters in the past. It is important to realize that matters of equality, fairness, and justice are not simply worked out in the abstract. They are filtered through the realities of history and human behavior. For this reason some historical background is necessary to fully appreciate their significance.

Equality, Race, and Integration

The issues involving the relationships between education and race are a direct outgrowth of the ideas of equality and opportunity. Fueled by long-standing civil rights abuses, issues of equality and race came to the forefront of American education in the 1950s and led to judicial intervention in the schooling process. To understand the recent history of the concept of equal educational opportunity, we must place it within the historical context of racism in the United States.

The psychology of racism is complex, but the facts of racism are easily identifiable and explainable. If blacks in the South had ever been able to show their real strength in numbers at the polls, the process of governance in the South would have been drastically altered. For years, literacy tests, poll taxes, white primaries, gerrymanded voting districts to dilute the black vote, and grandfather clauses had disfranchised blacks and kept political control in the hands of whites. Segregated schooling, and in many cases no schooling for blacks, was a simple extension of the policy of exclusion and disfranchisement in the political arena.

The constitutional mandate to desegregate schools was laid down in *Brown v. Board of Education of Topeka* (1954). In *Brown* the Court was faced with an extremely difficult fact-finding situation regarding the psychological effects of racial segregation. The Court concluded that children were indeed deprived of equal educational opportunity by virtue of their segregation. Segregation by race, said the Court, "generates a feeling of inferiority as to their status in the community that may affect their hearts and minds in a way unlikely ever to be undone." The United States Supreme Court explicitly rejected the *Plessy v. Ferguson* decision, which had stood since 1896, and concluded the "doctrine of 'separate-but-equal' has no place."[8]

Not every county or region was affected in the same way by the *Brown* decision. White politicians in so-called black belts of the South were intransigent in their opposition to integration. The United States Supreme Court and the federal judiciary system walked a fine line between pushing too hard, which would have led to widespread violence, and pushing too little, which would have resulted in only token desegregation.[9]

The years immediately following the landmark decision of *Brown* served to highlight the absence of equality of educational opportunity and the miserable performance of public schools in addressing great discrepancies in academic achievement between white and black children. The racism inherent in segregated schools before 1954 persisted in the decade following. Across the South and Southwest, achievement tests in reading showed black youth in the elementary grades lagging behind white youth by one to three and a half grade levels. A similar pattern was apparent in mathematics. The Commission on Civil Rights reported in 1962 that black students lagged one to two grade levels behind white students. Desegregated schools responded to these differences in achievement by "initiating or expanding grouping and tracking systems." The results were there for all to see: college preparatory tracks were almost all white, while basic tracks were mainly black.[10]

In the North, black children had long attended segregated schools that were "systematically inferior." One researcher estimated that in 1952 "about a fourth of black school children in northern elementary schools and about half in high school were 'physically integrated'." Throughout the 1950s and early 1960s segregated schooling increased, sometimes as a result of residential segregation but more commonly as a result of gerrymandering school boundaries. The list of cities in which systematic segregation was present was long, with the cases of Detroit, Philadelphia, New York, St. Louis, Oak Park Michigan, Berkeley, California, Portland, Oregon, Bridgeport, Connecticut, and Chicago being the most publicized and documented.[11]

As in the South, some of the segregation was "by school," but the more insidious was within. In St. Louis schools all high school students were distributed in one of three tracks. Comparisons of black and white students showed that in predominantly black schools the numbers in the lowest track were six times the number in predominantly white schools. Standardized achievement tests given in the cities mentioned above consistently reported black students lagging one to one and a half grade levels behind white students.[12]

Following passage of the 1964 Civil Rights Act, attacks on segregated schools began anew. Both the Department of Justice and the Department of Health, Education, and Welfare (HEW) took on the task of integration. In the process they offended many recalcitrant local school districts where racism was deeply embedded in community values. These districts often could not demonstrate that they had actually produced a racial mix in their schools.

Meyer Weinberg has pointed out that in the four years following the passage of the 1964 Civil Rights Act much more desegregation occurred than in the years spanning the period from *Brown* to the Civil Rights Act itself. In the latter years of the 1960s, boycotts, sit-ins, demonstrations, and picketing protested segregated schools in unprecedented numbers. The social drama played out on the stage of desegregation also was accompanied by an important shift in the thinking of the federal courts.

Using the Fourteenth Amendment of the United States Constitution, *Brown* had forbid states to compel or authorize segregation of public schools. Yet the reasoning in *Brown* was basically negative in that it forbid the state to force children to attend segregated schools. For years this was interpreted by other courts to mean "state neutrality allowing 'freedom of choice.'" Gradually, however, neutrality shifted to affirmative action. The key case in this important shift in constitutional doctrine was *Green v. County School Board of New Kent County* (1968). The court in this case ruled that school boards have "the affirmative duty to take whatever steps might be necessary to convert to a unitary system in which racial discrimination would be eliminated root and branch."[13] *Alexander v. Holmes County Board of Education* (1969) reaffirmed the obligation of every school district to terminate dual school systems.[14] This was followed in 1971 by the famous *Swann v. Charlotte-Mecklenberg Board of Education* case, which spoke specifically to the connection between residential segregation and school segregation. The court did not allow administrative convenience or residential patterns to interfere with the necessity to achieve fairness.[15]

When the course of desegregation litigation made its way to large urban areas—in both the South and the North—it faced a problem that, although legally similar, was qualitatively and quantitatively different. Patterns of segregated housing and deeply entrenched loyalties to neighborhood schools made pupil reassignment exceedingly difficult. Arguments in favor of the strategy of busing seemed commonsensical but, in fact, had little intellectual or practical merit, since they did not attack the problem of racism at its more basic psychological and cultural levels. It was busing as an issue that brought to light the depth of racism in American life.

In 1972, the percentages of black schoolchildren in selected cities attending schools with more than 50 percent black students were: New York, 83.5 percent; Los Angeles, 91.9 percent; Chicago, 98.3 percent; Philadelphia, 93.3 percent; and Detroit, 92.8 percent.[16] One of the most widely publicized failures to integrate schools in a northern city emerged from Judge W. Arthur Garrity's 1974 finding of intentional school segregation in the city of Boston. South Boston and Charlestown turned out to be the major problems and represented in stark form the distinct and divisive ethnic, racial, religious, and socioeconomic residential divisions in this historic city.

With the opening of school in September 1974, integration proceeded peacefully in most of Boston, but the pairing of South Boston High (Irish) and Roxbury (black) for purposes of busing led to violence and public expression of racial hatred in these two areas. The violence did not subside quickly and continued into the second year (second phase) of the integration plan, when mandatory busing affected approximately 21,000 students. The seemingly inevitable "white flight" began and continued during the period from 1974 to 1976. Students, indeed, did ride buses, but many also chose (with the support of their parents) absenteeism or enrollment in nonpublic schools as better alternatives.[17]

The years 1974 and 1978 were peak periods for school desegregation cases, but overall there has been a steady decline since 1975. Melvin Jarvis has pointed out that the reason for this probably stems from decisions by federal courts to "relinquish their supervision over the districts which still had suits pending."[18] In effect these decisions meant that the Supreme Court and appellate courts no longer saw a constitutional obligation to be involved.

By the end of the 1970s a general change in the public's attitude toward integrated schools was observable in the South. In 1959 opinion polls registered a 72 percent white opposition rate to integration, even when only a few blacks were attending. By 1975 only 15 percent of the whites polled opposed integration. Even when those polled were asked if they objected to integration when a school was "half" black, the opposition rate still dropped from 83 to 38 percent in these years. It is significant, though, that whites overwhelmingly rejected busing as a way to achieve integration. They did so by 75 to 80 percent.[19]

The situation in the North, particularly the Northeast, showed continued resistance to desegregation. As in the South, opposition to busing was widespread. A variety of factors contributed to this, including discrimination in location of new schools, resistance to changing "neighborhood" school policy after a segregated school system had developed, and school board failure to adopt proposed integration plans. These factors, however, overlaid major demographic changes that altered the black-white ratios of central cities. Whites increasingly moved to suburbs, and cities in the Northeast became increasingly black. Not all cities, of course, were affected equally by these changes. Some, particularly in the Northwest, had small minority constituencies. These were desegregated easily. In others, white flight was accompanied by black flight—middle-class and professional blacks moving out of the inner city—so that the major problem became poverty, not racism.[20]

The issue of busing and attempts to desegregate American schools forced Americans to reconsider the purposes of American public schooling. Because busing collided with residential patterns—which were, in turn, the basis for neighborhood schools—school officials, parents, and courts had to consider the more basic problem of justice in America and how that ideal was to be reconciled with freedom of choice and community values. Despite the centralization of authority at the state level and large amounts of federal funding for education, the school itself is perceived by many to be an extension of family and community life. As such, it is thought to represent the values embedded in them. (It is interesting that in many cases resegregation within schools occurs once desegregation has taken place). Historically, the school has paid tribute to the meritocratic ideal with its emphasis on fair play and just rewards. Yet that ideal itself has seldom transcended the community values of which it is a part.

The history of education for Mexican Americans was marked by many of the same difficulties as for African Americans. Even though "Mexican American" is an ethnic not a racial classification, federal courts, for purposes of education, treated ethnicity in the same manner as race. In *Cisneros v. Corpus Christi Independent School District* (1970) Mexican Americans were identified as an "ethnic minority with a past pattern of discrimination." In *United States Texas Education Agency* (1972) a federal appeals court, referring to *Brown*, said: "We see no reason to believe that ethnic segregation is any less detrimental than racial segregation."[21]

Separate and inferior school facilities, refusal to acknowledge Spanish as a "legitimate" language of instruction, and discriminatory practices in grouping and tracking had been present since the early twentieth century at least.[22] In many instances no schooling was provided for Mexican Americans. The case of Texas is well documented for the twentieth century. Not unexpectedly, says Meyer, "deprivation and failure were built into the Texas public school system." Ability grouping was a persistent feature of public schooling that adversely affected Mexican-American children.[23]

The long history of inequitable treatment and segregation resulting in high secondary school dropout rates and low scores on reading achievement tests were documented in the six-volume United States Civil Rights Commission report titled *Mexican American Education Study* (1971–1974).[24] The commission concluded that the education of Mexican Americans had been characterized by:

> (1) a high degree of segregation, (2) extremely low academic achievement, (3) a predominance of exclusionary practices by schools, and (4) a discriminatory use of public finance.[25]

Public financing, it said, was discriminatory because it:

> (1) implicitly assumed that Mexican-American children required no more than Anglo children; (2) guaranteed, nevertheless that Anglo children would receive

significantly more from the state; and (3) forced heavy dependence on local property taxes that were incapable of supporting equal, let alone equitable, expenditures.[26]

EXTENDING *BROWN*

Funding

Today, virtually no part of the educational process is untouched by some major court decision involving equal opportunity and equity. In fact, virtually every important aspect of school policy has been affected by federal court decisions. In a recent study of the impact of federal court intervention in public education, Jarvis notes that in the ten-year period from 1973 to 1982, there were at least 1,370 important cases (137 per year) affecting the "organization, administration and programs of the public schools."[27] This astonishing figure should give pause to anyone considering the degree to which local school systems guide the education of their students. In the succeeding pages we will take a brief historical look at the ways in which litigation has affected dimensions of the equality of opportunity problem other than segregation.

Following litigation over segregation, it took little time for issues of equity to appear that were related to school funding. There was an assault on uneven pupil expenditures within school districts and among school districts within the same state. In *Hobson v. Hansen II* (1971) a federal court addressed the problem of unequal funding within the Washington, D.C., school district by ordering the following:

> Per pupil expenditures for all teachers' salaries and benefits from the regular D.C. budget in any elementary school shall not deviate more than plus and minus five percent from the mean of all elementary schools.[28]

Problems with equity in funding were apparent in a number of states. Courts in New Jersey, California, and Connecticut all presumed a relationship between cost and quality. They reasoned that disparities in funding caused disparities in quality and therefore contributed to unequal educational opportunities. Costs and quality were *not* presumed to be causally related by courts in Texas, Idaho, Oregon, and Washington. Thus, court decisions about equity in funding differed from state to state.

The best known of these cases were *Serrano v. Priest* (1971) in California and *San Antonio v. Rodriguez* (1973) in Texas, where the state system of school financing was challenged. In *Serrano v. Priest* the California Supreme Court decided that the state's system of financing public education, discriminated against pupils in property-poor districts. These students, it was determined, did not receive the equal protection of the laws of the state.[29]

Hopes by plaintiffs challenging unequal funding in Texas, however, were crushed by the *San Antonio v. Rodriguez* decision. Interestingly, it was found in *Rodriguez* that there were inequities in the Texas school financing system. It was determined, however, that these did not violate the equal protection clause of the Fourteenth Amendment to the United States Constitution. The Court's position was that the state's foundation program (state funding for local schools) provided at least a minimum funding and that no one was completely deprived of educational opportunities.[30]

Bilingual Education

Bilingual education is one of those issues that cuts across America's cultural topography. At the heart of the issue of bilingual education is the question of power. Like the control of information, the control of language enables control of the socialization process itself. The earliest systemwide attempt at bilingual education in the United States occurred simultaneously with the rapid expansion of common schooling in the nineteenth century. This first attempt was in Cincinnati, Ohio, in 1840. Acting in response to political pressure as well as a concern for the assimilation of the children of immigrant German families, the state of Ohio made it lawful to provide German schools for youth desiring to learn German, or English and German together.

The first real revival of bilingual education did not occur until 1961 when Dade County, Florida, instituted a program for Cuban refugees. Two years later, the Ford Foundation supported this effort with a major grant. A significant piece of federal legislation, the Bilingual Education Act (BEA), followed in 1968. A second Bilingual Education Act (1974) was more specific. Instruction was to be given "with appreciation for the cultural heritage of such children" and was to "be in all courses or subjects of study which will allow a child to progress effectively through the educational system."[31]

The judicial test of bilingual legislation came with the Supreme Court decision in *Lau v. Nichols* (1974). This case was originally brought by Chinese students against the San Francisco Unified School District where approximately 1,800 Chinese students did not receive services to meet their linguistic needs. It was claimed that the result of instruction in a language they could not understand was a denial of a minimally adequate education. When the case eventually reached the Supreme Court, the Court reasoned that offering the same opportunities for Chinese students as for English-speaking students did not constitute equal treatment. In effect, the students had fewer opportunities because of their language differences.[32]

Since *Lau*, the bilingual education movement has encountered resistance because of the expense of bilingual programs, the mixed research results on their effectiveness, and the debate over the extent to which bilingual programs work against the acquisition of proficiency in English. The recent decision in *Castaneda v. Pickard* (1981), involving discrimination against Mexican-American students in the Raymondville, Texas, Independent School District, did not find discriminatory practices. The Court did, however, find that the school system was not taking appropriate action to help students overcome language barriers.

Attacks on the strategy of bilingual education as a way to provide equal educational opportunity have increased markedly since 1890. Criticisms of the bilingual strategy are not only technical, but reflect the stormy history of the assimilation of immigrant groups into the dominant Anglo-American culture.

In tune with President Reagan's professed skepticism about bilingual education programs, others have voiced concern that second language usage in schooling will be an obstacle to the assimilation of subcultures and linguistic minorities into the American cultural mainstream. Albert Shanker, President of the American Federation of Teachers, has called the bilingual strategy bad for children and harmful to the nation. Former Congressman John Ashbrook of Ohio has intimated that the strategy will create a breeding ground for welfare recipients.[33] Underlying much of the criticism of bilingual education programs is a long-standing xenophobia and concern about the potential disruption of the American political and social order.

Handicapped Students

Like bilingual education, education for the handicapped has been a direct extension of *Brown* and subsequent court decisions involving equal opportunity. We find, again, the courts intervening and determining the course of educational policy. The actual exclusion of an "entire class of children from access to education" was taken up in the landmark case of *Pennsylvania Association for Retarded Children (PARC) v. Commonwealth of Pennsylvania* (1972). This case challenged a Pennsylvania statute that "treated severely retarded students as 'incapable of benefitting' from publicly subsidized instruction."[34] The court noted, however, that all children are capable of benefiting from education, even if the result is simply being less dependent on others. The case of *Mills v. Board of Education of District of Columbia* (1972), which quickly followed *PARC*, extended the right to education to all handicapped children, not just the retarded.

The legislative result of this litigation was the passage of a series of laws elaborating and protecting the right to education of the handicapped. The best known of these was the Education for All Handicapped Act of 1975, better known as PL (Public Law) 94-142. The most critical provision of PL 94-142, the individualized education plan (IEP), was upheld in a 1982 United States Supreme Court decision. Thus, even though it was found that the Hendrick Hudson Central School District did not have the obligation to provide Amy Rowley with a sign language interpreter, the case affirmed that the child's "individualized education plan (IEP) should be reasonably calculated to enable the child to achieve passing marks and advance from grade to grade."[35] PL 94-142 went further than any previous legislation in *prescribing* how an educational experience should be designed. For this reason, and because it has been a very expensive piece of legislation, its provisions have been much debated.

Equality and Equity for Women

It must be remembered that the problem of equity for women has its context in both women's rights and civil rights. Historically, women reformers like Elizabeth Cady Stanton and Lucy Stone in the 1840s compared the condition of women to that of slaves. The civil rights movement of the 1950s provided an important impetus to women's rights, although the leadership of the two movements was not the same. Antiwar protest and counterculture groups, too, helped to create a climate of liberation. The formation of a national Commission on the Status of Women in 1961 and the subsequent formation of many similar state commissions helped to bring the more conservative element into the women's rights movement. Out of this wave of interest, the National Organization for Women (NOW) eventually emerged as the most powerful organization seeking equality and equity for women.

The chief educational impact of the women's rights movement has been felt through Title IX of the Educational Amendments of 1972. Title IX is to women what the Voting Rights Act (1965) and the Civil Rights Act (1964) are to blacks. It "prohibits discrimination on the basis of sex in education programs or activities" receiving federal funding.[36] The purpose of Title IX was to guarantee equal access for women in the academic world and in athletics. As part of the attempt to legislate sex equity, Congress also passed the Women's Educational Equity Act, the purpose of which was to provide funds to eliminate sex stereotyping in educational programs, including vocational education. Amendments to the Vocational Education Act in 1976 also were geared to eliminate sex bias and stereotyping.[37]

The Nixon administration was slow to enforce Title IX, and it took three years before regulations were approved by the Department of Health, Education, and Welfare (HEW). It was not until 1982 that the Supreme Court ruled on the HEW regulations in *North Haven Board of Education v. Bell*. The issue in this case was whether or not the statute covered employment. The Court held that the legislation was intended to cover both students and employees in federally funded projects. Significant as this was from an institutional standpoint, the greatest difficulty with the decision was that it was "program-specific." In other words it applied only in cases where discrimination was found in a federally funded program. The Court, however, did not define "program" and the eventual implications of the case are not yet clear.[38]

In addition to Title IX, federal courts have addressed sex discrimination in other contexts, such as single-sex public high schools, admission to special college-preparatory public high schools, and extracurricular activities. Most of these cases were brought before the courts because of alleged violations of the equal protection clause of the Fourteenth Amendment of the United States Constitution. *Vorckheimer v. School District of Philadelphia* (1976) was a particularly troublesome case because it challenged the prerogative of a school district to operate a single-sex, very selective high school.

The United States Court of Appeals upheld the policy of Philadelphia that permitted such schools, as did the Supreme Court of the United States a year later. Neither court was unanimous, however. The dissenting opinion by Circuit Judge Gibbons argued that the "separate but equal" principle of *Plessy* ought not to be revived to support sexual discrimination. Moreover, said Gibbons, the Equal Educational Opportunities Act of 1974 prohibited as Congress intended, a dual system of single-sex public schools that violated the equal protection clause of the Fourteenth Amendment.[39]

In *Berkelman v. San Francisco Unified School District* (1974) the United States Court of Appeals heard arguments on admission standards to a "preferred" public high school. In this case the San Francisco Unified School District used a double standard for admission to Lowell High School—a standard which used for admission a higher grade-point average for females than males. The school board justified this policy on the basis of balancing the number of males and females in the high school. The court, however, found that the policy was a violation of the equal protection clause.[40]

In 1978 a United States District Court heard a case involving female participation on an interscholastic basketball team in Yellow Springs School District, Ohio. This case, *Yellow Springs School District v. Ohio High School Athletic Association* (1978), occurred because the school board refused to allow two female students to participate on the Morgan Middle School basketball team. The girls had competed for and won places on the team, but the school board had denied them membership because a rule of the Ohio High School Athletic Association prohibited mixed-gender interscholastic athletic competition. The association threatened to exclude the team from competition unless the females were dropped from the team.

Under this threat the school board removed them and created, instead, a separate girls' basketball team. In its decision, the court concluded that girls "must be given the opportunity to compete with boys in interscholastic contact sports if they are physically qualified."[41] The court said that separate teams could be satisfactory, but could not be used as an "excuse to deprive qualified girls positions on formerly all boy teams, regardless of the sport."[42] The court concluded:

> It may well be that there is a student today in an Ohio high school who lacks only the proper coaching and training to become the greatest quarterback in professional football history. Of course the odds are astronomical against her, but isn't she entitled to a fair chance to try?[43]

CONCLUSION

Thus far we have seen that the question of justice and its relationship to education covers a wide range of judicial and legislative activity. Since the 1950s, federal and state courts have taken a much more active role in guiding educational policy at all levels. Teachers and administrators have had to be increasingly mindful about whether their behavior in a particular situation might be considered unfair or discriminatory. There is virtually no aspect of a teacher's life today that has gone untouched by court decisions and legislation related to civil rights.

The court decisions and legislative activity that have directly affected schools in recent years are extensions of larger philosophic issues that have come to the forefront of American education. The central issues, we have seen, are those of social justice and fairness. These, in turn, are very much related to other fundamental concepts in our culture such as merit, equality, and equal opportunity. These concepts are guideposts for determining how rewards are distributed to individuals in our society. Each also has an important place in our conception of how education functions in the overall reward system.

NOTES

[1] Aristotle, *Nicomachean Ethics,* trans. and intro. by Martin Oswald (New York: Bobbs-Merrill, 1962), Book 5.

[2] James Coleman, "The Concept of Equality of Educational Opportunity," *Harvard Educational Review* 68 (Winter 1968), p. 137.

[3] Ibid.

[4] Michael J. Sandel, *Liberalism and the Limits of Justice* (Cambridge: Cambridge University Press, 1982), p. 25.

[5] Ibid., p. 88.

[6] Robert Nozick, *Anarchy, State, and Utopia* (New York: Basic Books, 1974), Chapter 7, passim.

[7] Kenneth A. Strike, *Educational Policy and the Just Society* (Urbana: University of Illinois Press, 1982), pp. 182, 227.

[8] *Brown v. Board of Education of Topeka,* 74, Sup. Ct. 686 (1954).

[9] Harvie Wilkinson III, *From Brown to Bakke: The Supreme Court and School Integration, 1954–1978* (Oxford: Oxford University Press, 1979), pp. 76–84.

[10] Meyer Weinberg, *A Chance to Learn, A History of Race and Education in the United States* (Cambridge: Cambridge University Press, 1977), pp. 98–99.

[11] Ibid., p. 102.

[12] Ibid., pp. 102–103.

[13] 391 U.S. 430, 88 Sup. Ct. 1698; as in Arval A. Morris, *The Constitution and American Education,* 2nd ed., *American Casebook Series* (St. Paul, Minn.: West Publishing Co., 1980), p. 763.

[14] 396 U.S. 19, 90 Sup. Ct. 29; as in Morris, *Constitution,* p. 727.

[15] 402 U.S. 1, 91 Sup. Ct. 1267; as in Morris, *Constitution,* pp. 733–741.

[16] Wilkinson, *Brown to Bakke,* p. 202.

[17] Ibid., pp. 203–215.

[18] Melvin E. Jarvis, "Current Trends in Federal Court Intervention in Public Education." Paper presented at the Annual Meeting of the American Educational Research Association, New Orleans, April 23–27, 1984, p. 20.

[19] Frederick M. Wirt and Michael W. Kirst, *The Politics of Education: Schools in Conflict* (Berkeley: McCutchan, 1982), pp. 260–261.

[20] Ibid., pp. 261–265.

[21] 324 F. Supp. 599; 462 F. 2d 848; as in Weinberg, *A Chance to Learn,* 174.

[22] Weinberg, *Chance to Learn,* Chapter 4.

[23] Ibid., p. 147.

[24] Ibid., pp. 150–151.

[25] Ibid., p. 177.

[26] Ibid., p. 164.

[27] Jarvis, p. 9.

[28] Arthur E. Wise, *Legislated Learning: The Bureaucratization of the American Classroom* (Berkeley: University of California Press, 1979), p. 136. For a survey of the U.S. Supreme Court's activity in educational matters, see E. Edmund Reutter, Jr., *The Supreme Court's Impact on Public Education* (Bloomington, Ind.: Phi Delta Kappa and National Organization of Legal Problems of Education, 1982).

[29] David L. Kirp, "Law, Politics, and Equal Educational Opportunity: The Limits of Judicial Involvement," *Harvard Educational Review* 47 (1977), p. 122.

[30] Reutter, p. 166.

[31] Theodore Anderson and Mildred Boyer, *Bilingual Schooling in the United States* (Austin, Tex.: National Educational Laboratory Publishers, 1978), pp. 21–24. Herbert Teitelbaum and Richard Hiller, "Bilingual Education: The Legal Mandate," *Harvard Educational Review* 47 (1977), pp. 139–141.

[32] *Lau v. Nichols*, 94 Sup. Ct. 786 (1974).

[33] Stanley S. Seidner and Maria Medina Seidner, "In the Wake of Conservative Reaction: An Analysis," in *Theory, Technology, and Public Policy on Bilingual Education*, ed. Raymond V. Padilla (Rosslyn, Va.: National Clearing House for Bilingual Education, 1983).

[34] 343 F. Supp. 279.

[35] *Board of Education of Hendrick Hudson Central School District v. Rowley*, 50 U. S. L. W. 4925, 4932–4933 (U.S. June 28, 1982), 102 Sup. Ct. 3034.

[36] Reutter, p. 176.

[37] "An interview on Title IX," *Harvard Educational Review* 49 (Nov. 1979): 521.

[38] Reutter, p. 176.

[39] Arval A. Morris, *The Constitution and American Education*, 2nd ed., *American Casebook Series* (St. Paul, Minn.: West Publishing Co., 1980), pp. 829, 832.

[40] Ibid., p. 844.

[41] Ibid., p. 849.

[42] Ibid.

[43] Ibid., p. 850.

2

Readings on Equal
Educational Opportunity

The readings in this chapter show in chronological order the ideal and practice of equal opportunity in American education. Together they represent a common concern with the problem of inequality and fair opportunity. Their treatment of the varying dimensions of this problem help us to see its complexity as well as hope for resolution.

In the first selection, Horace Mann, one of the great common school reformers of the nineteenth century, argues the case for equal access to schools. His arguments should be understood in the context of attempts to extend elementary education to all children in this period. As did other reformers of his time, Mann saw opportunity as accessibility. Once access to school was provided, it was an individual's responsibility to make the most of school experiences. Close attention should be paid to Mann's arguments about the relationship between education and individual economic mobility as well as education and public welfare.

Excerpts from the landmark decisions in *Brown v. Board of Education of Topeka* (1954) and *PARC v. Commonwealth of Pennsylvania* (1972), and the essay by James Coleman show the extent to which the concept of equal educational opportunity had changed in the century between Mann's report and the advent of the Civil Rights movement in the United States. In *Brown* one clearly sees the influence of research in the social sciences on the Court's decision. This historic decision rejected the separate-but-equal doctrine of previous courts and forcefully extended the Fourteenth Amendment of the United States Constitution into the area of education. The PARC case illustrates the extension of civil rights and due process decisions to groups other than racial minorities. Litigation has been extensive in the area of the handicapped since the early 1970s.

Coleman's essay on "Equal Schools or Equal Students" reflects the growing concern over whether or not it is sufficient to talk about equal educational opportunity only in terms of "inputs"—resources going into the educational system. From the mid-1960s on, educational reformers increasingly thought of opportunity in terms of outputs (performance), not merely inputs. Like earlier reformers, Coleman stresses the power of the school to reshape the lives of children while recognizing the limitations imposed by home and culture. His "modest proposal," however, moves the school into the limelight of social policy.

T. H. Bell's essay written for the *Harvard Educational Review* is a statement of the new federalism in American education. It should be remembered that the great social and educational reforms of the 1960s and early 1970s were brought about by massive federal involvement. By the time Ronald Reagan was elected President the new right was gaining political momentum. Reagan's federalism signaled a rapid retreat from federal involvement with educational policy. In Bell's essay we see an advocate of the position that responsibility for civil rights, equity legislation, and equal opportunity should be transferred to state and local levels of government. For many, the resurgence of this idea has raised serious concerns about the capability of American society to maintain and extend progress in the areas of equal opportunity and equity. After all, they argue, it was the lack of assertiveness at the state and local levels that led to massive federal involvement in the first place.

The last essay in this section assesses the present state of education for black Americans. The author, Director of Education Programs for the NAACP in New York City, outlines the extent to which the major goals of equality and equity have or have not been achieved for black Americans. She ties her assessment to the educational practices of tracking and testing, federal policies on spending for education, and the goals of education in a democracy. The actual and potential conflicts between student classification and a meritocratic system of rewards on the one hand and commitment to democratic principles on the other are cited by the author.

Certain basic questions emerge from these readings that deserve further discussion. To what extent do the concepts of equal opportunity and meritocracy belong to the democratic creed? What concept of social justice is democracy committed to? What is the proper balance between state and federal authority in education? Is it possible to reconcile the ideal of equality with the aims of utilitarianism?

HORACE MANN

INEQUALITY IN THE MEANS OF EDUCATION

The inequality in the means of education possessed by the children in the different towns and sections of the State, is a subject of great moment, and not treated of in any former Report. . . .

Much has been, and much still continues to be, both said and written respecting that equality in the laws, and equality under the laws, which

From Horace Mann, *Fifth Annual Report to the Board of Education of Massachusetts*, 1842. Boston: Lee and Shepard, 1891, pp. 69–86.

constitutes the distinctive feature of a Republican government. By abolishing the right of primogeniture, and entails, by the extension of the elective franchise, and in other ways, much has been done towards realizing the two grand conceptions of the founders of our government, viz., that political advantages should be equal, and then, that celebrity or obscurity, wealth or poverty, should depend on individual merit. But the most influential and decisive measure for equalizing the original opportunities of men, that is, equality in the means of education, has not been adopted. In this respect, therefore, the most striking and painful disparities now exist. One source of this difference, indeed, is to be found in the almost unlimited freedom of action exercised by the different towns . . . in appropriating money for the support of schools. . . . In this respect, the towns resemble individuals. One parent will make all sacrifices, he will economize in his pleasure, dress, shelter, and even in his food, to save the means of educating his children; while another,—perhaps his nearest neighbor,—will sell the services of his children for a few pence a day, through the whole year, that he may hoard their earnings, or spend them in dissipation. . . .

On a broad survey of the State, and an inquiry into the causes which have led to the superior intelligence and respectability of some towns, as compared with others, it will almost uniformly be discovered, that the foundations of their prosperity were laid by a few individuals,—in some cases by a single individual,—in elevating the condition of their Common Schools. . . .

No other fact has ever exhibited so fully the extent of obligation which some towns are under to a few individuals, who have had the forecast and the energy, in the midst of difficulties and opposition, to sustain their schools. I have met many individuals, who, having failed to obtain any improvement in the means of education in their respective places of residence, have removed to towns whose schools were good, believing the sacrifice of a hundred, or even of several hundred dollars, to be nothing, in comparison with the value of the school privileges secured for their children by such removal. Still more frequently, when other circumstances have rendered a change of domicile expedient, has this principle of selection governed in choosing a residence.

• • •

For the present, the general remark must suffice,—a remark which, after five circuits made through all parts of the State, after a perusal and careful examination of every Return and Report made by the school committees, and after extensive correspondence and frequent interviews with the friends of education, I feel not wholly incompetent to make,—that, as a general fact, the great work of enlightening the intellect and cultivating the manners and morals of the rising generation, is going forward most rapidly and successfully in those towns whose appropriations are most generous; while, on the other hand, a noncompliance with the requisitions of the law, in employing unapproved teachers, in diverting school moneys to illegal purposes, in resisting a uniformity of books, and in the manifestation of indifference or hostility towards the measures recently adopted for the improvement of the schools, have most commonly been found in those towns whose appropriations look rather to the question, how little money will suffice to escape from penalty or forfeiture, than how much, through the alchemy of this institution, can be transmuted into knowledge and wisdom and virtue.

Here, then, it is obvious, are grounds of wide and permanent distinction, among the rising generation, as it happens to be their good or ill fortune to belong to one place or to another. As one State, where education is neglected and disdained, falls, in its wealth, in its social standing, and in the number of its distinguished men, below another State, where this great interest is fostered and exalted; so must some of our own towns fall below others, in all the elements of prosperity, and respectability, and honor. This, however, is a distinction which does not call upon the less favored portions of the community to curtail the privileges of the more favored, but to strive honorably to elevate themselves to a level with their fellows. It calls upon the more favored, also, by motives which should be all-powerful, to lend a helping-hand,—to practise upon those political principles which regard all men as equals, and upon those Christian principles which regard all men as brethren, in elevating their inferiors to the height of their own standard. All other means ever devised by which to approximate the idea of a Republican government, are insignificant when compared with the possession of equal education privileges. . . .

The government which should attempt to enforce an equality of external circumstances among men, while it permitted these educational inequalities to exist, would have daily and hourly occasion for the renewal of its work. . . . But, if equal opportunities of improvement are offered to all, the responsibility of using or neglecting them, may justly be cast upon each individual. Society does not exhibit a more instructive or salutary lesson, than those inequalities of actual condition which result from an unequal use of equal opportunities.

It was in the hope of seeing the opportunities of education more equally diffused, that I suggested, in a former report, the expediency of encouraging the purchase of a Common School library, for each school district, by the State's granting a small bonus or gratuity for the purpose. As I there intimated, the poorer and more sparsely populated districts will not be likely to obtain this indispensable auxiliary to a good school, without assistance from the government. So far, the result verifies the prediction. There have now been sold in the State, of the library prepared under the superintendance of the Board of Education, about three hundred sets; and, as a general fact, these have been purchased by the more wealthy and populous districts. A few districts, however, form a gratifying exception to this statement; for, though small in numbers, and of moderate wealth, these disadvantages have been counterbalanced by zeal and public spirit, in their members. The number of Public Schools in the State, last year, was three thousand one hundred and three, so that there are now not less than twenty-eight hundred of our Public Schools destitute of a school library. . . .

Having now established, beyond the possibility of denial or doubt, the extraordinary and heretofore unrecognized inequalities existing between different towns in the Commonwealth, as it respects the educational advantages they bestow upon their children, the natural course of the argument would lead, at once, to an exposition or development of the consequences which must grow out of this wide departure, on each hand, from a common standard. . . .

If it can be proved that the aggregate wealth of a town will be increased just in proportion to the increase of its appropriations for schools, the opponents of such a measure will be silenced. The tax for this purpose, which they now look upon as a burden, they will then regard as a profitable investment. Let it be shown that the money which is now clung to by the parent, in the hope of increasing his children's legacies, some six or ten per cent., can be so invested as to double their patrimony, and the blind instinct of parental love, which now, by voice and vote, opposes such outlay, will become an advocate for the most generous endowments. When the money expended for education shall be viewed in its true character, as seed-grain sown in a soil which is itself enriched by yielding, then the most parsimonious will not stint the sowing, lest the harvest, also, should be stinted, and, thereby, thirty, sixty, or a hundred fold, should be lost to the garners. . . .

I have novel and striking evidence to prove that education is convertible into houses and lands, as well as into power and virtue.

• • •

During the past year I have opened a correspondence, and availed myself of all opportunities to hold personal interviews with many of the most practical, sagacious and intelligent business men amongst us, who for many years have had large numbers of persons in their employment. My object has been to ascertain the difference in the productive ability,—where natural capacities have been equal,—between the educated and the uneducated,—between a man or woman whose mind has been awakened to thought and supplied with the rudiments of knowledge, by a good Common School education, and one whose faculties have never been developed, or aided in emerging from their original darkness and torpor by such a privilege. For this purpose I have conferred and corresponded with manufacturers of all kinds, with machinists, engineers, rail-road contractors, officers in the army, &c. These various classes of persons have means of determining the effects of education on individuals, equal in their natural abilities, which other classes do not possess.

• • •

No observing man can have failed to notice the difference between two workmen, one of whom,—to use a proverbial expression,—always hits the nail on the head, while the other loses half his strength and destroys half his nails, by the awkwardness of his blows; but perhaps few men have thought of the difference in the results of two such men's labor, at the end of twenty years.

But when hundreds of men and women work side by side, in the same factory, at the same machinery, in making the same fabrics, and, by a fixed rule of the establishment, labor the same number of hours each day; and when, also, the products of each operative can be counted in number, weighed by the pound, or measured by the yard or cubic foot,—then it is perfectly practicable to determine with arithmetical exactness, the productions of one individual and one class as compared with those of another individual and another class.

So where there are different kinds of labor, some simple, others complicated, and of course requiring different degrees of intelligence and skill, it is easy to observe what class of persons rise from a lower to a higher grade of employment.

This too is not to be forgotten, that in a manufacturing or mechanical establishment, or among a set of hands engaged in filling up a valley or cutting down a hill, where scores of people are working together, the absurd and adventitious distinctions of society do not intrude. The capitalist and his agents are looking for the greatest amount of labor, or the largest income in money from their investments; and they do not promote a dunce to a station, where he will destroy raw material, or slacken industry, because of his name, or birth, or family connections. The obscurest and humblest person has an open and fair field for competition. That he proves himself capable of earning more money for his employer, is a testimonial, better than a diploma from all the colleges.

Now many of the most intelligent and valuable men in our community, in compliance with my request,—for which I tender them my public and grateful acknowledgments,—have examined their books for a series of years, and have ascertained both the quality and the amount of work performed by persons in their employment; and the result of the investigation is a most astonishing superiority in productive power, on the part of the educated over the uneducated laborer. The hand is found to be another hand, when guided by an intelligent mind. Processes are performed, not only more rapidly, but better, when faculties which have been exercised in early life, furnish their assistance. Individuals who, without the aid of knowledge, would have been condemned to perceptual inferiority of condition, and subjected to all the evils of want and poverty, rise to competence and independence, by the uplifting power of education. In great establishments, and among large bodies of laboring men, where all services are rated according to their pecuniary value, where there are no extrinsic circumstances to bind a man down to a fixed position, after he has shown a capacity to rise above it—where, indeed, men pass by each other, ascending or descending in their grades of labor, just as easily and certainly as particles of water of different degrees of temperature glide by each other,—there it is found as an almost invariable fact,—other things being equal,—that those who have been blessed with a good Common School education, rise to a higher and a higher point, in the kinds of labor performed, and also in the rate of wages paid, while the ignorant sink, like dregs, and are always found at the bottom.

SELECTIONS FROM *BROWN ET AL. v. BOARD OF EDUCATION OF TOPEKA*

ISSUE: Segregation

OPINION: These cases come to us from the States of Kansas, South Carolina, Virginia, and Delaware. They are premised on different facts and different local conditions, but a common legal question justifies their consideration together in this consolidated opinion.

• • •

In each of the cases, minors of the Negro race, through their legal representatives, seek the aid of the courts in obtaining admission to the public schools of their community on a nonsegregated basis. In each instance, they have been denied admission to schools attended by white children under laws requiring or permitting segregation according to race. This segregation was alleged to deprive the plaintiffs of the equal protection of the laws under the Fourteenth Amendment. In each of the cases other than the Delaware case, a three-judge federal district court denied relief to the plaintiffs on the so-called "separate but equal" doctrine announced by this Court in *Plessy v. Ferguson.* Under that doctrine, equality of treatment is accorded when the races are provided substantially equal facilities, even though these facilities be separate. In the Delaware case, the Supreme Court of Delaware adhered to that doctrine, but ordered that the plaintiffs be admitted to the white schools because of their superiority to the Negro schools.

The plaintiffs contend that segregated public schools are not "equal" and cannot be made "equal," and that hence they are deprived of the equal protection of the laws. . . .

Reargument was largely devoted to the circumstances surrounding the adoption of the Fourteenth Amendment in 1868.

• • •

This discussion and our own investigation convince us that, although these sources cast some light, it is not enough to resolve the problem with which we are faced. . . .

An additional reason for the inconclusive nature of the Amendment's history, with respect to segregated schools, is the status of public education at that time. In the South, the movement toward free common schools, supported by general taxation, had not yet taken hold. Education of white children was largely in the hands of private groups. Education of Negroes was almost nonexistent, and practically all of the race were illiterate. In fact, any education of Negroes was forbidden by law in some states. Today, in contrast, many Negroes have achieved outstanding success in the arts and sciences as well as in the business and professional world. It is true that public school education at the time of the Amendment had advanced further in the North, but the effect of the

From *Brown et al. v. Board of Education of Topeka, Shawnee County, Kansas et al.* and Companion Cases, 74 Sup. Ct. 686 (1954).

Amendment on Northern States was generally ignored in the congressional debates. Even in the North, the conditions of public education did not approximate those existing today. The curriculum was usually rudimentary; ungraded schools were common in rural areas; the school term was but three months a year in many states; and compulsory school attendance was virtually unknown. As a consequence, it is not surprising that there should be so little in the history of the Fourteenth Amendment relating to its intended effect on public education.

• • •

Our decision . . . cannot turn on merely a comparison of these tangible factors [buildings, curricula, salaries of teachers] in the Negro and white schools involved in each of the cases. We must look instead to the effect of segregation itself on public education.

In approaching this problem, we cannot turn the clock back to 1868 when the Amendment was adopted, or even to 1896 when *Plessy v. Ferguson* was written. We must consider public education in the light of its full development and its present place in American life throughout the Nation. Only in this way can it be determined if segregation in public schools deprives these plaintiffs of the equal protection of the laws.

Today, education is perhaps the most important function of state and local governments. Compulsory school attendance laws and the great expenditures for education both demonstrate our recognition of the importance of education to our democratic society. It is required in the performance of our most basic public responsibilities, even service in the armed forces. It is the very foundation of good citizenship. Today it is a principal instrument in awakening the child to cultural values, in preparing him for later professional training, and in helping him to adjust normally to his environment. In these days, it is doubtful that any child may reasonably be expected to succeed in life if he is denied the opportunity of an education. Such an opportunity, where the state has undertaken to provide it, is a right which must be made available to all on equal terms.

We come then to the question presented: Does segregation of children in public schools solely on the basis of race, even though the physical facilities and other "tangible" factors may be equal, deprive the children of the minority group of equal educational opportunities? We believe that it does.

• • •

To separate [children] from others of similar age and qualifications solely because of their race generates a feeling of inferiority as to their status in the community that may affect their hearts and minds in a way unlikely ever to be undone. The effect of this separation on their educational opportunities was well stated by a finding in the Kansas case by a court which nevertheless felt compelled to rule against the Negro plaintiffs:

> Segregation of white and colored children in public schools has a detrimental effect upon the colored children. The impact is greater when it has the sanction of law; for the policy of separating the races is usually interpreted as denoting the inferiority of the Negro group. A sense of inferiority affects the motivation of a child to learn. Segregation with the sanction of law, therefore,

has a tendency to [retard] the educational and mental development of Negro children and to deprive them of some of the benefits they would receive in a racial-[ly] integrated school system.

Whatever may have been the extent of psychological knowledge at the time of *Plessy v. Ferguson*, this finding is amply supported by modern authority. Any language in *Plessy v. Ferguson* contrary to this finding is rejected.

We conclude that in the field of public education the doctrine of "separate but equal" has no place. Separate educational facilities are inherently unequal. Therefore, we hold that the plaintiffs and others similarly situated for whom the actions have been brought are, by reason of the segregation complained of, deprived of the equal protection of the laws guaranteed by the Fourteenth Amendment. This disposition makes unnecessary any discussion whether such segregation also violated the Due Process Clause of the Fourteenth Amendment.

James S. Coleman

EQUAL SCHOOLS OR EQUAL STUDENTS?

The Civil Rights Act of 1964 contains a section numbered 402, which went largely unnoticed at the time. This section instructs the Commissioner of Education to carry out a survey "concerning the lack of availability of equal educational opportunities" by reason of race, religion or national origin, and to report to Congress and the President within two years. The Congressional intent in this section is somewhat unclear. But if, as is probable, the survey was initially intended as a means of finding areas of continued intentional discrimination, the intent later became less punitive-oriented and more future-oriented: *i.e.*, to provide a basis for public policy, at the local, state, and national levels, which might overcome inequalities of educational opportunity.

In the two years that have intervened (but mostly in the second), a remarkably vast and comprehensive survey was conducted, focussing principally on the inequalities of educational opportunity experienced by five racial and ethnic minorities: Negroes, Puerto Ricans, Mexican Americans, American Indians, and Oriental Americans. In the central and largest portion of the survey, nearly 600,000 children at grades 1, 3, 6, 9, and 12, in 4000 schools in all 50 states and the District of Columbia, were tested and questioned; 60,000 teachers in these schools were questioned and self-tested; and principals of these schools were also questioned about their schools. The tests and questionnaires (administered in the fall of 1965 by Educational Testing Service) raised a considerable controversy in public school circles and among some parents, with concern ranging from Federal encroachment on the local education system to the spectre of invasion of privacy. Nevertheless, with a participation rate of about 70% of all the schools sampled, the survey was conducted; and on July 1, 1966, Commis-

From James S. Coleman, "Equal Schools or Equal Students?" *The Public Interest* 4 (Summer 1966), pp. 70–75. Reprinted with permission of the author. Copyright © 1966 by National Affairs.

sioner Howe presented a summary report of this survey. On July 31, the total report, *Equality of Educational Opportunity,* 737 pages, was made available (Government Printing Office, $4.25).

The summary of the report has appeared to many who have read it to be curiously "flat," lacking in emphases and policy implications. Much of the same flatness can be found in the larger report. The seeming flatness probably derives from three sources: the research analyst's uneasiness in moving from description to implications; the government agency's uneasiness with survey findings that may have political repercussions; and, perhaps more important than either of these, the fact that the survey results do not lend themselves to the provision of simple answers. Nevertheless, the report is not so uncontroversial as it appears. And some of its findings, though cautiously presented, have sharp implications.

Perhaps the greatest virtue of this survey—though it has many faults—is that it did not take a simple or politically expedient view of educational opportunity. To have done so would have meant to measure (a) the objective characteristics of schools—number of books in the library, age of buildings, educational level of teachers, accreditation of the schools, and so on; and (b) the actual extent of racial segregation in the schools. The survey did look into these matters (and found less inequity in school facilities and resources, more in the extent of segregation, than is commonly supposed); but its principal focus of attention was not on what resources go into education, but on what product comes out. It did this in a relatively uncomplicated way, which is probably adequate for the task at hand: by tests which measured those areas of achievement most necessary for further progress in school, in higher education, and in successful competition in the labor market—that is, verbal and reading skills, and analytical and mathematical skills. Such a criterion does not allow statements about absolute levels of inequality or equality of education provided by the schools, because obviously there are more influences than the school's on a child's level of achievement in school, and there are more effects of schools than in these areas of achievement. What it does do is to broaden the question beyond the school to all those educational influences that have their results in the level of verbal and mathematical skill a young person is equipped with when he or she enters the adult world. In effect, it takes the perspective of this young adult, and says that what matters to him is, not how "equal" his school is, but rather whether he is equipped at the end of school to compete on an equal basis with others, whatever his social origins. From the perspective of society, it assumes that what is important is not to "equalize the schools" in some formal sense, but to insure that children from all groups come into adult society so equipped as to insure their full participation in this society.

Another way of putting this is to say that the schools are successful only insofar as they reduce the dependence of a child's opportunities upon his social origins. We can think of a set of conditional probabilities: the probability of being prepared for a given occupation or for a given college at the end of high school, conditional upon the child's social origins. The effectiveness of the schools consists, in part, of making the conditional probabilities less conditional—that is, less dependent upon social origins. Thus, equality of educational opportunity

implies, not merely "equal" schools, but equally effective schools, who
ences will overcome the differences in starting point of children from ̹
social groups.

THE WIDENING EDUCATIONAL GAP

This approach to educational opportunity, using as it does achievement on
standardized tests, treads on sensitive ground. Differences in average achievement between racial groups can lend themselves to racist arguments of genetic
differences in intelligence; even apart from this, they can lead to invidious
comparisons between groups which show different average levels of achievement. But it is precisely the avoidance of such sensitive areas that can perpetuate
the educational deficiencies with which some minorities are equipped at the end
of schooling.

What, then, does the survey find with regard to effects of schooling on test
achievement? Children were tested at the beginning of grades 1, 3, 6, 9, and 12.
Achievement of the average American Indian, Mexican American, Puerto Rican,
and Negro (in this descending order) was much lower than the average white or
Oriental American, at all grade levels. The amount of difference ranges from
about half a standard deviation to one standard deviation at early grade levels.
At the 12th grade, it increases to beyond one standard deviation. (One standard
deviation difference means that about 85% of the minority group children score
below the average of the whites, while if the groups were equal only about 50%
would score below this average.) The grade levels of difference range up to 5
years of deficiency (in math achievement) or 4 years (in reading skills) at the 12th
grade. In short, the differences are large to begin with, and they are even larger at
higher grades.

Two points, then, are clear: (1) *these minority children have a serious educational deficiency at the start of school, which is obviously not a result of school;* and (2)
*they have an even more serious deficiency at the end of school, which is obviously in part a
result of school.*

Thus, by the criterion stated earlier—that the effectiveness of schools in
creating equality of educational opportunity lies in making the conditional
probabilities of success less conditional—the schools appear to fail. At the end of
school, the conditional probabilities of high achievement are even *more* conditional upon racial or ethnic backgrounds than they are at the beginning of school.

There are a number of results from the survey which give further evidence
on this matter. First, within each racial group, the strong relation of family
economic and educational background to achievement does not diminish over
the period of school, and may even increase over the elementary years. Second,
most of the variation in student achievement lies within the same school, very
little of it is between schools. The implication of these last two results is clear:
family background differences account for much more variation in achievement
than do school differences.

Even the school-to-school variation in achievement, though relatively small, is itself almost wholly due to the *social* environment provided by the school: the educational backgrounds and aspirations of other students in the school, and the educational backgrounds and attainments of the teachers in the school. *Per pupil expenditure, books in the library, and a host of other facilities and curricular measures show virtually no relation to achievement if the "social" environment of the school—the educational background of other students and teachers—is held constant.*

The importance of this last result lies, of course, in the fact that schools, as currently organized, are quite culturally homogeneous as well as quite racially segregated: teachers tend to come from the same cultural groups (and especially from the same race) as their students, and the student bodies are themselves relatively homogeneous. Given this homogeneity, the principal agents of effectiveness in the schools—teachers and other students—act to maintain or reinforce the initial differences imposed by social origins.

One element illustrates well the way in which the current organization of schools maintains the differences over generations: a Negro prospective teacher leaves a Negro teacher's college with a much lower level of academic competence (as measured by the National Teacher's Examination) than does his white counterpart leaving his largely white college; then he teaches Negro children (in school with other Negro children, ordinarily from educationally deficient backgrounds), who learn at a lower level, in part because of his lesser competence; some of these students, in turn, go into teacher training institutions to become poorly-trained teachers of the next generation.

Altogether, *the sources of inequality of educational opportunity appear to lie first in the home itself and the cultural influences immediately surrounding the home; then they lie in the schools' ineffectiveness to free achievement from the impact of the home, and in the school's homogeneity which perpetuates the social influences of the home and its environs.*

A MODEST, YET RADICAL PROPOSAL

Given these results, what do they suggest as to avenues to equality of educational opportunity? Several elements seem clear:

a) For those children whose family and neighborhood are educationally disadvantaged, it is important to replace this family environment as much as possible with an educational environment—by starting school at an earlier age, and by having a school which begins very early in the day and ends very late.

b) It is important to reduce the social and racial homogeneity of the school environment, so that those agents of education that do show some effectiveness—teachers and other students—are not mere replicas of the student himself. In the present organization of schools, it is the neighborhood school that most insures such homogeneity.

c) The educational program of the school should be made more effective than it is at present. The weakness of this program is apparent in its inability to overcome initial differences. It is hard to believe that we are so inept in its inability to overcome initial differences. It is hard to believe that we are so inept in educating our young that we can do no more than leave young adults in the same relative competitive positions we found them in as children.

Several points are obvious: It is not a solution simply to pour money into improvement of the physical plants, books, teaching aids, of schools attended by educationally disadvantaged children. For other reasons, it will not suffice merely to bus children or otherwise achieve pro forma integration. (One incidental effect of this would be to increase the segregation within schools, through an increase in tracking.)

The only kinds of policies that appear in any way viable are those which do not seek to improve the education of Negroes and other educationally disadvantaged at the expense of those who are educationally advantaged. This implies new kinds of educational institutions, with a vast increase in expenditures for education—not merely for the disadvantaged, but for all children. The solutions might be in the form of educational parks, or in the form of private schools paid by tuition grants (with Federal regulations to insure racial heterogeneity), public (or publicly-subsidized) boarding schools (like the North Carolina Advancement School), or still other innovations. This approach also implies reorganization of the curriculum within schools. One of the major reasons for "tracking" is the narrowness of our teaching methods—they can tolerate only a narrow range of skill in the same classroom. Methods which greatly widen the range are necessary to make possible racial and cultural integration within a school—and thus to make possible the informal learning that other students of higher educational levels can provide. Such curricular innovations are possible—but, again, only through the investment of vastly greater sums in education than currently occurs.

It should be recognized, of course, that the goal described here—of equality of educational opportunity through the schools—is far more ambitious than has ever been posed in our society before. The schools were once seen as a supplement to the family in bringing a child into his place in adult society, and they still function largely as such a supplement, merely perpetuating the inequalities of birth. Yet the conditions imposed by technological change, and by our post-industrial society, quite apart from any ideals of equal opportunity, require a far more primary role for the school, if society's children are to be equipped for adulthood.

SELF-CONFIDENCE AND PERFORMANCE

One final result of the survey gives an indication of still another—and perhaps the most important—element necessary for equality of educational opportunity for Negroes. One attitude of students was measured at grades 9 and 12—an attitude which indicated the degree to which the student felt in control of his own fate. For example, one question was: "Agree or disagree: good luck is more important than hard work for success." Another was: "Agree or disagree: every time I try to get ahead someone or something stops me." Negroes much less often than whites had such a sense of control of their fate—a difference which corresponds directly to reality, and which corresponds even more markedly to the Negro's historical position in American society. However, despite the very large achievement differences between whites and Negroes at the 9th and 12th grades, *those Negroes who gave responses indicating a sense of control of their own fate achieved higher on the tests than those whites who gave the opposite responses. This attitude was more highly related to achievement than any other factor in the student's background or school.*

This result suggests that internal changes in the Negro, changes in his conception of himself in relation to his environment, may have more effect on Negro achievement than any other single factor. The determination to overcome relevant obstacles, and the belief that he will overcome them—attitudes that have appeared in an organized way among Negroes only in recent years in some civil rights groups—may be the most crucial elements in achieving equality of opportunity—not because of changes they will create in the white community, but principally because of the changes they create in the Negro himself.

SELECTIONS FROM *PENNSYLVANIA ASSOCIATION FOR RETARDED CHILDREN v. COMMONWEALTH OF PENNSYLVANIA*

ISSUE: Education for the Handicapped

OPINION: This civil rights case, a class action, was brought by the Pennsylvania Association for Retarded Children and the parents of thirteen individual retarded children on behalf of all mentally retarded persons between the ages 6 and 21 whom the Commonwealth of Pennsylvania, through its local school districts and intermediate units, is presently excluding from a program of education and training in the public schools. Named as defendants are the Commonwealth of Pennsylvania, Secretary of Welfare, State Board of Education and thirteen individual school districts scattered throughout the Commonwealth. In addition, plaintiffs have joined all other school districts in the Commonwealth as class defendants of which the named districts are said to be representative.

From *Pennsylvania Association for Retarded Children v. Commonwealth of Pennsylvania,* 343 F. Supp. 279 (1972).

ORDER AND INJUNCTION

This 5th day of May, 1972, it is ordered that the Amended Stipulation and Amended Consent Agreement are approved and adopted as fair and reasonable to all members of both the plaintiff and defendant classes.

It is further ordered that the defendants; the Commonwealth of Pennsylvania, the Secretary of the Department of Education, the State Board of Education, the Secretary of the Department of Public Welfare, the named defendant school districts and intermediate units and each of the school districts and intermediate units in the Commonwealth of Pennsylvania, their officers, employees, agents and successors are enjoined as follows:

(a) from applying the Public School Codes so as to postpone or in any way deny to any mentally retarded child access to a free public program of education and training;

(b) from applying the School Code so as to postpone, to terminate or in any way deny to any mentally retarded child access to a free program of education and training;

(c) from applying the School Code so as to deny to any mentally retarded child access to a free public program of education and training;

(d) from applying the School Code so as to deny tuition or tuition and maintenance to any mentally retarded person except on the same terms as may be applied to other exceptional children, including brain damaged children generally;

(e) from denying homebound instruction to any mentally retarded child merely because no physical disability accompanies the retardation or because retardation is not a short-term disability;

(f) from applying the School Code so as to deny to any mentally retarded child access to a free public program of education and training;

(g) to provide, as soon as possible but in no event later than September 1, 1972, to every retarded person between the ages of six and twenty-one years as of the date of this Order and thereafter, access to a free public program of education and training appropriate to his learning capacities;

(h) to provide as soon as possible but in no event later than September 1, 1972, wherever defendants provide a preschool program of education and training for children aged less than six years of age, access to a free public program of education and training appropriate to his learning capacities to every mentally retarded child of the same age.

(i) to provide notice and the opportunity for a hearing prior to a change in educational status of any child who is mentally retarded or thought to be mentally retarded;

(j) to re-evaluate the educational assignment of every mentally retarded child not less than every two years, or annually upon the parents' request, and upon such re-evaluation, to provide notice and the opportunity for a hearing.

T. H. BELL

THE FEDERAL ROLE IN EDUCATION

I appreciate the invitation of the *Harvard Educational Review* to come here to discuss the evolving federal role in education and relate it to our New Federalism theme. Since this is a Sunday afternoon I would like to begin by talking a little bit about Moses. As you know, Moses was summoned to the top of Mount Sinai, and there the Lord appeared to him in the form of a fiery cloud. And to the accompaniment of thunder and lightning, God presented him with the Ten Commandments. I want to be a little bit like that this afternoon.

My hope is to lead you atop a metaphorical mountain and briefly examine the federal role in education as viewed by one who occupies a controversial and somewhat wobbly chair at the cabinet table of the Reagan administration. I do not propose to describe the federal role on behalf of this administration, because we're still arguing about that. A few of my colleagues would simply say that there should be no federal role, and others would say that if there is one, it ought to be somewhat different from what I will describe. Let me emphasize that these are *my* perceptions of this role as a Republican who considers himself a conservative but who recently has been accused of being far too liberal. I hope that this description will make a contribution to the growing public debate over the federal role in education, and perhaps to the growing controversy over public education as a whole.

Federalism is a uniquely American contribution to mankind's political storehouse. President Ronald Reagan quite eloquently explained portions of the philosophy of federalism in his 1981 address to the National Conference of State Legislatures:

> The designers of our Constitution realized that in federalism there is diversity. The Founding Fathers saw the federal system as constructed something like a masonry wall. The states are the bricks, the national government is the mortar. For the structure to stand plumb with the Constitution there must be a proper mix of that brick and mortar. Unfortunately, over the years many people have come to believe that Washington is the whole wall.

Federalism allows compromises that serve both local and national interests, simultaneously safeguarding the nation from excessive parochialism and protecting the community from unchecked centralism. President Reagan's New Federalism consists of certain initiatives such as block grants, strong efforts at deregulation, and the return of tax resources to the states. These policies reflect what the administration terms a "capacity-building strategy." Although in the area of education state governments are the pivots of this delicate balance, local governments and private institutions must be considered as well.

In my view, education is clearly the most important responsibility of our state governments. However, a limited federal role in education is required because despite past progress and acceptable responsiveness, the states have not done well recently. They have been unresponsive to clear signals for change.

State legislatures, governors, and other policymakers must initiate changes in such areas as teacher personnel policies that will make the educational profession more attractive to bright and talented young men and women. State and local leaders should also strengthen other well-known problem areas such as achievement in mathematics, science, and technology, as well as foreign language instruction. We all recognize a need for state legislatures to produce better equalization formulas to protect localities from unfair funding burdens that cause property tax rebellions like those in California and Massachusetts, and also to protect students from vast differences between school systems in financial resources. These areas have long been in need of state attention.

Rather than local governments turning to the federal government out of exasperation with unresponsive state legislatures, a better solution is to strengthen state governments and thereby preserve the diversity within what has been the hallmark of American democracy. To say that education is a state, local, and private responsibility is not to minimize its importance. On the contrary, because it is so important we must ensure its administration by the most appropriate levels of government. To eliminate the waste of human potential, education must provide a more productive return on invested human capital. The Reagan administration sees the federal role in education as one of enhancing the capacity of states and localities to make education more productive. The federal government should continue to play a role in education. As I see it, this role is fivefold.

First, the federal government has a responsibility for protecting civil rights, through education, negotiation, mediation, and as a last resort, enforcement. The Office of Civil Rights in the Department of Education is charged with this role, and we consider it to be a very significant part of our department. We receive complaints of discrimination and violation of rights, and we are required to investigate them. We are striving to involve more local and state officials in compliance activities. I believe that the states have left the burden of civil rights enforcement to the federal government. While the federal government should not shirk this responsibility, the states should assume a more assertive role. We have put as much emphasis as possible on persuasion, but have needed to resort to enforcement several times during my tenure as Secretary of Education.

The second aspect of this fivefold role is leadership, advocacy, and constructive criticism of all aspects of American education. The federal role is not to command or direct, but through research to discern nationwide trends, call attention to weaknesses, and recognize excellence. Currently, one of the most important aspects of this responsibility is the work of the National Commission on Excellence in Education. If the findings of this commission are persuasive, the federal government can use its leadership role to make an impact upon American education by convening meetings, stimulating debate, and increasing awareness and concern about the status of both public and private schooling. This important aspect of the federal role has not received sufficient attention.

The third aspect of the federal role concerns educational research and development. We need to learn more about learning and be involved in implementing what we learn. This important responsibility is managed by the National Institute of Education and other parts of the research arm of the Department of Education. The large amount of money needed to carry out this research can be more effectively allocated on the federal level. That is not to suggest that the federal government should do all of the research, but through coordination and leadership we can commission and finance studies that would not otherwise be funded because of the large amount of money involved. There is no need for 50 separate state education departments and 16,000 local school districts to pursue many of these endeavors independently.

The fourth aspect of this role is the capacity-building function I mentioned earlier. Currently, the major portion of the Department of Education's $13 billion budget is devoted to carrying out this responsibility. Although there are certain nationwide populations that are being ignored or insufficiently served, we believe that we ought to be playing a limited role. The allocation of funds to assure equal educational opportunity and access to higher education through student aid programs is part of this role. In addition, we recognize the need for some limited federal funding in aiding special populations such as the handicapped, the disadvantaged, and children with limited proficiency in English. In such a broad and diverse system as ours, there will be target populations that need special attention, and we recognize the necessity to provide this attention. Had it not been for the federal government, much of the attention currently focused on these target populations would not exist.

Our approach to this problem is through the capacity-building function. Decisions concerning the amount and purpose of financial assistance are obviously important considerations in any discussion of the federal role as it relates to this capacity-building strategy. If the purpose of federal financial assistance is to enhance the capacity of others to carry out their responsibilities, then there should be a gradual building and strengthening of the capacities of individual schools, school systems, and the states to assume more responsibility—the responsibility that we argue is theirs more than it is ours. Had they carried out their responsibility in the past, there would be no need to give them federal funds now.

Although it is frequently charged that our ultimate aim is to totally abandon any federal financial assistance, let me emphasize that we are not suggesting abandonment. This capacity-building may be a long-range strategy, so we are not suggesting an abrupt shutoff of funds. But ultimately federal financial assistance ought to be so successful in enhancing the capacity of those whose proper responsibility it is to meet these needs, that we can terminate federal financing and move on to other areas where there are nationwide deficiencies.

We should never consider any particular program as permanent; nor should we assume the full financial burden, or guarantee a certain specified percentage of the budget to any given program. We do not agree with the National Education Association that any specified fraction of the cost of education should be assumed by the federal government. The capacity-building strategy recognizes that education is a federal *concern,* but a local, state, and institutional *responsibility.* At some levels, we would argue that it is a responsibility of the family and the individual. Federal resources should be used to help people to help themselves, and this is not accomplished by helping those who do not need help. For example, recent amendments to the student loan program qualified everyone, regardless of income level and need, to receive a federally subsidized student loan. From the conservative perspective, this goes much too far. One does not strengthen or build capacity by taking over total responsibility, or by assuming more of the burden than is necessary. It is not beneficial to help someone by picking up and carrying the entire burden oneself.

Let me reemphasize that we advocate equality of opportunity. Our laws assume fundamental civil rights, and we champion those ideals. We champion an opportunity for everyone who can benefit from education to have an equal chance, or as nearly equal a chance as possible. There need not be any conflict between equality of opportunity and the concept of capacity building. It is a matter of how we try to strengthen those who are responsible for ensuring equality of opportunity. For example, we do not want to displace students' parents from their traditional role of overseeing their children's education, and students' responsibility to do as much as can reasonably be expected to finance their own education beyond high school. Assistance should be given only where it is indispensable, and it must be carefully measured, restrained, and limited. We suggest that the amendments to the Federal Higher Education Act of 1980 went far beyond this restrained assistance. In passing these amendments, the federal government said that every person in the United States is entitled to federal financial assistance regardless of their income level, and that it should be available to everyone regardless of need.

Some argue that our budget cuts are too drastic. In connection with this complaint, I want to discuss the history of the federal government's role in meeting the needs of disadvantaged children. In 1965 Congress passed the Elementary and Secondary Education Act, which contained many titles. Title I had the largest funding and was intended to have the greatest impact. Next to the Student Loan Program, it is still the largest program funded by the Department of Education. It has been very successful, and I have used the data related to that success in my arguments for the program's continued funding. The program has also had modest success as a capacity-building strategy. Many states now have their own state compensatory education program; none of them had it when the program began. If the program had been more effective at building capacity throughout its seventeen-year history, disadvantaged students would now be served much more effectively by their state and local school systems. The federal government should soon be shifting its resources to other priorities. This does not mean that we ought to pull out permanently and leave students without service. In fact, this imminent lack of funds has been my central concern in urging the Reagan administration to maintain the current funding level.

This desire to maintain the present level of funding for the disadvantaged is related to our decision to reduce the amount allocated to the guaranteed student loan program. We have a tremendous budget problem right now, and it is impossible for the federal government to meet all of our country's educational needs, especially the needs of the huge guaranteed student loan program. We do not propose to take over the traditional responsibility of the local school board, the state equalization program, and the state legislature in funding the needs of all students. We should defer to the state and local governments and attempt to strengthen them and enhance their capacity to meet these needs themselves. We should remember that when our system of government was established, the federal government did not delegate to the states the responsibility for education. On the contrary, the states created the federal government, and the states reserved to themselves those powers—such as education—which are not specified as federal responsibilities.

The fifth federal role in education is to strengthen national research capabilities, particularly university-based research. In contrast to the four other major educational roles, this is not primarily a responsibility of the Department of Education, but a government-wide responsibility. In fact, we are less involved in this role than other departments. Our colleges and universities have been responsible for the country's innovations—the great new discoveries, ideas, and inventions that have contributed so much to our life-style. I believe that the importance of university-based research is one of the great untold stories in America today. The contributions of our great research universities to the betterment of our daily lives, our national security, our storehouse of knowledge, and our understanding of one another have not been fully described to the general public. This research capability is important in medicine, agriculture, industrial and manufacturing practices, communications, and national defense. The federal government has a significant role to play here.

In summary, we are concerned about the autonomy, the diversity, and the strengthening of our people, as well as our local and state governments. We are also concerned about both public and private institutions, because they are essential to our nation's education. We assert that the federal government has an interest in preserving this great, diverse, and decentralized system, in maintaining its autonomy, in keeping it free from the stringent controls of centralism, and in encouraging choice as well as access. The question is, how do we accomplish this? Republicans and conservatives want to place a great deal of emphasis on a strategy of leverage for every federal dollar. We want to be very frugal about how many dollars are spent, and how they are spent. In areas that are clearly the responsibility of other levels of government, we want to ensure that the federal government does not pick up the load to such an extent that in the long haul the state and local levels become unable to carry it. We want to avoid rushing in with overly abundant federal dollars. We admit to wanting to keep a bit of creative tension in the system, a bit of pressure—if you please—on those who are truly responsible. When we talk about student aid, we look to students, parents, and the private sector. When we talk about maintaining the elementary and secondary system, we turn to local and state tax dollars. These points are key to the Republican view that emerges from the conservative perspective of limited help and limited government, with heavy emphasis upon private enterprise, local autonomy, and restrained decisionmaking in Washington. We deny that we are lacking in compassion and concern. We say that what we stand for is what is best for the individual. We suggest that you look first at the end of your own right arm when you need a helping hand. Why? Because that is where self-respect, independence, character, productivity, and the will to achieve are all to be found. You can weaken by helping too much. We say, "Hold back on the public help, use it frugally, be sparing with it." One can be concerned and filled with compassion and love and still be a bit tough-minded and tightfisted and wise to ways that do not strengthen others, but weaken them.

This then, is the rationale behind our effort to make budget cuts. How much should we spend in the Department of Education? Others in the administration would spend less than I would, because I am partisan for my department. However, I do believe that we have provided too much student aid in the past, and that with respect to Title I, we have not concentrated enough on strengthening other levels of government that have a responsibility. I do not believe that it is the intent of this administration to abandon all federal financial assistance. We would like to be so successful in our capacity-building efforts that we could move on to other emerging priorities and make it possible for others to carry out their responsibilities more effectively by not helping them too much.

BEVERLY P. COLE

THE STATE OF EDUCATION FOR BLACK AMERICANS

The struggle to obtain equal access to quality education for black Americans has been long and arduous. Before the Civil War, every slave state had laws against blacks being educated. When the education of blacks was finally permitted, it was established on a separate and decidedly unequal basis. Not until 1954 (*Brown v. Board of Education*) did the Supreme Court hand down its historic decision that, in the field of education, the doctrine of separate but equal had no place. The court further declared that "It is doubtful that any child may reasonably be expected to succeed in life if he is denied the opportunity of education. Such an opportunity is a right which must be made available to all on equal terms."

In the 1980's, this right is being greatly undermined at the Federal level by anti-busing legislation, severe budget cuts in education and student assistance, proposals for tuition tax credit, the granting of tax-exempt status to schools that blatantly discriminate, the exemption of certain schools from civil rights regulations, the revision of affirmative action requirements, and the abdication to the states of the Federal government's role of monitoring and enforcing equal access to quality education.

On the local level, the right to a quality education is being denied by

From Beverly P. Cole, "The State of Education for Black Americans," *USA Today*, May 1983. Reprinted with permission of the author.

indifferent and insensitive teachers and administrators, by the lack of school accountability, low expectations of students' potential, pushing-out due to discriminatory disciplinary practices, inadequate equipment, poor curricular and career counseling, racially isolated schools, labeling, tracking, and discriminatory school financing policies.

In spite of these obstacles, blacks have made some progress educationally. There has been a significant increase in school enrollment, with 51% of blacks aged 25 or older graduating from high school. Today, more blacks stay in school longer and go on to college than they did a quarter of a century ago.

On the other hand, this progress has been inadequate to close the gap between black and white educational attainments and, indeed, is minuscule when compared to the overwhelming educational needs of blacks. In many ways, the progress can be described as one step forward and two steps backwards.

In evaluating the educational attainments of blacks, one must not only look at enrollment rates, but also at completion rates, as well as the quality of the education experience.

- The dropout rate of blacks in high school is 28%, as compared to 17% for whites. Although blacks comprise 10% of the college population, whites are still twice as likely as blacks to be college graduates. Many attribute these statistics to an unresponsive school system.
- In most inner-city schools, where approximately 75% of black students are in attendance, achievement levels are usually two or more years behind the national norm.
- Studies have shown that black children tend to drop below grade level in elementary school and fall further behind as they get older, until, at age 16, at least 35% are below their modal grade.

Many theories have been offered to explain this disgrace; most built upon the notion of "blaming the victim." "Cultural deprivation," "the culture of poverty," the deficit model, "the disadvantaged"—all explained why the low socioeconomic student could not overcome the problems of poverty and social pathology and be expected to learn.

Nevertheless, the results of the "effective schools" research clearly demonstrate that children can be educated successfully, regardless of their family background. However, one of the main prerequisites is a belief and expectation on the part of the teacher and principal that this feat can be accomplished. Schools must demonstrate respect for the dignity of all students and be committed to the principle that all students are educable, regardless of their race or economic background.

Educators know what practices make schools effective, but in many cases are unwilling to implement them. We must hold schools accountable and stop entertaining excuses. As parents and interested citizens, we must also accept our fair share of the responsibility for motivating students, supporting them, and serving as advocates to insure that they receive a quality education.

IMPROVING THE QUALITY OF EDUCATION

NAACP branches across the nation are attempting to improve the deteriorating quality of education received by blacks by insisting upon:

- Equal access to quality integrated education at all levels from pre-school to professional schools.
- High expectations on the part of teachers in terms of achievement and behavior.
- Basic academic skills being taught and mastered at an early age (reading, mathematics, written and oral communications).
- A curriculum that develops skills of logic, analysis, problem-solving, and test-taking.
- Multi-cultural textbooks and materials.
- Teachers trained in multi-ethnic education/relations with more inner-city student teaching experiences.
- The utilization of a multi-method approach to evaluation and assessment.
- The elimination of tracking or homogeneous grouping.
- More teacher accountability.
- Counseling programs that encourage and advise students concerning varied career opportunities, the required courses, financial assistance, and other resources needed to pursue post-secondary education or other experiences consistent with their career goals and potential.
- Policies and procedures which insure racial fairness in classrooms and schools such as fair grading and evaluations, fair involvement in student activities, and fair discipline.
- Participation of parents and community leaders in the school process.
- Affirmative action in the hiring and promotion of black teachers and administrators to ensure that black students have appropriate role models.

These goals and objectives were chosen because of various reasons. Black children continue to be confined to separate and unequal schools; over 70% of black students are in predominantly minority schools. When desegregation occurs, research such as the seven-year study on The Effectiveness of School Desegregation produced by Vanderbilt University has shown that the achievement scores of minority students increase significantly and the achievement gains are likely to be maximized when desegregation is begun in the early grades. These findings notwithstanding, "neighborhood school proponents or anti-busing foes are accusing mandatory pupil assignments—for purposes of desegregation—of destroying public education and blighting entire communities across the country with its divisive impact." This is a myth and a gross exaggeration. Approximately 50% of schoolchildren are bused to school and, of this number, only three per cent are bused for purposes of desegregation. It is obvious that busing is not the real issue. The real issue is avoidance of quality integrated education.

Busing is not the goal, but only a means of technique for accomplishing the goal. If the purpose of education were only to teach selected academic subjects, then perhaps there would be no need for the desegregation of schools. All that would be needed is the enhancement of the present racially isolated schools. However, since the education institution is one of society's primary means of socialization, then it needs to teach our children to associate with different races and economic groups in order to exist compatibly in this pluralistic country and the world. Integration is an essential component of a quality education for everyone—black, white, brown, yellow, and red. The anti-busing amendment recently passed by the Senate as well as local initiatives are threatening to prevent this ideal from ever becoming a reality.

As was alluded to earlier, teacher expectation is one of the most crucial determinants of student effort, motivation, and achievement. Rosenthal's famous Pygmalion experiment demonstrated how teacher expectation creates self-fulfilling prophecy. If teachers expect that some children will fail, more than likely the children will fail. This occurs because the varied expectations, based often on race and income, are translated into different behavior. This treatment communicates to the students what behavior and achievement the teacher expects from them and affects their self-concepts, achievement motivation, and levels of aspiration.

The curriculum is another major source of concern. Students must be offered competent instruction in reading, writing, mathematics, and the process of logical thought. Beyond the minimum basic skills, the curriculum should be challenging in order to stimulate students to develop skills of logic, analysis, problem-solving, and test-taking—all of which they will need in this highly technological society. Stressing minimum basic skills is good only if the minimum does not become the maximum offered.

Secondly, our society is a pluralistic one, and the textbooks and materials must reflect this. Black children need to know about the contributions that their race has made to America. They can not learn to be proud of their heritage if all they encounter in school are the achievements of whites. In an effort to enhance the self-image and sense of worth of minority students, as well as to inform white youth, school officials should replace all biased and stereotyped schoolbooks and curriculum aids with materials which accurately reflect in text and illustrations the history and participation of blacks and other minorities.

In order for teachers to be responsive to the needs of minority children, they need more training in multi-cultural/multi-ethnic education and they need more inner-city student teaching experiences. Most teachers have very little knowledge of the poor's urban experiences. For this reason, teachers and administrators should be required to attend in-service training programs geared toward helping them come to terms with their own behavior and attitudes toward students from different cultural, ethnic, racial, and social backgrounds.

In addition, we must press for affirmative action in the hiring of black teachers and administrators to insure that black students have appropriate role models. In order to achieve this, educational systems must set goals and timetables in order to measure the effectiveness of recruitment, retention, and promotion efforts.

In terms of teacher accountability, administrators should expect more and demand more. New procedures need to be instituted for relieving the school system of those teachers who are indifferent, ineffective, and unwilling or unable to improve.

The I.Q. tests, the standardized aptitude tests, and the recent competency tests have been greatly misused in relation to black students and have caused great harm in terms of damaging self-images and life chances. Tests have been used for channeling black students into "slow tracks" and mentally retarded classes and for screening them out of higher education and jobs. For blacks, tests have meant exclusion, rather than inclusion into America's mainstream, and thus have been used to further stratify the society.

It is obvious that some type of assessment is needed, and testing for purposes of evaluation or diagnosis, when used in order to improve skills of the student, is both meaningful and desirable. A good assessment program utilizes a multi-method approach for evaluation. No one sole criterion should be used for such critical determinations as graduation, promotion, certification, college entrance, and hiring. Yet, the reality is that it is much easier to accept a standardized test score than to analyze systematically the strengths and weaknesses of students by multiple means. Therefore, accuracy has been sacrificed for expediency.

Culturally biased I.Q. tests are infamous for causing a disproportionate number of blacks to be placed into "special education" and mentally retarded classes. It would amaze you to know the number of outstanding black professionals who at one time in their early life were labeled in this manner.

Competency testing, which is being used by some 38 states, tends to place the burden of accountability solely on the students. This form of testing should be done at a stage where remedial action can be taken, and teachers as well as students should be held accountable in terms of which skills have been introduced and which skills have been mastered. In those school systems which use competency tests for purposes of promotion, students should be assigned to non-graded classes where they can advance according to their individual achievement and where the stigma of repeating a grade would be avoided.

"Tracking" or homogeneous grouping is synonymous with "trapping" at a very early age. This procedure can cause a child to view himself as being incompetent and consequently establish the self-fulfilling prophecy. Based on test scores, students are often placed into a "slow group" and kept there in the less rigorous dead-end curricula all the way through school, which often creates segregation within a desegregated school. No child is slow in everything. In a heterogeneous environment, there is opportunity for the strong to help and inspire the weak.

Another area that requires careful monitoring is guidance and counseling. The counseling is very limited in inner-city schools; often, a student will not see a counselor unless he is in trouble. It is important that when advice is given it is not based on false assumptions about presumed abilities and aspirations because of the student's racial or class identification. Counseling programs must be provided that will encourage and advise students concerning the required courses and available financial aid to attend college, post-secondary education, or other experiences consistent with their career goals and potential.

In terms of administrative practices, there is a need for the elimination of dehumanizing and exploitative practices for all students. Policies and procedures must be designed to insure racial fairness in classrooms and schools such as fair grading and evaluations, fair involvement in student activities, and fair discipline and suspension. It has been shown that, at the high school level, blacks are suspended three times as often as whites. While minority students are about 25% of the school population, they constitute about 40% of all suspended and expelled students. Furthermore, black students are suspended for longer periods of time. All schools need to examine carefully those conditions at the school which precipitate pushouts and dropouts.

Parental and community involvement are essential ingredients for quality education. Confidence in the school and support for its endeavors occur when parents believe that they have access to school personnel and have some influence over what happens to their children. The family and community must support school efforts and the school must serve the community. Lack of parental involvement in the education system to a large extent has been primarily because parents feel intimidated and unwelcomed, and lack the skills and information to impact upon the school system. Therefore, many black parents become disenchanted and withdrawn from the educational process. Yet they still hold high hopes for their children's education, for they know that education is the means to employment, upward social mobility, recognition, and esteem.

Another factor that explains the difference in the scope, content, and quality of the education that blacks receive is the inequitable distribution of revenues and resources to inner-city schools. Despite the overwhelming need, our society spends less money educating inner-city children than children of the suburbs. This is due largely to the declining city tax base and increasing competition from municipal needs (*e.g.*, police, welfare, fire) for the tax dollar. The suburbs, where these demands are less, allocate twice the proportion of their total budgets to education as do the cities. Several judicial decisions have attempted to make school spending independent of property values in order to reduce the gap in per-pupil expenditures between wealthy and low-income school districts.

Researchers have also studied the relationship between students' socioeconomic status and the amounts of school resources made available to them and have found that school districts allocate substantially fewer dollars to schools in poor and black neighborhoods. The intra-district disparities are often just as great as inter-district ones. Other formulas and methods for financing need to be devised.

THE BUDGET SQUEEZE

The Reagan Administration has taken steps that will widen the gap between black and white education attainment. The budget requested for education for 1983 is $10,300,000,000, as compared to $13,000,000,000 proposed to be spent on education in the fiscal year 1982. These proposed budget cuts adversely affect minority education programs the most and represent a big step backward in educational opportunities for the disadvantaged.

The Council of Great City Schools is an organization that represents the nation's 28 largest urban school districts, serving 5,000,000 students, of which 75% are minorities. This council stated that the proposed cuts in education would be especially severe in their areas, where 16% of big-city school revenues come from Washington, as compared to the national average of eight per cent.

These school systems estimate a loss of $300,000,000, which will have the cumulative effect of jeopardizing 12,000 jobs and curtailing or eliminating services to about 235,000 inner-city youngsters. The bulk of the cuts would occur in Title I funding, a program designed for low-achieving students in low-income areas. Some 78% of U.S. school districts receive Title I aid and approximately 50% of the children served are from minority groups—29% being black.

Several research studies have shown that the Title I program has been very successful in improving achievement, especially for minority students. The National Assessment of Educational Progress indicated improvement in the relative performance of black youth at ages nine and 13 in five learning areas. It is believed that this may be attributed to Federal programs designed to foster equal educational opportunity, especially Title I.

In spite of Title I's success, the President is proposing to cut its funds by 40% from the 1981–82 funding level. If Congress approves the proposed budget cuts, it would eliminate nearly 2,500,000 children from the program, leaving only 27% of the nation's children who need the services actually receiving them.

Another move which would restrict access to higher education—and consequently to the mainstream of society—is the drastic reduction in student financial assistance. Proposed for 1983 is a 44% reduction in the over-all student assistance program, which will impact approximately 2,000,000 needy students. Since over 80% of all black students enrolled in post-secondary institutions receive some Federal assistance either through a loan or a grant or both, black progress in higher education stands to be severely impeded.

The Pell Grant program, the largest of the Education Department's major aid programs for needy students, has been cut by 36% for 1983, requiring parents to contribute more for their children's education. Changes in the eligibility criteria for Pell Grants would eliminate about 1,000,000 students by 1983. Three programs—Supplemental Grants, State Incentive Grants, and National Direct Student Loans—would not receive any funds for 1983. The proposed reduction of college workstudy funding would eliminate 250,000 needy students from the program. The trio program specifically designed for the disadvantaged would be reduced by 47%. The budget would kill three of the five trio programs. The precollege counseling programs—Talent Search and Equal Opportunity Centers—would vanish under the proposal. Graduate and professional opportunity fellowships as well as assistance to needy students in the law school Cleo program would be eliminated.

Graduate students would be eliminated from the Guaranteed Student Loan program under the new proposal. Six hundred thousand students, more than half the current graduate school enrollment, depend on guaranteed student loans, and the majority of them probably will not be able to stay in school if the Administration's proposal to withdraw graduate aid entirely is approved by Congress. In addition, the Social Security Administration is planning top phase out payments to children of deceased, retired, or disabled parents at the rate of 25% each year until the program ends in 1985—with no checks being issued for the summer months. Any student not enrolled in college full-time by May, 1982, would not be eligible for Social Security aid. It is estimated that over 150,000 high school seniors will become ineligible for Social Security assistance for college.

The cumulative effect of such cuts, at a time of rising college costs (15% to 20%) and reductions in other programs, can tip the balance between the student's looking to education to better his employment possibilities or giving up. For blacks, attrition in higher education to a great extent is affected by financial aid policies. The dropout rate for blacks who do not receive any aid is 46%, as compared to 29% for whites.

COSTS TO SOCIETY

The costs to our society of not educating one person in terms of crime, welfare expenditures, and foregone productivity are far higher than the expense of a quality education from birth. When considering the cost effectiveness of programs like Title I, we should remember that it costs $26,000 a year to keep a man in prison.

The black community is quite concerned about Congress placing educational categorical programs such as the Teacher Corps and the Emergency School Aid Act—a program designed to assist school districts struggling with problems of racial isolation and desegregation—into block grants. It is feared that the objectives of these programs will be lost, and that the special needs of the poor and minorities will be left to the discretion of thousands of state and local officials, whose decisions about the allocation of funds will be based upon the political pressure in their jurisdictions. Past experiences have shown that states have not provided sufficient funds for the disadvantaged and minorities, and their funding formulas have been discriminatory.

Increased Federal legislation had to be developed in order to address the needs of the poor and minorities. If more control is relinquished to the local school systems, then the Federal government in turn must ensure that minority and disadvantaged students will receive adequate and appropriate resources.

With the proposed dismantling of the Department of Education and replacing it with the Foundation for Education Assistance, the Administration has decided to redefine the Federal role from one of promoting and ensuring equal access to quality integrated education to one of data collection and analysis, administration of block grants, and student financial assistance. The Foundation's civil rights role is limited to providing counsel, advice, and technical assistance concerning civil rights compliance upon request to recipients of Federal aid. Civil rights enforcement, however, would be turned over to the Justice Department.

Regardless of what happens to the Office of Civil Rights in the Department of Education, the Administration has made it clear that the role of the Federal government is one of advancing civil rights, not enforcing it, using cooperation rather than threatened sanctions to achieve its objectives.

The laws and regulations that took decades to achieve are being dismantled in a matter of months. The new affirmative action regulations would require fewer employers to file affirmative action plans and subject them to fewer reviews. Approximately 80% of the colleges and universities which previously were investigated and ordered to draw up detailed affirmative action plans to hire and promote women and minorities will be exempt. This poses a serious problem not only in terms of employment for minority professionals, but decreases appropriate role models for minority youth as well.

In addition, the Reagan Administration has decided to exempt from antidiscrimination laws those colleges at which guaranteed student loans are the only form of Federal aid. The new rules would significantly limit the number of colleges and universities that must comply with civil rights laws. This shift in policy and reinterpretation of what constitutes Federal assistance is designed to have the same effect as the decision to grant tax-exempt status to schools which racially discriminate.

Finally, the President has introduced tuition tax credit legislation. When you begin to analyze the implications of these actions, you can not help but conclude that access to the mainstream is being deliberately restricted by those who have a stake in their privileged position. When you see being proposed at both the local and national levels legislation that would provide tuition tax credits for parents of children enrolled in private schools, you realize that these tax credits are not designed to provide all parents with a choice concerning the education of their children, for it would not help the 8,600,000 blacks below the poverty level. It was designed to provide relief for the tax-burdened middle class and to encourage escape from the urban public schools with their growing enrollment of poor and minority youngsters. If enacted, these measures would increase social class and racial isolation by establishing a two-tiered educational system in this country—the private schools for the white and middle class and the public schools for the poor and minority. Private education should not be enhanced at the expense of public education, which is the cornerstone of our democracy.

Much remains to be done to finish the uncompleted task of guaranteeing all children in this nation an equal chance at a quality education. The issues of the 1980's are difficult, but not impossible. More concerted effort is needed on the part of all to ensure that black children will receive the kind of training that will equip them to thrive in the pluralistic technological society of which they are a part. We can no longer afford to point the finger and pass the blame. We should all heed the words of Thomas Carlyle: "That there should be one man [to] die ignorant who had the capacity for knowledge, this I call a tragedy."

DISCUSSION QUESTIONS FOR CHAPTER 2

1. Discuss the major points of the meritocratic ideal as set forth in Mann's report on the inequality of educational opportunity in mid-nineteenth-century Massachusetts. In so doing, look at the purposes of the meritocratic ideal as well as obstacles to its achievement as he saw them.
2. Discuss the reasoning behind *Brown v. Board of Education of Topeka,* paying particular attention to the relationship between achievement and the psychological effects of segregation.
3. Compare the "output" model for equal educational opportunity sketched by James S. Coleman with the "input" model as sketched by Horace Mann. What key observations led Coleman to alter the traditional "input" way of thinking about equal educational opportunity?
4. What arguments could be made to support the contention that periodic reevaluation of a student's placement in an educational program should be done for *all* students? What would the major arguments against such a contention be?
5. What are the major points of the "new federalism" in education? How do you think this change in the funding of education will affect equal educational opportunity?
6. What are the major points with which Cole takes issue regarding the "new federalism?" Discuss the validity of each of these.

PART TWO

Education and Human Diversity

3

Human Diversity and the Difference It Makes

In this chapter we deal with the ways in which schools respond to differences in intelligence, socioeconomic status, race, ethnicity, language, and gender. Our concern is general, so we touch on teaching methods only to the extent that they suggest solutions to problems arising from human diversity.

We respond to human differences in three general ways. First, we can ignore the differences. Second, we can subordinate differences to similarities. And third, we can elevate differences to a more important position than similarities. In the last two instances, we frequently associate differences with social roles and status or class positions in a society. The fact of human diversity is so obvious and its influence so prevalent that it is seldom ignored in the planning of school policy, curricula, and instruction. Yet, for all of this, people are seldom satisfied with the ways we deal with human diversity. In this chapter we will be dealing with how diversity (heterogeneity) is seen in relation to homogeneity in the larger society and how differences among human beings are translated into school practice.

The constantly changing features of our population in the United States affect the ways in which human diversity can be accommodated within the major institutions of government, workplace, and school. Try to imagine the difficulty that the approximately 83,000 public schools with a total enrollment of approximately 40 million have in accommodating the following facts, all of which have an impact on students' academic success:

- In 1988, 4.4 percent of the total families (excluding most of those in the Armed Forces) had less than $5,000 income and 22.9 percent had incomes over $50,000. Among whites, these figures were 3.2 percent below $5,000 and 24.4 percent over $50,000. Among blacks the corresponding figures were 13.5 percent below $5,000 and 9.5 percent over $50,000. In 1988 10.1 percent of whites were living below the poverty line. Comparable figures for blacks and Hispanics were 31.6 percent and 26.8 percent.

- Between 1961 and 1987, 11,882,600 immigrants came to the United States. Of these, 36.2 percent came from North America, 33.5 percent came from Asia, and 20.9 percent came from Europe.
- As of July 1, 1988, with the exception of the Hispanic population, females generally outnumbered males. For example, among whites there are 95.7 males for every 100 females; among blacks, 90.2 males for every 100 females; and, in other races, 95.7 males for every 100 females. The startling death rate among young males is evident when we realize that for whites, blacks, and other races *under* age 14 the males outnumbered females by an average of approximately 104 males to every female.
- In 1988, 59.4 percent of white householders lived in family households headed by married couples; 2.8 percent of white households were headed by single males, and 9.2 percent by single females (no spouse present). Among black householders in 1988, 36.1 percent were in family households headed by married couples, while 4.1 percent were headed by a single male and 30.2 percent by a single female. In Hispanic households there were 56.2 percent headed by a married couple, 5.5 percent by a single male head, and 18.8 percent by a single female head.[1]

These four descriptions representing some of the basic social, economic, cultural, and demographic facts of the United States are only the tip of the diversity iceberg. Remember that one individual belongs to many groups and that an individual's behavior simultaneously reflects all the groups to which he or she belongs. These group characteristics combined with unique mental, emotional, and physical characteristics result in a bewildering array of behaviors for every individual. This is multiplied millions of times for the entire population enrolled in the nation's schools.

INTELLIGENCE, CLASSIFICATION, AND HUMAN DIVERSITY

In most teacher education courses, discussion about intelligence tests and their uses centers around technical features of intelligence testing. Statistical problems of reliability and validity are better left to courses on testing and measurement and psychological foundations. We offer a different perspective here. As in the first chapter, matters of social justice and fairness are foremost in our considerations.

The concept of intelligence is far from fixed. Different concepts of intelligence are tied to different theories of the structure of the mind and how it functions. Some emphasize the genetic determinants of intelligence, others emphasize cognitive development, while still others see the mind as an information processing system much like a computer. Since the early twentieth century the most common approach to the study of intelligence has been the psychometric approach. It was the intelligence test and the concept of IQ that made a scale of numbers the central feature of student classification. When the degree of intelligence of a person is referred to today, it is most often in terms of a number on a scale. Even if the reference is not to a specific number, it is to larger categories such as "above average" or "below average" and so on.

The intelligence *test* developed alongside and was linked to a genetic conception of intelligence. More than any other theoretical conception of intelligence, the genetic explanation has led to intense debates over the fairness of its use. For this reason, it is important to look at the ways intelligence and genetics have been linked together historically and in debates among educators.

A HISTORICAL PERSPECTIVE

The concepts of intelligence that emerged in the early twentieth century alongside the development of intelligence testing had two competing standards of reference: hereditarian and behavioral. This division has tended to dominate our thinking about intelligence for the past two-thirds of a century.

Much of the early work on IQ testing was carried out in an attempt to improve the classification and instruction of "mentally defective" children. It was motivated by the practical concerns of diagnosing and "placing" the feebleminded and ill-behaved. According to Binet and Simon, the purpose of the intelligence scale was "to be able to measure the intellectual capacity of a child who is brought to us in order to know whether he is normal or retarded."[2]

Binet and Simon recognized that "special" children did not profit much from ordinary schools, but they were also concerned that special schools for these children were not doing their job. They hoped, moreover, that teachers in special schools would be attentive to the economic and occupational prospects for these "special" children.

The central question in this regard, as Binet and Simon viewed it, was "what becomes of the defectives on leaving school, and what percentage [have been placed] in situations with a suitable salary?" "To judge well, to comprehend well, to reason well," said Binet, "are the essential activities of intelligence."[3] It should be remembered, however, that the context for studying intelligence was the school itself. Thus, the standard of reference was progress in school. Binet's conclusions about the relationship between intelligence and scholastic level were not startling but nonetheless helped to lay the groundwork for the use of IQ as a predictor of academic success. Binet reported a "remarkable correlation" between level of intelligence and scholastic achievement.

The international interest in the Binet scale of intelligence, the fact that it underwent two revisions only a few years following its initial publication, and its immediate practicality in the area of student classification made it a promising instrument for dealing with the problem of retardation in public schools. Psychologists in the United States were quick to recognize its value.

The broad social significance of applying intelligence testing to the selecting and sorting of the feebleminded was addressed explicitly by Lewis Terman, author of *The Measurement of Intelligence* (1916):

In the near future intelligence tests will bring tens of thousands of these high grade defectives under the surveillance and protection of society. This will ultimately result in curtailing the reproduction of feeble-mindedness and in the elimination of an enormous amount of crime, pauperism, and industrial inefficiency.[4]

Terman was equally as forceful in his remarks about the gifted. It was a deplorable waste, he said, to let these children of high ability go unidentified and without special treatment. The "welfare of the country" and the progress of civilization depended upon genius. The "handicapping influences of poverty, social neglect, physical defects, or educational maladjustments" have hidden many of the gifted from view, said Terman.[5]

He was enthusiastic also about the possibilities for using intelligence tests for grade promotion and for "vocational fitness." Of the former, said Terman, "it would be desirable to make all promotions on the basis chiefly of intellectual ability." Of the latter, it was his opinion that research on intelligence would result in identifying "the minimum 'intelligence quotient' necessary for success in each leading occupation." The result would be great savings by industries who presently hire people "not equal to the tasks they are expected to perform."[6] By employing a psychologist, companies could achieve great savings in the long run, said Terman.

As an institution for mass education the school demanded techniques that would help manage large numbers of people. It was not surprising, then, that educators enthusiastically welcomed the Alpha and Beta mass-produced intelligence tests used by the United States Army in 1917. The piloting of the Army intelligence tests was done in the fall of 1971 using four cantonments (85,000 men, including 5,000 officers). Its purposes were classification, selection for positions, and the sorting out of the mentally incompetent. When in 1918 Robert M. Yerkes lectured on the results of this testing, he announced that the uses of mental testing far exceeded the original expectations. In addition to sorting out the feebleminded, unstable, and incorrigible, the tests were useful in identifying those of superior intelligence, organizing battalions to achieve "uniform mental strength," selecting personnel for further education, and providing data enabling each man to "receive instruction suited to his ability to learn."[7]

Like Terman, Yerkes envisioned intelligence testing as a way to rationalize the schooling process. Yerkes's argument rested upon hopes that the school could be made more efficient by a more systematic and early classification of pupils. It was also justified on grounds of equality of opportunity, he said. Yerkes was aware that early classification by intelligence tests could be construed as undemocratic, but, he claimed, it was in fact exactly the opposite. It was his position that educators were "seriously discriminating against individuals because of our failure to take their characteristics and needs into account." Said Yerkes:

> Equality of opportunity in our schools necessitates classification in accordance with ability, individualized treatment, recognition of limitations and of practical limits of educability, differentiation of courses, and vocational direction and

training which shall enable the individual to avoid failure by reason of under-taking the impossible or waste because of the choice of an occupation which makes slight demand upon the ability of the individual.[8]

INTELLIGENCE AND HEREDITY

As we proceed with a discussion of intelligence, it should be remembered that debates over the sources of intelligence are often ideological in nature. In other words, the positions people take on the issue are often motivated by social or political views that are much more comprehensive than the issue of intelligence itself. For example, the views of critics of hereditarian theories of intelligence might be shaped by a particular view of justice that sees hereditarianism as undermining any hope of equal educational opportunity and hence a fair distribution of social and economic rewards. Proponents of hereditarianism might view their position as supportive of a larger educational mission to sort and select talent. This intellectual elite could then be channeled in directions that make it most useful for achieving the social, political, and economic goals established by political and corporate leaders. Whatever side of hereditarianism people line up on, it is highly likely that their choices will be a reflection of the values and purposes they think are legitimate for society and government.

In *The Mismeasure of Man*, Stephen Jay Gould reminds us of a commonly misunderstood distinction between the facts of genetic transmission and a hereditarian theory of intelligence. Though genetic codes are inherited, they do not necessarily result in predetermined kinds of behaviors or limitations. Obvi-ous examples are near-sightedness and far-sightedness which, though inherited, are easily modified. There is, in other words, no inevitable outcome of the inherited condition.[9]

A second source of confusion, Gould notes, is that between individual heredity and group characteristics. Intelligence test scales are applied to individ-uals, of course, and the variations in scores (IQs) show variations among the individuals. To attempt to draw conclusions about differences among groups on the basis of differences among individuals, however, is extremely risky.

The problem Gould finds with the hereditarian theory of intelligence is its focus on a *number* which is supposed to represent something called intelligence. Gould's attack on the hereditarian fallacy was provoked in part by the work of Arthur Jensen, theoretician, clinician, and psychometrician at the University of California at Berkeley. Jensen's work is worth examining because he is an able researcher whose published work over the past quarter century has been the object of great controversy and popularization by the mass media.

Jensen has consistently supported the idea that there exists a general intelligence (g) that cannot be described in terms of specific content or tasks. He has also supported the arguments for "heritability" of intelligence. Says Jensen:

> The heritability of intelligence can only mean that individual differences in IQ and scholastic aptitude are largely a biological, rather than a psychological,

phenomenon, and that the main causes of individual differences are the developmental outcome factors already coded in the DNA at the moment of conception.[10]

Jensen concludes that "successful attempts to alter *g* materially will most probably require biological, rather than purely psychological interventions."[11]

Jensen made many of his arguments in a well-known essay titled "How Much Can We Boost IQ and Scholastic Achievement?" published in the *Harvard Educational Review* in 1969. It immediately caused a storm of criticism, including charges of racism. He began his essay by challenging what he called the "deprivation hypothesis," which, he claimed, explains academic failure or "academic lag" on the basis of environmental factors such as "social, economic and educational deprivation and discrimination. . . ."[12] At the same time Jensen questioned the efficacy of compensatory education programs designed to combat the effects of a "deprived" environment. In a more recent paper given before the American Educational Research Association meeting in 1984, Jensen reiterated the "plain truth," as he put it, "that compensatory programs have not resulted in any appreciable, durable gains in the IQs or scholastic achievements of those to whom they have been administered."[13]

The relationship between race and intelligence was almost a taboo subject in the 1960s. In the beginning of the subsection titled "Race Differences" in his 1969 essay, Jensen took great care to explain the difference between the "individual" and a "population," but his discussion of racial differences in intelligence touched a sensitive chord. The context of Jensen's remarks was the problem of fairness (or unfairness) in "society's multiple selection process." The disproportionately lower number of racial minority individuals entering higher-order occupations obviously raised the issue of discrimination. Yet it also pointed to the possibility that there were "real average differences among groups. . . ."[14]

Jensen then went on to cite evidence showing that "Negroes test about 1 standard deviation (15 IQ points) below the average of the white population in IQ. . . ." Environmental explanations for these differences in IQ were not adequate, according to Jensen. Genetic differences resulting from a different racial gene pool, he said, would have to be considered as a possible explanatory factor.[15]

"Like it or not," said Jensen, "the educational system is one of society's most powerful mechanisms for sorting out children to assume different roles in the occupational hierarchy." It is this screening process, he said, that, in fact, helps to create the positive correlation between socioeconomic status and intelligence. Though Jensen allowed that the selecting and sorting process was not "fair in any absolute sense," he maintained that the "best we can ever hope for is that true merit, given equality of opportunity, [will] act as a basis for the natural assorting process."[16]

Jensen's arguments immediately caused a storm of protest. Critics attacked his research as well as the inferences he drew from it. Scholars and researchers like Jerome Kagan and J. McV. Hunt pointed out that Jensen's research failed to take sufficient account of the early formative years of a child's life and thus failed to recognize the important developmental and environmental interactions that influence intelligence. Lee J. Cronbach of Stanford University pointed to Jensen's misuse of genetic arguments, particularly his suggestions that the "gene pools" of blacks are inferior. Cronbach pointed out that different environments themselves will produce different findings about the heritability of intelligence.[17]

More recently, Steven Selden has traced the history of student classification as it relates to intelligence testing. He has pointed out that biological determinism of the type that Jensen enunciates has led to many historical abuses of human welfare in the name of equal opportunity. The arguments of men such as Albert E. Wiggam (*The New Decalogue of Science*, 1923), Charles C. Peters (*Foundations of Educational Sociology*, 1924), and Henry C. Goddard (*The Kalikak Family*, 1912), he states, were shaped by their assumptions about inequalities among people and their commitment to a meritocratic system for distributing educational and social benefits. These assumptions, in turn, led to educational policies based on the segregation of exceptionality. Ironically, such policies were defended on the basis of equal opportunity, when it is far more likely that they reinforced already existing inequalities.[18]

Debates over the heritability of intelligence have been particularly heated because the idea of genetic determination has such profound implications for how the economic, social, and political systems of a country should be structured. The issues raised by the heritability of intelligence are highly charged with ethical considerations.

One of the questions which the measurement of intelligence and genetic endowment forces us to confront is whether or not, or how much, knowledge about genetic endowment should be used to control the development and employment of human resources. Though the genetic endowment of an individual is not a matter of his or her choice, the use of knowledge about that endowment is. Its use involves ethical questions.

One might justifiably ask, at this point, "Where do we stand?" and "Why has there been so much concern over genetic endowment and heritability?" The answer is deceptively simple. We wish to know how human diversity may be dealt with in a fair and equitable manner. It will not do to simply apply a technical answer to an ethical issue. It is not difficult to classify people or to devise measurements that will be reliable for doing so. What is difficult is to respect human diversity rather than viewing it as an obstacle to greater technical proficiency in the management of human resources. Throughout this chapter we will emphasize the problems schools encounter in dealing with human diversity and how they can respond in a reflective, humane, and just way.

RACE, ETHNICITY, AND AMERICAN SCHOOLING

In the first chapter we outlined the problem of justice as it relates to race and racism, including the ways in which federal legislation and federal courts addressed the persistent problems of racism and racial strife. These included the rejection of the "separate but equal" doctrine ensconced in *Plessy v. Ferguson*

(1896) with the ground-breaking decision in *Brown v. Board of Education of Topeka* (1954); the passage of the 1964 Civil Rights Act and 1965 Voting Rights Act; the application of *Brown* to Hispanic minorities in *Cisneros v. Corpus Christi Independent School District* (1970); the extension of the reasoning of *Brown* to issues of equity in *Hobson v. Hansen II* (1971), *Serrano v. Priest* (1971), and *San Antonio v. Rodriquez* (1973); and Title IX of the Educational Amendments of 1972.

Historically, the term *race* has denoted human groups distinguished either by unique physical characteristics and/or cultural differences. Biologically, the term has been used to designate subgroups of the species Homo sapiens. These groups are often based on differences in presumed "gene pools" that are shared by reproductive communities. In turn, these groups sometimes have been defined by geographical boundaries. The difficulty of using physical, genetic, and geographical standards of reference for race can be seen in the simple historical fact that estimates by anthropologists on the number of races have ranged from 2 to 200.[19]

Because of the difficulties in defining race, it is more useful to speak of race as a legal and cultural concept. The Supreme Court of the United States approved the use of race as a way of classifying human beings in *Plessy v. Ferguson* (1896). As we have seen, the *Brown* cases further legitimized "race" as a proper legal term. When dealing with educational issues, however, race as a *cultural* concept is better suited to understanding how people's beliefs about race affect learning, teaching, and educational policy.[20] Defining race as a cultural concept, for example, allows us to look at how *ethnocentrism* (perceiving one's own group as superior to other groups of people) leads to stereotyping, social distancing, racism, and, in general, the classification of groups of people into inferior and superior.[21]

As we have discussed in Chapter 1, equal educational opportunity as a means of achieving social justice has been a persistent theme in American education. The ideal of equal educational opportunity also has created the expectation that more schooling will "open doors" to minority youth and those from lower socioeconomic groups. Yet the numbers simply do not justify such an expectation. Among African Americans, the gap between middle- and low-income families has increased over the past twenty years. From 1976 to 1988 college enrollments of African Americans declined slightly as did the percent of those receiving a degree. For Hispanic Americans the drop was more precipitious. For low-income whites, however, college enrollments rose during the same period. Declining availability of student financial aid was a major factor in declining college enrollments for African Americans and Hispanic Americans. No matter what the cause, however, the expectations of equal educational opportunity were not being met.[22]

If we understand that the hard facts of numbers undercut claims of equal educational opportunity, then it becomes more understandable why so many minority youth do not share the "American dream." They are alienated from the dream and what it represents. The educational result of alienation is often some sort of openly hostile behavior, such as refusal to abide by school rules or dropping out of school. Alienation also results in "tuning out" (dropping out *in* school). For example, the persistent use of Black English (even when understanding standard English) may be a modest refusal to submit to the mainstream culture of white America. Chicanos and Cholos who wish to avoid conduct associated with "being white or gringo or quaddie or rich honkie" avoid behaviors associated with the dominant group. Thus participation in classroom discussion, carrying books to class, asking the teacher for help in the presence of other students, and aspiring to higher academic achievement must be avoided in order to maintain one's group identity.[23]

Dropping out of school is the ultimate form of resistence, while cutting classes is a milder form of protest. Descriptive statistics are plentiful which show high correlations between dropping out of school and factors such as poverty, minority culture, single-parent families, and pregnancies. Describing the characteristics of dropouts, however, does not *explain* dropping out. One way to understand the reasons for alienation and resistance, such as dropping out, is to look at the problem in terms of culture.[24]

Culture is a system of beliefs, behaviors, and ways of expression that constitute our social heritage. It is a "seamless webb" of *shared meanings* that gives meaning to our experience and gives us an identity larger than that of any individual.[25] Culture is part of individual behavior and thought and links us to others that share our culture. For this reason, it is easy to identify cultural *traits* that are unique, defining characteristics of a group. These traits are a source of strength for those who belong to the culture, but the same traits may be the target for prejudice, discrimination, and stereotyping by others. For example, in the case of Mexican Americans, there are many whose descendants predate European settlers and also speak only English in their homes. Yet these same people are often confused with "new immigrants," when peers and teachers say, "You sure speak English well."[26]

Literacy, Language, and Culture

Literacy is probably *the* most fundamental goal of public schooling in the United States. Other social and political purposes—the development of human capital and citizenship—are broader but assume that people are literate. By looking more closely at becoming literate in America we can bring into focus how cultural diversity affects the larger purposes of education in the United States.

Just as numeracy is more than arithmetic, so literacy is more than decoding skills and reading comprehension. The school inducts the young into literate culture by teaching them to read and write and by conveying the social norms associated with literate culture. The power of literacy is also the power of the system of beliefs which underlies literacy.

In a multicultural society, ethnicity and race are shapers of the meaning of literacy itself. For Puerto Ricans in the United States, for example, the Spanish language signifies their identity as Latinos, thus marking them apart from the majority culture.[27] Yet this same mark of identity can be a badge of failure when a *different* language is called a language *deficit*. The point is well made by the story of the first Puerto Rican member of the United States House of Representatives, who recalled his school days in New York City in the 1940s:

> I know . . . how amazed all the teachers were at the remarkable improvement of my intelligence quotient as I went from one grade to the other. . . . I did not have the heart to tell them that all that happened was that I learned to speak English.[28]

A more extreme example exists for many American-Indian children whose cultures "reinforce nonverbal communication, visual/spatial memory, visual/motor skills, and sequential visual memory over verbal skills." It should not be surprising that achievement tests conducted in English, a second language for many Indian children, show these children to "score very low on verbal skills."[29]

Because the policy of public schools is to provide equality of educational opportunity and because becoming literate is one of the major goals of schooling, the child's first encounter with a reading teacher is crucial to future academic success. In his studies of 5-year-olds learning to read, Gordon Wells has shown that the process of language acquisition in school follows a narrow model of instruction dominated by teacher questions and student response.

This teacher-centered model allows far fewer options for children to use a different language background in school. If the language patterns of the home and the significance attached to literacy are much the same as in school, there is little problem. In many so-called lower-class homes in which nonstandard dialects are spoken, however, there is a great divide between home and school. If the aim of the school is to overcome language deficiencies, the result is ironic because teachers often do not take advantage of the language the child already knows. We know that most children bring a wealth of language experience to school. Rather than using the resources that children already have, however, the strategy frequently is to restrict rather than expand language opportunities.[30] When we begin with a model of teaching that stresses disabilities, deficits, defects, and deficiencies, we see teaching as corrective. We come to stress what is wrong with the child's background rather than viewing the child's background as a resource upon which we can build.

Research on minority-language students has given us some hints on how teachers can best deal with this aspect of human diversity. A follow-up project to a suit filed in 1977 on behalf of fifteen elementary school children living in Ann Arbor, Michigan, investigated the way in which the dialect of the children (a black vernacular) influenced opportunities for learning in the classroom. The suit alleged that failure on the teacher's part to recognize and accept the fact that the dialect spoken in the home was different from the standard English of the classroom jeopardized student learning and made children feel ashamed of their language.

On the basis of their study of classroom interaction between teacher and students, the researchers concluded that children use language better in situations in which the dialect is recognized as acceptable. They suggest that teachers use the language competence that children already have to develop other language skills. And they argue that assessment procedures should include proficiency in dialects and/or language other than standard English. This would allow teachers to have the benefit of this knowledge.[31]

The work of Lucas, Henze, and Donato outlines several strategies for dealing with language-minority students. These authors studied students in six high schools which had been recognized for their success in teaching language-minority students. The authors found that these schools "celebrated diversity" by valuing and respecting the minority language. They also found that this respect promoted the "self-esteem necessary for student achievement." Minority-language students were allowed to speak their "primary language" except when instruction focused on learning English. The schools also offered lower- and advanced-content courses in the primary language and had many extracurricular activities to attract language-minority students.[32]

In the six high schools that Lucas and others studied, teachers had high expectations for their language-minority students. The schools also provided bilingual honors courses and assistance in applying for college and financial aid. Bilingual teachers were hired, and teachers were taught the principles of second-language acquisition and cross-cultural communication through staff development programs. Class size was relatively small, ranging from twenty to twenty-five students. There were academic support programs to help language-minority students make the transition from bilingual classes to mainstream classes taught in standard English. Parents were also involved through monthly parent nights and early-morning meetings. Finally, teachers were encouraged to give extra time to language-minority students and to participate in community activities in which they acted as advocates for Latinos.[33]

Clearly a combination of factors are needed to help language-minority students be successful. These range from a respect for different languages and nonstandard English, to high expectations for these students. No matter what the specific strategy, the teacher must view the language of the child as a foundation for language development rather than as a language deficit. Finally, the teacher must act as part of the student's community—not simply as one more school authority attempting to impose a system of values (including language) on an unwilling learner.

SOCIOECONOMIC STRATIFICATION

In this section we focus on the relationship of socioeconomic status to the common practices of ability grouping and tracking. About 75 percent of school districts in the United States use ability grouping despite the ruling in *Hobson v. Hansen* (1967) that declared it unconstitutional to group students into fast and slow tracks if these groupings resulted in an "unconstitutional segregation of minority and nonminority students."[34] Children come to school from a great variety of socioeconomic backgrounds, ranging from abject rural poverty to suburban affluence. Within and among schools the range of wealth and occupational status represented by students' families is enormous. Within families, other variables such as number of siblings, single-parent households, and working mothers make a tangled web for researchers attempting to assess the effects of socioeconomic status on educational opportunity and student learning.

For both teachers and administrators, differences in socioeconomic background are often seen as a problem to be overcome, a challenge to be met. The advice to treat each student as an individual is often compromised by demands for efficiency. This, in turn, leads to ability grouping (grouping on the basis of perceived and measured differences in achievement) and tracking (organization of the curriculum by *level* of instruction). Both of these methods of organizing instruction tend to reinforce already existing socioeconomic differences among students.

Grouping, Tracking, and Expectations

Following the publication of James Coleman and associates' *Equality of Educational Opportunity* (1966) and Christopher Jencks' *Inequality* (1972), educators became increasingly aware of the ways in which schools operate to preserve already existing socioeconomic inequalities. Prior to this, A. B. Hollingshead had observed in his *Elmtown's Youth* (1949) that when counseling parents about their children's school performance, teachers stressed the discipline problems of lower-class children and the academic problems of upper-class youth.[35]

Almost thirty years later in their *Schooling in Capitalist America* (1976), Bowles and Gintis argued that social relations in school (including curriculum organization) "reproduced" the class structure of the larger society. This was not by accident, they said, but because the "educational objectives and expectations of administrators, teachers, and parents (as well as the responsiveness of students to various patterns of teaching and control) differ for students of different social classes."[36] Though widely criticized for its Marxist explanations, the Bowles and Gintis thesis has remained plausible. The recent work of Farkas and others on cognitive performance suggests that teacher response to student effort and demeanor is selective. In turn, this affects how students respond to schooling.[37]

Tracking and ability grouping are the major ways in which schools select and sort students. For the most part, studies have focused on how tracking and grouping (1) affect opportunities for social mobility among students after they leave schools, (2) reinforce the socioeconomic differences that children bring with them to school, and (3) affect academic achievement.

Operating within these larger questions, researchers have focused on the problems of the self-fulfilling prophecy and teacher expectations. These were addressed in the now famous study of Robert Rosenthal and Lenore Jacobson in *Pygmalion in the Classroom* (1968). In this landmark study of the Oak School, the authors found that "children's gains in IQ . . . were correlated with teachers' perceptions of their classroom behavior." In addition, they observed that:

> The more the upper-track children of the experimental group gained in IQ, the more favorably they were rated by their teachers. The more the lower-track children of the control group gained in IQ, the more unfavorably they were

viewed by their teachers. . . . The more intellectually competent these [lower-track] children became, the more negatively they were viewed by their teachers.[38]

The results of the study confirmed George Bernard Shaw's poignant contrast of the lady and the flower girl in his famous play *Pygmalion:*

> You see, really and truly, apart from the things anyone can pick up (the dressing and the proper way of speaking, and so on), the difference between a lady and a flower girl is not how she behaves, but how she's treated. I shall always be a flower girl to Professor Higgins, because he always treats me as a flower girl, and always will; but I know I can be a lady to you, because you always treat me as a lady, and always will.

Ray Rist's work in the early 1970s deepened our understanding of how teacher expectations and academic grouping interact to affect student achievement. In his case study of one class of ghetto children during kindergarten, first, and second grades, Rist characterized teacher-student relations in terms of five propositions. These are useful signposts to better understand how teacher behavior affects student achievement:

1. the teacher has in mind an "ideal type" of student, the characteristics of whom are needed for success in and after school;
2. the teacher subjectively evaluates her students using the "ideal type" and organizes the class into "fast learners" and "slow learners";
3. the teacher gives the majority of her teaching time to the fast learners, but, for the slow learners, emphasizes control of behavior;
4. the teacher's treatment of the two groups becomes increasingly rigidified ("caste-like") and the gap in completion of academic material widens;
5. in the years following the initial grouping, information about past performance is used as the basis for classroom grouping.[39]

Rist describes the different behavior of the teacher toward the different reading groups. The acceptable behavior of those in the "middle-class" group (clean, attentive, highly verbal) were reinforced by the teacher. The "lower-class" group (dirty, smelly, low verbalization, and speakers of a dialect different from the teacher) were abused through ridicule and physical punishment. Both the social and academic distance among the groups, says Rist, increased to the point that they resembled "castes." Rist's conclusion was that the "system of public education in reality pepetuates what it is ideologically committed to eradicate—class barriers which result in inequality in the social and economic life of the citizenry."[40]

Numerous studies have built on the work of Rist, though few researchers talk in terms of "caste" today. It is widely assumed, however, that placement by track gives some students academic advantages over others. This is so obvious that it is virtually prima facie evidence that students are treated unequally. But does it mean that they are discriminated against? As we saw in Chapter 1 the case can be made that differential treatment is fair treatment because it takes into account the student's weaknesses when organizing instruction and curriculum.

Whether or not unequal treatment is discriminatory depends on both the intent and the effects of unequal treatment on the rights and opportunities of the student. Take, for example, a teacher who uses slow-paced instruction and highly structured written work as a technique for controlling student behavior rather than as a means for overcoming students' weaknesses in basic skills. One suspects that such behavior is discriminatory. If we know that these same techniques are a product of stereotyping, that the teacher has relatively low expectations for lower-track students, and that slow-paced instruction leaves lower-track students further and further behind academically, then we are led to the conclusion that such teacher behavior is discriminatory.

Other patterns of teacher behavior may also be suspect. If teachers of high-tracked students, compared to teachers of low-tracked students, give proportionately more instructional time to students and use less time telling them how to behave, then we are suspicious that the differences in instruction between the two tracks is discriminatory. This suspicion is confirmed when students themselves report that they "know" the high-track receives a better education and that low-track students aren't expected to do as well.

Jeanie Oakes's recent work *Keeping Track* (1985) is one of the most comprehensive and sobering accounts of the presumptions, fallacies, and effects of tracking in American public schools. In her study of twenty-five secondary schools, including 229 classes, Oakes examined the effects of tracking on the distribution of knowledge, opportunities to learn, classroom climate, and student attitudes.

Oakes's observations led her to conclude that four basic assumptions underlie the pervasive support of tracking found in our schools. The first assumption is that students learn better when tracked. The arguments are usually that bright students will be held back if grouped with "slow" students and that "slower" students can more easily be remediated if grouped together. The second assumption is that slower students, when tracked, will develop more positive self-concepts and that when mixed with brighter students will develop negative attitudes toward themselves. Third is the belief that the procedures we use to group students are accurate and fair, and "reflect past achievements and native abilities." Finally, there is the assumption that homogeneous grouping allows teachers to accommodate individual differences more easily, and that students are "easier to teach and manage."[41]

The idea that students learn better when grouped by ability is "simply not true," says Oakes. There are "mountains of research evidence indicating that homogeneous grouping doesn't consistently help *anyone* learn better." Occasionally, it has been found that bright students studying an enriched curriculum learn more when grouped with their peers, but most of the time this is not true. The second assumption about positive self-concept is likewise fallacious. Rather than fostering high self-esteem, homogeneous grouping tends to lower self-esteem. Moreover, students placed in lower tracks are seen by others as less intelligent.[42]

The third assumption, that placements are done in an accurate and fair way, presumes that the standardized test scores used to make placements are valid for such a use. Oakes reminds us that the questions included in these tests are selected for their ability to discriminate among student responses. Many questions that are accurate measures of a student's knowledge are discarded because too many students answer them correctly. The differences being measured conform to a normal distribution. Test-score differences, however, reflect only a very small proportion of the knowledge needed by the student to "know" the subject. The second point that relates to testing is fairness. Here the preponderance of evidence shows that poor and minority youth perform less well because their language background cannot be easily adapted to the language of the tests. Finally, the fourth assumption about ease of teaching and management seems to be valid—that is, if it is assumed that current teaching practices are the only ones that matter. But this is a self-serving justification at best. At worst, it is an excuse for lack of initiative and innovation.[43]

Overall, Oakes finds that the distribution of knowledge between lower- and higher-track students is not only unequal but probably influences opportunities beyond public schooling. High-track students are exposed to knowledge that is highly valued and classifies a person as educated. Moreover, having such knowledge permits greater access to higher education and hence higher social and economic status following school. Skills such as independent and critical thinking, creativity, and questioning are fostered in higher tracks. On the other hand, the knowledge and skills taught to lower-track students are not as prestigious and do not facilitate access to higher education and higher-status jobs. Functional literacy, computational skills, the ability to follow directions, and good work habits are "necessary" to success but hardly sufficient to permit access to higher-paying and higher-status jobs.[44]

Besides differences in academic content among tracks, Oakes and others have found that higher-track students get more teaching time and time on task, spend more time on homework, and receive the kind of instruction that motivates students to learn. These latter activities included field trips, research projects, role playing, narrative or expository writing, and making films or recordings. Activities that focused on active student involvement were noticeably absent in lower tracks These relative differences between higher and lower tracks, Oakes reminds us, must be placed against a common finding for all tracks—that there was little active student involvement and decision making in learning. Most of the time, all classrooms emphasized "passive activities" such as listening to the teacher, writing answers to questions, and taking tests.[45]

We conclude this section with a study done by Deborah Dillon of an eleventh grade low-track English reading classroom, in which 74 percent of the students were black and most were from low-income families. Most students were bused to and from school, and 75 percent participated in the free or reduced-cost lunch program. Dillon reported that the climate of the school was "free from racial or severe behavior problems." Most parents defined success for their youngsters as receipt of a diploma, and few parents were involved with their children's instruction.[46]

Dillon studied seventeen students, most of whom had low reading ability; the overall instructional reading level varied from sixth to eleventh grade. For purposes of her study Dillon defined teacher effectiveness as the ability to take account of the "backgrounds of [the] low socioeconomic, predominantly black students" and at the same time provide "meaningful experience for low-track remedial readers/writers."[47]

Several features of this highly effective teacher's instruction stood out. First, he was genuinely concerned for his students and worked hard to motivate them. His communications skills were excellent, he was confident, and he had a sense of purpose. He controlled his classroom without forcing control on his students, and he treated his students with respect. When selecting reading material, he matched it to his students' reading levels and interests. When teaching writing he used a process approach, including keeping journals and peer teaching. It was not, notes Dillon, the "watered-down, skill sheet commonly given to low reading/writing ability level students." The teacher (Appleby) "believed that his predominantly black students learned best when they were asked to listen, discuss, and work together cooperatively."[48]

Appleby allowed students to use their own natural language during lessons and transformed his own language to that of his students. This was particularly important to "bridging gaps between [the] background knowledge students have and new concepts and materials they are to learn." The students appreciated and admired Appleby's adaptation of his own language to theirs. He believed that students should learn actively and encouraged them to call out answers and make comments.[49]

There is little question that Appleby was a risk taker, confident in his abilities to succeed with these students. He was well informed about current educational research and modified his teaching on the basis of (1) his observations of his students and (2) new information about effective teaching. Yet Appleby could not have been innovative unless he was encouraged and allowed to be a risk taker, to try new teaching styles, and provided with time to reflect on his triumphs and mistakes. Thus, the climate of the school had to be supportive of him.

GENDER, CULTURE, AND EDUCATION

Historical Perspectives on Sex Roles

Sex and gender have been used to differentiate people in virtually every culture, regardless of geographic location, since the dawn of civilization. Family obligations, work status, property rights, political participation, and educational opportunity have all been defined by sex and gender. During much of the colonial period in America, education for women was very limited, seldom extending beyond reading, writing, arithmetic, and needlework. By the mid eighteenth century, however, there was sharp disagreement over what was an appropriate education for women. In 1787 Benjamin Rush, a famous physician in colonial Pennsylvania, published his "Thoughts Upon Female Education," a companion piece to his "Thoughts Upon the Mode of Education Proper in a

Republic" (1786). In a land that had embarked upon a great political experiment, both public and private enlightenment were important matters if the new republic called the United States was to succeed. Rush argued that the American woman must be different from her English counterpart. She should have a good knowledge of the basic skills, be acquainted with geography and history, music and dancing, be able to keep accounts, and have a good Christian instruction so as to model proper beliefs for her children.[50]

Rush's proposals were not radical, but did depart from English precedent insofar as they proposed a role for women that would ensure an upbringing of children that would suit them for life in a democracy. Across the Atlantic, Mary Wollstonecraft espoused a more radical view of women in her *Thoughts on the Education of Daughters* and *A Vindication of the Rights of Women*. Wollstonecraft acknowledged that a woman's duties were primarily domestic, but she wished to redefine a woman's role in the household. Women should be the intellectual companions of men, she said. Their relationship should not be one of sexual tyranny. Educationally, she supported equality of schooling for boys and girls at the elementary level. Moreover, the expectations for each sex should be equal, she said.[51]

We do not know how most women in the eighteenth and nineteenth centuries felt about sex differentiation and stereotyping. We do know, however, that as industrialization expanded during the nineteenth century, many young women were absorbed into the work force outside the home. Women's work was generally low-skilled compared to that of men. Thus in textile and paper mills, for example, women did work for lower wages using skills that were considered beneath those of men.

In the mid nineteenth century women were entering the industrial work force in large numbers, but the "ideal" woman remained a wife and homemaker. In fact the so-called cult of domesticity of the mid nineteenth century emphasized the mother as the guardian of moral, religious, and cultural values. This nurturing of virtue was accompanied by responsibilities for frugal household management. Manuals, treatises on domestic economy, and agricultural journals all contributed to what Carl Kaestle has called a "veritable crusade." The purpose of the crusade was to dignify womanhood itself.[52]

Education, Women, and Teaching

By the mid nineteenth century almost as many girls as boys attended elementary school. Actual school enrollments may have been affected by gender, but the overall increase in literacy rates for women in the first seventy years of the nineteenth century suggests that equalization of elementary schooling was taking place.[53]

At the same time that Victorian America was celebrating womanhood through motherhood, other voices and events were attempting to enrich the intellectual life of women. Catharine Beecher and Mary Lyon worked unceasingly to build academies for training teachers. They viewed teachers, especially those moving West, as institution builders, ready to raise public enlightenment to a level worthy of the new democracy. Through Catharine Beecher's National Popular Education Board (NPEB), 250 eastern teachers were placed in western schools during the 1840s and 1850s. In Oberlin College in Ohio, women, including the first black woman to obtain a college education in the United States, were inducted into an intellectual climate that allowed them, in turn, to teach in academies and female seminaries.[54]

On another, but related, front, Emma Willard, was introducing women to mathematics and science at Waterford Academy and Troy Female Seminary in upstate New York. Willard had taught herself geometry, algebra, trigonometry, and conics to a point where she felt confident to teach them to others. Mathematics and science became part of her students' intellectual heritage through Willard's teaching and by attendance at evening lectures at nearby Rensselaer Polytechnic Institute. The Troy Female Seminary placed many of its graduates in the West and South, as did the Boston's Ladies' Society for the Promotion of Education in the West. This latter society merged with the National Popular Education Board in 1852.[55]

In the larger metropolitan area of Philadelphia, women were also attending lectures on science at the Franklin Institute. This was the case at the Ohio Mechanics' Institute in Cincinnati as well. Though women were not part of the schools for apprentices operated by these mechanics' institutes, they were present in conspicuous numbers at the lecture series on natural and moral philosophy. The exhibitions sponsored at such institutes also typically included articles manufactured at home by women. Admittedly, women were on the periphery of the major purpose of these institutes, but there is no question they took part in acquiring the scientific and technical knowledge offered by this new type of educational institution.

During the nineteenth century women continued to build a foundation for respectability through teaching. By the twentieth century the names of women who were leaders in the progressive education movement were well known. They included Ella Flagg Young, the first woman superintendent of the Chicago schools, and Margaret Haley, feminist, progressive, and president of the Chicago Federation of Teachers. Julia Richman was the first Jewish woman superintendent of the New York City school system in the early twentieth century. Numbered among educational innovators were Marietta Johnson, founder of the Organic School in 1907; Caroline Pratt, who opened the Play School in 1914; Margaret Naumberg, founder of the Walden School in 1915; and Lucy Mitchell, who founded the Bureau of Educational Experiment (later the Bank Street College of Education) in 1916.[56]

Increased educational opportunities for women led many, in turn, to take up teaching themselves. There, however, they met the same wage discrimination that was present in the larger industrial economy. Women teachers worked for one-half to two-thirds the wages of men. The average weekly salary for women in urban school districts in 1841 was $4.44, compared to $11.93 for men. Proportionately, little had changed twenty years later when the figures were $6.91 and $18.07, respectively. In rural areas the situation was somewhat better, but female teachers still made only about two-thirds the average salary of men.

These differences in wages between male and female were, in part, an economic measure, not motivated by altruism. But they were also part of a larger strategy to improve the quality of education. By hiring female teachers at low salaries school boards were able to hire many more teachers than they otherwise could have at male salaries. The result was both the feminization of the teaching force and the improvement of education itself. Ironically, despite the inequities of the salary structure, women were able to enter teaching at a level of respectability far above those for female domestic servants and operatives of industrial machinery. Thus teaching provided paths for upward social mobility and respectability despite inequities in pay.

Women in the Labor Force

Current issues involving gender and education are rooted in the conflict between historically approved roles for women in American society and the emergence of equity issues brought about by feminists and others concerned with the fair treatment of women. As we noted in Chapter 1, federal courts in the United States addressed the problem of fair treatment for women during the 1970s in matters of single-sex public schools, selective school admission standards, and interscholastic sports. Historically, however, the effects of gender discrimination have been far broader than schooling.

Wage discrimination persisted in the late nineteenth and early twentieth century through the labor force. In the years 1890 and 1900 women in cotton mills, knitting mills, cigar making, and paper mills were paid approximately one-half to two-thirds the average wages of men. In bakeries, breweries, and shoe-making factories, they were paid, on the average, one-quarter to one-half the average wages of men. The proportion of females in the labor force increased from 14.7 percent to 24.8 percent between 1880 and 1910, but about 40 percent of these women "were employed as domestics—maids, cooks, nurses, and laundresses—in private homes." In the North many of these were recent immigrants, while most in the South were black. About 3 million women worked in the northeastern industries of garment making, cigar rolling, laundering, and food processing. These also were mainly immigrants, and few made a living wage.[57]

During the twentieth century stratification by gender remained a conspicuous feature of the work force. In the first half of the twentieth century single women and women from the lower socioeconomic strata, were pulled out of the home. Married middle-class women became increasingly isolated in the home. Today, approximately 55 percent of women are in the paid labor force. Most of these work in sex-segregated jobs, the largest proportion of which are in service work—the so-called pink-collar ghetto. Women today are certainly employed as professionals far more than in previous generations. Among professionals, however, there is persistent resentment on the part of both females and males. For the latter this is often expressed as sexual harassment motivated by the loss of status in areas of work once thought to be the sole prerogative of males. In the case of females, resentment grows over pay inequities and the constant threat of sexual harassment and assault. Even with the rise of women in the ranks of professionals, women continue to make up about 80 percent of administrative support workers, many of whom are clerical workers.[58]

When employed in blue-collar work, women are more likely to have low or semiskilled positions. Among all workers, women's pay averages about 66 percent of men's. If we look at unemployment, job displacement and poverty, the woman's place is not enviable. Despite great strides within professional ranks, women are usually the first to be laid off during economic slowdowns. Approximately 34 percent of single women who are heads of households live below the poverty line. This has dire consequences for their children, who, of course, also live below the poverty line.[59]

MODELS FOR INTERPRETING GENDER AND EDUCATION

Since the 1970s the literature on gender and education has grown impressively. Sex-role stereotyping and sex bias in instruction figure prominently in the literature. Included, also, are the differences between men and women in moral, emotional, and cognitive development and the ways in which women are denied equitable treatment in our major institutions, including schools. As we deal with gender in this chapter, keep in mind that there are several windows through which to interpret gender issues in education.

First, is what Fennema and Ayers call the *assimilation model.* This model assumes that in matters of learning, sex should be largely irrelevant. Differences in genitalia, physique, and physiological processes, though obvious and important in spheres other than education, are not relevant to the substance and the organization of instruction. Rather, the assimilationist argues that, for educational purposes, one should view students in an androgynous way. This means no stereotypes and no preconceived beliefs about differences in the ways boys and girls learn. This model includes both masculine and feminine characteristics that are positively valued.[60]

The *deficit model* assumes basic differences between sexes—such as differences in mathematical, verbal, or spacial-relations skills—that are educationally important. The origins of these differences may be genetic or environmental. In either case, however, the obligation of the teacher is to compensate for sex-related deficits. Thus, schools must provide equal educational opportunity by helping children to overcome sex-related deficits.[61]

Like the deficit model, the *pluralist model* assumes sex-related differences. Yet it differs from the deficit model in two important ways. First, it does not associate the word "difference" with "deficit." Second, it views sex-related differences as cultural (gender) rather than biological (sex). Thus the pluarlistic model speaks of male and female cultures rather than simply sex roles. This shift of focus is important because it recognizes maleness and femaleness as having meaning only within the context of shared beliefs (culture). Heterogeneity rather than homogeneity is the ideal of the pluralistic model. Heterogeneity, however, does not imply that females ought to accept male dominance. Instead, it implies that females can learn the knowledge and skills needed to compete in a male-dominated society. In other words, pluralism is acknowledged, but so is the right to the opportunity to participate in the dominant culture.[62]

Finally, the *justice model* assumes both similarities and differences among males and females. From Aristotle it borrows the view that equals should be treated equally and unequals should be treated differently. This means that in matters in which males and females are the same, there should be equal treatment; in matters in which they differ, they should be treated differently. The justice model assumes that it is humanness, not maleness or femaleness, that is most important. Sex, race, and ethnicity, for example, should not be relevant to a person's right to the benefits of society (freedom, security, sustenance) because these rights belong to human beings in general, not to a particular *type* of human being. To the extent that being male or female prevents sharing in society's benefits, then it is the obligation of government to make such sharing possible by eliminating barriers.

DIFFERENCES IN GENDER

Differences in Gender

On a December afternoon in 1872, Edward H. Clarke, a prominent Boston physician, delivered a guest lecture on female education to the New England Woman's Club. In his initial comments he spoke of a need for increased opportunity for women in higher education and noted that women had the capability for " 'equal eminence of attainment' with men." His remarks that followed, however, set off a debate that by 1905 was characterized by G. Stanley Hall, a leading American psychologist as a "holy war." What prompted this furor was Clarke's claim that women needed different methods of instruction from men because of their "peculiar" physical organization. The following year Clarke published *Sex in Education; or, a Fair Chance for the Girls,* arguing that if collegiate education for women were identical to that for men it would be a crime against nature. What Clarke was reviving was the age-old claim that women could not "physically withstand the rigors of intellectual training."[63]

Clarke had gone a long way beyond the late eighteenth century when it was necessary for J. Burton to prove that the "female mind is enduced with capacities sufficient for the acquisition of knowledge."[64] But Clarke insisted that physiological differences—different needs for nutriment and sleep and development of the reproductive organs—posed a problem for education. Moreover, he feared that to educate women without paying heed to their physiological differences would weaken the race to the point that "mothers in our republic [would have to] be drawn from transatlantic homes."[65]

Julia Howe's reply to Clarke's work was swift and sharp. Said Howe: "His book seems to have found a chance *at* the girls, rather than a chance *for* them. All could wish that he had not played his sex-symphony so harshly, so loudly, or in so public a manner."[66] Much of Howe's edited work *Sex and Education, A Reply to Dr. E. H. Clarke's "Sex in Education"* (1874) was a refutation of Clarke's "facts" and an assault on his authority in such matters. The last essay by Maria Elmore in Howe's work went to the heart of the matter. In this essay Elmore attacked the assumption that women must be educated to be wives and mothers. This was no more the case, she said, than the necessity for men to be educated to be husbands and fathers. Women's "highest" station may not be "wifehood" or "motherhood." Then Elmore added the final blow against Clarke's argument:

> Until men are willing to discuss woman's education in the same way they do that of their own sex, on the broad basis of individual need, individual taste and talent, and the necessity of thorough mental training of all. . . ; until men are convinced that the human being and its needs is paramount in importance, and that sex, with all its relations, is a secondary question. . . ; until, in short, men comprehend that they are not the guardians of women, and have no right to force her to education, or restrain her from the same . . . , every woman . . . will "persistently" and reasonably demand that the final decision in regard to her ability to endure mental or physical strain, her power of study, and her need for the same, shall rest with herself.[67]

The debate over a special curriculum for women did not disappear, but its force was tempered by expanding opportunities for women in higher education. Still, the question remains today. Currently, there is little talk of the peculiar physiological characteristics of women as there was a hundred years ago. Recent work on gender differences, however, have raised the debate in a new form. Instead of asking, What is the best curriculum for the "weaker sex"?, we ask, Are there distinctive patterns of gender development to which educators ought to respond? To ask the question in this way is not necessarily sexist. It is, rather, a way of opening up the issue of whether or not we can assume models of psychological and cultural development for women that are, in fact, based on studies of males.

The publication of Carol Gilligan's *In a Different Voice* (1982) was a major step forward in our understanding of women's psychological and moral development. Gilligan focused on the disparity between women's experience and major theories of psychological development. The disparity, she noted, has generally been interpreted as a "problem" with women's development. "Instead," said Gilligan, "the failure of women to fit existing models of human growth may point to . . . a limitation in the conception of [the] human condition, an omission of certain truths about life."[68]

Many of the differences between male and female psychological development may be traced to differences in relating to other people. It is customary for psychological theorists to associate maturity with individuation—that is, with the development of autonomy, individual responsibility, and the recognition of rights and rules. Children, it is argued, gradually learn to establish priorities by subordinating or excluding some relationships in favor of others. Typically, for example, boys choose up sides for a game by the method of exclusion, rather than inclusion. This type of behavior is seen as normal by most observers of psychological development. Yet the method of exclusion is peculiarly male, having been established as "normal" primarily on the basis of studies of boys.

Gilligan's studies of girls point to an alternative scheme of development. Autonomy, decision making on the basis of rights and rules, and the inclination to order people and things hierarchically are replaced by a world of human connection, not exclusion. This is a world organized around caring and interconnectedness rather than exclusion. As these early differences in female development are played out in young adulthood, it is the female who stresses interdependence and the male, independence. For the male, separation and independence lead to empowerment, while for the female, connectedness and attachment sustains the human community. Connectedness to others is *given* by the woman rather than *contracted,* as with the male. In matters of rights and responsibilities, male justice and female care may merge when people realize that "inequality adversely affects both parties in an unequal relationship [and] violence is destructive of everyone involved."[69]

We spent some time with Gilligan's work because it points up a difficulty much more basic than sex-role stereotyping and sex bias in schooling, both of which are obvious in teacher behavior and the content of many textbooks. Faculty in colleges of education and others studying and teaching about the psychological and moral development of children are the most obvious perpetuators of developmental theories that have an inherent male bias. Moreover, this bias is usually presented to students with scientific objectivity, making it seem as though there is no bias.

The same biases are part of several of the major reform reports of the 1980s. Sara Freedman has pointed out that the Carnegie report titled *A Nation Prepared: Teachers for the Twenty-First Century* presumed a "male model that emphasizes rationality, order, detachment, and the pursuit of profit/power above personal and emotional attachment." Likewise, Susan Laird points out that the Holmes Group publication titled *Tomorrow's Teachers* does not see care and empathy as an important part of the sensitivities needed by teachers. The model of teaching advocated by these reports does not view teaching from a woman's perspective. Thus, there is lacking in these two major reform documents a view of the classroom as a "net of relationships with people who care about each other's learning" rather than simply a classroom of teachers and students.[70] A similar view is expressed even more forcefully by Tetrault and Schmuck, who note that many of the major reform reports of the 1980s do not deal with gender as a crucial issue. Though these reports acknowledge the necessity for dealing with inequities among racial minorities, language minorities, and handicapped children, there is no mention of gender. It is, as they say, "not a relevant category in the analysis of excellence in schools. . . . The goal of excellence does not even have the female student in mind."[71]

Sex-Role Stereotyping

Sex-role socialization and stereotyping begin in infancy through verbal and nonverbal interaction with family members. Infants are socialized to gender through clothing, toys, tone of voice, and reinforcement of gender-specific activities. Socialization gradually becomes stereotyping as girls and boys are taught to exclude "inappropriate" expressions from their behaviors and to include only those identified with their sex. Books, television, movies, popular music, and advertisements teach children how to be women and men. To the extent that sexual stereotyping becomes a basis of discriminatory or prejudicial behavior of one sex toward the other, it is sexist in the same way that race discrimination is racist.[72]

Theories of sex-role socialization attempt to explain gender differences in terms of learning. That is, they explain gender-related behavior in psychological terms. This approach is valuable to the extent that we better understand how children come to behave in gender-specific ways. Yet, a psychological explanation of gender-specific behavior does not help us understand very well the *sources* of the behavior. As Margaret Anderson has pointed out, "such a perspective underestimates the influence of . . . institutionalized gender inequality in creating gender roles."[73] By looking at how gender differences are actually part of the *structure* of our institutions, we can see more clearly both the sources of inequality and possible solutions to problems of sex discrimination.

Students in most public schools are part of a large network of gender-defined activities. These range from curriculum and classroom organization to staffing. Recently, for example, much has been made of poor female performance on tests of quantitative and analytical skills. These claims, however, must be viewed with great caution. Gender-related differences in mathematical aptitude, for example, are not usually found among elementary school students. We do know, however, that males are encouraged more than females to enroll in mathematics courses. Thus, as students progress from elementary through secondary studies, males and females do not take the same number of courses in mathematics. Gradually, more females than males grow to dislike mathematics, and eventually mathematics becomes the province of men. Much the same pattern is found with courses in microcomputers.

The pattern of facts is not in question in the above instances. What is in question is their explanations. There is, for example, no need to attribute the differences in mathematical aptitude to genetic differences. In fact, the differences are statistically accounted for by the differences in number and level of mathematics courses taken by females and males. Keeping in mind that, for young students, there is usually no sex-related difference in mathematical aptitude, and that males are encouraged more than females to take mathematics courses, we begin to suspect that there are really no innate tendencies to like and achieve well in mathematics. Instead, we suspect that sex-related differences in mathematics are attributable to the way in which males and females are tracked through the curriculum.[74] We should be even more suspicious of arguments that males have a better aptitude for mathematics when we realize that teachers tend to misassign girls that have high aptitudes in mathematics. Sorensen and Halliman's study conducted in 1987 showed that girls with high mathematical aptitudes "were less likely to be assigned to high-ability math groups than boys with similar aptitudes."[75]

Other structural features of schooling are also gender-related. Patterns of staffing, for example, often reinforce curriculum choices for males and females.

More men than women teach in quantitative subject areas, and more women than men teach language arts and foreign languages. In addition, the administrative hierarchy is dominated by males to the extent that the educational historian David Tyack once labeled the school an "educational harem."

In textbooks, males frequently dominate the subject matter, particularly in history and in the history of science and technology. Basal reading texts have made some progress toward including females as main characters, but this has been accompanied by an increase in gender-neutral characters, such as talking trees and animals. In effect, then, one strategy of textbook publishers to deal with charges of *sexism* had been to avoid sex.[76]

Classroom methods and teaching strategies also reflect male priorities. For example, even though females mature earlier, have better small motor skills sooner, and are *ready* for learning verbal and mathematical skills at an earlier age than boys, we nevertheless organize instruction to "meet the needs of males who tend to develop at a slower pace." In addition, the very visible competitive climate of the classroom favors males who very early in life learn that competitiveness is a male trait. Teacher-student interaction also favors males. Teachers tend to call on male students more, and male students generally receive more attention from teachers: "more praise, more time, [and] also more reprimands and harsher discipline." Females, on the other hand, are ignored more, and high-achieving females "receive the least attention of all students."[77] All of these gender-related practices of schools help to reinforce broader social norms that portray women as less deserving, if not actually inferior to men. In this way schools are extensions of the social structure and the politics that created them.

CONCLUSION

We began this chapter by raising the general question of how to deal with human diversity while at the same time maintaining a system of education wherein student needs are fairly considered and rewards justly distributed. We pointed out that human diversity is so obvious that one does not need to demonstrate it. We do not infer from this, however, that human beings have no common traits. Indeed, they do. What matters is how we *deal with* both sameness and differences.

In the case of intelligence, we saw how assumptions about the measurements of intelligence led to questionable practices of grouping students. In the cases of race, ethnicity, language, and gender we saw the importance of accepting differences as legitimate rather than classifying them as deficits or disadvantages. We saw how racial, ethnic, language, and gender barriers have become part of the structure of schooling and how these barriers reflect and reinforce the same barriers present in the larger society. The general question that must be addressed here is, What can the school do about such barriers? To answer this question we looked at studies which showed how these barriers can be overcome if they are recognized as barriers in the first place.

Not everyone would agree that ability grouping, tracking, insistence upon standard English, and stratification by gender are necessarily bad things. Some would argue that it is natural to classify people according to intelligence, race, ethnicity, language, and gender. These same people would cite many historical examples of these classifications as proof of their point. Others might protest such classifications, but argue that there is nothing they can do anyway; that they can't change all of society, so why bother.

These are powerful emotive arguments that appeal to states of mind experienced by most people at one time or another. Unfortunately, that is all that such arguments do—appeal to a state of mind. The same arguments are usually self-serving and do not really address the critical question of what is fair or just. Unless one really wishes to defend discriminatory practices because they *are* discriminatory, then such arguments totally miss the point. They are excuses for inaction rather than logically constructed arguments. Seeking fairness and justice in the way we structure our educational institutions is exceedingly difficult. Moreover, protests against the status quo are not likely to make many friends. Yet one should consider seriously whether one wishes to defend an unjust system simply out of convenience. The stakes of fairness and justice are far higher than those of convenience, for it is in our treatment of others that we define ourselves and the values we stand for. This in itself should give us pause when we consider how we will deal with human diversity.

NOTES

[1] Bureau of the Census, United States Department of Commerce, *Statistical Abstracts of the United States, 1990* (Washington: GPO, 1990), pp. 10, 17–18, 38, 46, 423, 458. Generally, the householder is the adult(s) in whose name the home is owned or rented. A family "refers to a group of two or more persons related by birth, marriage or adoption and residing together in a household" (*Statistical Abstracts*, 1990, p. 5). There are many individuals who live in nonfamily households, and they are not included in the figures.

[2] Alfred Binet and Th. Simon, "New Methods for the Diagnosis of the Intellectual Level of Subnormals," *L'Année Psychologique*, 12 (1905) as in Kite (trans.) *The Development of Intelligence in Children* (Vineland, N.J.: Training School at Vineland, May 16, 1916), pp. 37–39.

[3] Ibid., p. 43.

[4] Lewis M. Terman, *The Measurement of Intelligence* (Boston: Riverside, 1916), p. 7.

[5] Ibid., p. 12.

[6] Ibid., pp. 16–17.

[7] Clarence S. Yoakum and Robert M. Yerkes, *Army Mental Tests* (New York: Holt, 1920), pp. xiii, xi, 9, 12.

[8] Ibid., p. 193.

[9] Stephen Jay Gould, *The Mismeasure of Man* (New York: Norton, 1981), p. 156.

[10] Arthur R. Jensen, "The Nonmanipulable and Effectively Manipulable Variables of Education," *Education and Society* 1 (1983), p. 56.

[11] Ibid.

[12] Arthur R. Jensen, "How Much Can We Boost IQ and Scholastic Achievement," *Harvard Educational Review*, Reprint Series No. 2 (June 1969), pp. 79, 81, 83.

[13] Arthur R. Jensen, "Cultural Deficit or Information Processing Deficit." Paper presented at the American Educational Research Association, New Orleans, April 24, 1984, p. 3.

[14] Jensen, "How Much Can We Boost IQ," pp. 79, 81, 83.

[15] Ibid.

[16] Ibid., pp. 13, 15.

[17] Jerome S. Kagan, "Inadequate Evidence and Illogical Conclusions"; J. McV. Hunt, "Has Compensatory Education Failed? Has It Been Attempted"; Lee J. Cronbach, "Heredity Environment and Educational Policy," *Harvard Educational Review*, Reprint Series No. 2 (June, 1969), pp. 127–128; 136, 141, 191.

[18] Steven Selden, "Biological Determinism and the Ideological Roots of Student Classification, *Journal of Education* 165, no. 2 (Spring 1983), pp. 177–191.

[19] Arval A. Morris, *The Constitution and American Education*, 2nd ed., American Casebook Series (St. Paul, Minn.: West Publishing Co., 1980), p. 708.

[20] Morris, *Constitution*, p. 709; Kathleen P. Bennett and Margaret D. LeCompte, *The Ways Schools Work, A Sociological Analysis of Education* (New York: Longman, 1990), p. 201.

[21] Bennett and LeCompte, *Ways Schools Work*, pp. 203–204.

[22] Joel Spring, *American Education, An Introduction to Social and Political Aspects* (New York: Longman, 1991), pp. 129–130.

[23] Matute Bianci as in Bernardo M. Ferdman, "Literacy and Cultural Identity," *Harvard Educational Review* 60 (May, 1990), pp. 181–204.

[24] Bennett and LeCompte, *Ways Schools Work*, pp. 217–218.

[25] Monica Heller, "The Role of Language in the Formation of Ethnic Identity," in J. S. Phinney and M. J. Rotheram (eds.), *Children's Ethnic Socialization: Pluralism and Development* (Newbary Park, Calif.: Sage, 1987), p. 184.

[26] Valerie Ooka Pang, "About Teachers and Teaching, Ethnic Prejudice: Still Alive and Hurtful" *Harvard Educational Review* 58 (August, 1988), p. 378.

[27] Bernardo M. Ferdman, "Literacy and Cultural Identity," *Harvard Educational Review* 60 (May, 1990), p. 190.

[28] As in Meyer Weinberg, *A Chance to Learn, A History of Race and Education in the United States* (Cambridge, Mass.: Cambridge University Press, 1977), p. 243.

[29] Carol Locust, "Wounding the Spirit: Discrimination and Traditional American Belief Systems," *Harvard Educational Review* 58 (August 1988), pp. 315–330.

[30] Gordon Wells, "The Language Experience of Five-Year-Old Children at Home and at School," in Jenny Cook-Gumperz (ed.), *The Social Construction of Literacy* (Cambridge, Mass.: Cambridge University Press, 1986); Kieran Egan, "Literacy and the Oral Foundations of Education," *Harvard Educational Review* 57 (Nov. 1987), pp. 445–472.

[31] Ceil Lucas and Denise Borders, "Language Diversity and Classroom Discourse," *American Educational Research Journal* 24 (Spring, 1987), pp. 119–141, passim.

[32] Tamara Lucas, Rosemary Henze, and Ruben Donato, "Promoting the Success of Latino Language-Minority Students: An Exploratory Study of Six High Schools," *Harvard Educational Review* 60 (August, 1990), pp. 310, 322.

[33] Ibid., pp. 324–325.

[34] Jeanne H. Ballantine, *The Sociology of Education, A Systematic Analysis*, 2nd ed. (Englewood Cliffs, N.J.: Prentice–Hall, 1989), p. 79.

[35] August B. Hollingshead, *Elmtown's Youth, The Impact of Social Classes on Adolescents* (New York: John Wiley and Sons, 1949), pp. 178–179.

[36] Samuel Bowles and Herbert Gintis, *Schooling in Capitalist America, Educational Reform and the Contradictions of Economic Life* (New York: Basic Books, 1976), p. 132.

[37] George Farkas, Daniel Sheehan, and Robert P. Grobe, "Coursework Mastery and School Success: Gender, Ethnicity, and Poverty Groups Within an Urban School District," *American Educational Research Journal* 27 (Winter, 1990), pp. 807–827.

[38] Robert Rosenthal and Lenore Jacobson, *Pygmalion in the Classroom* (New York: Holt Rinehart, 1968), pp. 178–179.

[39] Ray Rist, "Student Social Class and Teacher Expectations: The Self-Fulfilling Prophecy in Ghetto Education," *Harvard Educational Review* 40 (Aug., 1970), pp. 411–451.

[40] Ibid., pp. 443–449.

[41] Jeannie Oakes, *Keeping Track, How Schools Structure Inequality* (New Haven, Yale University Press, 1985), pp. 6–7.

[42] Ibid., p. 7.

[43] Ibid., pp. 8–14.

[44] Ibid., pp. 91–92.

[45] Ibid., pp. 111, 129–130.

[46] Deborah R. Dillon, "Showing Them That I Want Them to Learn and That I Care About Who They Are: A Microethnology of the Social Organization of a Secondary Low-Track English-Reading Program," *American Educational Research Journal* 26 (Summer, 1989), p. 231.

[47] Ibid., p. 228.

[48] Ibid., p. 243.

[49] Ibid., p. 245.

[50] H. Warren Button and Eugene E. Provenzo, Jr., *History of Education and Culture in America*, 2nd ed. (Englewood Cliffs, N.J.: Prentice–Hall, 1989), p. 69.

[51] Ibid., p. 70.

[52] Carl Kaestle, *Pillars of the Republic, Common Schools and American Society, 1780–1860* (New York: Hill and Wang, 1983), p. 84; Daniel Walker Howe (ed.), *Victorian America* (Philadelphia: University of Pennsylvania Press, 1976), p. 26.

[53] Kaestle, *Pillars*, p. 27; Lee Soltow and Edward Stevens, *The Rise of Literacy and the Common School in the United States, A Socioeconomic Analysis to 1870* (Chicago: University of Chicago Press, 1981), pp. 110–111.

[54] Kathryn Kish Sklar, "Female Teachers: 'Firm Pillars' of the West," in Paul Mattingly and Edward W. Stevens Jr. (eds.), *"Schools and the Means of Education Shall Forever Be Encouraged," A History of Education in the Old Northwest, 1787–1880* (Athens, Ohio: Ohio University Libraries, 1987), pp. 60, 64.

[55] Polly Welts Kaufman, *Women Teachers on the Frontier* (New Haven: Yale University Press, 1984), p. 6.

[56] Maxine Greene, *Landscapes of Learning* (New York: Teachers' College Press, 1978), p. 237.

[57] Thomas Woody, *A History of Women's Education in the United States*, vol. 2 (New York: Octogon Books, 1966), p. 36.

[58] Margaret L. Anderson, *Thinking About Women, Sociological Perspectives on Sex and Gender*, 2nd ed. (New York: Macmillan, 1988), pp. 22, 117–118.

[59] Ibid., p. 130, *Statistical Abstracts, 1990*, p. 411.

[60] Elizabeth Fennama and M. Jane Ayers (eds.), *Women and Education, Equity or Equality* (Berkeley, Calif.: McCutchan Publishing, 1984), pp. 3–6.

[61] Ibid., pp. 6–8.

[62] Fennema and Ayers, *Women and Education*, pp. 8–13; Bennett and LeCompte, *Ways Schools Work*, p. 224.

[63] Sue Zschoche, "Dr. Clarke Revisited: Science, True Womanhood, and Female Collegiate Education," *History of Education Quarterly* 29, no. 4 (Winter, 1989), pp. 545–548.

[64] J. Burton, *Lectures on Female Education and Manners,* vol. 1, 2nd ed. (New York: Source Book Press, 1970).

[65] Edward H. Clarke, *Sex in Education; or, A Fair Chance for the Girls* (Boston: James R. Osgood, 1873), p. 60.

[66] Mrs. Julia Ward Howe, *Sex and Education, A Reply to Dr. E. H. Clarke's "Sex in Education"* (Boston: Roberts Bros., 1874), p. 6.

[67] Ibid., pp. 187–188.

[68] Carol Gilligan, *In a Different Voice, Psychological Theory and Women's Development* (Cambridge, Mass.: Harvard University Press, 1982), pp. 1–2.

[69] Ibid., pp. 156, 174.

[70] Citing Carolyn Shrewsbury, "What is Feminist Pedagogy," in Susan Laird, "Reforming 'Woman's True Profession': A Case for 'Feminist Pedagogy' in Teacher Education?" *Harvard Educational Review* 58 (November, 1988), p. 460.

[71] As in Bennett and LeCompte, *Ways Schools Work,* p. 225.

[72] Ibid., pp. 224–229.

[73] Anderson, *Thinking About Women,* p. 97.

[74] Ibid., pp. 86–87.

[75] As in Bennett and LeCompte, *Ways Schools Work,* p. 231.

[76] Ibid., pp. 331–333.

[77] Ibid., pp. 235–236.

4

Readings on Human Diversity

Each of the essays in this chapter deal with one aspect of human diversity and its effects on the way our public schools are structured.

Robert Yerkes's early-twentieth-century report on the use of intelligence tests is a classic defense of student classification in the name of equal opportunity and fairness. The report should be read within the context of curriculum reforms of the time, which emphasized the need for a differentiated curriculum to serve the needs of a diversified student body. Like most current apologists for grouping and tracking, Yerkes sees the issue of fairness in terms of the capacity of the individual to profit from instruction. Thus, he assumes a close relationship between intelligence and equal opportunity.

Imani Perry's reflections on the two very different schools she attended reminds us that different schools structure success differently. In large urban schools having large numbers of minority students, the skills and knowledge taught do not foster creative thinking, says Perry. Moreover, the authority structure of the classroom creates a difficult environment for learning for many minority youth. At the root of this difficulty is the basic fact that the school is no longer an extension of the community values that underlie many urban neighborhoods. Perry characterizes the schooling she received at a public school as a blatant form of oppression and inequity.

The cultural pluralism of American society spans the dimensions of race, ethnicity, language, and socioeconomic position. Joan First's essay on immigrant students reminds us of the enormous task American schools have set for themselves in attempting to provide schooling for *all* children. The United States is a land of immigrants, and public schooling has been seen by successive immigrant populations as a means for upward socioeconomic mobility. As First reminds us, customs from different cultures often collide on the common meeting ground of the public school. Access, testing, and tracking all create their peculiar difficulties for children of other cultures. Thus, support services and teacher knowledge of multicultural education strategies are needed if immigrant students are to be given equal educational opportunity.

The final selection in this chapter focuses on the problems of equity and opportunity that are created by the ways in which gender differences are structured into the classroom. Pervasive differences (biases) in communications and teacher-student interactions create problems of self-esteem for females. The Sadkers argue convincingly that teachers and principals can be taught skills to help them eliminate gender bias from their behavior. The key to developing these skills is the teacher's and principal's own analysis of their behaviors. For most of us, the meanings of our behaviors to others are masked by our own perceptions. To look at our behaviors through the eyes of others is a first step in eliminating the cultural biases embedded in our actions.

ROBERT YERKES

THE MENTAL RATING OF SCHOOL CHILDREN

Children differ radically in physical traits; they differ no less markedly in intelligence and temperament. For this reason, both physical and mental measurements are of practical importance in connection with educational effort.

ARMY INTELLIGENCE TESTS

The application of methods of mental measurement in the army to more than one and three-quarters millions of men has demonstrated most convincingly the practicability of methods of mental testing for the classification and placement of men. The army method of examining men in large groups promptly supplied rough measurements of mental alertness or general intelligence which could be used, first as a basis of classification, and subsequently as a partial basis for occupational placement or for military training.

By grouping recruits in accordance with mental ratings, placing the highly alert men in one group, the mentally sluggish individuals in another, and the intermediates in a third group, it was possible for military instructors to adapt their procedures more satisfactorily than would otherwise have been the case to the individual's ability to learn. The alert group could progress most rapidly, the others at speeds proportionate to their intelligence.

EVERY MAN A PROPER CHANCE

Far from being unfair to the individual, this procedure gives every man his proper chance to learn. The quick individual is not retarded in this instance by the slow or the dull, and the latter, by contrast, is not forced beyond his capacity

From Robert Yerkes, "The Mental Rating of School Children," *National School Service* (February 15, 1919), pp. 6–7.

and either discouraged or harrassed by his inability to meet his instructors' expectations.

GROUP EXAMINATIONS FOR SCHOOLS

The lessons which psychological examining in the army and the military uses of mental ratings have taught us must not be lost to education. It is possible to devise methods of examining school children by groups and of securing thus mental ratings which shall be used in connection with grading and choice of methods of instruction.

INSURES EQUALITY OF OPPORTUNITY

Although this procedure at first appears undemocratic, it is in fact quite the reverse, for equality of opportunity is determined by the relation of the individual to his environment. A given educational opportunity or mode of instruction has the same value for two individuals only if they happen to be so much alike mentally that they can react in similar fashion. To place together in the same school class and to attempt to educate by precisely similar methods of instruction children who, although of approximately the same age, are of very different degrees of intelligence or mental ability, is just as unfair, and therefore as undemocratic, as it is to expect or require the same kinds and amounts of physical activity or achievement from different individuals.

It happens that we admit today the necessity of adapting physical instruction to the characteristics of the pupil, but we still deny or overlook the necessity of similarly adapting our procedures of intellectual training to the mental characteristics and capacity of the child.

MUST NOT IGNORE INDIVIDUALITY

Our ostensibly democratic public school system fails of just treatment to the individual because it largely ignores the principal facts of individuality. We must seriously inquire how this weakness may be remedied and how equality of educational opportunity may be achieved.

The solution of this problem which we desire to suggest is reasonably simple and also, we believe, practicable. [See Figure 1.]

CLASSIFICATION OF SCHOOL CHILDREN

It is proposed that as they enter school, children shall be mentally rated, and in accordance with their ratings, which must of course be reliable, placed in one of three mental groups, which we may designate as A, B, and C. In A would appear

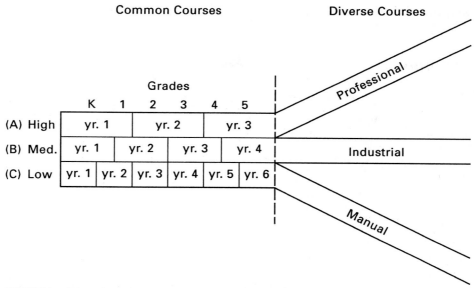

FIGURE 1 Mental Classification and Educational Plan.

all individuals possessing mental alertness or general intelligence of high degree; in C those of relatively low intelligence; and in B, the intermediates.

The pupils of a given grade when classified mentally would constitute three class sections in a given room, or, if the school were large, the units of three separate class rooms; but whether these sections worked in the same or in different rooms, they should be permitted and required to progress in their school work in accordance with their respective abilities.

TEACHINGS OF EXPERIENCE

It has already been demonstrated abundantly by school experimenters that the A group can progress about twice as rapidly as the C group. It is therefore reasonable to assume that the A group would accomplish as much grade work in one year as the B group would in one and one-half years and the C group in two years.

The accompanying rough diagram represents the arrangement which we are attempting to describe. It shows the segregation of a class into high, medium, and low sections (A, B, and C) and the progress by years of study of each of these sections through kindergarten and grades one to five.

School experience in relation to practical mental measurement indicates that by the time the fifth grade is reached a new sort of difference, in addition to that of rapidity of progress, will appear between the sections. Pupils of the A section may show slight change in educational response or mental attitude, but many of the pupils in the C section will exhibit signs of inability to profit by their school work. They may even fail repeatedly of promotion. Stated baldly this means that some of the pupils have already practically reached the limit of educability in the lines of our present elementary school curriculum. The necessary inference is that if their education is to be continued at all profitably it must be in a somewhat different direction and by a different pedagogical procedure.

DIVERGENT COURSES

It is for this reason that, following the fifth grade, the educational channels of sections A, B, and C are shown in the diagram as diverging from one another.

The diagram may be interpreted as implying the existence of three types of school, which should carry their pupils either as far as educability permits or to the point of preparedness for intelligent choice of a vocation. Roughly, the educational procedures and aims of these three schools would be professional, industrial, and manual. Pupils of section A, possessing excellent intelligence, can, if they so desire, proceed successfuly and profitably in the professional channel, fitting themselves for vocations which require facility in mental work and a high degree of intellectual training. By contrast, pupils of section C, with a relatively low degree of intellectual ability, will follow usually the channel of manual training, thus fitting themselves for vocations which are primarily dependent upon physical strength, manual dexterity and skill instead of mental initiative, insight, and originality of thought. Pupils of the intermediate section may profitably follow the industrial channel, thus fitting themselves for various types of skilled labor and for the lower grades of intellectual occupation.

RE-RATING AND TRANSFER OF CHILDREN

It is of the utmost importance, if mental classification of pupils and differentiation of training beyond the fifth grade be introduced, that all children be re-rated at intervals and, as necessary, re-classified within the school system. Moreover, it would be absolutely essential to permit transfer of children among the three divergent courses; thus, for example, on indication of suitable ability a pupil might be transferred from the manual to the industrial course, or from the professional to the industrial, or from the industrial to the manual or to the professional. There should be nothing fixed so far as the individual is concerned, and the sole purpose of the system should be to supply to every pupil the maximum and the optimum of opportunity for educational and vocational training.

PROVIDES VOCATIONAL GUIDANCE

The proposed plan is quite as important in its vocational as in its strictly educational bearings. It would, we believe, do more than any educational system has yet accomplished toward suitably directing children early in their school careers toward that group or general range of occupations for which they are best adapted.

Finally, it should once more be emphasized that the plan is alike fair to all industrial classes or levels and that the child of the poorest laborer has precisely the same opportunity to achieve a place in the A section and in the professional channel of training as has the economically more fortunate child of the laborer's employer. Instead of tending to develop class distinctions within the social or economic sphere, the plan should lead to the free intermingling of children of the various strata in any given intelligence section. The basis of classification then would be mental ability and educability, and that classification would be established and maintained in the interests wholly of educational efficiency, equality of opportunity, and justice to the individual.

IMANI PERRY

A BLACK STUDENT'S REFLECTION ON PUBLIC AND PRIVATE SCHOOLS

Which are more effective, private or public schools? This is an age-old question to which many educators and researchers have offered their answers. In this compelling essay, Imani Perry, a fifteen-year-old high school student, offers an interpretation of the differences between her private and public school experience that adds new insight into this question. Perry provides rich examples to support her main argument that, in her experience, public schools deny students their identity as intellectual beings, and repress the intellectual development of minority students in particular. Private schools, on the other hand, are culturally isolating for minority students. Perry does not advocate the abandonment of public for private school, but offers a clear analysis of those aspects of public schools that must be changed if public schools are to serve the needs of minority students. This is an analysis that could only come from a minority student who has experienced both worlds.

My name is Imani Perry. I am a fifteen-year-old Black female who has experienced both private and public education. These experiences have led me to believe there are significant differences between the two types of education that deserve to be acknowledged and resolved by society as a whole.

After ten years in private schools I made the decision to attend a public school. I left because I felt isolated as a person of color. I yearned to have a large,

From Imani Perry, "A Black Student's Reflection on Public and Private Schools," *Harvard Educational Review* 58 (August, 1988):332–336. Reprinted by permission.

strong Black community be a part of my development. I believed that I would find such a community in the public high school of my city, which is a fairly urban school with approximately 2,600 students, 20 percent of whom are Black.

Despite the fact that I had never been in a traditional public school environment, when I decided to go to one I had certain expectations about the teaching. I assumed that the teaching philosophy would be similar to that of the private schools I had attended. I expected that any teaching differences that did exist would be limited to less sophisticated reading, or a less intense work load. As I quickly learned, the differences were more substantial.

I believe the differences I found in the teaching between the private and public schools that I attended would best be illustrated by several examples of what I encountered. My initial realization of this difference began with an argument I had with a math teacher over a point value on a test. I felt that he should give partial credit for problems with computational errors rather than procedural errors, or conceptual misunderstanding. I presented this point to the math teacher, who responded by saying math is computation and the theories and concepts of math are only used to compute. I was astonished by this statement. Coming from a school where the teachers' stated goal for freshman math was to begin to teach you how to become a "theoretical mathematician," my entire perception of math was different. Perhaps that emphasis on theoretical math was also extreme; nevertheless, I believe that a good math teacher believes that computation in math should be used to assist in the organization of theories. Computation is a necessary but not sufficient step toward math knowledge. I felt this teacher was probably the product of schooling that did not emphasize the artistic qualities of math. While I could sympathize with his position, I felt that all I loved about math—new ideas, discussing unproved theorems, and developing personal procedures—was being ignored. I withdrew from this course only to find the ideological differences emerged again in my advanced English class at the public school, particularly in essay writing.

In this class, once we wrote a paper—mind you, with no assistance from the teacher—the process ended. We did not discuss papers, receive constructive criticism, or improve them through rewriting. Despite the fact that there was no proofreading assistance offered, 10 percent of the grade was taken off for sentence errors. It seemed as if the teacher assumed we no longer needed to continue developing our writing skills.

In my last school, which had an abundance of excellent essayists, my English teacher would give a detailed description of what he felt about each paper. At points where he felt one deserved praise or criticism, he would make comments in the margin. He would not neglect to correct punctuation errors— such as commas instead of semicolons—but these errors were not the sole criteria for our grades, especially if the writing was good. The emphasis was upon improving intellectual and organizational skills to raise the quality of the writing.

These examples illustrate my belief that my learning environment had changed from a place where thought and theory were emphasized to a place where form and precision were emphasized. The teaching system at the public school appears to assume that at some point in our education, learning and thinking are no longer important. Schooling in this situation becomes devoted to making things look correct. This is in sharp contrast to my private schools, where proper form was something I learned was necessary, but secondary in importance to the content and organization of what is produced.

Because of this difference in the concept of teaching and learning, there is also a difference in what and who teachers consider intelligent. The teaching at the public school has less to do with thinking and processing ideas, and more to do with precision and detail in appearance. Therefore, students who are considered intelligent by the public school faculty possess different skills than those at the private schools I have attended. In the public schools a student is considered intelligent if he or she is well-behaved and hard working. The ability to grasp a subject in its entirety—from theory to practice—is not valued.

For example, in the fall of 1987 there was an academic contest, where my school was competing against other public schools. All the teachers I encountered were very enthusiastic about it. The students who were selected to participate were raised on a pedestal. These students, most of whom were clean-cut and apparently straight-laced, were to serve as our models of very intelligent students. They were drilled in formulas, book plots, and other information for several days a week. It seemed as if the teachers were not concerned with whether the students digested the depth of these subjects and resources as long as the students completed all the reading, memorized the facts, and could repeat the information. The contest was more a demonstration of a memory function than anything else. In my opinion there is nothing wrong with such a contest, but it should be recognized for what it is and is not. One thing it is not is a true measure of knowledge and ability. This was never recognized by the school.

Another example of how a different view of intelligence is manifested in this public school is the school's view of two students whom I know. I will identify them as Student A and Student B. Student B is an intellectual. She reads, is analytical in her discussion and is knowledgeable. Student A is very precise with his homework, answers the patronizing questions the teachers ask ("What color was the horse?" "Black with a white spot!" "Correct!"), and is very "all-American" in behavior and appearance. Student A is considered more intelligent at this public school because he displays skills that are considered signs of intelligence at this school. The intelligence criteria at this school are more related to superficial qualities such as appearance, knowing facts, etc., rather than the intellectual qualities that student B possesses. Student B displays an ability to learn and write in creative and analytical formats. I left a school where the criterion for intelligence was the student's thought process resulting from the information, for a school where the information was the measure of intelligence.

In reflecting on schooling it is important to realize that all people, including teachers, have biases based on the physical appearances of other people. On the train most people are more likely to sit next to the clean-shaven Harvard freshman than next to the Mohawked, multiple-earringed punk-rocker. In teachers, however, these biases should diminish as they begin to know a student. Unfortunately, in the public school there is an absence of teacher-student contact.

Because of this lack of contact there are no criteria by which intelligence can be determined, besides grades, appearance, and behavior. As I mentioned before, the grading system at this school often reflects one's ability to memorize and not one's thinking and analytical abilities. Moreover, since people are biased in their acceptance of different appearances, students who look different are judged differently. The only way they can make up for this difference is to be "well-behaved," and, as I will mention later, the definition of well-behaved is arbitrary.

All these issues I have discussed have every negative effects for students from minority groups, more specifically the Black and Hispanic youths who make up a large percentage of most urban schools. It is those Black and Hispanic students who retain strong cultural characteristics in their personalities who are most negatively affected by teachers' emphasis on behavior, appearance, and respect for authority.

Public schools' emphasis on the teaching of form merely trains students for low-powered or menial jobs that do not require analytical thought. It is evident when most students are discussing what they intend to be that their goals are most often focused toward areas and professions about which they have some idea or knowledge. If in class you've never spoken about how language and colloquialisms are reflections of the society you are studying, you definitely will not be thinking of being a linguist. And if you are only asked to type a paper summarizing the book, rather than writing an analysis of it, the primary skill shown is typing. This should not be the main skill which is emphasized.

The neglect of intellectual development also occurs in higher-level classes, but at least the resources, books, etc., available to students are not altogether lacking in intellectual value. Occasionally these resources will have depth and content, be philosophical, or insightful. But in lower-level classes, where minority students are most often found and where bad textbooks are used without outside resources, the reading has less content, and the point of reading is to perfect reading skills, not to broaden thinking skills or gain knowledge of how the subject is currently affecting us. It is often not possible to broaden your thinking skills or knowledge with the books used in lower-level classes, which are more often stripped of any content. In an upper-level class, if you have a parent who wants you to know the subject in depth, and to think about it, it is possible to do that detached from the school environment, because the subject matter may have content, or have some meaning beyond the words. My high-level sophomore English class read *Moby Dick* as an outside reading. We didn't discuss the symbolism or religious qualities of it, but I am aware of them because I read critical essays and discussed them with my mother. If one is reading a book which has been stripped of meaningful content, it is not helpful to do outside research, because it is lacking in meaning.

Many students from minority groups are being trained only in form and not in creative ways of thinking. This I believe causes disenchantment among students. Upper-class students are not as affected, because of their social class, and their "social responsibility" to be achievers. This is especially true of upper-class students in a public school whose social-class peers are in private schools. But instead of striving to be true learners, they quickly learn how to be good students by being well-behaved. What well-behaved means is always taking the teacher's word as absolute truth and never questioning the teacher's authority. This definition of well-behaved is of course culturally based and can be in opposition to cultures of Black and Hispanic students.

In Black and Hispanic cultures, respect and obedience come and develop with the relationship. Rather than being automatic, respect must be earned. For example, one will occasionally hear a Black child say to a stranger, "You can't tell me what to do, you're not my mother." But at the same time, often one will see Black kids following the orders and rules of an adult friend of the family, whom they would under no circumstances disrespect. In addition, in Black and Hispanic cultures it appears that adult and child cultures are more integrated than those of other ethnic groups. For example, parties in the Hispanic community will often have an age range from toddler to elderly. Children are often present in the conversation and socializing of adults and are not treated as separate, as they may be in other cultures.

When this relationship is not made between teacher and student, it is not an acceptable educational situation, because the Black and Hispanic students are now expected to respect someone in a different manner than their culture has socialized them to. Often students are not aware of the fact that the demands being placed on them by the relationship conflict with those of their culture. They then show signs of what a teacher views as a lack of the respect that he/she deserves. The student might feel it is just a sign that they do not know the teacher and have no obligation to him or her. Many times I have seen a dumbstruck student of color sent to detention; when asked what he or she did, the student will seriously say that he or she has no idea; perhaps that he or she sucked his or her teeth in dismay, or something of that sort.

Black and Hispanic students have less of a chance at building strong relationships with any teachers because their appearance and behavior may be considered offensive to the middle-class White teachers. These students show signs of what White teachers, and some teachers of color, consider disrespect, and they do not get the nurturing relationships that develop respect and dedication. They are considered less intelligent, as can be seen in the proportion of Blacks and Hispanics in lower-level as opposed to upper-level classes. There is less of a teacher-student contact with "underachievers," because they are guided into peer tutoring programs. Perhaps this is understandable, because the teachers have less of a vested interest in the achievement of students that are not of their community, or have less of an idea of how to educate them. Public school teachers are no longer part of the same community as the majority of their students. The sad part of the situation is that many students believe that this type of teaching is what academic learning is all about. They have not had the opportunity to experience alternative ways of teaching and learning. From my experience in public school, it appears that many minority students will never be recognized as capable of analytical and critical thinking.

In the beginning of this article I spoke about my decision to leave my private school because of feeling isolated. After three months at a large urban public school I found myself equally isolated—intellectually as well as racially.

My thinking process has gradually affected my opinions and character. I am in upper-level classes in which there are barely any kids of color, except Asians. Black and Hispanic students have been filtered down into lower-level classes. Most of the students I meet are kind, interesting people whom I like and respect. However, because the environment of the school is one in which ideas are not valued or fostered, I find it difficult to discuss issues with them, because my thoughtfulness has flourished, while others have been denied an opportunity to explore their intellectual development. I am now at a point of deciding which isolation is worse, cultural/racial or intellectual-opinion-based and slightly racial. This is a decision many Black students who have attended private schools at some time are wrestling to make, a decision that will affect their development, knowledge, and viewpoint of education, and their relationships to educators—those supposed possessors of greater knowledge than themselves.

Afterword: Since the writing of this article I have returned to a private school with the feeling that one's educational development is too much to sacrifice. I now attend a private high school with a strong unified Black community, as well as academic merit. Even though I did not remain at the urban public school, I valued my experience there, mostly because through it I learned one of the most blatant forms of oppression and inequity for lower-class students in American society, and I appreciate the opportunities with which I have been blessed.

JOAN M. FIRST
IMMIGRANT STUDENTS IN U.S. PUBLIC SCHOOLS: CHALLENGES WITH SOLUTIONS

Rosario Anaya, a member of the board of the San Francisco Unified Schools, has strong opinions about the American response to the challenge of educating immigrant students. "While we talk about democracy and equal opportunity," Anaya says, "in reality many of our students are barely given a chance to get out of the gate. We resist meeting immigrant children even halfway. The basic question is not how we can teach these children, but whether we really want to."[1]

Extensive immigration to the U.S. during the last 15 years has resulted in historic levels of enrollment of immigrant students in public schools. These new arrivals—largely from Asia, Latin America, and the Caribbean—are a vital resource for this country's future. But their extraordinary cultural diversity and unique backgrounds present difficult challenges that must be met if this promise is to be fully realized.

From Joan M. First, "Immigrant Students in U.S. Public Schools: Challenges with Solutions, *Phi Delta Kappan* 70 (November, 1988):205–210. Reprinted with permission.

COMING TO A NEW LAND

The lives and hopes of recently arrived immigrant students are shaped by three dominant forces: the traumas of war and violence in their native lands, the isolation of racism, and the struggle to survive economically in a new land.

War and Violence

Vietnam, Cambodia, and Laos have suffered from decades of almost unimaginable brutality, ranging from bloody civil wars and protracted revolutions to foreign invasions. El Salvador, Guatemala, and Nicaragua have been convulsed by civil wars, marked by terrorism and torture, that inevitably have affected the neighboring states of Honduras and Costa Rica. In Haiti, beatings and executions have kept a series of repressive governments in power.

A man from El Salvador tells of "countless situations where children were in the classroom and their teacher was killed." A New York City education advocate counsels an 8-year-old girl who "saw her father put up against the wall and shot by government troops. He died before her eyes." A child psychiatrist in Los Angeles notes that "random shooting, skirmishes, aerial bombardments, and other war-related acts of violence were commonplace in the lives of these youngsters."[2]

The trial of fleeing their homes was extended for many. Vietnamese refugees escaping by boat risked assaults by pirates who robbed, raped, and murdered on the open seas. Young people crossing the U.S.-Mexican border were piled in automobile trunks, 10 at a time, or were stuffed in hidden compartments near the engines; some were severely burned. Many Southeast Asians were confined in refugee camps for months or years.

Racial Tension

Once in the U.S. immigrants face a population that is only beginning to acknowledge its increasing ethnic variety. Discussions with immigrant parents and students across the country reveal racial tension between newcomers and native-born Americans and among immigrant groups themselves.

Cambodians and Puerto Ricans face off in Lowell, Massachusetts; Hispanics and Southeast Asians bicker in Providence, Rhode Island; Haitians tangle with American blacks in Miami; Hispanic, black, white, and Asian youngsters argue and fight in school gyms in Philadelphia, Boston, and California. In some cities, ethnic gangs fight to defend their turf and boost their members' self-esteem. Although conflicts are frequent, they should not be exaggerated: the majority of immigrant students reject fighting and have made friends with both native-born Americans and with other immigrants.

Economic Struggle

Most immigrant families arrive in the U.S. with few material resources. They must settle wherever they can afford housing, find work, and join other immigrants in a supportive community. Often they tend to settle in poor, urban areas. Unless they have been granted refugee status, recent immigrants are not eligible for government services that provide housing, food stamps, and health care. They are, however, eligible for such federal education and nutrition programs as Chapter 1, Head Start, Supplemental Security Income, child welfare programs, and guaranteed access to emergency medical care.

The limited financial resources of new immigrants are further strained by the need to support family members who remain in their native countries. A community worker in Cambridge, Massachusetts, reports, "A lot of people—13- to 14-year-old boys, for example—who have come into the United States alone . . . know they have sisters, they have brothers, they sometimes have parents waiting for them to support them. And they cannot do it by attending school."[3]

CROSS-CULTURAL CONFLICTS

One of the first experiences of children who enter the U.S. is the clash between their primary cultures and the norms of their new home. In a land in which relatively few citizens can speak or write any language other than English, language is the primary barrier faced by immigrants.

Because most recently arrived immigrants speak little or no English to their children, the home is not a fertile place to improve children's skills in English. Public schools remain the front lines in the effort to provide immigrant children with equal access to a productive future. As one young Vietnamese girl observed, to be successful in the U.S. "you have to know English." She added: "And it helps to be white."[4]

Young immigrants enter U.S. classrooms with cultural scripts modeled on the material and social environments of their homelands. Their behavioral norms stem from lives they are no longer living but cannot forget. To survive, they must integrate old scripts with their new environment.[5]

While the millions of immigrants who compose the most recent migration have much in common, they are also remarkably diverse and face differing problems and pressures. Miren Uriarte, a professor at the University of Massachusetts, explains:

> Collectively, they share the fact that they are Third World people in the U.S. . . . beginning to understand the meaning of being a person of color in American society. They also share the fact that they are adjusting to a different culture, learning a new language, that they have families which cannot be very helpful in understanding the ways of American life.
>
> But clearly, how they entered the U.S. and the policies that greeted them are different for each group. The problems of documentation, the differences in resources available for refugees versus those available for nonrefugees or undoc-

umented people, and the differences in class and educational background among groups have to be taken into account.[6]

Cultural distinctions account for different ways of learning and may affect classroom behavior and participation. Cultural misunderstandings on the part of teachers and fellow students can be a major source of conflict for young immigrants. In a simple example, crossed fingers—used by native-born Americans to invite good luck—are considered obscene by Southeast Asians.

The unique experiences faced by many immigrant children in their native lands and after arrival in the U.S. can leave them vulnerable. Coming to America with mixed educational backgrounds, with varying languages and cultures, and bearing emotional burdens unknown to most of us, these children have been forced by circumstances to assume extraordinary responsibilities while still young.

CHALLENGES AND SOLUTIONS

Public schools across the U.S. are now struggling to meet the unique and often urgent needs of recently arrived immigrant students. A number of factors play a critical role in meeting these needs, including access to school and school programs, assessment and placement, tracking and ability grouping, school climate, the availability of support services, and the participation of parents and communities.

Access to School

The U.S. Supreme Court ended years of political controversy and litigation in Texas when it ruled in 1982 in *Plyler v. Doe* that the state has an obligation to educate the children of undocumented immigrants. While acknowledging the complexity and far-reaching implications of its decision, the Court clearly expressed its ultimate concern: ". . . the deprivation of education takes an inestimable toll on the social, economic, intellectual, and psychological well-being of the individual, and poses an obstacle to individual achievement. . . . [Thus] its cost to the innocent children may properly be considered."[7]

While most public school personnel are now aware of the ruling in *Plyler*, problems continue. Immigrant children are sporadically discouraged from attending school—both directly (by school personnel who illegally press for documents providing legal status) and indirectly (by the failure of schools to inform immigrant families of their rights).

The U.S. Immigration and Naturalization Service (INS) should prepare and distribute to immigrant families information explaining their educational rights, written in their native languages. The federal government should inform school officials of these rights and of its determination to see that they are upheld, and the INS should refrain from entering school buildings or grounds in search of undocumented immigrants. This is particularly important in the wake of the

Immigration Reform and Control Act of 1986, which has increased fears of deportation within the immigrant community.

State and local education agencies should be sure that their personnel understand the educational rights of immigrants and should prepare and distribute to immigrant families information written in their native languages. Policies should be adopted to prohibit any local or state agency or organization from entering schools or collaborating with school officials in ways that infringe on the rights of immigrants.

Access to the Classroom

Because most immigrant families settle in inner-city neighborhoods, the public schools they attend are often short on resources, poorly staffed, badly maintained, and overcrowded. One New York City superintendent observed, "We have been overcrowded for years. The space problem impinges on every action we take and makes the solution to our problems immensely more difficult."[8] An assistant superintendent in Los Angeles noted that "*Time* magazine has called our school district 'Ellis Island of the West' because . . . we are growing [by] almost a classroom a month."[9]

To help address the problem of overcrowding, state education agencies must recognize the higher cost of educational services in metropolitan areas and must work to insure a more equitable allocation of funding. The U.S. Department of Education can play an important role by providing fiscal incentives to states that provide adequate resources to their overburdened inner-city schools.

Access to a Comprehensible Education

One of the most common access issues facing immigrant students who may have a limited command of English is the problem of securing equal educational opportunity. Estimates of the number of students with limited proficiency in English who are enrolled in U.S. public schools range from 3.5 million to 5.5 million.[10] It is also estimated that as many as two-thirds of them are not receiving the assistance they need to succeed in their studies.[11]

Language assistance services are uneven in quality, ranging from simple immersion in a classroom filled with English speakers to bilingual education programs designed to improve students' skills in English and in their native languages at the same time. When immigrant students do not receive basic instruction in their native languages, at least until they can become fully proficient in English, their chances of succeeding in school are tragically undercut. Moreover, their lifelong success is threatened if they are unable to learn English at all. The complexity of providing native-language instruction in an underfunded inner-city school system struggling with 40 or 50 languages is profound, particularly when standard English-as-a-second-language (ESL) programs by themselves do not provide the needed support for academic success.

A more realistic approach is embodied in "English Plus," which was developed by the League of United Latin American Citizens, an organization based in Washington, D.C. "English Plus" makes use of special strategies to supplement existing ESL programs. These strategies might include providing the necessary language support for children—as they learn English and their other subjects in an all-English program—by using teachers who speak the students' native languages or by using peer and adult tutors. "English Plus" shows respect for a student's primary language and culture. In addition, "English Plus" provides better access to the mainstream curriculum and provides role models to bolster students' self-confidence and encourage their aspirations.

Assessment and Placement

The great wave of immigration of the last 15 years seems to be on a collision course with the school reforms of the 1980s, as an increasingly diverse student population confronts an increasingly rigid school environment. One of the most troublesome practices for new immigrants is the lock-step use of standardized testing.

Newcomers tend not to score well on standardized tests for a number of reasons: the failure to provide native-language instruction while children are learning English; the premature termination of instruction in English; the cultural bias of the tests; and students' lack of test-taking skills. A legal advocate familiar with the problems faced by immigrant students in southern Florida testified at a public hearing on the Immigrant Student Project in Miami, "If you are going to test immigrant students, at least you should teach them the things that you are testing them about."[12]

Immigrant children also have difficulty with rigid grade levels and with the accompanying expectation that every child is expected to progress by a full year every year. Students who are learning a second language, adjusting to a new culture, or recovering from emotional trauma may well need more than nine months to complete the learning associated with a given grade level.

Schools most often respond to this need for more time by labeling the children as failures and requiring them to repeat a grade or by assigning them to special education classes. The current widespread use of retention ignores research findings that show that most students learn better when promoted and given additional assistance.[13] And the steep climb in the number of referrals to special education classes has fueled concern that immigrant students are likely to be misassigned to such classes.

A Miami specialist in immigrant relations with the Dade County public schools told the Immigrant Student Project, "Teachers thought these kids were dumb, that they could not learn . . . [but in reality] their problems could have been that they had never gone to school, or they were placed in sixth grade when they [had] only completed first grade. . . . There are some schools that have mostly Haitian kids in their special education classes."[14]

Schools seeking to meet the needs of immigrant students must avoid lock-step assessment, placement, and instruction. Flexible strategies best accommo-

date differences in language, culture, and learning style, as explained by Paul
Cheng, principal of Newcomer High School in San Francisco:

> We know for a fact that what these youngsters need is time: time in the school
> system; time to develop a sense of spontaneity about speech, making friends,
> having a vision of what their life will be like in America, having an idea of
> what the ultimate goal of being a human being should be in this country.[15]

Tracking and Ability Grouping

As today's immigrants enter U.S. public schools, they encounter persistent
grouping and tracking—a direct inheritance from the last great wave of immigration at the beginning of this century. Researcher Jeannie Oakes notes that
turn-of-the-century educators, faced with increasing diversity among students,
responded with "tracking and ability grouping—providing a differentiated
curriculum to accommodate the needs of these 'new' students, as well as
fulfilling the more traditional function of providing 'high status' preparation for
upper-class students. . . . High schools that were tracked along the lines of race
and class provided an acceptable solution to the considerable social disequilib-
rium."[16]

Most public schools track children because it is commonly assumed that
students learn best in homogeneous groupings. But contemporary research
concludes that little evidence supports this widely held assumption.[17] Immigrant
students, who often experience initial difficulties in social development and in
academic achievement, are more likely than their native-born peers to be placed
in lower tracks. As a New York City case worker observed, "[Immigrant
students] tend to become tracked for failure and geared toward low-level jobs.
They are steered away from college-prep courses."[18]

John Goodlad and Jeannie Oakes argued in 1984 that schools should
"detrack" their curricula by eliminating ability grouping for instruction; by
designing curricula around central ideas and themes, rather than according to a
'scope and sequence' chart; by including cooperative activities and other strategies to facilitate learning in mixed-ability classrooms; and by rejecting the
assumption that some students can't or won't learn.[19]

School Climate

Immigrant children and adolescents, many of whom have survived wars,
political oppression, and economic deprivation, find that their problems are not
over when they enter American public schools. Confronted with hatred, prejudice, and violence in U.S. schools, many newcomers are left asking what they
have done to deserve such treatment. One Vietnamese student spoke for many
when he said, "I like school here. But I wish there would be more friendships
among immigrants and American students."[20]

A supportive social environment in the schools will emerge only with
strong adult leadership. Administrators and teachers are responsible for in-

suring that all students are treated respectfully, by peers and school staff alike. This is particularly important when students differ in physical appearance, language, and culture. There must be no tolerance of harassment.

In the classroom, high-quality multicultural education can teach children to respect and understand diversity. Immigrant students then experience their native languages and cultures as sources of pride, not of conflict. The alternative, as expressed by one New York City student, is chilling:

> I came upon a world unknown to me, a language I did not understand, and a school administration which made ugly faces at me every time I spoke Spanish. Many teachers referred to us as animals. Believe me, maintaining a half-decent image of yourself wasn't an easy thing. . . . I had enough strength of character to withstand the many school personnel who tried to destroy my motivation. But many of my classmates didn't make it.[21]

Support Services

A particularly serious barrier to equal educational opportunity is the shortage of school personnel who have the language skills needed for effective teaching, who are sensitive to and well-informed about different cultures, and who reflect the ethnic and cultural diversity evident in the student population.

Of the skills in short supply, language skills are the most urgently needed. Burgeoning enrollments of immigrant students have contributed to an acute shortage of bilingual teachers. State education agencies must implement plans for recruiting and training bilingual educators. Teacher education programs must expand their efforts to prepare qualified graduates to meet the growing demand. Barriers that now prevent foreign-born teachers from gaining their U.S. credentials should be removed.

However, improving the language skills of the teaching force may not be enough. The traumatic backgrounds of some young immigrants have left them badly scarred. Counseling and other mental health services are needed to help heal their wounds, resolve their learning and behavioral problems, and ease their transition into U.S. culture.

Parents and Community

By themselves, public schools cannot be expected to fill the educational, social, and medical needs of young immigrants. Nor do they have to. Schools should use the broad spectrum of community-based services available in many areas and recognize that immigrant communities have unique resources that need only to be properly tapped. Unfortunately, schools often seem unwilling to seek partnerships with parents and community organizations in immigrant neighborhoods. Sometimes they even discourage these groups from becoming involved.

However, active parental involvement in schools can help insure a culturally sensitive academic and social environment and can help narrow the gap between children's experiences at home and in school. When educators involve minority parents in the education of their children, they send a powerful message that the school cares.

Schools sometimes view community groups as unprofessional—even as adversaries. But overburdened and underfinanced schools will find that community groups can be rich sources of information and support. Many community groups can provide staff training, help with the identification and recruitment of bilingual personnel, offer counseling and other mental health services for students, and provide structured social activities, resettlement services, and legal support. Community activists are also effective as role models for young immigrants learning to live in the U.S.

Easing the transition to life in America for the latest wave of immigrants poses difficult problems—for society and for the schools. But most immigrant families are profoundly committed to their children's education. As a Vietnamese mother expressed it, "I am willing to give up everything in order for my son to succeed in school." Surely such caring and determination must not be wasted.

NOTES

[1] Joan M. First et al., *New Voices: Immigrant Students in U.S. Public Schools* (Boston: National Coalition of Advocates for Students, 1988), p. 39.

[2] Ibid., p. 22.

[3] Ibid., p. 27.

[4] Ibid., p. 16.

[5] Wendy Walker, "The Other Side of the Asian Academic Success Myth: The Hmong Story," unpublished paper, Graduate School of Education, Harvard University, October 1987.

[6] First, p. 19.

[7] *Plyler v. Doe*, 457 U.S. 202 (1982).

[8] First, p. 42.

[9] Ibid.

[10] Ibid., p. 49.

[11] Ibid.

[12] Ibid., p. 45.

[13] Ibid., p. 46.

[14] Ibid., p. 48.

[15] Ibid., p. 88.

[16] Ibid., p. 96.

[17] Ibid.

[18] Ibid., p. 48.

[19] Ibid., p. 97.

[20] Ibid., p. 60.

[21] Ibid., p. 51.

Myra Sadker and David Sadker

SEXISM IN THE CLASSROOM: FROM GRADE SCHOOL TO GRADUATE SCHOOL.

From grade school to graduate school to the world of work, males and females are separated by a common language. This communications gender gap affects self-esteem, educational attainment, career choice, and income. But its hidden lessons generally go unnoticed.

For the past six years we have conducted research on classroom interactions in elementary and secondary schools and in institutions of higher education. In this article, we will discuss four conclusions of our research.

- Male students receive more attention from teachers and are given more time to talk in classrooms.
- Educators are generally unaware of the presence or the impact of this bias.
- Brief but focused training can reduce or eliminate sex bias from classroom interaction.
- Increasing equity in classroom interaction increases the effectiveness of the teacher as well. Equity and effectiveness are not competing concerns; they are complementary.

Our first study of classroom interaction was conducted from 1980 to 1984. With funding from the National Institute of Education (NIE), researchers trained in the INTERSECT Observation System collected data in more than 100 fourth-, sixth-, and eighth-grade classrooms in four states and the District of Columbia. The sample included urban, suburban, and rural classes; classes that were predominantly white, predominantly black, and predominantly integrated. The teachers observed in this study were both male and female; they represented both white and minority groups; they taught in the areas of language arts, social studies, and mathematics. While the sample reflected the diversity of American students and teachers, the observations revealed the pervasiveness of sex bias.[1]

At all three grade levels and in all subjects, we found that male students were involved in more interactions than female students. It did not matter whether the teacher was black or white, female or male; the pattern remained the same. Male students received more attention from teachers.

But the matter was not as simple as boys winning and girls losing the battle for the attention of the teacher. Classrooms were characterized by a more general environment of inequity; there were the "haves" and the "have nots" of teacher attention. Students in the same classroom, with the same teacher, studying the same material were experiencing very different educational environments.

About a quarter of the elementary and secondary students typically did not

From Myra Sadker and David Sadker, "Sexism in the Classroom: From Grade School to Graduate School," *Phi Delta Kappan* 67 (March, 1986), pp. 512–515. Reprinted with permission.

interact with the teacher at all during class. These were the silent ones, spectators of classroom interaction. A second group was involved in a nominal level of interaction—typically one interaction per class session. The majority of students fell within this group. The final category consisted of interaction-rich students who participated in more than three times their fair share of interactions with the teacher. Only a few students (typically less than 10%) fell into this category; these were the stars, the salient students.

The quality as well as the quantity of classroom interaction is also distributed inequitably. Teacher interactions involving precise feedback were more likely to be directed to male students. We identified three types of precise teacher reactions: praise (positive reactions to a student's comment or work), criticism (explicit statements that an answer is incorrect), and remediation (helping students to correct or improve their responses). A fourth, less-specific teacher reaction consisted of simple acceptance of student comments, including such teacher comments as "okay" or "uh-huh." More than half of the teachers' comments fell into this category. This high rate of acceptance responses created classroom environments best characterized as flat, bland, and unexciting.

When teachers' reactions were more precise, remediation comments designed to correct or improve students' answers were the most common. These accounted for about one-third of all teacher comments. Praise constituted approximately 10% and criticism 5% of teacher interactions. Male students received significantly more remediation, criticism, and praise than female students. There was more equity in the distribution of acceptance responses—the ones that pack the least educational wallop.

Although our research has made the inequities of classroom interaction more apparent, the reasons why males capture more and better teacher attention remains less clear. Sex segregation may be part of the problem. The majority of classrooms in our study were sex-segregated, and teachers tended to gravitate to the boys' sections, where they spent more of their time and attention.

Another explanation is that boys demand more attention. Our research shows that boys in elementary and secondary schools are eight times as likely as girls to call out and demand a teacher's attention. However, this is not the whole story; teachers behave differently depending on whether the student calling out is a boy or a girl. When boys call out, teachers tend to accept their answers. When girls call out, teachers remediate their behavior and advise them to raise their hands. Boys are being trained to be assertive; girls are being trained to be passive—spectators relegated to the sidelines of classroom discussion.

These findings cannot be dismissed as a mechanistic and irrelevant game of counting who talks more often. National measures of academic progress support the thesis that girls and boys are experiencing different educational environments. In the early grades, girls' scores on standardized tests are generally equal to or better than boys' scores. However, by the end of high school, boys are scoring higher on such measures as the National Assessment of Educational Progress and the Scholastic Aptitude Test.

Given our findings about classroom interaction, common sense suggests that this is what should happen. The most valuable resource in a classroom is the teacher's attention. If the teacher is giving more of that valuable resource to one group, it should come as no surprise that that group shows greater educational gains. The only real surprise is that it has taken us so long to see the problem.

Nor is bias in classroom interaction confined to schools in the U.S. Recently we returned from Great Britain, where we had been discussing sexism in classroom instruction. Unlike American educators, who are often taken aback by the subtle but significant bias in teacher/student interaction, British educators were not surprised by evidence of bias in the classroom. Indeed, over the past few years debate in Britain has focused on strengthening girls' schools as a way of avoiding this bias. Such a separate-but-equal approach would be far less palatable in the U.S., where the memory of struggles to end racial segregation is still fresh.

Following completion of our three-year NIE study of elementary and secondary schools, we received support from the Fund for the Improvement of Postsecondary Education (FIPSE) to train college faculty members in equity and excellence in classroom instruction.[2] Joan Long conducted a doctoral dissertation study of this two-year project.[3]

Field researchers, who had been trained in a postsecondary version of the INTERSECT Observation System, collected data in 46 classes in a wide range of academic and professional disciplines at American University. The data indicate that the patterns established in elementary and secondary school continue in higher education. Male students receive significantly more attention, and sex bias persists.

The need for teacher training at the college level is evident. The data from the observations of college classrooms showed that the overall amount of interaction decreased and that the number of silent students increased. In fourth-, sixth-, and eighth-grade classes, 25% of the students did not interact with the teacher at all; in college classes this number rose to half. The "okay" classroom was prevalent at the university level. There was more acceptance than praise, criticism, and remediation combined.

Research also shows that college women experience a decline in self-esteem as they progress through college.[4] It is likely that a key factor in this decline is the inequitable communication women experience inside and outside the college classroom.[5]

TRAINING THAT WORKS

For both our NIE and our FIPSE projects, we designed and evaluated intensive four-day programs of training for teachers. At the elementary and secondary levels, more than 40 teachers from several states have participated in the training.

Initially, many of these teachers were skeptical. Some said, "Girls get better grades on their report cards. What's the problem?" Others felt that boys did receive more attention but that this was true in some other teachers' classrooms, not in their own. One teacher who was an active member of the National

Organization for Women (NOW) said, "I'm delighted that you're doing this project. Of course, I won't have to change anything I do in the classroom. This is an issue I've been concerned about for years." But, as these teachers became more involved in the training, their perceptions of and attitudes toward classroom interaction underwent substantial change.

In the training session, the teachers viewed videotapes and films that demonstrated the research findings about bias in student/teacher interaction. In a modified microteaching setting, the teachers practiced equitable teaching skills, received feedback on their performance, and practiced again. They were surprised to look at videotapes showing, irrefutably, their own bias in classroom interaction. The teacher who was also a NOW member was stunned. But all the teachers saw the need for change.

Changing instructional patterns in the college classroom was a more difficult challenge because inservice training in postsecondary institutions rarely addresses specific teaching skills (nor does preservice training, for that matter). When we proposed our microteaching design, many K–12 educators expressed serious reservations. "Professors will talk about teaching," they said, "but they'll never be willing to have their teaching observed, videotaped, and critiqued by their colleagues."

Nevertheless, we were able to recruit American University professors from a wide range of academic disciplines—from anthropology to computer science, from biology to economics, from chemistry to community studies. We did not find aversion to clinical training, but rather a thirst for it. For many experienced professors, this project was the first opportunity in their professional lives to systematically analyze and improve their teaching skills. Some professors, who had lectured (and only lectured) all their lives, had to learn questioning skills. Others, who had received awards for their teaching skills, were surprised to see videotapes showing that half of their students didn't receive a fair share of teacher time. These professors, committed as they were to good teaching, also wanted to change.

In both of these studies, trained teachers and professors were matched with control groups, and the performance of the two groups was evaluated. The trained instructors at all levels achieved equity in verbal distribution; they included male and female students in numbers that reflected their distribution in the classroom. The differences between the trained groups and the control groups were statistically significant. Moreover, the trained instructors had higher rates of interaction, more precise reactions, more academic contacts, and a greater number of student-initiated comments. In short, the training resulted in more intentional and more direct teaching. Developing equity in teaching had promoted excellence as well.

LANGUAGE OF MEETINGS

But sex bias in communication does not stop at the classroom door. Many studies have found key sex differences in how men and women communicate in meetings and other professional settings. Males exhibit more powerful behaviors and are more likely to influence the group discussion. Women's comments are more likely to be ignored. This gender gap in communication leads to ineffective discussions and can put female administrators and teachers at a disadvantage in seeing that their ideas are heard and implemented.

Despite the stereotypical image of women as garrulous, studies consistently show that men talk more than their fair share of the time.[6] In mixed groups, sex is a status characteristic, and men talk more than women. They emerge as group leaders,[7] and they are more successful at influencing groups to accept new ideas.[8]

One of the ways that men dominate professional meetings is through interruptions. When men and women talk with one another, almost all interruptions are by male speakers. Males interrupt females more frequently than they interrupt other males. Men also gain verbal dominance by answering questions that are not addressed to them.

Women, even female administrators and managers, often collaborate with men in this game of verbal domination of professional communication. When women are interrupted, they typically do not assert themselves in an effort to hold the floor. Rather, following an interruption, women are usually quiet for an extended period. They are more likely to ask questions and to do the housekeeping chores of keeping conversations going by making encouraging and supportive remarks. In one study, over 96% of the topics men introduced were developed in the discussion. Only 36% of those introduced by women were similarly developed.[9]

Women are aware that the dynamics of a group interaction can constitute a barrier to their influence and advancement. In a recent study of problems facing professional women, 43% of respondents identified their own failure to speak up in mixed groups as their greatest problem. Another 22% said that their greatest problem in group meetings was interruptions by males.[10] Minority women appear to face an even greater challenge in seeing that their contributions are heard. The socialization of 12, 16, or more years of schooling is not easily shed.

PRINCIPALS CAN HELP, TOO

With support from the Women's Educational Equity Act, we have created the Principal Effectiveness-Pupil Achievement (PEPA) Project, through which we are currently developing a model program to improve the equity and effectiveness of classroom interaction and professional communication. The project does not focus directly on the classroom teacher, but rather on principals in their role as instructional leaders.

The initial group of principals to be trained in the PEPA Program will be selected from the Mid-Atlantic region. After this pilot testing, the PEPA Program and materials will be made available to principals nationwide. Principals involved in PEPA will acquire the skills to analyze both classroom interaction and professional communication. Through the use of videotapes, a trainer's manual, and micro-supervision, the PEPA Program will give principals the skills they need to lead the improvement of instructional equity and effectiveness in their schools.

The experience of female students in U.S. schools is unique. What other group starts out ahead—in reading, in writing, and even in math—and 12 years later finds itself behind? We have compensatory education for those who enter school at a disadvantage; it is time that we recognize the problems of those who lose ground as a result of their years of schooling.

Bias in classroom interaction inhibits student achievement. Bias in workplace interaction inhibits the nation's productivity and efficiency. The tools to solve these problems have been forged. It is up to educators to pick them up and put them to use.

NOTES

[1] David Sadker and Myra Sadker, *Year III: Final Report, Promoting Effectiveness in Classroom Instruction* (Washington, D.C.: NIE Contract No. 400-80-0033, March 1984).

[2] Myra Sadker and David Sadker, *Final Report: Faculty Development for Effectiveness and Equity in College Teaching* (Washington, D.C.: FIPSE, November 1985).

[3] Joan Long, "The Effects of Sex Equity and Effectiveness Training on Classroom Interaction at the University Level" (Doctoral dissertation, American University, 1986).

[4] Alexander Astin, *Four Critical Years: Effects of College on Beliefs, Attitudes, and Knowledge* (San Francisco: Jossey-Bass, 1977).

[5] Roberta Hall and Bernice Sandler, *The Classroom Climate: A Chilly One for Women* (Washington, D.C.: Project on the Status and Education of Women, Association of American Colleges, 1982).

[6] Barbara Eakins and Gene Eakins, *Sex Differences in Human Communication* (Boston: Houghton Mifflin, 1978).

[7] Marlaine Lockheed and Katherine Hall, "Conceptualizing Sex as a Status Characteristic: Applications to Leadership Training Strategies," *Journal of Social Issues*, vol. 32, 1976, pp. 111–124.

[8] James DeBerardinis, Kathy Ramge, and Steve Levitt, "Risky Shift and Gender of the Advocate: Information Theory Versus Normative Theory," *Group and Organization Studies*, vol. 9, 1984, pp. 189–200.

[9] Donald Zimmerman and Candace West, "Sex Roles, Interruptions, and Silences in Conversation," in Barrie Thorne and Nancy Henley, eds., *Language and Sex: Differences and Dominance* (Rowley, Mass.: Newbury House, 1975).

[10] P. Shockley and Constance Staley, "Women in Management Training Programs: What They Think About Key Issues," *Public Personnel Management*, vol. 9, 1980, pp. 214–224.

DISCUSSION QUESTIONS FOR CHAPTER 4

1. Discuss the ways in which Yerkes's view of equal opportunity differs from and is similar to those expressed in Chapter 2. What are the assumptions that Yerkes makes about the purposes of education?

2. Discuss how teachers may inadvertently commit acts of oppression in their class-rooms. Discuss how these may be avoided.
3. Explain how the concepts of sexism and racism are similar, including both their assumptions and their effects.
4. Discuss ways in which you believe that differences in cultures may be overcome within the context of the classroom.

PART THREE

Schooling and Ideology

5

Forming a National Character

In the first two sections of this book we saw how the concepts of opportunity, equality, and meritocracy have shaped major debates over the process and purposes of schooling in America. It was pointed out that what we think or believe about these concepts shapes our ideas about how children should be treated in school and whether or not the outcomes of schooling are fair and just. In this chapter we introduce the concept of ideology as a way of further explaining how social and educational policies are guided by systems of beliefs that underlie our educational and social ideals. We examine how belief systems (ideologies) come to shape the way we see schooling and how ideologies are translated into school policies. In Part Four we discuss the public face, or political aspects, of school decision making. In this section we look at the more covert origins of school practices: those that begin with our ideas about social justice, equality, and meritocracy.

Ideology, simply defined, is "the body of doctrine, myth, symbol, etc., of a social movement, institution, or class."[1] In every society ideology functions in two ways. First, ideology is the dominant belief system that explains or justifies the status quo. For example, the notion of Divine Right of Kings was an ideology that justified whatever action a monarch might take.

Second, competing ideologies that challenge the status quo can usually be found in any social system. In opposition to Divine Right of Kings, for example, there arose in Europe the ideology of self-determination and self-government. It eventually replaced the ideology that had supported monarchical governments. In turn, it helped to justify the American and French Revolutions and the development of a constitutional monarchy in Great Britain.

The crucial point with regard to an ideological system in any society is how it is established and maintained. This question was first raised by Karl Marx when he claimed that "the ideas of the ruling class are in every epoch the ruling ideas."[2] That is, the dominant ideology in a society is that belief system which justifies, or legitimates, the position of the ruling class. But why? Certainly those who do not benefit from the status quo would find it to their advantage to oppose the beliefs that keep them at the bottom. How are we all convinced that one system of belief better serves us than another? Part of the answer is found in the ideological messages received by children in schools.

THE "HIDDEN CURRICULUM"

Does the school operate to produce and reproduce a dominant American ideology? To find out, we look at what has often been called the "hidden curriculum." To see if schools are in the business of perpetuating the status quo requires looking beyond lists of curriculum objectives, test scores, and dollars spent. Alternatively, we look at what values, norms, and beliefs (ideology) are taught through the structure of the school day, the instructional materials used, the behavior of teachers, and the school organization itself. These constitute the hidden curriculum—the meanings, beliefs, and truths that students take from the daily routine of schooling.

In 1968 two studies, Philip Jackson's *Life in Classrooms* and Robert Dreeben's *On What Is Learned in School*, opened research into school culture in order to study the socialization process. Both writers were concerned with the "daily grind" of school life, but they arrived at contradictory conclusions about "the cultural significance of the humdrum elements of human existence."[3] According to Dreeben, students learned "to form transient social relationships, submerge much of their personal identity, and accept the legitimacy of categorical treatment," thus making it possible to maintain a "democratic polity."[4] For Jackson, on the other hand, these very same values helped to teach children how to behave as "members of crowds, as potential recipients of praise or reproof, and as pawns of institutional authorities" in order that they might become the unimaginative "company man."[5]

As a result of these studies, the attention of researchers was diverted from seeing the outcomes of schooling as merely a set of test scores. Instead they began to focus on the ideological disposition resulting from schooling—a disposition that helped children fit neatly into a technological, hierarchical, yet democratic society. A consensus has since emerged

> [t]hat schools are indeed agencies of socialization and so do more than simply teach subject matter and technical skills . . . what is being hotly debated among educators is not whether the hidden curriculum exists so much as the function and consequences of such a curriculum.[6]

Of course, the ideological consequences, or what are often called the socializing functions of schooling, have varied depending on social need. In what follows we explore both the ideological intent and outcomes of public schooling in America.

CREATING AMERICANS

During the American colonial period the ideological messages of schools were not, in fact, very hidden. One of the early educational statutes in the colonies, the Massachusetts "ould deluder Satan" act of 1647, was specifically designed to prevent Satan's influence upon children. The opening paragraph of the Massachusetts act justified the mandating of reading and writing schools in towns of fifty or more and grammar schools in those of one hundred or more in the following strong language:

> It being one chiefe project of that ould deluder, Satan, to keepe men from the knowledge of the Scriptures, as in former times by keeping them in an unknowne tongue, so in these latter times by perswading from the used of tongues, that so at least the true sence and meaning of the originall might be clouded by false glosses of saint-seeming-deceivers, that learning may not be buried in the grave of our fathers in the church and commonwealth. . . .[7]

The purpose of the curriculum, which focused on teaching children to read, was to aid in individual salvation and the religious well-being of the colony.

Following independence, a variety of proposals were put forth for the schooling of children in the new nation. Behind each of these was the intent to mold a new citizen, an American. We can see these sentiments in the writings of American educational reformers and political leaders such as Benjamin Rush, Thomas Jefferson, and Noah Webster. For these men schooling was not merely educating in the sense of transmitting academic skills. More importantly, education was to shape a set of attitudes, dispositions, and beliefs (an ideology) designed to support the young nation.

American educators in the late 1700s held that teaching was fundamentally a moral endeavor. If America was to fulfill its promise, it was presumed that the task would fall upon the shoulders of the common man. It was crucial that this new citizen be prepared to play his role in this important mission. The idea of citizenship was as much a moral as a civic concept.

For some, like Rush, this meant that schools would have to give students a strong dose of religious education. He argued that Protestantism and Americanism were one and the same and that the foundation for education in the new republic was religion. "Without this," he wrote in 1786, "there can be no virtue, and without virtue there can be no liberty, and liberty is the object and life of all republican governments."[8]

Jefferson's educational system, proposed in "A Bill for the More General Diffusion of Knowledge" to the Virginia Legislature in 1779, separated religion and education. Yet the proposed system of schooling was firmly based on a moral concept of citizenship. Moreover, all levels of schooling included education in "democratic principles" so that citizens would fulfill their civic duties and obligations. Jefferson proposed a three-tiered educational system that began with three years of common schooling. A selecting and sorting process based on achievement was to reduce the number of students who could proceed to higher levels of learning at public expense. From the common schools a natural aristocracy was to emerge that would be further educated to assume political leadership.

Noah Webster felt the key to Americanization was the standardization of language. His *Grammatical Institute of the English Language, Part I*, first published in 1783, was retitled *The American Spelling Book*. The purpose of the text was to teach children American speech and spelling in a non-British way. But more importantly, the text contained stories containing moral lessons. Piety, morality, and patriotism played a leading role. To make certain that no one would miss the moral teachings, the text ended with "The History of the THRIFTY AND UNTHRIFTY" and "A Moral Catechism."

Schools were explicitly moral agents in the process of nation building. It was expected that teachers would teach by example and be "grave in their manners, gentle in their tempers, exemplary in their morals, and of sound principles in religion and government." Indeed, the business of schooling was closely attached to the task of governing:

> Our schools of learning, by producing our general and uniform system of education, will render the mass of the people more homogeneous and thereby fit them more easily for uniform and peaceable government.[9]

In these late eighteenth-century examples we see how schools served a particular social and ideological role as well as met individual academic needs. The new nation needed both informed and loyal citizens. As it emerged from a war for independence, still under siege from the British in the North and the Spanish in the Southwest, the building of a secure nation-state was vital. Reflected in both the ideal agrarian democracy of Jefferson and the nationalistic language of Webster was the drive to mold the American citizen.

We also find a broader message here. Schooling in virtually any society is designed to perform a socializing function. That is, it is designed to inculcate in the young the values held in the society at large and, in so doing, to perpetuate the society itself. Thus, schools are always committed to a particular set of values and a particular way of life.

This is often not as simple as it seems. As we saw in Parts One and Two, values are frequently contested, especially when they concern equality and social justice. For example, is it appropriate to socialize students to believe in a meritocratic system when meritocracy may have the effect of keeping political and economic elites in place?

The socialization of children becomes even more problematic in a democratic society. On the one hand there is the drive to maintain the status quo, to hold the society where it is and prepare the citizens and workers to take their place in the current social order. On the other hand there is the promise of democracy in which each generation is empowered to mold society in whatever way it sees fit. For example, if minorities or women are at a disadvantage in the culture at large, should the school shape minority or female students to take their given place? Or, should schools work to develop in these students the political and social tools they will need to democratically change society? It is this tension that underlies much of the debate over the ideological function of schooling.

HORACE MANN AND THE AMERICAN CREED

By the mid-1800s the United States was relatively secure from external threat. Economic growth was rapid, as was territorial expansion. Already the hopes for the young country were being challenged, however. Waves of immigrants from poverty-ravaged European nations seemed to threaten the emerging American character. The growth of industry brought with it the crowding of many workers into cities, challenging the preeminence of Jefferson's farmer-citizen.

These twin pressures aided the first major push for mass public schooling in the United States and with it a new ideological mission for public education. As the country underwent industrial expansion in the mid- to late 1800s, reformers such as Horace Mann, Henry Barnard, and Abbott Lawrence pushed for public schooling as a way to prevent poverty, establish good work habits, and instill the American creed in a growing number of children from immigrant families. Mann, the first state superintendent of schools in Massachusetts, felt that education would be the key component in establishing equality of opportunity. In his famous and often quoted *Fifth Annual Report to the Board of Education* (1842), Mann invoked this vision:

> Education, then, beyond all other devices of human origin, is the great equalizer of the conditions of men—the balance-wheel of the social machinery. . . . It [education] does better than to disarm the poor of their hostility towards the rich; it prevents being poor.[10]

Mann saw a system of universal education as being the key to solving the problems of poverty. Workers were to become more productive, thus commanding a higher wage. Schools simultaneously increased the workers' general store of knowledge and, more importantly, inculcated proper values and behaviors. Lawrence, a leading Massachusetts industrialist, echoed Mann's sentiments when he said: "Let your common school system go hand in hand with the employment of your people; you may be quite certain that the adoption of these systems at once, will aid each other."[11]

Mann and his fellow reformers were centrally concerned with two issues. First, they were appalled by the poverty of industrial towns and wanted to find some way to equalize opportunity so that the poor could rise above their condition. Thus, while the curriculum was made up of reading, writing, and arithmetic, these studies were couched in lessons that stressed hard work, perseverance, self-denial, and promptness. Similar lessons were taught in the popular literature of the day. Later, Horatio Alger novels featured "ragged Dick" and other young men who moved from rags to riches on the basis of hard work and virtue. The meritocratic ideology was clearly stated in a textbook often used during the period:

> If he has good health and is industrious, even the poorest boy in our country has something to trade upon; and if he be well-educated and have some skill in any kind of work, and add to this moral habits and religious principles, so that his employers may trust him and place confidence in him, he may then be said to set out in life with a handsome capital, and certainly has as good a

chance of becoming independent and respectable, and perhaps rich, as any man in the country. Every man is the maker of his own fortune.[12]

Like the colonists before them, reformers in the mid-1800s faced a changing and uncertain environment. America, which had been an agrarian nation governed by the rhythm of the seasons and the motion of the sun, was undergoing a fundamental change. Steam had been harnessed and with it came the promise of an industrialized economy. But industrial production necessitated that work be governed by the clock, and that workers become accustomed to artificial, man-made time divisions. Thus, the second component of the hidden curriculum was the organization of the school with its segmented day, and its bureaucratically organized system of authority and regimented drill. All this helped to prepare the work force to leave the field for the factory.

Classrooms during this period were structured in a way that would characterize most of public education for the next one hundred years. Barbara Finkelstein examined descriptions of over 1,000 elementary school classrooms of the period 1820–1890 and found that teachers were in virtually total control of the classroom setting. Students were expected to uniformly complete assignments and behave in ways consistent with teacher expectations. Teachers told students "when they should sit, when they should stand, when they should hang their coats, and when they should turn their heads. . . ." Frequently student activities took the form of recitation in reading or writing.[13]

Near the end of the nineteenth century Joseph Rice, a pediatrician-journalist and critic of much of what he saw in education, observed 1,200 teachers in thirty-six cities over a six-month period in the year 1892. He published a series of popular magazine articles depicting teaching as grim, dreary, and mechanical. Perhaps the last term is the most important to this discussion. He described the majority of classroom work as made up of drill, memorization, and busywork done under the teacher's direction. Typical of his exchange with educators of the day was one with a New York principal whom Rice queried as to whether or not children were allowed to turn their heads. The response: "Why should they look behind them when the teacher is in front of them?"[14]

In both the school structure and curriculum we see the emergence of a new ideological role for schools. The aim was no longer the one that so concerned Jefferson, Rush, and Webster—to prepare the democratic citizen. The new ideological task was to prepare students to accept their place in an emerging industrial order, a task that was to gain increasing preeminence in the early 1900s.

EDUCATING THE WORKER-CITIZEN

The twentieth century was ushered in by technological and industrial advances that threatened the cultural fabric of the republic. Both educators and political leaders looked to the school to resolve major social issues created by the urbanization and industrialization of America. It is this debate which continues today.

The early part of the century was fraught with contradiction and conflict. With the growth of American industrial power and the parallel increase in national wealth, many perceived growing inequalities of wealth and power. Industrial capitalism was spawning a productive system previously unmatched in human history. Occurring simultaneously with the mass production of goods and the amassing of large fortunes, however, was poverty on a scale larger than previously witnessed. Workers were crammed into city slums and paid minimal wages for long hours of exhausting work. Children were often required to work as many as twelve hours a day for pennies in order to supplement meager family incomes. The Great Depression of the 1930s brought Americans face to face with the weaknesses of the capitalist system.

Clearly, something had to be done about these "crimes against humanity" suffered daily by many American workers. For some this meant challenging the capitalist system that gave rise to these conditions. Labor unions such as the Industrial Workers of the World (IWW), which called for working people to control or own a greater share of the productive processes, experienced rapid growth and widespread support. The Socialist party candidates for president, Eugene V. Debs and Norman Thomas, were the major opposition to the mainstream political parties. Socialists in various states were successful in electing state representatives, judges, and other political officials. George Counts, a leading educator, summed up the challenge to capitalism this way:

> Unless the democratic tradition is able to organize and conduct a successful attack on the economic system, its complete destruction is inevitable. . . . This clearly means that, if democracy is to survive in the United States, it must abandon its individualistic affiliations in the sphere of economics [and] insist on two things: first, that technology be released from the fetters and the domination of every type of special privilege; and second, that the resulting system of production and distribution be made to serve directly the masses of people.[15]

The hope of Counts and other "social reconstructionists" was that teachers would lead the campaign for economic democracy both in the schools, through their teaching, and in the community, through their labor unions.

The increasing contradictions between American political democracy and the economics of capitalism attracted the attention of both social and educational reformers. If the American political system was to become a democracy made up of political equals, clearly the problem of economic inequality, and the resultant political inequality, had to be addressed. The answer offered by the socialists and others was that the economic system that produced such disparity had to be brought under democratic control in order to preserve democracy.

Aware of the conflict swirling about them, educational reformers of the period went to work trying to change individuals rather than the system. The argument, simply put, was that the system worked fine for those with the requisite skills. That is, it offered an equal opportunity to all who were willing and able to take advantage of it. Certainly corruption needed to be eliminated and trusts "busted." But these abuses of the system were seen as merely aberrations, a "fly in the ointment" that could be legislated out of existence. On one hand the strategy was to tinker with the system in order to get the bugs out. On the other hand, and most important for education, the desire was to improve individuals so that they could take advantage of the equal opportunities offered them. It was this dual effort that reformers of the period believed would save both democracy and capitalism simultaneously.

Schools were thus called upon to expand their role in the socialization of children. Rather than become active agents for social change, as Counts and others proposed, teachers were asked to focus on the role of children in the future perfectability of society. Consistent with most reform of the period, the mission of the school was not to "solve inequality—or poverty . . . . in the present, but to equalize opportunity for the future."[16]

Children, says Richard deLone, were seen as "bearers of the American dream." The meritocratic ideology of equal opportunity had, by this time, displaced any broader notion of equality, which seemed unobtainable in the face of disparities in wealth and income. The public agenda was thus made one of providing for "equal educational opportunity" for children in order that they might lift themselves out of poverty and strife. For schools, fairness was defined as opportunity, and the just system of rewards was tacitly agreed to be the system that provided equal opportunity.

As they had been in the mid-nineteenth century, schools were called upon to be a central institution in the struggle to maintain democracy (or at least one version of it) in the face of privilege. The structure of schooling—curriculum, administration, and student classification—was designed to produce one clear and overriding message: that America was indeed the land of opportunity and only personal limitations stood between each individual and success. This meant using the school again as the great panacea for social ills. Educational reformers did little to attack the barriers to political and economic inequality, barriers that the poor, women, and minorities were to find nearly impossible to overcome. Instead, the scenario for educational reform saw the school as a sorting mechanism that rewarded each fairly according to his or her talents.

The Curriculum

The curriculum of the public schools was directed more and more toward preparing students for industrial work. Given the rapid expansion of industry, it seemed logical to many that poverty could be eliminated on an individual basis through work in the expanding productive sectors of the nation's economy. Schools in the early 1900s came under increasing attack for a curriculum that was not "practical." They were accused of being preoccupied with "mere scholastic learning" while not equipping students with the tools for making a living. Summarizing and agreeing with this critique was a piece in the March, 1911, issue of *Educational Review:*

One hears many protests from the business house, the factory, the farm, and from every form of industry, that the boys and girls come from the schools with little preparation for work. We are told that the schools have given the children an "education" which does not fit them to earn a living, and which even in some cases unfits them for this desired end. . . .[17]

Generated by a perceived need for schools to prepare workers for industrial occupations, a tide of narrow utilitarianism swept over public schooling. In this view the moral and cultural effects of schooling were of secondary importance. Instead, they were seen as side effects of an education that increased efficiency and augmented income. Educators were asked to "drop their platitudes and put the schools in a position of aiding industrial progress."[18]

The business of the school curriculum was to be business, and this was the not-so-hidden curriculum in the first part of the century. The ability of an individual to succeed in society was enhanced by an education that stressed punctuality, the ability to follow orders, "practical" as opposed to intellectual studies, and an adaptation to a hierarchical, routinized, and standardized social system. Children were indoctrinated into such a system by the organization of the school itself, which came to mirror the industrial model.

Scientific Management and School Administration

Along with demands for a more "practical" curriculum were calls for a more "efficient" educational system. Schools followed the lead of industry toward scientific management and efficiency engineering. For educators committed to scientific management it made sense that if students were to learn industrial values they ought to do it in a school modeled on industrial production.

In industry, the work of Frederick W. Taylor, summed up by him in *The Principles of Scientific Management* (1911), led to a transformation of the very nature of work and management. Preoccupied by what Raymond Callahan has labeled the "cult of efficiency," Taylor was devoted to making industrial production as efficient as possible. He engaged in time-management studies, breaking down each job into its constituent parts and attempting to describe in detail each movement of the worker. This prescribed formula, which specified what, how, and when something was to be done, was put in the hands of managers who took over control of the production process. The essence of this transformation was to keep control over work away from the worker and put it in the hands of managers for the sake of more efficient production. The model was the epitome of specialized labor:

[Taylor] saw his theory as providing an "almost equal division of the work and the responsibility between the management and the workman." For Taylor this meant that "one type of man is needed to plan ahead and an entirely different type to execute the work." Managers were to analyze, plan and control. The worker's "equal division" was to do what he was told by management. A mechanic working under Taylor reported that Mr. Taylor told him he was "not supposed to think; there are other people paid for thinking around here."[19]

Arthur Wirth has recounted the tragic side effects of such work organization. Workers became alienated from their work, efficiency did not increase as dramatically as hoped, work became routine and dehumanizing, and the expertise of workers was lost to the workplace. But more important for us is the effect the industrial model had on schooling at the time.

The efficiency movement swept rapidly through the public schools. This meant three things for school organization. First and foremost was the drive to organize the school as a workplace along the lines of the efficiency model proposed by Taylor. Educational administrators across the country subscribed to the idea put forth by John Franklin Bobbitt, an influential professor of educational administration, that "education is a shaping process as much as the manufacture of steel rails."[20] Thus the process of teaching and learning was to be divided into its smallest parts, every act standardized, coordinated by a foreman (or principal), and constantly measured against agreed upon standards of efficiency. This led to calls for devising "test(s) or a system of measuring the work of pupils which will enable us to ascertain a value to any product or result of instruction which any other observer could verify, and to report these values with as great definiteness as is possible—that is, to be scientific in measuring the efficiency of instruction."[21]

Both instruction and the use of the school building were to meet the highest levels of efficiency. The noted "Gary Plan," named for the city of Gary, Indiana, attempted to use every classroom every minute of the school day and on weekends. By 1929, this plan, or variations of it, was used in approximately 1,068 school districts affecting over 730,000 pupils in 202 cities. Formulas were developed to measure the efficiency of a school system based on the year-to-year progress of students.

Finally, the teacher-student ratio and time spent on subject matter were also reviewed through the lens of industrial efficiency. Realizing that teachers can lecture to large classes as well as small ones, class sizes were increased. This met the goals of scientific management, including more production per worker accompanied by a decrease in costs. Similarly, the costs of "recitations" in various subject matters were computed so that administrators could compare costs among schools. Based on these cost accounting methods, widely disseminated by Bobbitt, superintendents chose the courses to be offered and identified the optimal class size. Seemingly the logic of the workplace was to control the entire process of schooling.

As Larry Cuban has pointed out, instruction continued to reflect the ethos of the workplace. Many schools did embrace the progressivism of John Dewey, whose work and influence will be discussed later in this chapter, but "the dominant pattern of instruction . . . remained teacher centered." In his extensive review of reports on teaching written from 1900 to 1940, Cuban found teaching similar in most sites:

> Elementary and secondary teachers persisted in teaching from the front of the room, deciding what was to be learned, in what manner, and under what conditions. The primary means of grouping for instruction was the entire class.

The major daily classroom activities continued with a teacher telling, explaining, and questioning students while the students listened, answered, read, and wrote.[22]

Motivated by a reasonable desire to overcome political corruption, educational reformers and reformers in other social services turned to the model of industrial capitalism, which seemed so successful. The efficiency-oriented programs mentioned above, and many others like them, were feverishly undertaken. Those who launched them, however, forgot that educating children was not the same as producing steel rails. The ideological messages from such a culture seem relatively clear. First, all social enterprises are best organized along routinized and standardized lines, and authority flows from the top with orders issued from superiors who expect to be obeyed. Second, the rewards handed out by schools (later to be turned into earning power) will be fundamentally fair and just because they are based on objective measures of student abilities. It is to this last covert message we now turn.

Student Classification

Between 1910 and 1945 the not-so-hidden curriculum was marked by the development of more sophisticated techniques to measure intelligence, sort talent, and track students. In an era that was seemingly relentless in its drive to measure and classify, it made sense that students themselves fell under the quantifier's gaze. If the curriculum was to prepare workers in an institution devoted to the "efficient" use of resources, then it was necessary to apply the laws of scientific management to the raw material of schools—children. Bobbitt saw it this way:

> [The] fourth principle of general scientific management is: Work up the raw material into that finished product for which it is best adapted. Applied to education this means: Educate the individual according to his capabilities. This requires that the materials of the curriculum be sufficiently various to meet the needs of every class of individuals in the community; and that the course of training and study be sufficiently flexible that the individual can be given just of things that he needs.[23]

Once the curriculum was diversified it required an appropriate way to measure and sort students (raw material) as well.

We have seen previously that the development of IQ tests that claimed to be measures of inherited intellectual ability provided the scientific measures needed for tracking students. The testing of intelligence and standardized achievement tests became a central feature of public education. It was thought that students classified according to the results of such tests would receive equal opportunity through differentiated educational programs. The idea was neatly put by Boston's school superintendent in 1908: "Until very recently, [schools] have offered equal opportunity for all to receive *one kind* of education, but what will make them democratic is to provide opportunity for all to receive such education as will fit them *equally well* for their particular life work."[24]

Tracking based on testing became a common feature of schooling. Students were assigned curricula leading to employment suitable for their aptitudes. Prior to entering the workplace, children could be sorted, ranked, and then instructed in ways that would suit them for a particular brand of work. Those with a "motor type of mind, with neither tastes nor ability to abstract intellection," could be guided to vocational education. On the other hand, "if one is clearly of the intellectualistic type of mind, preparing for a professional career, it may be desirable to give him a maximum of the general studies, and a smaller amount of the concrete activities."[25]

The ideal of a unified curriculum gave way to the ideal of differentiating students for predetermined places in the work force. On the one hand this desire to treat students as individuals was motivated by a genuine concern among some reformers to meet the needs of students. But when coupled with the curriculum offered, the bureaucratic nature of schooling, and the assumption that intelligence as tested was inherited and thus unchanging, the tracking plans can be seen in a more disturbing light. The supposedly scientific process assured every student an equal chance at educational opportunity, but clearly some students were more equal than others.

An Alternative View

It would be misleading to suggest that all educators accepted the scientific management model for schooling. In fact a broad-based and vital movement led by George Counts, John Dewey, Ella Flagg Young, and others worked to make schools democratic hothouses. Here students would gain a genuine sense of personal political empowerment, and teachers might work directly for social change.

Counts was a leader of the social reconstructionists. He and others believed that the fundamental threat to democracy was the concentration of economic and political power. In his best-remembered treatise, *Dare the School Build a New Social Order*, written during the Depression, he wrote forceably about the economic threat to democracy and compassionately about the toll it was taking on children: "Breakfastless children march to school past bankrupt shops laden with rich foods gathered from the ends of the earth."[26]

The social reconstructionist solution to the problem of revitalizing American democracy was that teachers become agents of social change. Directly this meant that teachers should organize to support social programs that would expand democracy and alleviate the suffering of the poor. Indirectly, it meant altering the ideological messages of the school. Schools were to inculcate in children the values of egalitarian democracy. Schools were to be "centers for the building, and not merely for the contemplation, of our civilization." They were asked to actively inculcate in children a vision of democracy that ran counter to the meritocratic ideology and put industry to the task of promoting "the welfare of the great masses of the people."[27]

Counts worked most of his life to realize his vision. He believed that teachers represented the interests of all the people, without regard to class, race, or sex. Thus, said Counts, teachers should "seek power and then strive to use that power fully and wisely and in the interests of the great masses of the people."[28] To that end he was active in the Progressive Education Association, was a founder of the journal *The Social Frontier*, and helped organize the American Federation of Teachers.

John Dewey was the best known of the educators called the progressives, and his work continues to have a major impact on educational thought. He is, perhaps, the most influential of all American educators. To Dewey, the key task for the school was to rekindle the flames of democracy. He recognized the importance of assisting students to orient themselves vocationally, but his priority remained that of preparing democratic citizens, not merely workers. For Dewey the school was a place where teachers prepared students for democratic living by equipping them with the necessary skills for self-governance.

This put Dewey and other progressives in direct opposition to much of the efficiency-minded reform of the times. For example, Dewey argued against the fragmentation of curriculum, proposing instead an integration of subject matter by topic. He argued that schooling should not be seen as a preparation for specific occupations and that schools should be places where the basis is laid for lifelong learning.[29]

Dewey's ideas influenced a great many educators and were a major source of inspiration for those who opposed the trend toward organizing schools on a factory model. Educators such as Ella Flagg Young, superintendent of schools in Chicago, worked to implement Dewey's ideas, much to the dismay of many industrialists.[30] Many progressive classrooms reflected Dewey's ideas as children learned through experience, enjoyed an integrated curriculum, and developed critical thinking and decision-making skills.

It is important to note that the progressives' rejection of the meritocratic ideology stemmed from the role they sought for public education. In their minds a just society was a democratic one. To violate democratic principles with the classification of students and the subordination of fairness to efficiency was to abandon the school's finest social role. To prepare democratic citizens was the highest calling of the school, not to be debased by narrow vocationalism.

THE COLD WAR, EQUAL RIGHTS, AND MERITOCRACY

In the late 1950s the Cold War began to overshadow issues of social justice, equality, and democracy in debates about the social role of public schools. On October 4, 1957, the Soviet Union launched the first artificial earth satellite, Sputnik. This event caused widespread concern over the ability of the United States to keep up technologically with its Cold War adversary. But Sputnik was made into a symbol much larger than a mere spacecraft. The real challenge faced was not Sputnik per se but, according to then Senator James W. Fulbright of Arkansas, a challenge involving "the very roots of our society. It involves our educational system, the source of our knowledge and cultural values."[31]

Much of the blame for our inferior space program was placed on the public schools and their inability to produce needed scientists. The popular media were filled with "Johnny" vs. "Ivan" stories. Why Ivan could read (write, add, spell, etc.) better than Johnny was America's most widely discussed question.

The educational reforms generated by this public outcry were epitomized by the National Defense Education Act (NDEA) of 1958, which provided federal aid to promote the improved teaching of mathematics, science, and foreign languages:

> The present emergency demands that additional and more adequate educational opportunities be made available. The defense of this Nation depends upon the mastery of modern techniques developed from complex scientific principles. . . . This requires programs that will give assurance that no students of ability will be denied an opportunity for higher education because of financial need; will correct as rapidly as possible the existing imbalances in our educational programs which have led to an insufficient proportion of our population educated in science, mathematics, and modern foreign languages and trained in technology.
>
> It is therefore the purpose of this Act to insure trained manpower of sufficient quality and quantity to meet the national defense needs of the United States.[32]

Thus, as national needs shifted, so did the ideological function of the schools. They were to continue to promote equal opportunity. But now it was equal opportunity to become a scientist or soldier. Trends in curriculum and instruction reflected this new role of public education. Additional resources were allocated for the teaching of science and math, new texts were developed, and a new wave of testing for scientific and mathematical aptitude was promoted. The curriculum was to get back to the basics of science, math, English, and history. In these ways, and others, the schools were expected to help meet national defense needs.

In the years following World War II an unfinished agenda of equal opportunity remained for the schools. While much attention was devoted to the Cold War between the United States and the Soviet Union, a series of historic battles was being fought on the home front. The struggle against racism that was played out on buses and at lunch counters found its way to the schoolhouse door as well.

Until the 1950s one of the major elements of the hidden curriculum was the promotion of white superiority. Although President Harry Truman desegregated the Armed Forces in 1948, blacks and sometimes other minorities were still excluded from school attendance with whites in most parts of the United States, either by law or simply in fact (*de facto*). With the advent of the civil rights movement, however, this ideological role of public schooling was challenged. The extension of the meritocratic ideology and of equal opportunity to various minority groups became the goal for many school reformers. The major impetus for change began with court-ordered desegregation of schools initiated by the *Brown* decision in 1954. It continued through a variety of legislative and judicial actions that applied not only to racial minorities but also to women, linguistic minorities, and the handicapped.

In the 1960s widespread poverty generated new questions about the social and ideological role of schooling. Dramatically illustrated in Michael Harrington's *The Other America* (1962), a work often credited with launching the War on Poverty in the 1960s, poverty seemed not to have been diminished in the least. In a country that pictured itself as the land of opportunity, 40 to 50 million of its citizens were poor and had little or no hope of improving their lot. In Harrington's words:

> . . . until these facts shame us, until they stir us to action, the other America will continue to exist, a monstrous example of needless suffering in the most advanced society in the world.[33]

To witness the way in which America responded to the plight of the poor is to witness how deeply ingrained the American meritocratic ideology is. Rather than focus reform on the nature of the economic system itself, War on Poverty programs were designed to improve individuals in order that they might better be able to compete for America's bounties. Most prominent among these programs were those grouped under Title I of the Economic Opportunity Act of 1964. Here over $412 million were set aside for a Job Corps (direct training programs), work-training programs (funds to employ young people while they worked toward a high school degree), and work-study programs (funds for the part-time employment of undergraduate, graduate, or professional students from low-income families). All of these programs were designed to increase the individual's "employability"—or merit, if you will—so that he or she would be better able to take advantage of society's opportunities.

The largest educational program of the War on Poverty was project Head Start. This program targeted children who, because of their parents' poverty, risked school failure and, consequently, failure in getting and keeping jobs. Head Start centers were set up throughout the country, primarily in large cities, where parents and their young children gathered to play and learn. The program's concern was "improving the nutrition and health of the children in the hope of increasing their readiness for school."[34] Head Start, along with other educational programs such as Upward Bound (designed to help disadvantaged high school students get a head start on college), was devoted to the idea of preparing youths for a more equal educational opportunity. In this way, argued Senator Hubert Humphrey, we would eliminate or at least greatly reduce poverty:

> The facts show that education holds the key to escape from the mire of poverty. An education is the best insurance policy against poverty our youths have. It prevents them from being one-skill workers subject to the ravages of the machine. Education gives people mobility and a variety of employable skills.[35]

In the 1970s legislation and litigation additionally focused on women, the handicapped, and language minorities with respect to equal opportunity. The histories of all of these programs, Title IX, PL 94–142, and Bilingual Education, were discussed previously in Part One, but it is important to return here to the purposes of these efforts, which are reflected in the excerpts that follow:

> (Title IX) No person in the United States shall, on the basis of sex, be excluded from participation in, be denied the benefits of, or be subjected to discrimination under any program or activity receiving Federal financial assistance. . . .[36]

> (PL 94–142) It is the purpose of this Act to assure that all handicapped children have available to them . . . a free appropriate public education which emphasizes special education and related services designed to meet their unique needs. . . .[37]

Clearly the legislative agenda was to open up equal opportunity to groups previously discriminated against, as set forth by the Equal Educational Opportunities Act of 1974:

> The Congress declares it to be the policy of the United States that all children enrolled in public schools are entitled to equal educational opportunity without regard to race, color, sex, or national origin.[38]

As public concern with artificial limits to equal access to schools increased, attention also focused on what happened *within* the school. The claim was increasingly heard that due to the bias inherent in textbooks and teacher practices many students were denied equal educational opportunity. It was argued that children were exposed to stereotypical behavior associated with gender and race and treated in a differential manner according to probable future social status and occupations. Reformers pressured schools to keep step with the culture at large and alter these now rejected stereotypes.

Gender typing and racial stereotyping were blatant in school texts. The occupational and social roles portrayed for female characters were drastically limited as compared to those held by males. Such limitations were seen by critics as "inadequate for female children," because they included "few of the activities, possible occupational goals, and characteristics which are accorded greater prestige and held higher in esteem in our society."[39] Similar claims were made about the role of minorities in texts:

> For decades black characters were presented as shuffling, lazy, shiftless, singing, subhumans. Without mind, purpose, or aspirations, blacks danced across the pages of children's books fostering prejudice and ignorance in the minds of young readers. The only saving grace was that for many years, in the vast majority of children's books, black characters simply never existed.[40]

The argument was that such stereotypes and biases operated in opposition to our stated national goals of equalizing opportunities for all. Books for children, it was argued, should be free of stereotypes, biases, and prejudiced treatment:

> Reading materials should include more female characters in leadership roles which depict them as intelligent, capable human beings with the ability to

create, generate new ideas and resolve problems. Reading materials need to expand the quality and quantity of career roles shown for females.[41]

Similar arguments were made for all minorities.

Attacking the problem of discrimination in textbooks was relatively easy because it was substantiated by research findings. More than any other single factor, texts dictate curriculum, so it seemed logical to first attack the problem at that level. And, in fact, important strides have been made in this area, though much is left to be done.

The issue of prejudicial teacher behaviors remained, however, and was not so easily overcome. As more women, minorities (racial and language), and handicapped students entered schools, the practices of teachers toward these groups came under close scrutiny. Ways in which teachers varied their instructional behaviors toward these groups came under close scrutiny and were challenged. For example, students who spoke a variation of standard American English were labeled slow or handicapped. These classifications were challenged by those who argued that there were a variety of American dialects. This led to attempts to remove cultural language biases from testing and teacher evaluations of student work. The goal of some reformers was to aid students in becoming proficient in both their own dialect and in standard American English while not depriving them—through criticism of their speech patterns, of an equal educational opportunity.

Mathematics education has been the focus of similar efforts toward equal opportunity for women. Given the structure of the American job market, a solid mathematics background provides access to some of the most lucrative employment fields. This includes access to training in engineering, physical sciences, medicine, commerce, and the like. Yet women seem not to succeed in math classes and are thus generally excluded from opportunities to compete in these fields. It is only recently that research has been devoted to this phenomenon, locating much of its source in the daily practices of teachers and guidance counselors who steer girls clear of math and related coursework.

Throughout the 1960s and 1970s great strides were taken in making schools places where students received fairer treatment. Artificial limits on students due to race, class, or sex were challenged and many practices changed. This is not to say that all the problems faced by minorities were solved and that they now have equal opportunity. In fact, some have suggested that the job is only half done and that we need to recommit ourselves to genuine equal educational opportunities for all students.[42] Because many of the *de jure* limits placed on students have been struck down by judicial ruling or mitigated by legislative action, the more pressing issue for those concerned with the social role of schooling is what goes on inside schools. This is where our understanding of the hidden curriculum helps us see the ideological function of schooling. Regardless of the legislative and judicial changes, helpful as they may be, it is the daily actions of the school that will determine what students can do when they leave school. Unfortunately, it seems that day-to-day life in school has been little changed, as a variety of studies point out.

SCHOOLING AND CITIZENSHIP

Throughout this chapter we have presented an argument that schooling both reflects and projects ideological commitments. We have seen how those commitments are reflected in curricular and pedagogic decisions. Throughout we have seen that the dominant view of American schooling is that it should prepare students to take their places in society, places dependent on each individual's merit.

Certainly, reforms in the 1960s and 1970s called some of these premises into question. They attacked, for example, the whole idea that equal opportunity could exist when many citizens were denied a fair chance at schooling (and hence other social rewards) merely by virtue of race or sex. These challenges led to the removal of artificial barriers to schooling as well as attempts to overcome unfortunate circumstances beyond an individual's control, such as being born into poverty.

Yet the argument is still forcibly made that the covert or hidden curriculum of schooling still sends ideological messages. While the school appears to be a neutral system in which each child succeeds or fails due to his or her merits, it is actually a rigged race. The very structure of the school, particularly its tracking and sorting function, is designed to assure the success of some at the expense of others. And yet the supposedly scientific objectivity of the system keeps the losers in the race from protesting their poor finish.

Some may argue that the messages that schools send to children about their worth and their place in society are justified. These arguments are tightly linked to the vocational dimensions of public schooling. If indeed schools are primarily to serve as a training ground for future employment, we should, early on, be preparing people for life in the world of work. And the work world is one of ranking and sorting, regimented routine, and taking orders. Certainly we should eliminate artificial barriers, such as race and gender, to success in climbing up the vocational ladder, the argument goes. Aside from that, schools are justified in promoting a meritocratic ideology.

But such an argument only works if we grant that schooling is primarily about preparing workers. As we saw earlier in the chapter, the initial rationale for creating public schools was *not* to prepare workers. Rather, what Jefferson and his peers envisioned was an educational system that prepared citizens for self-governance. Today many educators are returning to that original purpose of public schooling and raising questions about how the hidden curriculum of schooling helps or hinders such an agenda.

Again, most of these issues are raised in terms of the daily life of students in schools. As we saw earlier, this concern with preparing democratic citizens was what caused Philip Jackson to first examine the socialization functions of schools. Today researchers are returning to this issue, asking if the ways children are treated in schools makes it possible for them to function as citizens of a democracy.

For example, in Chapter 3 we looked at the practice of ability grouping or tracking and its effect on minority, poor, and female students. As we saw, a disproportionate number of each of these groups of students fell into lower academic tracks, receiving a more limited education. Thus, one argument against tracking is that it unfairly discriminates.

However, a second, perhaps just as powerful, argument can be made that ability grouping also violates the democratic principle of equality. That is, tracking teaches some children they are better, or worse, than others. Students internalize this belief, as indeed they are treated better (or worse) by adults and peers in the school. When they leave school and enter the public world, young people carry these beliefs with them and are unable to perceive one another as political equals. When one adds to this the research pointing out that there are no academic benefits from tracking, we can see what a potentially anti-democratic practice it is.[43]

Similar arguments could be made about a wide variety of school practices. For example, if a citizen of a democracy needs to be able to ask questions and find information on his or her own, how do we reconcile that with the fact that most children do nothing more than sit and listen during school? Or, if as citizens we have to be able to cooperate to solve our public problems, how do we reconcile that with most schoolwork being individual or competitive? Further, if citizens of a democracy have to be good decision makers, why do young people in school get so little practice at making decisions?

In effect, we are returning to the questions John Dewey and the progressives asked over half a century ago. Central to all of these issues is the role we expect our public schools to play in our society. If it is one of simple job preparation, then instilling in children an ideology of meritocracy is probably sufficient. But if it is one of preparing citizens who can live in a democratic society with all that that entails, it probably means we need to rethink much of what the hidden curriculum teaches our children. These and other related issues are taken up in the readings that follow.

NOTES

[1] *The Random House College Dictionary* (New York: Random House, 1983), p. 659.

[2] Karl Marx and Frederick Engels, *The German Ideology,* trans. and ed. R. Pascal (New York: International, 1947, orig. 1844, 1845), p. 39.

[3] Philip Jackson, "The Daily Grind," in Henry Giroux and David Purpel (eds.), *The Hidden Curriculum and Moral Education* (Berkeley, Calif.: McCutchan, 1983).

[4] R. Dreeben, *On What Is Learned in School* (Reading, Mass.: Addison-Wesley, 1968), p. 147.

[5] P. Jackson, "The Daily Grind," pp. 35, 59.

[6] Henry Giroux and David Purpel (eds.), *The Hidden Curriculum and Moral Education* (Berkeley: McCutchan, 1983), p. ix.

[7] As in David B. Tyack (ed.), *Turning Points in American Educational History* (Waltham, Mass.: Blaisdell, 1967), p. 15.

[8] Benjamin Rush, *A Plan for the Establishment of Public Schools and the Diffusion of Knowledge in Pennsylvania* (Philadelphia: Dobson, 1786), p. 23.

[9] Noah Webster, *A Collection of Essays* (Boston: I. Thomas and E. T. Andrews, 1790), p. 17.

[10] Horace Mann, *"Twelfth Annual Report to the Board of Education,"* in *Life and Works of Horace Mann,* Vol. 4 (Boston: Lee and Shephard, 1891), p. 251.

[11] Quoted in Merle Curti, *The Social Ideas of American Educators* (Patterson, N.J.: Littlefield, Adams, 1959), p. 112.

[12] Quoted in Lawrence A. Cremin, *The American Common School: An Historic Conception* (New York: Bureau of Publications, Teachers College, Columbia University, 1951), p. 41.

[13] Barbara Finkelstein, *"Governing the Young: Teacher Behavior in American Primary Schools"* (Unpublished Ed.D. Dissertation, Teachers College, Columbia University, 1970).

[14] Joseph M. Rice, *The Public School System of the United States* (New York: Arno, 1969).

[15] George S. Counts, *Dare the School Build a New Social Order?* (Carbondale, Ill.: Southern Illinois University Press, 1978, first published 1932), pp. 51–52.

[16] Richard deLone, *Small Futures: Children, Inequality, and the Limits of Liberal Reform* (New York: Harcourt Brace Jovanovich, 1979), p. 54.

[17] M. C. Wilson, *"Some Defects in Our Public School System,"* *Educational Review* (May 1911), pp. 238–239.

[18] Simon N. Pattern, *"An Economic Measure of School Efficiency,"* *Educational Review* (May 1911), pp. 476–477.

[19] Arthur Wirth, *Productive Work in Industry and Schools: Becoming Persons Again* (New York: University Press of America, 1983), p. 12.

[20] John Franklin Bobbitt quoted in Raymond E. Callahan, *Education and the Cult of Efficiency* (Chicago: University of Chicago Press, 1962), p. 68.

[21] George Drayton Strayer, *"Is Scientific Accuracy Possible in the Measurement of Efficiency of Instruction?"* *Education* 34, no. 4 (December 1913), p. 251.

[22] Larry Cuban, *How Teachers Taught* (New York: Longman, 1984), p. 137.

[23] John Franklin Bobbitt, *"The Elimination of Waste in Education,"* *The Elementary School Teacher* 12, no. 6 (February 1912), p. 269.

[24] Quoted in deLone, *Small Futures,* p. 62.

[25] Bobbitt, *"Elimination of Waste,"* p. 270.

[26] George S. Counts, *Dare the Schools Build a New Social Order?* (Carbondale, Ill.: Southern Illinois University Press, 1978; first published 1932), p. 30.

[27] Ibid., pp. 34, 40.

[28] Ibid., p. 27.

[29] John Dewey, *Democracy and Education* (New York: Macmillan, 1916).

[30] See a discussion of Flagg and other progressives in David Tyack and Elisabeth Hansot; *Managers of Virtue* (New York: Basic Books, 1982).

[31] Quoted in William Manchester, *The Glory and the Dream,* Vol. 2 (Boston: Little, Brown, 1973), p. 965.

[32] *U.S. Statutes at Large,* Vol. 72, part 1, 85th Congress, 1958, pp. 1581–1582.

[33] Michael Harrington, *The Other America* (New York: Macmillan, 1962), p. 174.

[34] Sar A. Levitan, *The Great Society's Poor Law* (Baltimore: Johns Hopkins Press, 1969), p. 141.

[35] Hubert H. Humphrey, *War on Poverty* (New York: McGraw-Hill, 1964), p. 130.

[36] *U.S. Statutes at Large,* Vol. 86, 92nd Congress, 1972, p. 373.

[37] *U.S. Statutes at Large,* Vol. 89, 94th Congress, 1975, p. 775.

[38] *U.S. Statutes at Large,* Vol. 88, 93rd Congress, 1974, p. 514.

[39] Romona Frasher and Annabelle Walker, "Sex Roles in Early Reading Textbooks," *The Reading Teacher* 25, no. 8 (May 1972), p. 747.

[40] Myra Sadker and David Sadker, *Now Upon a Time: A Contemporary View of Children's Literature* (New York: Harper and Row, 1977), p. 129.

[41] Gwyneth E. Britton, "Sex Stereotyping and Career Roles," *Journal of Reading* 17, no. 3 (November 1973), p. 147.

[42] National Coalition of Advocates for Children, *Barriers to Excellence: Our Children at Risk* (Boston: National Coalition of Advocates for Children, 1985).

[43] Jeannie Oakes, *Keeping Track* (New Haven: Yale University Press, 1985).

6

Readings on Ideology: Historical Perspectives

In this chapter we review the historical evolution of the ideological functions of schooling in America. Horace Mann, in his 1842 report to the Board of Education of Massachusetts, set the stage for schooling for equal opportunity. His ideas about social justice and equality emphasize the importance of the self-motivation of the individual. The school was to be the place where any, and apparently every, child could rise above poverty. This idea of social justice was to be the foundation on which American public schooling was built.

By the early 1900s the United States was in a period of rapid economic growth. Ideas of social justice and equality were still linked to the ideal of equality of opportunity, but the context for opportunity was now in industrial workplaces. To prepare children for their future roles in this new industrial order, they were placed in schools that mirrored the factory organization. John Franklin Bobbitt's discussion of the "Gary Plan" demonstrates how the ideological messages of schools were found not only in the subject matter taught there but in the organization of the schools themselves.

There were voices raised that suggested alternative ideological roles for schooling; among them was that of Margaret Haley, president of the Chicago Federation of Teachers. Haley led a progressive feminist movement in the Chicago schools that called for adequate schooling for all children, payment of delinquent taxes by businesses, better pay for teachers, and an education that embraced democracy over industry. In the selection presented here she attacks schools organized along the lines of a factory model. She sees them as preparing children to blindly accept the dictates of efficiency-minded industrialists.

In the last selection, George Counts attacks more directly the ideological messages of the schools. Counts was working on two fronts. First, he objected to schools teaching children that capitalism was more important than democracy. He saw these two ideals as incompatible. Second, he objected to those progressive educators who were so child-centered that they were afraid of imposing anything on children. Counts argued that capitalism was clearly in trouble (he was writing during the Great Depression) and that economic concentration threatened democratic rule. He felt that teachers ought to be the most altruistic members of society and that they should help build a new social order by teaching children to value democracy above all else.

In considering the arguments made in these selections, the reader should keep several questions in mind: How do the authors envision a just society? How are these beliefs reflected in the ideological functions they propose for the school? Whose needs is the school to serve in performing these ideological functions? And finally, how are these historical debates still with us today?

HORACE MANN

INTELLECTUAL EDUCATION AS A MEANS OF REMOVING POVERTY AND SECURING ABUNDANCE

Another cardinal object which the government of Massachusetts, and all the influential men in the State, should propose to themselves, is the physical well-being of all the people,—the sufficiency, comfort, competence, of every individual in regard to food, raiment, and shelter. And these necessaries and conveniences of life should be obtained by each individual for himself or by each family for themselves, rather than accepted from the hand of charity or extorted by poor-laws. It is not averred that this most desirable result can, in all instances, be obtained; but it is, nevertheless, the end to be aimed at. True statesmanship and true political economy, not less than true philanthropy, present this perfect theory as the goal, to be more and more closely approximated by our imperfect practice. The desire to achieve such a result cannot be regarded as an unreasonable ambition; for, though all mankind were well fed, well clothed, and well housed, they might be but half civilized.

• • •

According to the European theory, men are divided into classes,—some to toil and earn, others to seize and enjoy. According to the Massachusetts theory, all are to have an equal chance for earning, and equal security in the enjoyment of what they earn. The latter tends to equality of condition; the former, to the grossest inequalities. Tried by any Christian standard of morals, or even by any of the better sort of heathen standards, can any one hesitate, for a moment, in declaring which of the two will produce the greater amount of human welfare, and which, therefore, is the more comfortable to the divine will? The European theory is blind to what constitutes the highest glory as well as the highest duty of a State. Its advocates and admirers are forgetful of that which should be their highest ambition, and proud of that which constitutes their shame. How can any one possessed of the attributes of humanity look with satisfaction upon the splendid treasures, the golden regalia, deposited in the Tower of London or in Windsor Palace, each "an India in itself," while thousands around are dying of

From Horace Mann, *Twelfth Annual Report to the Board of Education of Massachusetts, 1849*. Boston: Dutton and Wentworth, 1849, pp. 53–60.

starvation, or have been made criminals by the combined forces of temptation and neglect? The present condition of Ireland cancels all the glories of the British crown. The brilliant conception which symbolizes the nationality of Great Britain as a superb temple, whose massive and grand proportions are upheld and adorned by the four hundred and thirty Corinthian columns of the aristocracy, is turned into a loathing and a scorn when we behold the five millions of paupers that cower and shiver at its base. The galleries and fountains of Versailles, the Louvre of Paris, her Notre Dame, and her Madeleine, though multiplied by thousands in number and in brilliancy, would be no atonement for the hundred thousand Parisian *ouvriers* without bread and without work. The galleries of painting and of sculpture at Rome, at Munich, or at Dresden, which body forth the divinest ideals ever executed or ever conceived, are but an abomination in the sight of Heaven and of all good men, while actual, living beings—beings that have hearts to palpitate, and nerves to agonize, and affections to be crushed or corrupted—are experimenting all around them upon the capacities of human nature for suffering and for sin. Where standards like these exist, and are upheld by council and by court, by fashion and by law, *Christianity is yet to be discovered;* at least, it is yet to be applied in practice to the social condition of men.

● ● ●

But, is it not true that Massachusetts, in some respects, instead of adhering more and more closely to her own theory, is becoming emulous of the baneful examples of Europe? The distance between the two extremes of society is lengthening, instead of being abridged. With every generation, fortunes increase on the one hand, and some new privation is added to poverty on the other. We are verging towards those extremes of opulence and of penury, each of which unhumanizes the human mind. A perpetual struggle for the base necessaries of life, without the ability to obtain them, makes men wolfish. Avarice, on the other hand, sees, in all the victims of misery around it, not objects for pity and succor, but only crude materials to be worked up into more money.

I suppose it to be the universal sentiment of all those who mingle any ingredient of benevolence with their notions on political economy, that vast and overshadowing private fortunes are among the greatest dangers to which the happiness of the people in a republic can be subjected. Such fortunes would create a feudalism of a new kind, but one more oppressive and unrelenting than that of the middle ages. The feudal lords in England and on the Continent never held their retainers in a more abject condition of servitude than the great majority of foreign manufacturers and capitalists hold their operatives and laborers at the present day. The means employed are different; but the similarity in results is striking. What force did then, money does now. The villein of the middle ages had no spot of earth on which he could live, unless one were granted to him by his lord. The operative or laborer of the present day has no employment, and therefore no bread, unless the capitalist will accept his services. The vassal had no shelter but such as his master provided for him. Not one in five thousand of English operatives or farm-laborers is able to build or own even a hovel; and therefore they must accept such shelter as capital offers them. The baron prescribed his own terms to his retainers: those terms were peremptory, and the serf must submit or perish. The British manufacturer or farmer prescribes the rate of wages he will give to his workpeople; he reduces these wages under whatever pretext he pleases; and they, too, have no alternative but submission or starvation. In some respects, indeed, the condition of the modern dependent is more forlorn than that of the corresponding serf class in former times. Some attributes of the patriarchal relation did not spring up between the lord and his lieges to soften the harsh relations subsisting between them. Hence came some oversight of the condition of children, some relief in sickness, some protection and support in the decrepitude of age. But only in instances comparatively few have kindly offices smoothed the rugged relation between British capital and British labor. The children of the work-people are abandoned to their fate; and notwithstanding the privations they suffer, and the dangers they threaten, no power in the realm has yet been able to secure them an education; and when the adult laborer is prostrated by sickness, or eventually worn out by toil and age, the poor-house, which has all along been his destination, becomes his destiny.

• • •

Now, surely nothing but universal education can counterwork this tendency to the domination of capital and the servility of labor. If one class possesses all the wealth and the education, while the residue of society is ignorant and poor, it matters not by what name the relation between them may be called: the latter, in fact and in truth, will be servile dependents and subjects of the former. But, if education be equally diffused, it will draw property after it by the strongest of all attractions; for such a thing never did happen, and never can happen, as that an intelligent and practical body of men should be permanently poor. Property and labor in different classes are essentially antagonistic; but property and labor in the same class are essentially fraternal. The people of Massachusetts have, in some degree, appreciated the truth, that the unexampled prosperity of the State—its comfort, its competence, its general intelligence and virtue—is attributable to the education, more or less perfect, which all its people have received: but are they sensible of a fact equally important; namely, that it is to this same education that two-thirds of the people are indebted for not being to-day the vassals of as severe a tyranny, in the form of capital, as the lower classes of Europe are bound to in the form of brute force?

Education, then, beyond all other devices of human origin, is the great equalizer of the conditions of men,—the balance-wheel of the social machinery. I do not here mean that it so elevates the moral nature as to make men disdain and abhor the oppression of their fellow-men. This idea pertains to another of its attributes. But I mean that it gives each man the independence and the means by which he can resist the selfishness of other men. It does better than to disarm the poor of their hostility towards the rich: it prevents being poor. Agrarianism is the revenge of poverty against wealth. The wanton destruction of the property of others—the burning of hay-ricks and corn-ricks, the demolition of machinery because it supersedes hand-labor, the sprinkling of vitriol on rich dresses—is only agrarianism run mad. Education prevents both the revenge and the madness. On the other hand, a fellow-feeling for one's class or caste is the common instinct of hearts not wholly sunk in selfish regards for person or for family. The spread of education, by enlarging the cultivated class or caste, will open a wider area over which the social feelings will expand; and, if this education should be universal and complete, it would do more than all things else to obliterate factitious distinctions in society.

The main idea set forth in the creeds of some political reformers, or revolutionizers, is, that some people are poor *because* others are rich. This idea supposes a fixed amount of property in the community, which by fraud or force, or arbitrary law, is unequally divided among men; and the problem presented for solution is, how to transfer a portion of this property from those who are supposed to have too much to those who feel and know that they have too little. At this point, both their theory and their expectation of reform stop. But the beneficent power of education would not be exhausted, even though it should peaceably abolish all the miseries that spring from the co-existence, side by side, of enormous wealth and squalid want. It has a higher function. Beyond the power of diffusing old wealth, it has the prerogative of creating new. It is a thousand times more lucrative than fraud, and adds a thousand-fold more to a nation's resources than the most successful conquests. Knaves and robbers can obtain only what was before possessed by others. But education creates or develops new treasures,—treasures not before possessed or dreamed of by any one.

JOHN FRANKLIN BOBBITT

THE ELIMINATION OF WASTE IN EDUCATION

Six years ago the site where Gary now stands was a region of waste and sand-dunes covered here and there with patches of stunted trees. Today there stands upon this site at the southern end of Lake Michigan the most complete system of steel mills west of Pittsburgh, and a rapidly growing city of some twenty-five thousand inhabitants.

The rapid growth of the city has brought to the school department a financial problem of peculiar difficulty. The population consists for the most part of immigrant foreign laborers, possessing but little taxable property. The city having been practically created by the United States Steel Corporation, naturally its plants are undervalued in the assessments for taxation. Still further embarrassment grew out of the fact that according to the laws of the state of Indiana, school revenues for any given year are obtained upon an assessment of property made almost two years before. In a city where the population has been doubling each year, the result was that the revenues for any given year were based upon an assessment made when the population was only about one-quarter as great. Furthermore, the method of distributing the state school revenues failed to

From John Franklin Bobbitt, "The Elimination of Waste in Education," *The Elementary School Teacher* 12, no. 6 (February 1912), pp. 259–271.

recognize the pressing needs of a rapidly growing city. Revenues were apportioned on the basis of an enumeration made the previous April; but the enumeration was increasing 50 percent between April and September, and another 50 percent before the end of the school year.

Along with these unusual difficulties in the raising of current revenues there were on the other hand unusual immediate demands. In a city of slow growth, the school plant grows slowly and the yearly increase is no great burden upon the community; but in a new city having no school plant there was the immediate necessity of creating a complete school plant in addition to the annual cost of instruction and maintenance.

There were two ways of meeting the situation. One was to build inferior buildings, omit playgrounds, school gardens, laboratories, workrooms, and assembly halls, to employ cheap teachers, to increase the size of classes, to cut down the yearly term to eight months, or to accommodate two shifts of children in the same building each day by doing half-time work. The other possible method was to create a thoroughly modern school plant, equipped with every modern necessity; then to operate it according to recently developed principles of scientific management, so as to get a maximum of service from a school plant and teaching staff of minimum size.

The majority of cities suffering from a shortage of funds choose some portion of the former alternative. Illustrations are sufficiently numerous, from New York and Chicago on the one hand down to the poorest school district on the other. But the new city was being built by engineers, superintendents, and business managers who were familiar with the principles of scientific management in the steel industry; and when the educational engineer appeared and showed how it was possible to introduce similar principles of management into the operation of the school plant, his words fell upon understanding ears; and Gary, contrary to the usual plan, adopted the latter alternative.

The first principle of scientific management is to use all the plant all the available time.

In a school of the ordinary type, accommodating eight classes, let us say, of forty pupils each, but equipped in the most modern manner possible, there would be eight ordinary classrooms, each capable of seating forty children. In addition, there would be wide corridors, an assembly room, an indoor playroom or gymnasium, bathing and swimming-pool, shops and workrooms, science room, outdoor playground, and school garden. When all of the classrooms were in operation, the rest of the facilities of the plant would be lying idle. To the extent that the other facilities of the plant were actually being used, to that extent the classrooms would be lying idle. The result of such a policy is that half of the plant is idle half the time. In other words, the usual plant, if it is fully equipped is operated during school hours at about 50 percent of efficiency. The task of the educational engineer at Gary was to formulate a plan of operating his plant during school hours at 100 percent efficiency.

For a group of eight primary classes of forty pupils each he provided a plan of work as shown in Daily Program No. 1. For the eight classes only four regular schoolrooms are required. While these classrooms are occupied by four classes,

DAILY PROGRAM NO. 1

Time	Regular Studies				Special Activities				Time
	Class-room I	Class-room II	Class-room III	Class-room IV	Basement, Garden, Attic, Auditorium, Shops, Workrooms, Laboratories		Play-ground		
8:45–10:15	1A	2A	3A	4A	1B	3B	2B	4B	8:45–9:30
					2B	4B	1B	3B	9:30–10:15
10:15–11:45	1B	2B	3B	4B	1A	3A	2A	4A	10:15–11:00
					2A	4A	1A	3A	11:00–11:45
1:00–2:30	1A	2A	3A	4A	1B	3B	2B	4B	1:00–1:45
					2B	4B	1B	3B	1:45–2:30
2:30–4:00	1B	2B	3B	4B	1A	3A	2A	4A	2:30–3:15
					2A	4A	1A	3A	3:15–4:00

the other four classes are being accommodated half upon the playground and the other half in the workrooms, assembly room, school garden, science laboratory, or science excursions. The program is divided into regular and special studies. The regular studies in the elementary school consist of arithmetic, history, geography, and the formal language studies of reading, writing, spelling, and composition. The special activities are nature study, manual activities, drawing, literature, music, and play. Half the day is given by the pupil to the regular studies, and half the day to the special activities. The regular work consists of two periods of ninety minutes each, one in the forenoon, one in the afternoon. The special studies are likewise given a period of ninety minutes in the forenoon and ninety minutes in the afternoon.

The ninety-minute periods devoted to special activities are each divided into two forty-five minute periods as shown in the program. The ninety-minute periods devoted to the regular studies are divided as the teachers see fit. Each teacher has one class that is not divided into sections and a certain portion of the regular studies to be covered in the three hours given to her. She is free to divide the time as seems best. Theoretically she is supposed to divide the time equally between recitation periods and study periods. This gives her an opportunity to train pupils in methods of study, to supervise their study, and to give individual help to those in need of it. During these study periods she is expected to do all the paper work that falls to her for the day, so that when her six hours' schoolroom service is ended, her day's work is done.

The daily program for the four upper grades of the elementary school is shown in Daily Program No. 2. Putting the two programs together one has the daily program of a regular elementary school accommodating sixteen classes. This is done, however, with eight regular classrooms used in connection with

DAILY PROGRAM NO. 2   In actual practice it is found advisable to alternate the manual arts with the music, drawing, and literature so that each may have a ninety-minute period every other day.

Time	Regular Studies				Special Activities				Time
	Class-room V	Class-room VI	Class-room VII	Class-room VIII	Science	Man-ual Arts	Music, Draw-ing, and Litera-ture	Play	
8:45–10:15	5B	6B	7B	8B	5G	7G	6G	8G	8:45–9:30
					6G	8G	5G	7G	9:30–10:15
10:15–11:45	5G	6G	7G	8G	5B	7B	6B	8B	10:15–11:00
					6B	8B	5B	7B	11:00–11:45
1:00–2:30	5B	6B	7B	8B	5G	7G	6G	8G	1:00–1:45
					6G	8G	5G	7G	1:45–2:30
2:30–4:00	5G	6G	7G	8G	5B	7B	6B	8B	2:30–3:15
					6B	8B	5B	7B	3:15–4:00

special rooms and outdoor playgrounds. All the plant is used all the available time. None of it is idle any portion of the school day.

Although operating his plant six hours per day at the very high percentage of efficiency shown, still the educational engineer is not yet satisfied with the percentage of efficiency attained. The six-hour day is not enough. The plant might well be operated continuously from eight o'clock in the morning until six o'clock in the evening. The time once needed for chores at home is no longer used for that purpose in the majority of cases. It becomes "street and alley time," to borrow Superintendent Wirt's expressive phrase and tends toward the undoing of the work that is actually done under school conditions. A start has been made in an informal way toward remedying this lack. The playground teachers have charge of all of the playground facilities for an hour before school, during the noon hour, and for an hour or two after school. Since there is a larger number of playground teachers than usual, it is possible to divide this voluntary work among themselves so as not to require the attendance of any one of them for more than one of these extra periods per day. The plan is to be extended to the early and late use of laboratories and shops as well.

That an expensive plant should lie idle during all of Saturday and Sunday while "street and alley time" is undoing the good work of the schools is a further thorn in the flesh of the clear-sighted educational engineer. That the plant should lie idle is one loss. That work already done should be undone is a further loss. Scientific management demands that the school buildings be in use on Saturdays and Sundays. Gary has made a start in this direction by opening her buildings and placing the entire school plant at the disposal of the city's children for seven hours each Saturday. Attendance is voluntary; yet it amounts to about one-half of the total enrollment. One-half the teachers report for duty on Saturdays and are paid extra for all such voluntary services at the rate of one dollar per hour for those studies that are confining, and seventy-five cents per hour for the active and less exacting portions of the work. The Saturday sessions are proving popular with both teachers and pupils.

There is a further loss of efficiency in the use of the plant by closing the building during the two months of summer. This alone is a loss of some 16 per cent, no small item in the calculations of the efficiency engineer. Several years before, Superintendent Wirt had established the all-year school divided into four quarters, at Bluffton, Indiana. Pupils were required to attend three of the quarters or nine months of the year. They could take as their vacation the quarter that seemed most desirable.

Naturally this feature of scientific management seemed to be a desirable means of economy at Gary; but unfortunately the antiquated legal machinery of the state forbade. All that is permitted them yet is the ten months of regular school, and the two months of voluntary vacation school. Gary will have the all-year school, however, as soon as the state officials see fit to make it legally possible.

A second principle of scientific management is to reduce the number of workers to a minimum by keeping each at the maximum of his working efficiency.

In the usual school system, in a building containing sixteen classes of forty pupils each, there would be sixteen regular classroom teachers. But in addition to these sixteen regular teachers, if the special activities were carried on as fully as modern conditions are demanding, there would be needed the services of additional special teachers of drawing, music, manual activities, elementary science, and organized play; or, if not special teachers, then numerous special supervisors of these subjects to aid the regular teachers.

But Gary does away with the extra expense for extra teachers or the overhead expense of unnecessary supervision by having specialization within the group. According to their system, for every sixteen classes there are needed only sixteen teachers, eight regular and eight special. Both regular and special teachers can be experts in their particular fields, requiring no supervisors other than the regular building principals and the city school superintendent. The plan, if employed in a large city, would probably require the services of a small expert staff of special supervisors. It reduces the number of workers, however, to a minimum.

Maximum working efficiency is brought about here as everywhere by division of labor, special preparation, and the adjustment of the load to the strength and capacity of the worker. The objections to the departmental plan of organization are met by placing the pupils under a classroom teacher for all the regular traditional school work, and by keeping each class intact throughout the day.

Teachers are not expected to do school work of any kind except during the periods of the day for which they are regularly employed. They are to do paper work during study periods and they are not to take books or papers home at night. The highest working efficiency demands certain qualities of personality that are not to be had without normal association with one's fellows, nor without proper and normal leisure occupations. One cannot be a proper teacher if he does not engage in the many varied activities that are normal for every completely developed human creature. Teachers are expected to live like other people, and when their day's work is done to leave it behind them as completely as other classes of workers.

Under present conditions in order to secure even reasonable efficiency, the special activities must usually be taken care of by special teachers. It is argued that if the immature pupil is able to cover the whole range of subjects, that certainly the regular teacher ought to be able to do the same sufficiently for teaching him in his immaturity. But as a matter of fact the special activities require special points of view and special attitudes of mind of such diversity that under present conditions at least it is not possible to secure regular teachers who can assume the different mental attitudes at all adequately. To be a leader in organized play, for example, requires a special type of personality, special attitudes of mind, a special understanding of the needs of the child and of the many directions of individual and social development that have their roots in play. The work requires a special form of dress, a specially developed physique, special training that covers years. Without these things on the part of the teacher, the work will be slighted. It is certain almost to be undervalued by the regular teacher and her valuation of the matter as a school activity is certain unconsciously to be transmitted to the minds of the pupils and to the minds of the parents. The last few years have shown the indispensable nature of a large amount of organized play directed by the playground supervisor. Nobody but the specially trained playground teacher will do the work adequately in the face of the present general undervaluation on the part of the general community. It will never really get into the curriculum if left to the regular teacher.

The manual and industrial activities are in a similar position, as well as music, elementary science, school gardens, practical civic activities, and the like. Left to the regular teacher, they are academicized and devitalized simply because he cannot carry so many points of view. It may be possible for a few highly endowed individuals to see all these matters in so large a way that he can assume the various viewpoints and exchange mental and physical attitudes in passing from one to the other as frequently as required through the day; but it is not this type of individual that is teaching in the elementary grades of our public schools.

The burden must be adapted to the strength and capacity of the worker. To require so much of the elementary teacher of the usual type is to undermine physical vitality and mental integrity. It might well be different, however, if the so-called special studies were matters of the general community consciousness and if the teachers of our day have been effectively trained in all of them from their childhood up. The mental attitudes required by the special activities might then be as much matters of second nature as is the case with the regular studies. But for the immediate present it appears that teaching differentiation is the only practicable solution.

A third principle of efficient management is to eliminate waste. Ayers has given us the figures that measure the waste of retardation. Gulick and others have shown the waste that results from ill-health and lowered vitality. Social workers are pointing out the waste of undoing the pernicious effects of the vicious street and alley influences. Gary attempts to reduce retardation to a minimum by two or three methods. Teachers during the study periods give individual attention to the laggards, teaching them how to study, helping them to overcome difficulties. The voluntary Saturday classes and the summer vacation school classes receive a very large proportion of the backward pupils and aid in keeping them up to grade. Further, if a boy is weak in some particular subject, it is possible to give him double work in that subject. Let us say a 4A boy is weak in arithmetic. It is possible for a time for him to omit some of his special activities and take arithmetic with the 4B class also, thus permitting double time in arithmetic. If he is weak in all of his regular studies it is easy to drop him out of his special activities for a time and permit him to do double work in the regular studies. The special activities are of such a sort that he can return to his classes there without difficulty.

Waste due to ill-health and lowered vitality is in large measure eliminated by employing a large portion of their time in outdoor play under playground teachers specially trained for the work. Pupils of lowered physical vitality are sometimes given double work in the special subjects, the regular studies being wholly omitted until they are sufficiently built up physically. One boy, for example, who was pronounced by the physician wholly unable to attend school, was placed in the special classes for double time and after six months was wholly cured. It was a case of sending a boy to school to make him well rather than the usual situation of taking a child out of school to make him well. The system combines the virtues of the open-air school with those of the regular school.

There is an attempt to eliminate the waste of labor in counteracting the evils of street and alley influences by extending the regular school days, by introducing much healthy play during a portion of the day, and by occupying the pupil for an additional voluntary two hours each day under the regular playground teachers; and for several hours on Saturdays. There is the definite intention of making the school the recreation center for the use of the city. They attempt to gather up in a unitary way in the school system the various influences which in Chicago, for example, are to be found in part in the school system and in part in the small parks recreation centers. They would look upon the introduction of the separate municipal recreation centers such as are being introduced into so many of our cities as a disastrous backward step.

In this connection a statistical comparison, made by Superintendent Wirt, of the uses of the recreational facilities of the Emerson School at Gary with the uses of similar facilities in the recreation centers of the South Park system, which is considered the best of its kind in the world, shows the advantages of a unitary organization of educational facilities (Table 1). The table shows the Emerson School to be from four to eight times as efficient as the average of these twelve small parks and to be from two to five times as efficient as the most efficient of the small parks. This comparison is all the more striking when one remembers that the small parks of South Chicago are located in the most congested portions of the city whereas Gary has no congested district. And also that the recreation

TABLE 1   **Comparison of the Number of Uses of Various Recreational Facilities of the Twelve Small Parks of the Chicago South Parks System with the Number of Uses of the Corresponding Facilities at the Emerson School at Gary for Twelve Months**

	Chicago Recreation Parks		Emerson School
	Average	**Highest**	
Outdoor gymnasium	164,314	278,498	1,200,000
Indoor gymnasium	25,750	45,793	330,000
Swimming pools	60,400	115,542	240,000
Library reading-room	48,940	85,933	300,000

parks of the South Side vary in size from ten to sixty acres whereas the Emerson School plant includes only five acres.

As a means of caring for pupils that come from homes so vicious as to be subversive of all healthy educational influences, the Gary school system owns a farm of one hundred and sixty acres lying twelve miles outside the city. Here boys from twelve to eighteen years of age live in cottages that make up what they call "Boytown." They attend school during school hours and work about the cottages and upon the farm during out-of-school time. They are paid for their labor at a definite rate, usually fifteen cents per hour; and in turn they are expected to pay their board, at the rate of three dollars per week. The school is neither a parental school, however, nor an orphan home. The boys are neither delinquent nor dependent, and their attendance is voluntary.

The work-cards for two weeks of one of the boys will show the nature of their work outside of school hours (Table 2). During these two weeks the earnings of the boys ranged from a minimum of $9.30 to a maximum of $18.01. After deducting board for the two weeks, surplus earnings amounted to $3.30 as the lowest and $11.81 as the highest. This out-of-school work is looked upon as an integral portion of their education.

A fourth principle of general scientific management is: Work up the raw material into that finished product for which it is best adapted. Applied to education this means: Educate the individual according to his capabilities. This requires that the materials of the curriculum be sufficiently various to meet the needs of every class of individuals in the community; and that the course of training and study be sufficiently flexible that the individual can be given just the things that he needs.

The program as shown above for the elementary grades, and this, by the way, is continued through the high school, appears to go a long way toward meeting both these requirements. If an individual is of the motor type of mind, with his interests lying in the field of manual industry, with neither tastes nor ability for abstract intellection—the type that is prematurely forced out of our schools uneducated and unprepared for his share of the world's work—he can

TABLE 2   Work-Card for Two Weeks of One of the Boys in the Farm School

Date	Work Done	Time	Rate	Earned
December 18	Husking corn	2 hrs.	15c	$0.30
December 19	Shoveling clay	4 "	15	.60
December 20	Husking corn	3 "	15	.45
December 21	Mending tent	5 "	15	.75
December 22	Hauling wood	5 "	15	.75
December 23	Husking corn	3 "	15	.45
December 25	No work	0 "	15	.00
December 26	Laying linoleum	8 "	15	1.20
December 27	Laying linoleum	9 "	15	1.35
December 28	Laying linoleum	9 "	15	1.35
December 29	Teaming	6 "	15	.90
December 30	Painting	8 "	15	1.20
	Total earned			$9.30
	Board for two weeks			6.00
	Net earnings			$3.30

be given a maximum of work in the special activities and a minimum in the academic studies. Upon reaching the age when bookish studies tend to force him out of school, it is possible to give him double work along the line of manual activities and the correlated applied science, omitting the general studies entirely. This is being done at present for certain students who are taking trade courses in the high school. On the other hand, if one is clearly of the intellec-tualistic type of mind, preparing for a professional career, it may be desirable to give him a maximum of the general studies, and a smaller amount of the concrete activities. There might be periods when all his regular work should be for a time confined to studies of the academic sort, securing his physical exercise during out-of-school hours. The Gary plan is adapted to meet all such contingencies.

There is a very great degree of flexibility. A pupil can take all regular studies, and no special ones; three quarters, regular, and one quarter, special; half regular, and half special; one quarter regular and three quarters special; or all special. The schools are able to make an appeal to every type of student.

There is another aspect of this education according to need that is worthy of attention. The needs of boys are in part different from those of girls along lines of vocation, recreation, civic labors, and personal hygiene. The program of the grammar grades given above shows the separation of boys and girls beginning with the fifth grade. This is based upon no theoretical considerations as to the desirability or undesirability of coeducation. It is simply the practical and more or less unforeseen result of attempting to give to each pupil the thing that he needs.

The organization of classes for play, for gymnasium and swimming-pool, for manual activities, for applied science and mathematics as related to manual activities, brought about the placing of the boys in certain classes and of the girls in others. And further, at this age, it seems advisable that classes be kept together, and not broken up every hour as may be the case with departmental disorganization. The result is that the segregated classes formed for the special activities retain their unisexual character in the regular studies.

This in turn has its effect upon the teaching force. The boys require masculine leadership in many of their activities, and the girls, feminine leadership. These practical demands insure the employment of sufficient proportions of both men and women in the system. Cries of calamity have been arising rather numerously of late on account of the disappearance of men from the profession. But as long as school activities consist of little more than academic matters to be poured into the heads of pupils, a task that can usually be better performed and almost always more gladly performed by women teachers, these Jeremiahs are not likely to accomplish the desired results. But constructive work as at Gary, not even raising the question, is solving the problem in the way in which the country in general is likely to solve it.

Other aspects of the system are reserved for later discussion.

MARGARET A. HALEY
THE FACTORY SYSTEM

In the fight for and against the platoon school, we are witnessing a deadly conflict between two hostile American institutions struggling for supremacy—the public school and the factory. One or the other must yield; there can be no compromise. The development of the child physically, mentally, morally and spiritually is the ideal around which the public school is organized. In industry the making of material things is the supreme and only consideration; the welfare and development of character is not even a remote consideration.

Either the public schools must be reorganized to fit the children for industry as it is carried on today or else the industrial system must find some way to utilize human productive power without wrecking the ideals, aspirations, and hopes fostered in the schools, by making of human beings mere automatons. Children who are given the outlook that the public schools give today are not fitted for industry as it is organized. The public schools do not train a man to be a part of a machine.

There is a nation-wide movement to limit school opportunities in order to cut education costs. It is supported by a powerful combination which may win out before the public is aware of what is taking place. Any scheme for cheapening or lowering the cost of education of the masses meets with the approval of this combination. The platoon school is such a scheme. At the same time the platoon school, with its high degree of specialization, is the form of school organization which best lends itself to the work of fitting the masses of children for industry as now organized.

From Margaret A. Haley, "The Factory System," *The New Republic* Part 2, 40, no. 519 (November 12, 1924), pp. 18–19.

The platoon school is a plan of organization of the elementary school by which from ten percent to seventy percent more children are enrolled than there are seats for in class rooms. This is done by "dumping" the ten percent to seventy percent on the playground and into the auditorium or basement, and by keeping all the children rotating from room to room, teacher to teacher, so that the same ten percent to seventy percent may not be kept waiting longer than thirty consecutive minutes to get into class rooms. Even the six-year-old children have six or seven teachers a day, and as many as twelve or thirteen in some cities. Teachers handle as many as four hundred different pupils a day, and a thousand in a week. A mother who withdrew her children from the Detroit platoon school writes, "These long lines of little children—marching-marching-marching— looked to me like nothing so much as the lines of uncompleted Ford cars in the factory, moving always on, with a screw put in or a burr tightened as they pass— standardized, mechanical, pitiful."

Nine Chicago classroom teachers spent a week last December visiting the Detroit platoon schools and reported unanimously against the platoon system as detrimental to the children. A Chicago elementary principal, who was a member of a commission appointed by the Chicago Board of Education and who visited the platoon schools in Detroit and other cities, said in her report to the Board, "The platoon school is a mechanical system of departmentalization for the elementary schools. It is exactly the factory system applied to the education of the child." The classroom teachers sent by the Milwaukee Board of Education to visit platoon schools reported that the platoon school was unsound from the standpoint of health and hygiene because it over-stimulates the children to the point of exhaustion and offers great opportunities for the spread of contagious and infectious diseases. These teachers were in agreement with the Chicago teachers, and both groups declared the platoon school unsound educationally because it emphasizes the teaching of subject matter rather than the teaching of children, and it breaks down the personal and motherly contact between children and teachers and tends to cultivate bad mental habits.

The failure to build schools during and after the war [The Great War of 1914–1918], and the continued high cost of building, have left most boards of education with a serious housing problem to be met with wholly inadequate revenue. Here again the school as an institution finds itself in another deadly conflict with another institution, the antiquated, inequitable, unenforced and unenforceable taxing system which continues to exist in every state in the nation.

The boards of education find it easier to fall into line and adopt the platoon system than either to lead the teachers and the community, or to follow where the teachers are willing to lead, and attack the problem of securing the enforcement or revision of the taxing system. Boards of education are temporary, their terms are short; they are composed largely of citizens who have other, and to them more important, business to attend to. They are not disposed to enter into or to address themselves persistently to so difficult a problem as securing the necessary revenue to run the schools.

The lack of money gives the excuse for the organization of the schools on a mechanical basis. There are those who see that unless the growth and development of the public educational system is arrested it must and will result in a reorganization of the tax system. The same interests that do not want the tax system revised do not want the industrial system reorganized; and two powerful sets of interest are combined to push the organization of the platoon school.

It seems incredible that university professors, who recognize that the nonenforcement and inadequacy of the present tax system are responsible for the lack of school revenue, instead of advising communities to address themselves to enforcing or changing the tax system, recommend the limiting of school opportunities of children by the leaders in the communities. One of the most recent utterances of this kind from such a source is that of Professor Henry C. Morrison, Illinois Director of the staff of the Educational Finance Inquiry Commission under the auspices of the American Council on Education. In a study of public school costs in Illinois, published in 1924, Professor Morrison states the question very clearly when he says, "It is impossible to escape the conclusion that the development of a system of taxation more in accord with the economic organization of society is a condition precedent to the improvement of financial support of popular education in Illinois. If legislators prefer to wrangle over who should pay the tax and how much, they can doubtless do so, but they must choose between that and the maintenance of an enduring school system, as well as other public good." After stating that problem, Mr. Morrison runs away from it exactly as the boards of education do and proceeds to attack the school opportunities of children. He says, "The issue is perfectly clear. There is no way to reduce costs so as to make the trend parallel the population trend except by topping off the school enterprise above and beyond the elementary schools, wholly or in part."

The junior high school is the money saving device for lopping off three years at the top of the public school system, i.e., three years from the high school; the platoon system is the scheme for cutting costs at the bottom of the system— the elementary school. Both are acceptable to school administrators because they help solve their housing and budget problem. It is only the teacher who sees, knows, and understands the harm to the child involved in the platoon system with its inevitable lack of correlation and unity in education of the child and lack of opportunities for the influence of the personality of the teacher, the prime essential of character building.

To a nation that is fed on machines, eats, drinks and sleeps by their assistance, the evils of this mechanicalized system of education, the platoon schools, are too subtle to be seen and understood. There is a lack of any general understanding of educational principles. There is no intelligent, critical faculty developed so that they can detect essential weakness in a school. People take for granted that when children assemble in a schoolhouse, they have a school.

Honest, but superficial, observers judging external appearances give glowing reports on the mass formations and the machine-like movements of the children in platoon schools. They fail to recognize what the educator sees—the factory system carried into the public school, which needs only the closing-time whistle to make complete its identification with the great industrial plants.

GEORGE S. COUNTS

DARE THE SCHOOL BUILD A NEW SOCIAL ORDER?

If we may now assume that the child will be imposed upon in some fashion by the various elements in his environment, the real question is not whether imposition will take place, but rather from what source it will come. If we were to answer this question in terms of the past, there could, I think, be but one answer: on all genuinely crucial matters the school follows the wishes of the groups or classes that actually rule society; on minor matters the school is sometimes allowed a certain measure of freedom. But the future may be unlike the past. Or perhaps I should say that teachers, if they could increase sufficiently their stock of courage, intelligence, and vision, might become a social force of some magnitude. About this eventuality I am not over sanguine, but a society lacking leadership as ours does, might even accept the guidance of teachers. Through powerful organizations they might at least reach the public conscience and come to exercise a larger measure of control over the schools than hitherto. They would then have to assume some responsibility for the more fundamental forms of imposition which, according to my argument, cannot be avoided.

That the teachers should deliberately reach for power and then make the most of their conquest is my firm conviction. To the extent that they are permitted to fashion the curriculum and the procedures of the school they will definitely and positively influence the social attitudes, ideals, and behavior of the coming generation. In doing this they should resort to no subterfuge or false modesty. They should say neither that they are merely teaching the truth nor that they are unwilling to wield power in their own right. The first position is false and the second is a confession of incompetence. It is my observation that the men and women who have affected the course of human events are those who have not heistated to use the power that has come to them. Representing as they do, not the interests of the moment or of any special class, but rather the common and abiding interests of the people, teachers are under heavy social obligation to protect and further those interests. In this they occupy a relatively unique position in society. Also since the profession should embrace scientists and scholars of the highest rank, as well as teachers working at all levels of the educational system, it has at its disposal, as no other group, the knowledge and wisdom of the ages. It is scarcely thinkable that these men and women would ever act as selfishly or bungle as badly as have the so-called "practical" men of our generation—the politicians, the financiers, the industrialists. If all of these facts are taken into account, instead of shunning power, the profession should rather seek power and then strive to use that power fully and wisely and in the interests of the great masses of the people.

This suggests, as we have already observed, that the educational problem is not wholly intellectual in nature. Our Progressive schools therefore cannot rest

From George S. Counts, *Dare the School Build a New Social Order?* (Carbondale, Ill.: Southern Illinois University Press, 1978; first published 1932), pp. 25–27, 33–34, 44–52. Reprinted by permission.

content with giving children an opportunity to study contemporary society in all of its aspects. This of course must be done, but I am convinced that they should go much farther. If the schools are to be really effective, they must become centers for the building, and not merely for the contemplation, of our civilization. This does not mean that we should endeavor to promote particular reforms through the educational system. We should, however, give to our children a vision of the possibilities which lie ahead and endeavor to enlist their loyalties and enthusiasms in the realization of the vision. Also our social institutions and practices, all of them, should be critically examined in the light of such a vision.

The important point is that fundamental changes in the economic system are imperative. Whatever services historic capitalism may have rendered in the past, and they have been many, its days are numbered. With its deification of the principle of selfishness, its exaltation of the profit motive, its reliance upon the forces of competition, and its placing of property above human rights, it will either have to be displaced altogether or changed so radically in form and spirit that its identity will be completely lost. In view of the fact that the urge for private gain tends to debase everything that it touches, whether business, recreation, religion, art, or friendship, the indictment against capitalism has commonly been made on moral grounds. But today the indictment can be drawn in other terms.

Capitalism is proving itself weak at the very point where its champions have thought it impregnable. It is failing to meet the pragmatic test; it no longer works; it is unable even to organize and maintain production. In its present form capitalism is not only cruel and inhuman; it is also wasteful and inefficient. It has exploited our natural resources without the slightest regard for the future needs of our society; it has forced technology to serve the interests of the few rather than the many; it has chained the engineer to the vagaries and inequities of the price system; it has plunged the great nations of the earth into a succession of wars ever more devastating and catastrophic in character; and only recently it has brought on a world crisis of such dimensions that the entire economic order is paralyzed and millions of men in all the great industrial countries are deprived of the means of livelihood. The growth of science and technology has carried us into a new age where ignorance must be replaced by knowledge, competition by cooperation, trust in providence by careful planning, and private capitalism by some form of socialized economy.

Already the individualism of the pioneer and the farmer, produced by free land, great distances, economic independence, and a largely self-sustaining family economy, is without solid foundation in either agriculture or industry. Free land has long since disappeared. Great distances have been shortened immeasurably by invention. Economic independence survives only in the traditions of our people. Self-sustaining family economy has been swallowed up in a vast society which even refuses to halt before the boundaries of nations. Already we live in an economy which in its functions is fundamentally cooperative. There remains the task of reconstructing our economic institutions and of reformulating our social ideals so that they may be in harmony with the underlying facts of life. The man who would live unto himself alone must retire from the modern world. The day of individualism in the production and distribution of goods is gone. The fact cannot be overemphasized that choice is no longer between individualism and collectivism. It is rather between two forms of collectivism: the one essentially democratic, the other feudal in spirit; the one devoted to the interests of the people, the other to the interests of a privileged class.

The objection is of course raised at once that a planned, coordinated, and socialized economy, managed in the interests of the people, would involve severe restrictions on personal freedom. Undoubtedly in such an economy the individual would not be permitted to do many things that he has customarily done in the past. He would not be permitted to carve a fortune out of the natural resources of the nation, to organize a business purely for the purpose of making money, to build a new factory or railroad whenever and wherever he pleased, to throw the economic system out of gear for the protection of his own private interests, to amass or to attempt to amass great riches by the corruption of the political life, the control of the organs of opinion, the manipulation of the financial machinery, the purchase of brains and knowledge, or the exploitation of ignorance, frailty, and misfortune. In exchange for such privileges as these, which only the few could ever enjoy, we would secure the complete and uninterrupted functioning of the productive system and thus lay the foundations for a measure of freedom for the many that mankind has never known in the past. Freedom without a secure economic foundation is only a word: in our society it may be freedom to beg, steal, or starve. The right to vote, if it cannot be made to insure the right to work, is but an empty bauble. Indeed it may be less than a bauble: it may serve to drug and dull the senses of the masses. Today only the members of the plutocracy are really free, and even in their case freedom is rather precarious. If all of us could be assured of material security and abundance, we would be released from economic worries and our energies liberated to grapple with the central problems of cultural advance.

Under existing conditions, however, no champion of the democratic way of life can view the future with equanimity. If democracy is to be achieved in the industrial age, powerful classes must be persuaded to surrender their privileges, and institutions deeply rooted in popular prejudice will have to be radically modified or abolished. And according to the historical record, this process has commonly been attended by bitter struggle and even bloodshed. Ruling classes never surrender their privileges voluntarily. Rather do they cling to what they have been accustomed to regard as their rights, even though the heavens fall. Men customarily defend their property, however it may have been acquired, as tenaciously as the proverbial mother defends her young. There is little evidence from the pages of American history to support us in the hope that we may adjust our difficulties through the method of sweetness and light. Since the settlement of the first colonists along the Atlantic seaboard we have practiced and become inured to violence. This is peculiarly true wherever and whenever property rights, actual or potential, have been involved. Consider the pitiless extermination of the Indian tribes and the internecine strife over the issue of human slavery. Consider the long reign of violence in industry, from the days of the Molly Maguires in the [eighteen-]seventies down to the strikes in the mining regions of Kentucky today. Also let those, whose memories reach back a dozen years, recall the ruthlessness with which the privileged classes put down every expression of economic or political dissent during the period immediately following the World War. When property is threatened, constitutional guarantees are but scraps of paper and even the courts and the churches, with occasional exceptions, rush to the support of privilege and vested interest.

This is a dark picture. If we look at the future through the eyes of the past, we find little reason for optimism. If there is to be no break in our tradition of violence, if a bold and realistic program of education is not forthcoming, we can only anticipate a struggle of increasing bitterness terminating in revolution and disaster. And yet, as regards the question of property, the present situation has no historical parallel. In earlier paragraphs I have pointed to the possibility of completely disposing of the economic problem. For the first time in history we are able to produce all the goods and services that our people can consume. The justification, or at least the rational basis, of the age-long struggle for property has been removed. This situation gives to teachers an opportunity and a responsibility unique in the annals of education.

In an economy of scarcity, where the population always tends to outstrip the food supply, any attempt to change radically the rules of the game must inevitably lead to trial by the sword. But in an economy of plenty, which the growth of technology has made entirely possible, the conditions are fundamentally altered. It is natural and understandable for men to fight when there is scarcity, whether it be over air, water, food, or women. For them to fight over the material goods of life in America today is sheer insanity. Through the courageous and intelligent reconstruction of their economic institutions they could all obtain, not only physical security, but also the luxuries of life and as much leisure as men could ever learn to enjoy. For those who take delight in combat, ample provision for strife could of course be made; but the more cruel aspects of the human struggle would be considerably softened. As the possibilities in our society begin to dawn upon us, we are all, I think, growing increasingly weary of the brutalities, the stupidities, the hypocrisies, and the gross inanities of contemporary life. We have a haunting feeling that we were born for better things and that the nation itself is falling far short of its powers. The fact that other groups refuse to deal boldly and realistically with the present situation does not justify the teachers of the country in their customary policy of hesitation and equivocation. The times are literally crying for a new vision of American destiny. The teaching profession, or at least its progressive elements, should eagerly grasp the opportunity which the fates have placed in their hands.

Such a vision of what America might become in the industrial age I would introduce into our schools as the supreme imposition, but one to which our children are entitled—a priceless legacy which it should be the first concern of our profession to fashion and bequeath. The objection will of course be raised that this is asking teachers to assume unprecedented social responsibilities. But we live in difficult and dangerous times—times when precedents lose their significance. If we are content to remain where all is safe and quiet and serene, we shall dedicate ourselves, as teachers have commonly done in the past, to a role of futility, if not of positive social reaction. Neutrality with respect to the great issues that agitate society, while perhaps theoretically possible, is practically tantamount to giving support to the forces of conservatism. As Justice Holmes has candidly said in his essay on Natural Law, "we all, whether we know it or not, are fighting to make the kind of world that we should like." If neutrality is impossible even in the dispensation of justice, whose emblem is the blindfolded goddess, how is it to be achieved in education? To ask the question is to answer it.

To refuse to face the task of creating a vision of a future America immeasurably more just and noble and beautiful than the America of today is to evade the most crucial, difficult, and important educational task. Until we have assumed this responsibility we are scarcely justified in opposing and mocking the efforts of so-called patriotic societies to introduce into the schools a tradition which, though narrow and unenlightened, nevertheless represents an honest attempt to meet a profound social and educational need. Only when we have fashioned a finer and more authentic vision than they, will we be fully justified in our opposition to their efforts. Only then will we have discharged the age-long obligation which the older generation owes to the younger and which no amount of sophistry can obscure. Only through such a legacy of spiritual values will our children be enabled to find their place in the world, be lifted out of the present morass of moral indifference, be liberated from the senseless struggle for material success, and be challenged to high endeavor and achievement. And only thus will we as a people put ourselves on the road to the expression of our peculiar genius and to the making of our special contribution to the cultural heritage of the race.

DISCUSSION QUESTIONS FOR CHAPTER 6

1. Why do you think that Bobbitt was so concerned with the issue of efficiency in education? Are there ways in which his concern with efficiency continues to affect schooling today?
2. What was the basis for Haley's and Counts's objections to the system of schooling proposed by Bobbitt et al.? Be sure to address any differences that there seemed to be in terms of ideology and democracy.
3. Who would you say has the greatest influence upon public education today—Mann and Bobbitt or Haley and Counts? In what specific ways do you see that influence present today?

7

Readings on Ideology: The Classroom and the Curriculum

In Chapter 6 we laid some of the historical foundations for debates over the ideological functions of schooling. It was not until the middle of this century, however, that serious investigation was launched into the nature of these functions. Beginning with the work of pioneers like Philip Jackson, schools were looked at as places where the context of the school day taught students as much as the content of the curriculum.

Jean Anyon looks at the nature of schoolwork to find ideological messages children receive. In the differentiation of schoolwork for students of different socioeconomic backgrounds she finds a strong ideological bias toward the preparation of children for predetermined work roles. Her conclusion, simply put, is that schools often implicitly say to children that they will work where their parents worked and should be prepared for that role. Walter Parker finds a similar ideological function in many of the current reforms offered for the schooling of poor, inner-city youth.

At first glance such schooling might appear to run contrary to the equality-of-opportunity ideology that has traditionally guided American education. However, if we accept ideas of social justice that give priority to the meeting of individual "needs," these practices do seem to make sense. Each child is tracked at the level ostensibly best suited to his or her needs and thus has an equal opportunity to succeed. Success or failure in such a system is merely a function of individual merit.

Ken Sirotnik's essay suggests that we look beyond the issue of tracking to the treatment of all students to find ideological messages. The passive instructional techniques and lackluster classrooms faced by many students (Sirotnik's sample includes over 1,000 classrooms) seem designed to teach political apathy. We are asked if this is what we really want from our schools.

As the reader considers the disturbing arguments and evidence in these sections, several questions should be kept in mind. What are the various sources of ideological messages that children might get from school? What is the content of the messages—that is, what are children being led to believe? Are there

153

consequences beyond the school of these messages—for students and society? Are there desirable ways for teachers to project alternative messages about social justice and equality and their relationship to democracy?

PHILIP W. JACKSON

THE DAILY GRIND

The crowds, the praise, and the power that combine to give a distinctive flavor to classroom life collectively form a hidden curriculum which each student (and teacher) must master if he is to make his way satisfactorily through the school. The demands created by these features of classroom life may be contrasted with the academic demands—the "official" curriculum, so to speak—to which educators traditionally have paid the most attention. As might be expected, the two curriculums are related to each other in several important ways.

As has already been suggested in the discussion of praise in the classroom, the reward system of the school is linked to success in both curriculums. Indeed, many of the rewards and punishments that sound as if they are being dispensed on the basis of academic success and failure are really more closely related to the mastery of the hidden curriculum. Consider, as an instance, the common teaching practice of giving a student credit for trying. What do teachers mean when they say a student tries to do his work? They mean, in essence, that he complies with the procedural expectations of the institution. He does his homework (though incorrectly), he raises his hand during class discussion (though he usually comes up with the wrong answer), he keeps his nose in his book during free study period (though he doesn't turn the page very often). He is, in other words, a "model" student, though not necessarily a good one.

It is difficult to imagine any of today's teachers, particularly those in elementary schools, failing a student who tries, even though his mastery of course content is slight. Indeed, even at higher levels of education rewards sometimes go to the meek as well as the mighty. It is certainly possible that many of our valedictorians and presidents of our honor societies owe their success as much to institutional conformity as to intellectual prowess. Although it offends our sensibilities to admit it, no doubt that bright-eyed little girl who stands trembling before the principal on graduation day arrived there at least in part because she typed her weekly themes neatly and handed her homework in on time.

This manner of talking about educational affairs may sound cynical and may be interpreted as a criticism of teachers or as an attempt to subvert the virtues of neatness, punctuality, and courteous conduct in general. But nothing

From Philip W. Jackson, *Life in Classrooms*. New York: Holt, Reinhart, and Winston, 1968, pp. 33–37.

of that kind is intended. The point is simply that in schools, as in prisons, good behavior pays off.

Just as conformity to institutional expectations can lead to praise, so can the lack of it lead to trouble. As a matter of fact, the relationship of the hidden curriculum to student difficulties is even more striking than is its relationship to student success. As an instance, consider the conditions leading to disciplinary action in the classroom. Why do teachers scold students? Because the student has given a wrong answer? Because, try as he might, he fails to grasp the intricacies of long division? Not usually. Rather, students are commonly scolded for coming into the room late or for making too much noise or for not listening to the teacher's directions or for pushing while in line. The teacher's wrath, in other words, is more frequently triggered by violation of institutional regulations and routines than by signs of his students' intellectual deficiencies.

Even when we consider the more serious difficulties that clearly entail academic failure, the demands of the hidden curriculum lurk in the background. When Johnny's parents are called in to school because their son is not doing too well in arithmetic, what explanation is given for their son's poor performance? Typically, blame is placed on motivational deficiencies in Johnny rather than on his intellectual shortcomings. The teacher may even go so far as to say that Johnny is *un*motivated during arithmetic period. But what does this mean? It means, in essence, that Johnny does not even try. And not trying, as we have seen, usually boils down to a failure to comply with institutional expectations, a failure to master the hidden curriculum.

Testmakers describe a person as "test-wise" when he has caught on to the tricks of test construction sufficiently well to answer questions correctly even though he does not know the material on which he is being examined. In the same way one might think of students as becoming "school-wise" or "teacher-wise" when they have discovered how to respond with a minimum amount of pain and discomfort to the demands, both official and unofficial, of classroom life. Schools, like test items, have rules and traditions of their own that can only be mastered through successive exposure. But with schools as with tests all students are not equally adroit. All are asked to respond but not everyone catches on to the rules of the game.

If it is useful to think of there being two curriculums in the classroom, a natural question to ask about the relationship between them is whether their joint mastery calls for compatible or contradictory personal qualities. That is, do the same strengths that contribute to intellectual achievement also contribute to the student's success in conformity to institutional expectations? This question likely has no definite answer, but it is thought-provoking and even a brief consideration of it leads into a thicket of educational and psychological issues.

It is probably safe to predict that general ability, or intelligence, would be an asset in meeting all of the demands of school life, whether academic or institutional. The child's ability to understand causal relationships, as an instance, would seem to be of as much service as he tries to come to grips with the rules and regulations of classroom life as when he grapples with the rudiments of plant chemistry. His verbal fluency can be put to use as easily in "snowing" the teacher as in writing a short story. Thus, to the extent that the demands of classroom life call for rational thought, the student with superior intellectual ability would seem to be at an advantage.

But more than ability is involved in adapting to complex situations. Much also depends upon attitudes, values, and life style—upon all those qualities commonly grouped under the term: *personality*. When the contribution of personality to adaptive strategy is considered, the old adage of "the more, the better," which works so well for general ability, does not suffice. Personal qualities that are beneficial in one setting may be detrimental in another. Indeed, even a single setting may make demands that call upon competing or conflicting tendencies in a person's makeup.

We have already seen that many features of classroom life call for patience, at best, and resignation, at worst. As he learns to live in school our student learns to subjugate his own desires to the will of the teacher and to subdue his own actions in the interest of the common good. He learns to be passive and to acquiesce to the network of rules, regulations, and routines in which he is embedded. He learns to tolerate petty frustrations and accept the plans and policies of higher authorities, even when their rationale is unexplained and their meaning unclear. Like the inhabitants of most other institutions, he learns how to shrug and say, "That's the way the ball bounces."

But the personal qualities that play a role in intellectual mastery are very different from those that characterize the Company Man. Curiosity, as an instance, that most fundamental of all scholarly traits, is of little value in responding to the demands of conformity. The curious person typically engages in a kind of probing, poking, and exploring that is almost antithetical to the attitude of the passive conformist. The scholar must develop the habit of challenging authority and of questioning the value of tradition. He must insist on explanations for things that are unclear. Scholarship requires discipline, to be sure, but this discipline serves the demands of scholarship rather than the wishes and desires of other people. In short, intellectual mastery calls for sublimated forms of aggression rather than for submission to constraints.

This brief discussion likely exaggerates the real differences between the demands of institutional conformity and the demands of scholarship, but it does serve to call attention to points of possible conflict. How incompatible are these two sets of demands? Can both be mastered by the same person? Apparently so. Certainly not all of our student council presidents and valedictorians can be dismissed as weak-willed teacher's pets, as academic Uriah Heeps. Many students clearly manage to maintain their intellectual aggressiveness while at the same time acquiescing to the laws that govern the social traffic of our schools. Apparently it *is* possible, under certain conditions, to breed "docile scholars," even though the expression seems to be a contradiction in terms. Indeed, certain forms of scholarship have been known to flourish in monastic settings, where the demands for institutional conformity are extreme.

Unfortunately, no one seems to know how these balances are maintained, nor even how to establish them in the first place. But even more unfortunate is the fact that few if any school people are giving the matter serious thought. As institutional settings multiply and become for more and more people the areas in which a significant portion of their life is enacted, we will need to know much more than we do at present about how to achieve a reasonable synthesis between the forces that drive a person to seek individual expression and those that drive him to comply with the wishes of others. Presumably what goes on in classrooms contributes significantly to this synthesis. The school is the first major institution, outside the family, in which almost all of us are immersed. From kindergarten onward, the student begins to learn what life is really like in The Company.

The demands of classroom life discussed in this chapter pose problems for students and teachers alike. As we have seen, there are many methods for coping with these demands and for solving the problems they create. Moreover, each major adaptive strategy is subtly transformed and given a unique expression as a result of the idiosyncratic characteristics of the student employing it. Thus, the total picture of adjustment to school becomes infinitely complex as it is manifested in the behavior of individual students.

Yet certain commonalities do exist beneath all the complexity created by the uniqueness of individuals. No matter what the demand or the personal resources of the person facing it there is at least one strategy open to all. This is the strategy of psychological withdrawal, of gradually reducing personal concern and involvement to a point where neither the demand nor one's success or failure in coping with it is sharply felt.

JEAN ANYON

SOCIAL CLASS AND THE HIDDEN CURRICULUM OF WORK

Scholars in political economy and the sociology of knowledge have recently argued that public schools in complex industrial societies like our own make available different types of educational experience and curriculum knowledge to students in different social classes. Bowles and Gintis,[1] for example, have argued that students in different social-class backgrounds are rewarded for classroom behaviors that correspond to personality traits allegedly rewarded in the different occupational strata—the working classes for docility and obedience, the managerial classes for initiative and personal assertiveness. Basil Bernstein, Pierre Bourdieu, and Michael W. Apple,[2] focusing on school knowledge, have argued that knowledge and skills leading to social power and regard (medical, legal, managerial) are made available to the advantaged social groups but are withheld from the working classes, to whom a more "practical" curriculum is offered (manual skills, clerical knowledge). While there has been considerable argumentation of these points regarding education in England, France, and North America, there has been little or no attempt to investigate

From Jean Anyon, "Social Class and the Hidden Curriculum of Work," *Journal of Education* 162, no. 1 (Winter 1980), pp. 67–92. Reprinted by permission.

these ideas empirically in elementary or secondary schools and classrooms in this country.[3]

• • •

THE SAMPLE OF SCHOOLS

With the above discussion as a theoretical backdrop, the social-class designation of each of the five schools will be identified, and the income, occupation, and other relevant available social characteristics of the students and their parents will be described. The first three schools are in a medium-sized city district in northern New Jersey, and the other two are in a nearby New Jersey suburb.

The first two schools I will call *working-class schools*. Most of the parents have blue-collar jobs. Less than a third of the fathers are skilled, while the majority are in unskilled or semiskilled jobs. During the period of the study (1978–1979), approximately 15 percent of the fathers were unemployed. The large majority (85 percent) of the families are white. The following occupations are typical: platform, storeroom, and stockroom workers; foundrymen, pipe welders, and boilermakers; semiskilled and unskilled assembly-line operatives; gas station attendants, auto mechanics, maintenance workers, and security guards. Less than 30 percent of the women work, some part-time and some full-time, on assembly lines, in storerooms and stockrooms, as waitresses, barmaids, or sales clerks. Of the fifth-grade parents, none of the wives of the skilled workers had jobs. Approximately 15 percent of the families in each school are at or below the federal "poverty" level;[4] most of the rest of the family incomes are at or below $12,000, except some of the skilled workers whose incomes are higher. The incomes of the majority of the families in these two schools (at or below $12,000) are typical of 38.6 percent of the families in the United States.[5]

The third school is called the *middle-class school,* although because of neighborhood residence patterns, the population is a mixture of several social classes. The parents' occupations can be divided into three groups: a small group of blue-collar "rich," who are skilled, well-paid workers such as printers, carpenters, plumbers, and construction workers. The second group is composed of parents in working-class and middle-class white-collar jobs: women in office jobs, technicians, supervisors in industry, and parents employed by the city (such as firemen, policemen, and several of the school's teachers). The third group is composed of occupations such as personnel directors in local firms, accountants, "middle management," and a few small capitalist (owners of shops in the area). The children of several local doctors attend this school. Most family incomes are between $13,000 and $25,000, with a few higher. This income range is typical of 38.9 percent of the families in the United States.[6]

The fourth school has a parent population that is at the upper income level of the upper middle class and is predominantly professional. This school will be called the *affluent professional school.* Typical jobs are: cardiologist, interior designer, corporate lawyer or engineer, executive in advertising or television.

There are some families who are not as affluent as the majority (the family of the superintendent of the district's schools, and the one or two families in which the fathers are skilled workers). In addition, a few of the families are more affluent than the majority and can be classified in the capitalist class (a partner in a prestigious Wall Street stock brokerage firm). Approximately 90 percent of the children in this school are white. Most family incomes are between $40,000 and $80,000. This income span represents approximately 7 percent of the families in the United States.[7]

In the fifth school the majority of the families belong to the capitalist class. This school will be called the *executive elite school* because most of the fathers are top executives (for example, presidents and vice-presidents) in major United States-based multinational corporations—for example, ATT, RCA, City Bank, American Express, U.S. Steel. A sizable group of fathers are top executives in financial firms in Wall Street. There are also a number of fathers who list their occupations as "general counsel" to a particular corporation, and these corporations are also among the large multinationals. Many of the mothers do volunteer work in the Junior League, Junior Fortnightly, or other service groups; some are intricately involved in town politics; and some are themselves in well-paid occupations. There are no minority children in the school. Almost all the family incomes are over $100,000, with some in the $500,000 range. The incomes in this school represent less than 1 percent of the families in the United States.[8]

Since each of the five schools is only one instance of elementary education in a particular social class context, I will not generalize beyond the sample. However, the examples of schoolwork which follow will suggest characteristics of education in each social setting that appear to have theoretical and social significance and to be worth investigation in a larger number of schools.

SOCIAL CLASS AND SCHOOLWORK

There are obvious similarities among United States schools and classrooms. There are school and classroom rules, teachers who ask questions and attempt to exercise control and who give work and homework. There are textbooks and tests. All of these were found in the five schools. Indeed, there were other curricular similarities as well: all schools and fifth grades used the same math book and series (*Mathematics Around Us,* Scott Foresman, 1978); all fifth grades had at least one boxed set of an individualized reading program available in the room (although the variety and amounts of teaching materials in the classrooms increased as the social class of the school population increased); and, all fifth-grade language arts curricula included aspects of grammar, punctuation, and capitalization.[9]

This section provides examples of work and work-related activities in each school that bear on the categories used to define social class. Thus, examples will be provided concerning students' relations to capital (for example, as manifest in any symbolic capital that might be acquired through schoolwork); students' relation to persons and types of authority regarding schoolwork; and students' relation to their own productive activity. The section first offers the investigator's interpretation of what schoolwork *is* for children in each setting and then presents events and interactions that illustrate that assessment.

Working-Class Schools

In the two working-class schools, work is following the steps of a procedure. The procedure is usually mechanical, involving rote behavior and very little decision making or choice. The teachers rarely explain why the work is being assigned, how it might connect to other assignments, or what the idea is that lies behind the procedure or gives it coherence and perhaps meaning or significance. Available textbooks are not always used, and the teachers often prepare their own dittos or put work examples on the board. Most of the rules regarding work are designations of what the children are to do; the rules are steps to follow. These steps are told to the children by the teachers and are often written on the board. The children are usually told to copy the steps as notes. These notes are to be studied. Work is often evaluated not according to whether it is right or wrong but according to whether the children followed the right steps.

The following examples illustrate these points. In math, when two-digit division was introduced, the teacher in one school gave a four-minute lecture on what the terms are called (which number is the divisor, dividend, quotient, and remainder). The children were told to copy these names in their notebooks. Then the teacher told them the steps to follow to do the problems, saying, "This is how you do them." The teacher listed the steps on the board, and they appeared several days later as a chart hung in the middle of the front wall: "Divide, Multiply, Subtract, Bring Down." The children often did examples of two-digit division. When the teacher went over the examples with them, he told them what the procedure was for each problem, rarely asking them to conceptualize or explain it themselves: "Three into twenty-two is seven; do your subtraction and one is left over." During the week that two-digit division was introduced (or at any other time), the investigator did not observe any discussion of the idea of grouping involved in division, any use of manipulables, or any attempt to relate two-digit division to any other mathematical process. Nor was there any attempt to relate the steps to an actual or possible thought process of the children. The observer did not hear the terms *dividend, quotient,* and so on, used again. The math teacher in the other working-class school followed similar procedures regarding two-digit division and at one point her class seemed confused. She said, "You're confusing yourselves. You're tensing up. Remember, when you do this, it's the same steps over and over again—and that's the way division always is." Several weeks later, after a test, a group of her children "still didn't get it," and she made no attempt to explain the concept of dividing things into groups or to give them manipulables for their own investigation. Rather, she went over the steps with them again and told them that they "needed more practice."

In other areas of math, work is also carrying out often unexplained fragmented procedures. For example, one of the teachers led the children through a series of steps to make a 1-inch grid on their paper *without* telling them that they were making a 1-inch grid or that it would be used to study scale. She said, "Take your ruler. Put it across the top. Make a mark at every number. Then move your ruler down to the bottom. No, put it across the bottom. Now make a mark on top of every number. Now draw a line from . . ." At this point a girl said that she had a faster way to do it and the teacher said, "No, you don't; you don't even know what I'm making yet. Do it this way, or it's wrong." After they had made the lines up and down and across, the teacher told them she wanted them to make a figure by connecting some dots and to measure that, using the scale of 1 inch equals 1 mile. Then they were to cut it out. She said, "Don't cut until I check it."

In both working-class schools, work in language arts is mechanics of punctuation (commas, periods, question marks, exclamation points), capitalization, and the four kinds of sentences. One teacher explained to me, "Simple punctuation is all they'll ever use." Regarding punctuation, either a teacher or a ditto stated the rules for where, for example, to put commas. The investigator heard no classroom discussion of the aural context of punctuation (which, of course, is what gives each mark its meaning). Nor did the investigator hear any statement or inference that placing a punctuation mark could be a decision-making process, depending, for example, on one's intended meaning. Rather, the children were told to follow the rules. Language arts did not involve creative writing. There were several writing assignments throughout the year, but in each instance the children were given a ditto, and they wrote answers to questions on the sheet. For example, they wrote their "autobiography" by answering such questions as "Where were you born?" "What is your favorite animal?" on a sheet entitled "All About Me."

In one of the working-class schools, the class had a science period several times a week. On the three occasions observed, the children were not called upon to set up experiments or to give explanations for facts or concepts. Rather, on each occasion the teacher told them in his own words what the book said. The children copied the teacher's sentences from the board. Each day that preceded the day they were to do a science experiment, the teacher told them to copy the directions from the book for the procedure they would carry out the next day and to study the list at home that night. The day after each experiment, the teacher went over what they had "found" (they did the experiments as a class, and each was actually a class demonstration led by the teacher). Then the teacher wrote what they "found" on the board, and the children copied that in their notebooks. Once or twice a year there are science projects. The project is chosen and assigned by the teacher from a box of 3-by-5-inch cards. On the card the teacher has written the question to be answered, the books to use, and how much to write. Explaining the cards to the observer, the teacher said, "It tells them exactly what to do, or they couldn't do it."

Social studies in the working-class schools is also largely mechanical, rote work that was given little explanation or connection to larger contexts. In one school, for example, although there was a book available, social studies work was to copy the teacher's notes from the board. Several times a week for a period of several months the children copied these notes. The fifth grades in the district were to study United States history. The teacher used a booklet she had purchased called "The Fabulous Fifty States." Each day she put information from the booklet in outline form on the board and the children copied it. The type of information did not vary: the name of the state, its abbreviation, state capital, nickname of the state, its main products, main business, and a "Fabulous Fact" ("Idaho grew twenty-seven billion potatoes in one year. That's enough potatoes for each man, woman, and . . ."). As the children finished copying the sentences, the teacher erased them and wrote more. Children would occasionally go to the front to pull down the wall map in order to locate the states they were copying, and the teacher did not dissuade them. But the observer never saw her refer to the map; nor did the observer ever hear her make other than perfunctory remarks concerning the information the children were copying. Occasionally the children colored in a ditto and cut it out to make a stand-up figure (representing, for example, a man roping a cow in the Southwest). These were referred to by the teacher as their social studies "projects."

Rote behavior was often called for in classroom work. When going over math and language art skills sheets, for example, as the teacher asked for the answer to each problem, he fired the questions rapidly, staccato, and the scene reminded the observer of a sergeant drilling recruits: above all, the questions demanded that you stay at attention: "The next one? What do I put here? . . . Here? Give us the next." Or "How many commas in this sentence? Where do I put them . . . The next one?

The four fifth-grade teachers observed in the working-class schools attempted to control classroom time and space by making decisions without consulting the children and without explaining the basis for their decisions. The teacher's control thus often seemed capricious. Teachers, for instance, very often ignored the bells to switch classes—deciding among themselves to keep the children after the period was officially over to continue with the work or for disciplinary reasons or so they (the teachers) could stand in the hall and talk. There were no clocks in the rooms in either school, and the children often asked, "What period is this?" "When do we go to gym?" The children had no access to materials. These were handed out by teachers and closely guarded. Things in the room "belonged" to the teacher: "Bob, bring me my garbage can." The teachers continually gave the children orders. Only three times did the investigator hear a teacher in either working-class school preface a directive with an unsarcastic "please," or "let's" or "would you." Instead, the teachers said, "Shut up," "Shut your mouth," "Open your books," "Throw your gum away—if you want to rot your teeth, do it on your own time." Teachers made every effort to control the movement of the children, and often shouted, "Why are you out of your seat??!!" If the children got permission to leave the room, they had to take a written pass with the date and time.

The control that the teachers have is less than they would like. It is a result of constant struggle with the children. The children continually resist the teachers' orders and the work itself. They do not directly challenge the teacher's authority or legitimacy, but they make indirect attempts to sabotage and resist the flow of assignments:

TEACHER: I will put some problems on the board. You are to divide.

CHILD: We got to divide?

TEACHER: Yes.

SEVERAL CHILDREN: (Groan) Not again. Mr. B., we done this yesterday.

CHILD: Do we put the date?

TEACHER: Yes. I hope we remember we work in silence. You're supposed to do it on white paper. I'll explain it later.

CHILD: Somebody broke my pencil. (Crash—a child falls out of his chair.)

CHILD: (repeats) Mr. B., somebody broke my *pencil!*

CHILD: Are we going to be here all morning?

(Teacher comes to the observer, shakes his head and grimaces, then smiles.)

The children are successful enough in their struggle against work that there are long periods where they are not asked to *do* any work but just to sit and be quiet.[10] Very often the work that the teachers assign is "easy," that is, not demanding and thus receives less resistance. Sometimes a compromise is reached where, although the teachers insist that the children continue to work, there is a constant murmur of talk. The children will be doing arithmetic examples, copying social studies notes, or doing punctuation or other dittos, and all the while there is muted but spirited conversation—about somebody's broken arm, an after-school disturbance the day before, and so on. Sometimes the teachers themselves join in the conversation because, as one teacher explained to me, "It's a relief from the routine."

Middle-Class School

In the middle-class school, work is getting the right answer. If one accumulates enough right answers, one gets a good grade. One must follow the directions in order to get the right answers, but the directions often call for some figuring, some choice, some decision making. For example, the children must often figure out by themselves what the directions ask them to do and how to get the answer: what do you do first, second, and perhaps third? Answers are usually found in books or by listening to the teacher. Answers are usually words, sentences, numbers, or facts and dates; one writes them on paper, and one should be neat. Answers must be given in the right order, and one cannot make them up.

The following activities are illustrative. Math involves some choice: one may do two-digit division the long way or the short way, and there are some math problems that can be done "in your head." When the teacher explains how to do two-digit division, there is recognition that a cognitive process is involved; she gives several ways and says, "I want to make sure you understand what you're doing—so you get it right"; and, when they go over the homework, she asks the *children* to tell how they did the problem and what answer they got.

In social studies the daily work is to read the assigned pages in the textbook and to answer the teacher's questions. The questions are almost always designed to check on whether the students have read the assignment and understood it: who did so-and-so; what happened after that; when did it happen, where, and sometimes, why did it happen? The answers are in the book and in one's understanding of the book; the teacher's hints when one doesn't know the answers are to "read it again" or to look at the picture or at the rest of the paragraph. One is to search for the answer in the "context," in what is given.

Language arts is "simple grammar, what they need for everyday life." The language arts teacher says, "They should learn to speak properly, to write business letters and thank-you letters, and to understand what nouns and verbs and simple subjects are." Here, as well, actual work is to choose the right answers, to understand what is given. The teacher often says, "Please read the next sentence and then I'll question you about it." One teacher said in some exasperation to a boy who was fooling around in class, "If you don't know the answers to the questions I ask, then you can't stay in this *class!* [pause] You *never* know the answers to the questions I ask, and it's not fair to me—and certainly not to you!"

Most lessons are based on the textbook. This does not involve a critical perspective on what is given there. For example, a critical perspective in social studies is perceived as dangerous by these teachers because it may lead to controversial topics; the parents might complain. The children, however, are often curious, especially in social studies. Their questions are tolerated and usually answered perfunctorily. But after a few minutes the teacher will say, "All right, we're not going any farther. Please open your social studies workbook." While the teachers spend a lot of time explaining and expanding on what the textbooks say, there is little attempt to analyze how or why things happen, or to give thought to how pieces of a culture, or, say, a system of numbers or elements of a language fit together or can be analyzed. What has happened in the past and what exists now may not be equitable or fair, but (shrug) that is the way things are and one does not confront such matters in school. For example, in social studies after a child is called on to read a passage about the pilgrims, the teacher summarizes the paragraph and then says, "So you can see how strict they were about everything." A child asks, "Why?" "Well, because they felt that if you weren't busy you'd get into trouble." Another child asks, "Is it true that they burned women at the stake?" The teacher says, "Yes, if a woman did anything strange, they hanged them. [sic] What would a woman do, do you think, to make them burn them? [sic] See if you can come up with better answers then my other [social studies] class." Several children offer suggestions, to which the teacher nods but does not comment. Then she says, "Okay, good," and calls on the next child to read.

Work tasks do not usually request creativity. Serious attention is rarely given in school work on *how* the children develop or express their own feelings and ideas, either linguistically or in graphic form. On the occasions when creativity or self-expression is requested, it is peripheral to the main activity or it is "enrichment" or "for fun." During a lesson on what similes are, for example, the teacher explains what they are, puts several on the board, gives some other examples herself, and then asks the children if they can "make some up." She calls on three children who give similes, two of which are actually in the book they have open before them. The teacher does not comment on this and then asks several others to choose similes from the list of phrases in the book. Several do so correctly, and she says, "Oh good! You're picking them out! See how good we are?" Their homework is to pick out the rest of the similes from the list.

Creativity is not often requested in social studies and science projects, either. Social studies projects, for example, are given with directions to "find information on your topic" and write it up. The children are not supposed to copy but to "put it in your own words." Although a number of the projects subsequently went beyond the teacher's direction to find information and had quite expressive covers and inside illustrations, the teacher's evaluative comments had to do with the amount of information, whether they had "copied," and if their work was neat.

The style of control of the three fifth-grade teachers observed in this school varied from somewhat easygoing to strict, but in contrast to the working-class schools, the teachers' decisions were usually based on external rules and regulations—for example, on criteria that were known or available to the children. Thus, the teachers always honor the bells for changing classes, and they usually evaluate children's work by what is in the textbooks and answer booklets.

There is little excitement in schoolwork for the children, and the assignments are perceived as having little to do with their interests and feelings. As one child said, what you do is "store facts up in your head like cold storage—until you need it later for a test or your job." Thus, doing well is important because there are thought to be *other* likely rewards: a good job or college.[11]

Affluent Professional School

In the affluent professional school, work is creative activity carried out independently. The students are continually asked to express and apply ideas and concepts. Work involves individual thought and expressiveness, expansion and illustration of ideas, and choice of appropriate method and material. (The class is not considered an open classroom, and the principal explained that because of the large number of discipline problems in the fifth grade this year they did not departmentalize. The teacher who agreed to take part in the study said she is "more structured" this year than she usually is.) The products of work in this class are often written stories, editorials and essays, or representations of ideas in mural, graph, or craft form. The products of work should not be like everybody else's and should show individuality. They should exhibit good design, and (this is important) they must also fit empirical reality. Moreover, one's work should attempt to interpret or "make sense" of reality. The relatively few rules to be followed regarding work are usually criteria for, or limits on, individual activity. One's product is usually evaluated for the quality of its expression and for the appropriateness of its conception to the task. In many cases, one's own satisfaction with the product is an important criterion for its evaluation. When right answers are called for, as in commercial materials like SRA (Science Research Associates) and math, it is important that the children decide on an answer as a result of thinking about the idea involved in what they're being asked to do. Teacher's hints are to "think about it some more."

The following activities are illustrative. The class takes home a sheet requesting each child's parents to fill in the number of cars they have, the number of television sets, refrigerators, games, or rooms in the house, and so on. Each child is to figure the average number of a type of possession owned by the fifth grade. Each child must compile the "data" from all the sheets. A calculator is available in the classroom to do the mechanics of finding the average. Some children decide to send sheets to the fourth-grade families for comparison. Their work should be "verified" by a classmate before it is handed in.

Each child and his or her family has made a geoboard. The teacher asks the class to get their geoboards from the side cabinet, to take a handful of rubber bands, and then to listen to what she would like them to do. She says, "I would like you to design a figure and then find the perimeter and area. When you have it, check with your neighbor. After you've done that, please transfer it to graph paper and tomorrow I'll ask you to make up a question about it for someone. When you hand it in, please let me know whose it is and who verified it. Then I have something else for you to do that's really fun. [pause] Find the average number of chocolate chips in three cookies. I'll give you three cookies, and you'll have to *eat* your way through, I'm afraid!" Then she goes around the room and gives help, suggestions, praise, and admonitions that they are getting noisy. They work sitting, or standing up at their desks, at benches in the back, or on the floor. A child hands the teacher his paper and she comments, "I'm not accepting this paper. Do a better design." To another child she says, "That's fantastic! But you'll never find the area. Why don't you draw a figure inside [the big one] and subtract to get the area?"

The school district requires the fifth grade to study ancient civilization (in particular, Egypt, Athens, and Sumer). In this classroom, the emphasis is on illustrating and re-creating the culture of the people of ancient times. The following are typical activities: The children make an 8mm film on Egypt, which one of the parents edited. A girl in the class wrote the script, and the class acted it out. They put the sound on themselves. They read stories of those days. They wrote essays and stories depicting the lives of the people and the societal and occupational divisions. They chose from a list of projects, all of which involved graphic representations of ideas: for example, "Make a mural depicting the division of labor in Egyptian society."

Each child wrote and exchanged a letter in hieroglyphics with a fifth grader in another class, and they also exchanged stories they wrote in cuneiform. They made a scroll and singed the edges so it looked authentic. They each chose an occupation and made an Egyptian plaque representing the occupation, simulating the appropriate Egyptian design. They carved their design on a cylinder of wax, pressed the wax into clay, and then baked the clay. Although one girl did not choose an occupation but carved instead a series of gods and slaves, the teacher said, "That's all right, Amber, it's beautiful." As they were working the teacher said, "Don't cut into your clay until you're satisfied with your design."

Social studies also involves almost daily presentation by the children of some event from the news. The teacher's questions ask the children to expand what they say, to give more details, and to be more specific. Occasionally she adds some remarks to help them see connections between events.

The emphasis on expressing and illustrating ideas in social studies is accompanied in language arts by an emphasis on creative writing. Each child wrote a rhebus story for a first grader whom they had interviewed to see what kind of story the child liked best. They wrote editorials on pending decisions by the school board and radio plays, some of which were read over the school intercom from the office and one of which was performed in the auditorium. There is no language arts textbook because, the teacher said, "The principal wants us to be creative." There is not much grammar, but there is punctuation. One morning when the observer arrived, the class was doing a punctuation ditto. The teacher later apologized for using the ditto. "It's just for review," she said. "I don't teach punctuation that way. We use their language." The ditto had three unambiguous rules for where to put commas in a sentence. As the teacher was going around to help the children with the ditto, she repeated several times, "Where you put commas depends on how you say the sentence; it depends on the situation and what you want to say." Several weeks later the observer saw another punctuation activity. The teacher had printed a five-paragraph story on an oak tag and then cut it into phrases. She read the whole story to the class from the book, then passed out the phrases. The group had to decide how the phrases could best be put together again. (They arranged the phrases on the floor.) The point was not to replicate the story, although that was not irrelevant, but to "decide what you think the best way is." Punctuation marks on cardboard pieces were then handed out, and the children discussed and then decided what mark was best at each place they thought one was needed. At the end of each paragraph the teacher asked, "Are you satisfied with the way the paragraphs are now? Read it to yourself and see how it sounds." Then she read the original story again, and they compared the two.

Describing her goals in science to the investigator, the teacher said, "We use ESS (Elementary Science Study). It's very good because it gives a hands-on experience—so they can make *sense* out of it. It doesn't matter whether it [what they find] is right or wrong. I bring them together and there's value in discussing their ideas."

The products of work in this class are often highly valued by the children and the teacher. In fact, this was the only school in which the investigator was not allowed to take original pieces of the children's work for her files. If the work was small enough, however, and was on paper, the investigator could duplicate it on the copying machine in the office.

The teacher's attempt to control the class involves constant negotiation. She does not give direct orders unless she is angry because the children have been too noisy. Normally, she tries to get them to foresee the consequences of their actions and to decide accordingly. For example, lining them up to go see a play written by the sixth graders, she says, "I presume you're lined up by someone with whom you want to sit. I hope you're lined up by someone you won't get in trouble with." The following two dialogues illustrate the process of negotiation between student and teacher.

TEACHER: Tom, you're behind in your SRA this marking period.

TOM: So what!

TEACHER: Well, last time you had a hard time catching up.

TOM: But I have my [music] lesson at 10:00.

TEACHER: Well, that doesn't mean you're going to sit here for twenty minutes.

TOM: Twenty minutes! OK. (He goes to pick out an SRA booklet and chooses one, puts it back, then takes another, and brings it to her.)

TEACHER: OK, this is the one you want, right!

TOM: Yes.

TEACHER: OK, I'll put tomorrow's date on it so you can take it home tonight or finish it tomorrow if you want.

TEACHER: (to a child who is wandering around during reading) Kevin, why don't you do *Reading for Concepts?*

KEVIN: No, I don't like *Reading for Concepts.*

TEACHER: Well, what are you going to do?

KEVIN: (pause) I'm going to work on my DAR. (The DAR has sponsored an essay competition on "Life in the American Colonies.")

One of the few rules governing the children's movement is that no more than three children may be out of the room at once. There is a school rule that anyone can go to the library at any time to get a book. In the fifth grade I observed, they sign their name on the chalkboard and leave. There are no passes. Finally, the children have a fair amount of officially sanctioned say over what happens in the class. For example, they often negotiate what work is to be done. If the teacher wants to move on to the next subject, but the children say they are not ready, they want to work on their present projects some more, she very often lets them do it.

Executive Elite School

In the executive elite school, work is developing one's analytical intellectual powers. Children are continually asked to reason through a problem, to produce intellectual products that are both logically sound and of top academic quality. A primary goal of thought is to conceptualize rules by which elements may fit together in systems and then to apply these rules in solving a problem. Schoolwork helps one to achieve, to excel, to prepare for life.

The following are illustrative. The math teacher teaches area and perimeter by having the children derive formulas for each. First she helps them, through discussion at the board, to arrive at A = W × L as a formula (not *the* formula) for area. After discussing several, she says, "Can anyone make up a formula for perimeter? Can you figure that out yourselves? [pause] Knowing what we know, can we think of a formula?" She works out three children's suggestions at the board, saying to two, "Yes, that's a good one," and then asks the class if they can think of any more. No one volunteers. To prod them, she says, "If you use rules and good reasoning, you get many ways. Chris, can you think up a formula?"

She discusses two-digit division with the children as a decision-making process. Presenting a new type of problem to them, she asks, "What's the *first* decision you'd make if presented with this kind of example? What is the first thing you'd *think*? Craig?" Craig says, "To find my first partial quotient." She responds, "Yes, that would be your first decision. How would you do that?" Craig explains, and then the teacher says, "OK, we'll see how that works for you." The class tries his way. Subsequently, she comments on the merits and shortcomings of several other children's decisions. Later, she tells the investigator that her goals in math are to develop their reasoning and mathematical thinking and that, unfortunately, "there's no *time* for manipulables."

While right answers are important in math, they are not "given" by the book or by the teacher but may be challenged by the children. Going over some problems in late September the teacher says, "Raise your hand if you do not agree." A child says, "I don't agree with sixty-four." The teacher responds, "OK, there's a question about sixty-four. [to class] Please check it. Owen, they're disagreeing with you. Kristen, they're checking yours." The teacher emphasized this repeatedly during September and October with statements like "Don't be afraid to say you disagree. In the last [math] class, somebody disagreed, and they were right. Before you disagree, check yours, and if you still think we're wrong, then we'll check it out." By Thanksgiving, the children did not often speak in terms of right and wrong math problems but of whether they agreed with the answer that had been given.

There are complicated math mimeos with many word problems. Whenever they go over the examples, they discuss how each child has set up the problem. The children must explain it precisely. On one occasion the teacher said, "I'm more—just as interested in *how* you set up the problem as in what answer you find. If you set up a problem in a good way, the answer is *easy* to find."

Social studies work is most often reading and discussion of concepts and independent research. There are only occasional artistic, expressive, or illustrative projects. Ancient Athens and Sumer are, rather, societies to analyze. The following questions are typical of those that guide the children's independent research. "What mistakes did Pericles make after the war?" "What mistakes did the citizens of Athens make?" "What are the elements of a civilization?" "How did Greece build an economic empire?" "Compare the way Athens chose its leaders with the way we choose ours." Occasionally the children are asked to make up sample questions for their social studies tests. On an occasion when the investigator was present, the social studies teacher rejected a child's question by saying, "That's just fact. If I asked you that question on a test, you'd complain it was just memory! Good questions ask for concepts."

In social studies—but also in reading, science, and health—the teachers initiate classroom discussions of current social issues and problems. These discussions occurred on every one of the investigator's visits, and a teacher told me, "These children's opinions are important—it's important that they learn to reason things through." The classroom discussions always struck the observer as quite realistic and analytical, dealing with concrete social issues like the following: "Why do workers strike?" "Is that right or wrong?" "Why do we have inflation, and what can be done to stop it?" "Why do companies put chemicals in food when the natural ingredients are available?" and so on. Usually the children did not have to be prodded to give their opinions. In fact, their statements and the interchanges between them struck the observer as quite sophisticated conceptually and verbally, and well-informed. Occasionally the teachers would prod with statements such as, "Even if you don't know [the answers], if you think logically about it, you can figure it out." And, "I'm asking you [these] questions to help you think this through."

Language arts emphasizes language as a complex system, one that should be mastered. The children are asked to diagram sentences of complex grammatical construction, to memorize irregular verb conjugations (he lay, he has lain, and so on . . .), and to use the proper participles, conjunctions, and interjections in their speech. The teacher (the same one who teaches social studies) told them, "It is not enough to get these right on tests; you must use what you learn [in grammar classes] in your written and oral work. I will grade you on that."

Most writing assignments are either research reports and essays for social studies or experiment analyses and write-ups for science. There is only an occasional story or other "creative writing" assignment. On the occasion observed by the investigator (the writing of a Halloween story), the points the teacher stressed in preparing the children to write involved the structural aspects of a story rather than the expression of feelings or other ideas. The teacher showed them a filmstrip, "The Seven Parts of a Story," and lectured them on plot development, mood, setting, character development, consistency, and the use of a logical or appropriate ending. The stories they subsequently wrote were, in fact, well-structured, but many were also personal and expressive. The teacher's evaluative comments, however, did not refer to the expressiveness or artistry but were all directed toward whether they had "developed" the story well.

Language arts work also involved a large amount of practice in presentation of the self and in managing situations where the child was expected to be in charge. For example, there was a series of assignments in which each child had to be a "student teacher." The child had to plan a lesson in grammar, outlining, punctuation, or other language arts topic and explain the concept to the class. Each child was to prepare a worksheet or game and a homework assignment as well. After each presentation, the teacher and other children gave a critical appraisal of the "student teacher's" performance. Their criteria were: whether the student spoke clearly, whether the lesson was interesting, whether the student made any mistakes, and whether he or she kept control of the class. On an occasion when a child did not maintain control, the teacher said, "When you're up there, you have authority and you have to use it. I'll back you up."

The teacher of math and science explained to the observer that she likes the ESS program because "the children can manipulate variables. They generate hypotheses and devise experiments to solve the problem. Then they have to explain what they found."

The executive elite school is the only school where bells do not demarcate the periods of time. The two fifth-grade teachers were very strict about changing classes on schedule, however, as specific plans for each session had been made. The teachers attempted to keep tight control over the children during lessons, and the children were sometimes flippant, boisterous, and occasionally rude. However, the children may be brought into line by reminding them that "It is up to you." "You must control yourself." "You are responsible for your work." You must "set your priorities." One teacher told a child, "You are the only driver of your car—and only you can regulate your speed." A new teacher complained to the observer that she had thought "these children" would have more control.

While strict attention to the lesson at hand is required, the teachers make relatively little attempt to regulate the movement of the children at other times. For example, except for the kindergartners the children in this school do not have to wait for the bell to ring in the morning; they may go to their classroom when they arrive at school. Fifth graders often came early to read, to finish work, or to catch up. After the first two months of school, the fifth-grade teachers did not line the children up to change classes or to go to gym, and so on, but, when the children were ready and quiet, they were told they could go—sometimes without the teachers.

In the classroom, the children could get materials when they needed them and took what they needed from closets and from the teacher's desk. They were in charge of the office at lunchtime. During class they did not have to sign out or ask permission to leave the room; they just got up and left. Because of the pressure to get work done, however, they did not leave the room very often. The teachers were very polite to the children, and the investigator heard no sarcasm, no nasty remarks, and few direct orders. The teachers never called the children "honey" or "dear" but always called them by name. The teachers were expected to be available before school, after school, and for part of their lunchtime to provide extra help if needed.

The foregoing analysis of differences in schoolwork in contrasting social class contexts suggests the following conclusion: the "hidden curriculum" of schoolwork is tacit preparation for relating to the process of production in a particular way. Differing curricular, pedagogical, and pupil evaluation practices, emphasize different cognitive and behavioral skills in each social setting and thus contribute to the development in the children of certain potential relationships to physical and symbolic capital, to authority, and to the process of work. School experience, in the sample of schools discussed here, differed qualitatively by social class. These differences may not only contribute to the development in the children in each social class of certain types of economically significant relationships and not others but would thereby help to *reproduce* this system of relations in society. In the contribution to the reproduction of unequal social relations lies a theoretical meaning and social consequence of classroom practice.

NOTES

[1] S. Bowles and H. Gintis, *Schooling in Capitalist America: Educational Reform and the Contradictions of Economic Life* (New York: Basic Books, 1976).

[2] B. Bernstein, *Class, Codes and Control, Vol. 3. Towards a Theory of Educational Transmission*, 2d ed. (London: Routledge & Kegan Paul, 1977); P. Bourdieu and J. Passeron, *Reproduction in Education, Society and Culture* (Beverly Hills, Calif.: Sage, 1977); M. W. Apple, *Ideology and Curriculum* (Boston: Routledge & Kegan Paul, 1979).

[3] But see, in a related vein, M. W. Apple and N. King, "What Do Schools Teach?" *Curriculum Inquiry* 6 (1977): 341–58; R. C. Rist, *The Urban School: A Factory for Failure* (Cambridge, Mass.: MIT Press, 1973).

[4] The U.S. Bureau of the Census defines *poverty* for a nonfarm family of four as a yearly income of $6,191 a year or less. U.S. Bureau of the Census, *Statistical Abstract of the United States: 1978* (Washington, D.C.: U.S. Government Printing Office, 1978), p. 465, table 754.

[5] U.S. Bureau of the Census, "Money Income in 1977 of Families and Persons in the United States," *Current Population Reports* Series P-60, no. 118 (Washington, D.C.: U.S. Government Printing Office, 1979), p. 2, table A.

[6] Ibid.

[7] This figure is an estimate. According to the Bureau of the Census, only 2.6 percent of families in the United States have money income of $50,000 or over. U.S. Bureau of the Census, *Current Population Report* Series P-60. For figures on income at these higher levels, see Smith and Franklin, "The Concentration of Personal Wealth, 1922–1969."

[8] Smith and Franklin, "Concentration of Personal Wealth."

[9] For other similarities alleged to characterize United States classrooms and schools but which will not be discussed here, see R. Dreeben, *On What Is Learned in School* (Reading, Mass.: Addison-Wesley, 1968); P. Jackson, *Life in Classrooms* (New York: Holt, Rinehart & Winston, 1968); and S. Sarasan, *The Culture of School and the Problem of Change* (Boston: Allyn & Bacon, 1971).

[10] Indeed, strikingly little teaching occurred in either of the working-class schools, and this naturally curtailed the amount that the children learned. Incidentally, it increased the amount of time that had to be spent by the researcher to collect data on teaching style and interaction.

[11] A dominant feeling, expressed directly and indirectly by teachers in this school, was boredom with their work. They did, however, in contrast to the working-class schools, almost always carry out lessons during class times.

WALTER C. PARKER

THE URBAN CURRICULUM AND THE ALLOCATING FUNCTION OF SCHOOLS

One hears more frequently now the suggestion that inner-city schools serving predominantly poor and minority children ought to have a curriculum different from that of other schools. The suggestion is at least in part a response to renewed cries from other quarters for a common curriculum for all.[1] The rationale often advanced for a special curriculum for inner-city youth is that these students are so unique in their goals, life styles, and orientations toward school, especially when compared to their economically advantaged counterparts attending suburban schools, that what they learn in school ought to be unique, too. The suggestion stems from what I believe is a perfectly appropriate belief that schools should recognize and respond to individual and group differences among students rather than present a single, monolithic curriculum that is oblivious to the diversity among students. It is important, however, that educators strive for both the goal of individualization in education and another goal of equal importance, namely, equal access to knowledge. Pursuing individualism at the expense of equal access to knowledge can result in diversified curricula that, whether intentionally or fortuitously, maintain existing social, political, and economic arrangements.

A central dilemma in an industrial democracy is the disjuncture between the sanctioned ideology of equal opportunity for vertical mobility, well represented by the log-cabin-to-White-House mythology, and the limited number of actual opportunities in the upper reaches of organizational hierarchies.

> Democracy asks individuals to act as if social mobility were universally possible; status is to be won by individual effort, and rewards are to accrue to those who try. But democratic societies also need selective training institutions, and hierarchical work organizations permit increasingly fewer persons to succeed at ascending levels. Situations of opportunity are also situations of denial and failure.[2]

While the prevailing belief in equal opportunity encourages individual aspirations to make it to the top, or at least to move up on the socioeconomic ladder, numerical realities in occupational hierarchies render upward mobility an impossibility for everyone. Consequently, an industrial democracy has the dual challenge of motivating achievement through effort while simultaneously maintaining the hierarchic order by denying access to many. The American dream is promoted *as though* it could be granted to all even though, clearly, it cannot. Sociologists point to the "dissociation between culturally instilled goals and institutionally provided means of realization,"[3] and argue that this dissociation is a structural source of individual failure, anomie, and, potentially, rebellion.[4] This structured discrepancy becomes all the more apparent as

From Walter C. Parker, "The Urban Curriculum and the Allocating Function of Schools," *The Educational Forum* 49, no. 4 (Summer 1985), pp. 445–450. Reprinted by permission.

industrial democracies move toward what Bell called a "post-industrial" model, one where natural resources and growth are recognized as limited.[5]

As recognized limits to growth put a more visible ceiling on the promise of vertical mobility for all, the gap between individual aspirations and their achievement is underscored.

> Now a generation is growing up with the dawning knowledge that in the future there may well not be enough affluence to go around. Many bright young people (dismayed by the prospect that "the best of times" are passing into history) are likely to be less motivated. This is because their future-focused role image leaves them with an image of living with limited opportunity in a world that demands voluntary frugality. "Why work when there's so little to gain?"—some feel now that the "carrot" of personal gain is of reduced influence.[6]

These words of Shane remind us that the school reflects the larger society and, more to the point, the school *serves* it. Any conception of schooling, any educational philosophy, will inevitably have to come to grips with the question: "Should the school develop young people to fit into present society as it is or does the school have a revolutionary mission to develop young people who will seek to improve society?"[7]

Either way, the school's relationship to the larger society is certainly not a neutral one. Freire makes the point more explicit.

> There is no such thing as a neutral educational process. Education either functions as an instrument which is used to facilitate the integration of the younger generation into the logic of the present system and bring about conformity to it, or it becomes the "practice of freedom"—the means by which men and women deal critically and creatively with reality and discover how to participate in the transformation of their world.[8]

One of the most important services the school has been expected to provide in the industrial era is the management of the discrepancy between aspiration and denial, that is, the monitoring of vertical mobility within the larger society. As Waller pointed out as early as in 1932, this is accomplished by a "sorting process" in which a few students "are carried by the express elevators of prep schools which do not stop below the college level,"[9] a few others drop out of school early and are allocated to the lowest status ranks in the occupational hierarchy, and the rest are sorted within and among schools. Applying the concept of Goffman,[10] Clark referred to the process of sorting students into the lower ranks as the "cooling out" function.[11] His analysis of junior colleges found an elaborate system for cooling out transfer students, who aspire to entry into a four-year college following a successful two-year stint at a junior college, into terminal students whose higher education will end after, if not before, the two-year junior college program.

The concept of "cooling out" is appropriate here because the management of the aspiration and denial dilemma is analogous to the classic *con game* in which the cooling out of the *mark*, who is the person conned by a con artist, by a *cooler*, a confederate of the con artist, is critical to the whole scheme. The cooler's job is to befriend the mark and keep him or her from calling the authorities or in some other way blowing the whistle on the con game. This is called "cooling out the mark."[12] Similarly, in school, those who are denied their aspirations must be skillfully handled so as to mollify them and adapt them to failure while the structural inevitability of their failure is concealed from them. Their disappointment is to be reduced through the provision of alternatives, counseling, and consolation. Above all, the less successful have "to be made to feel that their failure to attain was a personal failure and not the failure of the system."[13] This reduces their inclination to inveigh against the system that first raised their aspirations only to shut the door.

Comparing the status-allocating function of schools to a con game may seem extreme, but the structural similarities are undeniable. It is unlikely that schools will soon forfeit their control over this process, and perhaps, as some argue, it is done most fairly by the school. Consider the alternatives:

> If one's station in life is not to be earned through achievement in school, how else should it be earned? Should it be assigned by some form of ascription, by birth or heritage? Should differences in status be denied? To us, the first seems unfair and the second—unrealistic.[14]

The questions before educators considering a special curriculum for inner-city students are these: Given the allocating function of schools, would not a separate inner-city curriculum cool these students into the lower ranks? Given, further, the disproportionate number of poor and minorities in inner-city schools, would it not perpetuate current inequities?

Needless to say, there are apparently effective inner-city schools whose students are predominantly from poor and minority families. For example, George Washington Carver High School in Atlanta has received a good deal of attention from Congress, the press, and scholars.[15] But at what are such schools effective? Perhaps at production of students with marketable, vocational skills, but, if that were the case, should we be happy about their success? Is this really *good* news? Are not these students being cooled out? Jackson, too, noted that one might cheer Carver's successes if one were to take a *realistic* view of status differences in society, acknowledging the perennial presence of poor people and poor conditions. But,

> the realistic view carried to its logical conclusion says that things are not only as they *must* be, but as they *should* be, that they in fact represent some kind of social justice. Given their "place" in society or (less portentously) in the light of what they are going to wind up doing as adults, students like those attending Carver really do not *need* any more or any better schooling than they get. Or such youngsters really cannot *handle* any more or any better educational fare than a school like Carver offers. The quality of their schooling fits them as individuals. From here it is only a short step to the argument that students like those at Carver get the kind of education they *deserve*.[16]

Many people have advocated this "realistic" view over the years, and often to sympathetic ears. In fact, none other than John Locke suggested a special curriculum in separate schools for "the children of laboring people (who) are an ordinary burden to the parish."

> In order therefore to the more effectual carrying on of this work to the advantage of this kingdom, we further humbly propose that these schools be generally for spinning or knitting, or some other part of the woolen manufacture, unless in other countries [that is, districts] where the place shall furnish some other materials fitter for the employment of such poor children; in which places the choice of these materials for their employment may be left to the prudence and direction of the guardians of the poor.[17]

Were Locke's proposal advanced today in the United States, it would no doubt shock most educators into a rebuttal of the most righteous indignation. Jackson has imagined the reaction:

> Why the very *idea* is close to criminal. The thought of forcing children of laboring people to attend schools to learn how to diddle with bobbins and keep the floor swept clean, while the children of the well-to-do are taken on nature walks and have music lessons and begin the study of French in the third grade—and such gross inequities supported by tax dollars to boot—why it's downright unjust. It's unfair. It's undemocratic.[18]

Is it any less "undemocratic" to create a special curriculum for inner-city students which accepts tacitly both the existing status hierarchy *and* the allocating function of schools, and then proceeds matter-of-factly with the cooling of these youth into their respective *places?* Now that equal access to schools has become more of a logistical problem than an ideological one, educators must turn with what Maxine Greene calls "wideawakeness"[19] to the problem of equal access to knowledge *within* schools.[20] This is no mere logistical problem; it is ideological and political as any. The recognition of the aspiration and denial dilemma faced by this democratic society and of the cooling out function currently performed by schools will open the issue of status allocation to public debate. This is not going to be an easy debate, but surely it deserves a public forum.

NOTES

[1] Mortimer J. Adler, *The Paideia Proposal* (New York: Macmillan, 1982), and *Paideia Problems and Possibilities* (New York: Macmillan, 1983); the Carnegie Foundation, *High School: A Report on Secondary Education in America* (New York: Harper & Row, 1983); Charles W. Eliot's argument for a college preparatory curriculum for all high school students in *Charles W. Eliot and Popular Education,* ed. Edward A. Krug (New York: Teachers College Press, 1961).

[2] Burton R. Clark, "The 'Cooling-Out' Function in Higher Education," *The American Journal of Sociology* 65 (May 1960): 569–576.

[3] Clark, Ibid., p. 569.

[4] Robert K. Merton, "Social Structure and Anomie," in *Social Theory and Social Structure,* rev. ed. (Glencoe, Ill.: Free Press, 1957).

[5] Daniel Bell, *The Coming of Post-Industrial Society* (New York: Basic Books, 1973).

[6] Harold G. Shane, "Some Educational Consequences of Contemporary Social Disorientation," in *Bad Times, Good Schools*, ed. Jack Frymier (West Lafayette, Ind.: Kappa Delta Pi, 1983), p. 38.

[7] Ralph W. Tyler, *Basic Principles of Curriculum and Instruction* (Chicago: University of Chicago Press, 1949), p. 35.

[8] Paulo Freire, *Pedagogy of the Oppressed* (New York: Seabury Press, 1973), p. 15.

[9] Willard Waller, *The Sociology of Teaching* (New York: John Wiley and Sons, 1967).

[10] Erving Goffman, "Cooling the Mark Out: Some Aspects of Adaptation to Failure," *Psychiatry* 15 (November 1952): 451–463.

[11] Clark, "The 'Cooling-Out' Function."

[12] Goffman, "Cooling the Mark Out."

[13] Sally Geis, Jill Hilton, and William Plitt, "School Reform: Catching Tigers in Red Weather," *Educational Studies* 7 (Fall 1976), p. 249.

[14] Ibid., p. 250.

[15] Sara Lawrence Lightfoot, "Portraits of Exemplary Secondary Schools: George Washington Carver Comprehensive High School," *Daedalus* 110 (Fall 1981): 17–37; Philip W. Jackson, "Secondary Schooling for Children of the Poor," *Daedalus* 110 (Fall 1981): 39–57; Alonzo A. Crim, "A Community of Believers," *Daedalus* 110 (Fall 1981): 145–162.

[16] Jackson, "Secondary Schooling," p. 54.

[17] John Locke, quoted in Jackson, "Secondary Schooling," pp. 54–55.

[18] Jackson, "Secondary Schooling," p. 55.

[19] Maxine Greene, *Landscapes of Learning* (New York: Teachers College Press, 1978).

[20] Equal access to knowledge is one of the themes developed by John I. Goodlad in *A Place Called School* (New York: McGraw-Hill, 1983), and discussed in "Access to Knowledge," *Teachers College Record* 84 (Summer 1983): 787–800.

Kenneth A. Sirotnik

WHAT YOU SEE IS WHAT YOU GET: CONSISTENCY, PERSISTENCY, AND MEDIOCRITY IN CLASSROOMS

Since the turn of the century, we have seen educational configurations ranging from the one-room little red schoolhouse to the thirty-five plus student classroom complexes in highly institutionalized, densely populated, urban environments. We have seen fashionable philosophies of pedagogical practice, including traditional/fixed curricula approaches, progressive/experiential methods, open classroom/individualized learning systems, inquiry-driven/inductive learning techniques, and the ever-present back-to-basics tonic, most recently with a competency-based twist. We have seen all this within a rapidly evolving social context consisting of an industrial revolution, two world wars (and a number of undeclared ones), and an astounding technological revolution only in its infant stage of development.

From Kenneth A. Sirotnik, "What You See Is What You Get: Consistency, Persistency, and Mediocrity in Classrooms," *Harvard Educational Review* 53 (1983), pp. 1, 16–31. Copyright © by President and Fellows of Harvard College.

Yet, what we have seen and what we continue to see in the American classroom—the process of teaching and learning—appears to be one of the most consistent and persistent phenomena known in the social and behavioral sciences. To put it succinctly, the "modus operandi" of the typical classroom is still didactics, practice, and little else.

Historically, this observation can be verified by wading through the literature on classroom processes. For example, in a groundbreaking four-year study of secondary classrooms in the early 1900s, Stevens (1912) generated statistics in terms of teacher talk percentages, types of questioning, and classroom interactional configurations. She remarks: "The fact that one history teacher attempts to realize his educational aims through the process of 'hearing' the textbook, day after day, is unfortunate, but pardonable; that history, science, mathematics, foreign language, and English teachers, collectively are following in the same groove, is a matter for theorists and practitioners to reckon with" (p. 16).

More recently, Hoetker and Ahlbrand (1969) reviewed the literature on the so-called "recitation" syndrome. In study after study, with great variety in observational method, and with either "thick" descriptions of a few classes or "thin" descriptions of many classes, teacher lecturing or total class work on written assignments continue to emerge as the primary instructional patterns. (Other reviews can be found in Amidon and Hough, 1967; Dunkin and Biddle, 1974; and Peterson and Walberg, 1979.) Similarly, Goodlad and Klein looked behind the classroom door in the late 1960s and found that these patterns were among "the most monotonously recurring pieces of data" that they gathered (1970, p. 51).

Ten years later, these patterns were once again revealed in "A Study of Schooling" directed by Goodlad.[1] In the 1976–1978 school years, Goodlad and his associates collected data in over 1,000 elementary and secondary classrooms. The present article is based primarily on observational data from this study.

Assuming that these didactic patterns are old news to astute observers of the educational scene, what, then, are the purposes of another article discussing these findings? First, it is important to document empirically this pedagogical trend up to the 1980s. Hopefully, complacency has not yet prevented us from still being shocked—perhaps even shocked into action—when we see, once again, what goes on in schools and classrooms in the United States.

Second, it is important to begin the next step, namely, to raise some serious questions regarding the ways we educate students—questions which arise from a substantial body of empirical data. This discussion will be clearly value-based, growing out of the belief that the mastery of basic skills should not be the only goal of the teaching-learning process. Developing the capabilities for self-reflection, creativity, interpersonal communication, and social and political analysis, for example, should be equally important. From this perspective, I have used the term "mediocrity" in the title of this article to convey the narrowness of what goes on in classrooms in light of what could (and ought to) happen. My hope is that my article will stimulate continued critical inquiry by both researchers and practitioners into the phenomena we call teaching and learning.

SAMPLE, PROCEDURES, AND OBSERVATIONAL SYSTEM

A Study of Schooling was based on the assumption that improving schools requires knowing what is happening in and around them. We focused on collecting *contextual* data on commonplaces such as teaching practices, content, physical environment, resources, use of time, communication, decision making, goals, and the implicit (or "hidden") curriculum. These data were obtained from multiple sources (teachers, students, administrators, observers, and parents) in a hierarchy of contextual domains (the individual or personal domain, the class or instructional domain, the school or institutional domain, and the schooling or societal domain).

Included in the data base are observations of 129 elementary and 887 secondary classes (362 junior high and 525 senior high). Classes in each elementary school were randomly sampled at each grade level; in secondary schools, classes were randomly sampled to represent each of eight major subject areas.[2] The 38 schools (13 elementary, 12 junior high or middle, and 13 senior high) represent a purposive, nationwide sample with systematic variation in such factors as school size, economic status of the community, race/ethnicity of the student body, and geographic characteristics. (See Overman, 1979, for a complete description of the methodology used in A Study of Schooling.) Although the data base is not suitable for strict statistical generalization to all schools in the country, it is sufficiently representative to serve as a rich source for exploratory data analysis and heuristic speculation.

Each class was usually observed by one trained observer on three different occasions (full days at the elementary level and full periods at the secondary level) during the two-week period devoted to the observational phase of the study.[3] These data were accumulated into a single observational protocol for each classroom. Aggregating the results for each class serves to increase the validity of the data by increasing generalizability of the observations over time. Interobserver reliability was assessed for a subsample of the classes and found to be generally adequate (Sirotnik, 1981a).

The observational system was quite complex and has been more comprehensively described elsewhere (Giesen & Sirotnik, 1979). Briefly, the system was a modified version of that developed at the Stanford Research Institute by Stallings and her associates for the evaluation of Project Follow Through (Stallings & Kaskowitz, 1974). For the present study, there were four primary modifications: (1) it was generalized for use at both elementary and secondary schooling levels; (2) variables were separated out by course content; (3) variables were separated out by classroom *context*—instruction, behavior control, routines, and the remainder, labeled "social"; and (4) a daily summary section was included in each observation.

The data presented in this article come from the four major sections of this modified system: physical environment inventory (PEI), daily summary (DS), classroom snapshot (CS), and five-minute interaction (FMI). The PEI is designed to record the architectural arrangement of the classroom, seating and grouping patterns, furnishings, and materials and equipment. The DS provides an overview of the space and materials available as well as the decision-making processes of students and teachers.

The CS and FMI sections are considerably more complicated. The classroom snapshot provides information about what each adult (usually a teacher) and student in the classroom is doing, the size of student groups (if any) and the nature of the activities in progress at a given moment. These data can be transformed into percentages which represent the likelihood of finding students, at any given time, involved in designated activities, with or without the teacher, in one or more grouping configurations.

The five-minute interaction portion of the observation record is a more continuous accounting of how time is spent in the classroom, which focuses on the teacher and the interactive process between teacher and students. These data yield estimates of the percentage of class time various teacher-student interactional configurations occur—that is, *who* (teacher or student) is doing *what* (questioning, lecturing, correcting, responding, and so forth) to *whom* (teacher or student), *how* (for example, verbally, nonverbally, with positive affect, with guidance), and in what *context* (instruction, behavior control, routines, or social). Twelve FMI and CS records at the secondary level and forty-eight FMI and CS records at the elementary level were accumulated in the observation protocol for each classroom.

FINDINGS

Although we were aware of the documented patterns noted in the literature reviewed above, we were still startled by the paucity of variation in the observational results, both within and across schools. For example, in the elementary classes observed, we estimate that, on the average, just under 3 percent of the instructional time that the teacher spent interacting with students involved corrective feedback (with or without guidance). At the secondary level, this estimate is less than 2 percent. Moreover, the dispersion of class estimates around these means is minimal, ranging from 0 to 8 percent at the elementary level and 0 to 14 percent at the secondary level. Thus one of the most touted pedagogical features of classroom instruction—immediate corrective feedback—rarely occurs in our sample of classrooms during the three full observations recorded.[4]

Physical Environment and Daily Summary Data

From the PEI data, we find that approximately 95 percent of the classrooms observed are self-contained, with a capacity for thirty to thirty-five students. Eighty percent or more of the secondary classes have no adjacent, usable space; over 70 percent of the elementary classrooms can be similarly described. Seating typically consists of a combination of fixed and moveable chairs. Eighty percent of the junior high classes and nearly 90 percent of the senior high classes have no learning centers, compared with 60 percent of the elementary classes. Two-thirds of the elementary classes appear to have some alteration of their physical environment, such as plants, area rugs, and unusual bulletin board displays. At the secondary level, over half of the junior high and two-thirds of the senior high classes have little or no such elaboration of the basic four-wall classroom environment.

In the Daily Summary, only the variables relating to locus of decision making had sufficient interobserver reliability for further analysis. Nearly 100 percent of the elementary classes are entirely teacher-dominated. Moreover, the junior and senior high school classes are highly teacher-dominated, averaging nearly 90 percent and 80 percent, respectively.

Five-Minute Interaction Data

At both elementary and secondary levels, approximately 75 percent of class time is instructional, while most of the remaining time is spent on routines such as preparation for instruction, roll-taking, and cleanup. For example, the typical senior-high class period averaged 57 minutes in length in which roughly 43 minutes are spent on instruction, 12 minutes on routines, and the remaining 3 minutes on discipline, control, and miscellaneous social interactions. Nearly 70 percent of the total class time involves verbal interaction or "talk," mostly in the instructional context. Particularly interesting is the ratio of teacher-to-student talk. Approximately half of the verbal interaction time is devoted to teacher talk, mostly to either individual students or the entire class. Less than a fifth of the time involves student talk. Teachers, therefore, "out-talk" students by a ratio of nearly three to one.

If 70 percent of the class time involves teacher-student verbal interaction, how is the remaining time spent? Since our observation system was designed to focus on teachers, we can only account for their remaining time. Approximately 20 percent of their time is equally divided between working alone (usually at their desks) or monitoring and observing students. The remaining 10 percent of the average teacher's time is spent on such activities as moving around the classroom and responding nonverbally to students.

Scanning the array of teacher-to-student interactions, we find that barely 5 percent of the instructional time is spent on direct questioning—questioning which anticipates a specific response like "yes," "no," "Columbus," or "1492." Less than 1 percent of that time is devoted to open questions which call for more complex cognitive or affective responses. As noted above, corrective feedback is rarely observed, particularly at the secondary level. Providing corrective feedback in combination with additional information designed to help students understand and correct their mistakes is almost nonexistent. In fact, reinforcement of any kind is rarely noticed, whether in the form of specific, task-related acknowledgment and praise or general support and encouragement. Moreover, less than 5 percent of teachers' time is spent responding to students, which, as will be seen shortly, is less than the percentage of time students are observed initiating interaction with the teacher.

In contrast to teacher-to-student interactions, the array of student-to-

teacher interactions reveals that the modal interaction, that is, the most frequently occurring single interaction, is one of students *responding* to the teacher.
This occurs roughly 15 percent and 10 percent of the time at elementary and
secondary levels, respectively. None of the remaining student-to-teacher interaction categories accounts for more than 5 percent of class time. In summary, the
modal classroom patterns consist of (1) the teacher explaining or lecturing to the
total class or to a single student, asking direct, factual questions, or monitoring
students; and (2) the students ostensibly listening to the teacher or responding to
teacher-initiated interaction.

What kind of visible effect is present during these teacher-student interactions? Our data suggest little or none. Interactions defined as noticeably positive
would include comments like "I love this subject," "You did a good job,"
"Wow," and such behavior as shared laughter and overt enthusiasm. Noticeably
negative interactions would include "That's a stupid thing to do," "Go sit in the
corner," crying, or yelling. According to these definitions, less than 3 percent of
classroom time can be characterized as either positive or negative, regardless of
the level of schooling. In other words, the affect present over 95 percent of the
time can best be described as neutral.

Snapshot Data

The data derived from this aspect of the observation system both support and
augment the foregoing results. Each snapshot "locates" all individuals present
in the classroom at a given moment. This is accomplished by the simultaneous
consideration of three facets: (1) the *activity* in progress (such as preparing for
instruction, lecturing, discussion, or nontask behavior); (2) the *directorship* of the
activity (teacher working with students, students working cooperatively on a
common task, or students working independently); and (3) the *grouping* configuration (a single student, small, medium, or large groups, or total class). When the
data are aggregated and converted to percentages, they represent the likelihood
of students being found in each configuration. As such, these values are not as
easily interpretable as the five-minute interaction percentages since they do not
represent a continuous accounting of classroom time. They can be most useful,
however, for making *relative* comparisons. That is, the magnitudes of the actual
percentages themselves are less interesting than the contrasts they suggest
between the modal classroom configurations and those involving relatively few
students.

When the results for the activity facet are summarized across the directorship and grouping facets, the activities involving the most students alternate
between working on written assignments or being lectured to, depending on the
schooling level. The mean percentages of students involved in the explain/
lecture activity range from just under 20 percent at the elementary level to just
over 25 percent at the senior-high level. Conversely, working on written assignments steadily decreases from nearly 30 percent at the elementary level to 15
percent at the senior-high level. Routine activities either preparatory to or
following instruction also involve a relatively large number of students. In fact,

the likelihood of student involvement in noninstructional activities increases from over 15 percent in elementary classes to over 20 percent at the senior-high level. The only other secondary school activity which accounts for a relatively high proportion of student involvement (roughly 15 percent) is the practice of psychomotor skills, primarily in art, vocational, and physical education classes. Thus, it is evident from the data that most students can be found in the more "traditional" and "passive" learning activities, whether these involve practicing psychomotor skills in physical education classes or, its analogue, working on written assignments in English classes. The likelihood of students participating in other activities such as discussion, simulation, role playing, and demonstration is less than 8 percent. And these are activities which are ordinarily viewed as less traditional and more enriching, as well as more demanding, since students participate more actively in their own learning process.

These findings are echoed in the overall results for the directorship and grouping facets of the snapshot data. According to the directorship data, over 50 percent of the students, regardless of grade, are directed by the teacher. Over 33 percent are found working independently, usually on the same assignments, and only 10 percent or less are ever found working cooperatively on an assignment. According to the grouping configuration data, nearly 67 percent of the elementary students and 75 percent of the secondary students work as a total class. Less than 5 percent are found working individually and less than 10 percent are found working in small group configurations.

Finally, taking all three facets into account illuminates the findings even further. The modal three-facet configuration is clearly that of the teacher explaining or lecturing to the total class. Students working independently on written assignments in larger groups, or as a total class, is the second most typical configuration. Ranking third is the configuration of the teacher and total class involved in general routines, such as cleanup or preparation.

• • •

Discussion

Some years ago, Andy Warhol made a series of films portraying life events in the actual time frame they occurred—for example, six and one-half hours of a person sleeping. In his film *The Haircut*, we see what seems like hours of interminable sameness—a close-up of a man's face and head with little or no expression and the hands and tools of a barber at work. At one point the man twitches—not a big twitch—but, relative to what has been going on, a noticeable momentary change in countenance. The audience cheers in nearly hysterical relief from the accumulated boredom and strain of rationalizing their stay in the theater.

If Warhol were to have made a film of the typical American classroom, the data we just reviewed might easily have been the script. We would watch the secondary classroom scene unfold, fifty-seven minutes during which a hint of affect would be a cause for celebration—positive affect would be nice, but even negative would suffice, as a welcome change from the flat affective neutrality pervading the screen. If it were a physical education class, we would break out in applause were the teacher to actually spend time helping students perfect their baseball swing instead of monitoring whatever physical activities were in progress. If it were a science class, we would cheer wildly were the teacher to demonstrate the effects of air pressure and vacuums instead of explaining them or monitoring the class as students worked independently on their written assignments. Similar scenarios and positive audience response could be played out in other subject areas—small group poetry reading and discussion sessions in an English class, role-play simulations of civil liberty suits in a social studies class, and so forth.

What if we were forced to view the movie from the standpoint of the student? Depending upon the time frame, the film could run 330 minutes for the typical 6-period day, 495 hours for the typical 90-day semester, over 40 continuous 24-hour days for the typical school year. In all, typical secondary students play out their 6-year role involuntarily, subordinately, and in a physical setting that usually translates to no more than a 4-foot square of space per person including desks, tables, and so on. The scenario for elementary classes and students is nearly the same, if not more uneventful, considering how little variety is offered in course content beyond the three Rs. Placing observations such as these in a time perspective is not new. It was done far more eloquently fifteen years ago by Jackson (1968). His commentary on classroom life was based on over 1,000 hours of observation in a few elementary classrooms. As it turns out, he was also accurately portraying a few hours of observation of over 1,000 elementary and secondary classrooms nearly two decades later. The remainder of this paper will briefly discuss these findings from two perspectives, one narrower and one broader.[5]

The Narrower View

What we have seen portrayed in the observational data might be labeled either "good news" or "bad news," depending upon which brand of research on teaching you happen to prefer. The good news is that this monotonous scenario of teacher talk to total class and student work on written assignments is consistent with the recommendations emerging from current research on effective teaching practices: increasing quantity of schooling, specifically time-on-task or academically engaged time, raises scores on achievement tests. The roots of this line of research can be traced through the work of Carroll (1963), Wiley (1973), Bloom (1976), and a host of others. (See the reviews by Rosenshine and Furst, 1971; Rosenshine, 1979; Denham and Lieberman, 1980; and Frederick and Walberg, 1980). This research is useful in at least two respects. First, it reaffirms some fundamental premises implicit in our common form of pedagogy— didactics and practice. In particular, it reinforces the connection between concerted teacher-learner effort on specific skills and test scores which measure the attainment of these skills. Second, and more importantly, this research focuses attention on the complexity of mastery learning in the ordinary classroom setting and may eventually lead to more definitive studies of viable teaching strategies (see Stallings, 1980).

Unfortunately, the bad news is that time-on-task research may have also diverted attention from critical instructional variables such as discussion, demonstration, questioning at higher cognitive levels, praise, reinforcement, student decision making, and positive affective climate. These are practices which we rarely observed in our study, but which are valued teaching strategies by many educators and researchers and are correlated positively with achievement outcomes in many empirical studies.

Peterson (1979), in noting the empirical basis for a more comprehensive view of useful instructional practices, also recognized the cyclical nature of the orientation of research on teaching as it alternates between the "soft" (open, indirect, nontraditional, and inductive) and the "hard" (closed, direct, traditional, deductive) modalities of teaching. This dichotomy becomes particularly destructive as it feeds into the popular cry of "back to the basics" whenever education is in trouble. Witness the decline in achievement test scores since the late 1960s. Ironically, whether guided by Jackson's (1968) observations at the beginning of the decline or by those suggested in our data, navigating back to the basics should be easy. We never left.

Clearly, it is the *quality* more than the quantity of schooling which best serves as an educational and research focus. Quality of schooling includes not only time-on-task, but time *well spent*. It also includes, however, time spent on teaching practices such as encouragement, corrective feedback with guidance, small group discussions, individualization, and students' involvement in their own education; but not idle praise, corrective feedback without guidance, rambling verbal interactions, busy work as a control device, or token student decision making. Considerable research has been done which supports the former instructional practices. An incomplete but illustrative list includes the following work: Anderson (1970), Bossert (1979), Good, Biddle, and Brophy (1975), Johnson (1981), Moos and Moos (1978), Morrison (1974), Ripple (1965), Slavin (1977), Soar and Soar (1979), and Walberg (1977).

The literature, therefore, suggests, an array of teaching practices—some observed frequently and some rarely observed—which enhance student learning. But we have very little evidence suggesting how these practices can be combined given the variety of classroom exigencies encountered by the ordinary teacher. Research on teacher practices in the *context* within which they occur is a high priority if we are to continue the quest for an applied science of teaching. (See, for example, Bronfenbrenner, 1976; Doyle, 1977; Goodlad, 1975; and Tikunoff, 1979.)

The Broader View

Having focused on research in which achievement outcomes are the sine qua non for judging effective teaching practices, the foregoing perspective may convey the impression that schooling is unidimensional in purpose—that the raison d'être of schools is to provide instruction in basic skills of required subject matters. We might label this solid academic grounding as the "intellectual" function of schooling. But, in fact, schools fulfill a host of other functions, ranging from delivering glorified daycare services to providing a forum for the solution of societal problems such as racial segregation.

A thorough delineation of the functions of schooling would require explicit definitions within a historical and philosophical framework. Readers are advised to consult Goodlad (1979) for just such a presentation. It will suffice here simply to use the term "function" generically with appropriate modifiers. For example, advertised goals in curriculum guides, perceptions of what goes on in schools, and proclamations of what ought to go on could be classified, respectively, as the stated, apparent, and ideal functions of schooling. This discussion will focus on the apparent and ideal functions of schooling as the people who are involved in schooling—teachers, parents, and students—see them.

For this purpose, it is useful to summarize additional data from A Study of Schooling. We asked approximately 1,300 teachers, 8,500 parents, and 15,000 students what they thought to be the single most emphasized function at their school and, also, which function *should* be the most emphasized. Respondents were provided four alternative choices representing the stated function categories found in virtually all formal curriculum documents at the state, district, and school levels (Klein, 1980). These categories are intellectual development (as defined above); personal development (building self-confidence, creativity, ability to think independently, and self-discipline); social development (helping students learn to get along with other students and adults, preparing them for social and civic responsibility, and developing their awareness and appreciation of our own and other cultures); and vocational development (preparing students for employment, developing skills necessary for getting a job, developing an awareness of career choices and alternatives).

It should be clear from the results in Table 1 [renumbered from the original] that intellectual development is usually the single most emphasized apparent or ideal function. Equally revealing, however, is the substantial number of persons who view functions other than the intellectual as of primary importance. In fact, more high school students chose the vocational development category to be ideally more important than intellectual development. Of particular interest is the shift in primary importance from intellectual development to the other functions as the teachers, parents, and students shift from the apparent to the ideal perspectives. (See Overman, 1980, for more detailed analyses of these data.)

The important contrast here is between what teachers, parents, and students see as the apparent and ideal functions of schooling and what can be inferred from our observational data as the apparent functions of schooling. Making these inferences is a speculative process which the reader can engage in as well as I. Further, it is easier to make these inferences when they are grounded in empirical studies based upon commonly accepted student outcome criteria, such as achievement test scores. Thus, it is easier to make inferences regarding the intellectual function of schooling in light of the research on teaching which was discussed in the previous section. But we do not have commonly accepted student outcome criteria in the personal, social, and vocational functions. Nor do we have research which sorts out the more promising instructional strategies to

TABLE 1 Teacher, Parent, and Student Views of the Single Most Emphasized Apparent and Ideal Functions of Schooling[a]

		Function[3]							
		Intellectual		Social		Personal		Vocational	
Level & Data Source		Apparent	Ideal	Apparent	Ideal	Apparent	Ideal	Apparent	Ideal
Elementary	N[b]								
Teachers	278	78.5	48.9	12.2	14.0	6.1	33.5	3.2	3.5
Parents	1653	68.9	57.6	13.6	9.3	11.4	24.5	6.0	8.6
Students	1565	61.4	47.1	11.1	13.8	11.9	17.3	15.5	21.8
Junior High									
Teachers	392	64.4	46.7	16.3	13.9	8.7	29.3	10.7	10.1
Parents	5099	56.3	51.1	19.5	9.5	11.2	21.1	13.0	18.2
Students	4655	64.1	38.0	11.7	13.4	11.2	18.3	13.1	30.3
Senior High									
Teachers	653	52.2	45.6	18.0	9.9	6.8	29.7	23.0	14.8
Parents	3961	43.1	46.5	19.0	8.7	10.2	19.3	27.8	25.5
Students	6727	61.6	27.3	10.2	15.9	13.2	25.6	14.9	31.1

[a]Table entries are percentages.

[b]Average number of respondents.

achieve these outcomes. In fact, nearly all the research on teaching practices has focused on what 50 percent or more of the teachers, parents and students in our sample do *not* see as the primary function of schools—namely, intellectual development.[6]

Nevertheless, the inconsistencies between what people want and what goes on in classrooms suggest a host of questions and reflections:[7]

> Do we want an educated, informed and participating citizenry? If so, how does this square with the time spent on social studies at the elementary school (about 5 percent of a school day), or the time spent in active discussion, simulation, and role play in secondary social studies classes (9 percent of a class period)? Are we looking at the roots of the kind of national apathy that sends a leader to the White House with an overwhelming majority vote from an underwhelming minority of the eligible voting public?

> Do we want philosophers in the literal meaning of the word—people who value continuing their education beyond school, who might even enjoy learning and who can identify their educational needs as they arise? If so, how does this square with the degree of positive affect, encouragement, praise, and guidance students experience in the classroom (less than 3 percent of classroom time)? If children are not encouraged to learn, what will people do with increasing amounts of free time as technology escalates in exponential proportions?

Do we want people who can intellectually contribute to society or benefit from what society has to offer? Are independent and creative thinking valuable assets for solving pressing societal problems? If so, how does this square with the number of opportunities for decision making offered to students (about 5, 10 and 20 percent in elementary, junior and senior high, respectively), and the extent of innovative teaching practices requiring the active involvement of learners (approximately 8 percent)?

The point is this: the record of classroom experience presented in the data is very much out-of-sync with the wishes of both the providers and recipients of education.

The final irony, of course, is that in systematically deemphasizing the social, personal and vocational functions of schooling, we are communicating subtle messages to students. Consider again the modal classroom picture presented here: a lot of teacher talk and a lot of student listening, unless students are responding to teachers' questions or working on written assignments; almost invariably closed and factual questions; little corrective feedback and no guidance; and predominantly total class instructional configurations around traditional activities—all in a virtually affectless environment. It is but a short inferential leap to suggest that we are implicitly teaching dependence upon authority, linear thinking, social apathy, passive involvement, and hands-off learning. This so-called "hidden" curriculum is disturbingly apparent.

CONCLUDING REMARKS

It would be a grave mistake to interpret what I have reported and commented upon as an indictment of teachers and schools. There are exceptional schools and teachers quite atypical of the aggregated profiles presented here. But fundamental and pervasive changes cannot occur without restructuring societal values and priorities. With sufficient reorganization and endowment, schools can become more viable hosts for teacher-learner activities, and teachers can become more effective when trained properly, treated as professionals, and rewarded appropriately (see Goodlad, 1984).

The purpose of this article, however, has been to raise questions about what goes on in classrooms grounded in comprehensive, empirical inquiry—not to provide answers. We have seen that schools have changed little since we and those before us were there. What have changed, and what continue to change, are the economic, social, and political realities of the society in which we live. Schools and the people who care about them must be responsive to these changes. As Toffler (1974) has noted:

> Education . . . is not just something that happens in the head. It involves our muscles, our senses, our hormonal defenses, our total biochemistry. Nor does it occur solely within the individual. Education springs from the interplay be-

tween the individual and a changing environment. The movement to heighten future-consciousness in education, therefore, must be seen as one step toward a deep restructuring of the links between schools, colleges, universities and the communities that surrond them. (p. 13)

I suspect "future shock" has been upon us for some time. If we do not unplug ourselves from the "mediocrity" of our educational circuitry, we will never achieve a working correspondence between what we see in classrooms and what we want for our children.

NOTES

[1] More detailed information on A Study of Schooling can be found in the series of four sequential articles published in the *Phi Delta Kappan*. The first in this series, Goodlad, Sirotnik, and Overman (1979), includes a conceptual overview, the sample design, and the types of data collected. Additional information on the curriculum, student experience, and adult experience components of the study can be found, respectively, in Klein, Tve, and Wright (1979), Benham, Giesen, and Oakes (1980), and Bentzen, Williams, and Heckman (1980).

[2] These subject areas included English/reading/language arts, mathematics, social studies, science, the arts, foreign language, vocational/career education, and physical education.

[3] Four time periods (forty to sixty minutes each) were purposively sampled from each *elementary* class "day" to maximize the observation of instruction in the basic subject areas. Thus, the observed proportion of instructional time reported is likely to be an overestimate.

[4] A considerable number of tables are required to present even the minimal amount of data necessary to form an adequate frame of reference against which to interpret the relative presence or absence of various classroom processes. These tables are included in the technical report upon which this article is based. I will highlight the trends in these tables, reserving comments for the next section. However, in the interest of space, the tables themselves are omitted but with strong encouragement to readers to supplement what follows with the data presented in the technical report.

[5] A more in-depth treatment of these and other issues including recommendations for school improvements will be found in Goodlad (1984).

[6] I am not suggesting that the research focused on intellectual development has been a waste of time. Personally, I believe that intellectual development is the most important function of schooling. But I also believe that instructional strategies can be developed and implemented which emphasize important goals in the other function categories.

[7] Inferences of this type are fundamentally normative and reflect implicit values and beliefs. In my view, further systematic inquiry into these and similar issues requires active recognition of the connection between educational practice and the prevailing cultural-political interests. A critical theoretical analysis of this sort is approached in the work of Apple and King (1977), Apple (1979), and Giroux (1981) and would not be incompatible with the data presented here.

REFERENCES

Amidon, E. J., & Hough, J. B. (Eds.). *Interaction analysis: Theory research and application.* Reading, Mass.: Addison-Wesley, 1967.

Anderson, G. J. Effects of classroom social climate on individual learning. *American Educational Research Journal,* 1970, 7, 135–152.

Apple, M. W. *Ideology and the curriculum.* London: Routledge & Kegan Paul, 1979.

Apple, M. W., & King, N. What do schools teach? In R. H. Weller (Ed.), *Humanistic education: Visions and realities.* Berkeley: Calif.: McCutchan, 1977.

Benham, B. J., Giesen, P., & Oakes, J. A Study of Schooling: Students' experiences in schools. *Phi Delta Kappan,* 1980, 61, 337–340.

Bentzen, M. M., Williams, R. C., & Heckman, P. A Study of Schooling: Adult experiences in schools. *Phi Delta Kappan,* 1980, 61, 394–397.

Bloom, B. S. *Human characteristics and school learning.* New York: McGraw-Hill, 1976.

Bossert, S. T. *Tasks and social relationships in classrooms: A study of instructional organization and its consequences.* Cambridge, Eng.: Cambridge University Press, 1979.

Bronfenbrenner, U. The experimental ecology of education. *Teachers College Record,* 1976, 78, 157–204.

Carroll, J. B. A model for school learning. *Teachers College Record,* 1963, 64, 723–733.

Denham, C., & Lieberman, A. (Eds.). *Time to learn: A review of the beginning teacher evaluation study.* Washington, D.C.: National Institute of Education, U.S. Department of Education, 1980.

Doyle, W. Paradigms for research on teacher effectiveness. In L. S. Shulman (Ed.). *Review of research in education.* Itasca, Ill.: Peacock, 1977.

Dunkin, M. J., & Biddle, B. J. *The study of teaching.* New York: Holt, Rinehart & Winston, 1974.

Frederick, W. C., & Walberg, H. J. Learning as a function of time. *Journal of Educational Research,* 1980, 73, 183–194.

Giesen, P., & Sirotnik, K. A. *The methodology of classroom observation in* A Study of Schooling (*A Study of Schooling* Tech. Rep. No. 5). Los Angeles: Laboratory in School and Community Education, University of California, 1979. (ERIC Document Reproduction Service No. ED 214 875).

Giroux, H. A. *Ideology, culture and the process of schooling.* Philadelphia: Temple University Press, 1981.

Good, T. L., Biddle, B. J., & Brophy, J. E. *Teachers make a difference,* New York: Holt, Rinehart & Winston, 1975.

Goodlad, J. I. *Dynamics of educational change.* New York: McGraw-Hill, 1975.

Goodlad, J. I. *What schools are for.* Bloomington, Ind.: Phi Delta Kappa Educational Foundation, 1979.

Goodlad, J. I. *A place called school.* New York: McGraw-Hill, [1984].

Goodlad, J. I., Klein, M. F., & Associates. *Behind the classroom door.* Worthington, Ohio: Jones, 1970.

Goodlad, J. I., Sirotnik, K. A., & Overman, B. C. An overview of *A Study of Schooling. Phi Delta Kappan,* 1979, 61, 174–178.

Hoetker, J., & Ahlbrand, W. P. The persistence of the recitation. *American Educational Research Journal,* 1969, 6, 145–167.

Jackson, P. W. *Life in classrooms.* New York: Holt, Rinehart & Winston, 1968.

Johnson, D. W. Student-student interaction: The neglected variable in education. *Educational Researcher,* 1981, 10, 5–10.

Klein, M. F. *State and district curriculum guides: One aspect of the formal curriculum* (*A Study of Schooling* Tech. Rep. No. 9). Los Angeles: Laboratory in School and Community Education, University of California, 1980. (ERIC Document Reproduction Service No. ED 214 879).

Klein, M. F., Tye, K. A., & Wright, J. E. A Study of Schooling: Curriculum. *Phi Delta Kappan.* 1979, 61, 244–248.

Moos, R. H., & Moos, B. S. Classroom social climate and student absences and grades. *Journal of Educational Psychology,* 1978, 70, 263–69.

Morrison, T. L. Control as an aspect of group leadership in classrooms: A review of research. *Journal of Education,* 1974, 156, 38–64.

Overman, B. C. *A Study of Schooling: Methodology* (*A Study of Schooling* Tech. Rep. No. 2). Los Angeles: Laboratory in School and Community Education, University of California, 1979. (ERIC Document Reproduction Service No. ED 214 872).

Overman, B. C. *Functions of schooling: Perceptions and preferences of teachers, parents and students* (*A Study of Schooling* Tech. Rep. No. 10). Los Angeles: Laboratory in School and Community Education, University of California, 1980. (ERIC Document Reproduction Service No. ED 214 880)

Peterson, P. L. Direct instruction reconsidered. In P. L. Peterson & H. J. Walberg (Eds.), *Research on teaching.* Berkeley, Calif.: McCutchan, 1979.

Peterson, P. L., & Walberg, H. J. (Eds.). *Research on teaching.* Berkeley, Calif.: McCutchan, 1979.

Ripple, R. W. Affective factors influence classroom learning. *Educational Leadership.* 1965, 22, 476–480.

Rosenshine, B. V. Content, time, and direct instruction. In P. L. Peterson & H. J. Walberg (Eds.), *Research on teaching.* Berkeley, Calif.: McCutchan, 1979.

Rosenshine, B., & Furst, N. Research on teacher performance. in B. O. Smith (Ed.), *Research in teacher education: A symposium.* Englewood Cliffs, N.J.: Prentice-Hall, 1971.

Sirotnik, K. A. *An inter-observer reliability study of the SRI observation system as modified for use in* A Study of Schooling (*A Study of Schooling* Tech. Rep. No. 27). Los Angeles: Laboratory in School and Community Education, University of California, 1981. (a) (ERIC Document Reproduction Service No. ED 214 895).

Sirotnik, K. A. *What you see is what you get: A summary of observations in over 1000 elementary and secondary classrooms* (*A Study of Schooling* Tech. Rep. No. 29). Los Angeles: Laboratory in School and Community Education, University of California, 1981. (b) (ERIC Document Reproduction Service No. ED 214 897).

Slavin, R. E. Classroom reward structure: An analytical and practical review. *Review of Educational Research,* 1977, 47, 633–650.

Soar, R. S., & Soar, R. M. Emotional climate and management. In P. L. Peterson & H. J. Walberg (Eds.), *Research on teaching.* Berkeley, Calif.: McCutchan, 1979.

Stallings, J. Allocated academic learning time revisited, or beyond time on task. *Educational Researcher,* 1980, 9, 11–16.

Stallings, J., & Kaskowitz, D. *Follow Through classroom observation evaluation, 1972–1973* (SRI Project URU-7370). Stanford, Calif.: Stanford Research Institute, 1974.

Stevens, R. *The question as a measure of efficiency in instruction: A critical study of classroom practice.* New York: Teachers College, Columbia University, Contributions to Education No. 48, 1912.

Tikunoff, W. J. Context variables of a teaching-learning event. In N. Bennett & D. McNamara (Eds.), *Focus on teaching: Readings in the observation and conceptualization of teaching.* London: Longman, 1979.

Toffler, A. The psychology of the future. In A. Toffler (Ed.), *Learning for tomorrow: The role of the future in education.* New York: Vintage Books, 1974.

Walberg, H. J. Psychology of learning environments: Behavioral, structural or perceptual. In L. S. Shulman (Ed.), *Review of research in education* (Vol. 4). Itasca, Ill.: Peacock, 1977.

Wiley, D. E. Another hour, another day: Quantity of schooling, a potent path for policy. *Studies in Educative Processes* (No. 3). Chicago: University of Chicago, 1973.

DISCUSSION QUESTIONS FOR CHAPTER 7

1. What does Jackson mean when he refers to the "daily grind" of classroom life? How important does he judge this to be as compared to the more formal, set curriculum?
2. Anyon and Parker both suggest that the "hidden curriculum" of schooling serves some students better than others. Who seems to be best served by this "hidden curriculum" and how? What questions of justice and equality are raised by this phenomenon?
3. Discuss what Sirotnik feels are the hidden messages of schooling in terms of students' future political life. What are the conditions of the classroom that help send these messages?
4. What do you see as the possible outcomes of the "hidden curriculum" in terms of student learning? Which is more important in terms of student outcomes, the hidden or the formal curriculum?

PART FOUR

Schooling and Politics

8

Bureaucracy and Control in Education

In Part Three we focused on the socialization function of schooling. As we saw, the hidden curriculum is always a topic of debate among people of opposing opinions and goals. How these debates are resolved in the realm of school politics is the topic we explore in this section. We will see, in other words, the ways in which beliefs about social justice, equality, and meritocracy are turned into actual school practice.

Perhaps you have heard it said that it is too bad that politics have to interfere with schooling. In fact, as we point out later, school reformers have often based their efforts on an appeal to depoliticize the schools. As noble as this sentiment may seem, it hides more than it reveals. Pause for a moment to consider the alternatives to making public policy through politics. Would we perhaps prefer some type of coercion or dictatorial control of our educational decisions? In fact, arguments to remove politics from schools are usually a device to limit the number of people involved in school politics or decision making.

It is important to note that the definition of a politic individual is one who is "sagacious, prudent, shrewd" or whose actions are "judicious, expedient, [or] skillfully contrived."[1] Perhaps the goal in examining the politics of schooling should be to see how to make our personal actions more sagacious and our politics more judicious.

WHO RUNS THE SCHOOLS?

The culture, curriculum, and administration of the U.S. educational "industry" did not simply arise as a product of a general consensus on how schools should operate. Rather, continuing political debates have been waged over alternative conceptions of public schooling that grew from competing views of the socialization function of schooling. The key to understanding these debates is an awareness of the growing bureaucratization of schools and the various movements designed to limit the power of such bureaucracies.

When we look at the role of bureaucracy in modern government and in educational politics, the first point to be made is that it is probably impossible to run any government without some type of bureaucratic structure. A society or political entity must have ways to act consistently and to meet continued needs. Otherwise, a society would grind to a halt while attempting to make even the simplest of decisions. Every demand would be seen as original, requiring long periods of study and debate before responding. One function of a bureaucracy is to make regular responses to recurring events. In one sense, then, our objections to the bureaucratization of modern life are ill-founded. However, this should not be used as an argument for overlooking many of the basic tensions and contradictions between bureaucratic *administrative* structure and democratic *decision-making* structure.

Debate over the centralization of authority has a long history in American politics. The American Revolution was waged against a royal bureaucracy. Jeffersonian democracy was in part an attempt to resist the continuation of bureaucratic rule from colonialism to constitutionalism, and Jacksonian democracy was similarly a populist campaign against the perceived excesses of "big city" bureaucrats. Since the great common-school reforms of the mid-nineteenth century, educational politics in this country have often revolved around issues of democratic versus bureaucratic control and power. But what is meant by *bureaucracy?*

A wide variety of definitions have been offered by social scientists. Of most use to us in discussing school politics is one offered by Carl Friedrich:

> The six elements of a bureaucracy . . . fall naturally into two groups. Three of them order the relations of members of the organization to each other, namely, centralization of control and supervision, differentiation of functions, and qualification for office (entry and career aspects), while three embody rules defining desirable habit or behavior patterns of all the members of such an organization, namely, objectivity, precision and consistency, and discretion.[2]

We can see easily all of these characteristics in the school system. The school is governed by a hierarchy with power flowing from a central office (superintendent). He or she oversees individuals in specific, differentiated positions (principal, teacher, and so on) who attain their positions and advance in status by gaining appropriate certification. The process of schooling itself is carried out without respect to personal characteristics such as race and sex (objectivity), in a consistent manner across schools (use of same texts, for example), and with discretion exercised by those with authority (limited access to student records and evaluations of staff). Certainly there is much here with which no one would disagree. Why should teachers, for instance, worry about ordering cleaning supplies, and why should we not treat students somewhat objectively?

Yet some of the characteristics of bureaucracy operate to concentrate power in the hands of a few, a situation antithetical to democracy. For example, why should decisions on textbooks and curriculum flow down from the top? It would make more pedagogical sense to put such decisions in the hands of teachers and students who are in the classroom. Neither does it make much sense to differentiate functions to the point where a school principal never sees the inside of a classroom.

A series of more fundamental questions may also be raised. Do the qualifications commonly established for entry into a bureaucracy (state licensing requirements for teachers) really establish that someone is qualified to teach? Should we indeed treat all individuals objectively? What about students (perhaps *all* students) with special needs? Is it possible to be consistent and precise in education, a field dealing exclusively with human beings in all their complexity? How much privacy or discretion should be allowed in such a public process as educating a community's children?

When we ask these questions and at the same time consider the bureaucratic structure within which educators function, we begin to better understand school politics. The conflict between democratic and bureaucratic control has been part of political debates in all spheres of American life. In education this underlying conflict has often been overlooked because attention is focused on debates over local versus state or national control, the authority of school boards versus school superintendents, the legitimacy of teacher unions, the role parents should play in educational decision making, and the role students should have in school decision making. Each of these debates reflect the most important feature of school politics: the continuing bureaucratization of schools and the political challenges to that trend.

THE FORMATIVE YEARS, 1840–1880

We have to go back to the early 1800s to find a time in which schooling was relatively free from bureaucratization. Small one-room schoolhouses could be found in the majority of communities. These were usually maintained by one itinerant teacher or headmaster who was responsible for all elements of the school's functioning. In rural areas constituencies were usually neighboring families who "would bond together and sponsor such schools and educational activities as they collectively deemed proper."[3]

"Local" interests still dominated in the control of schooling through the Civil War. Beginning in the fourth decade of the nineteenth century, however, efforts increased to make the state more responsible for public education. Accompanying this trend was the development of state-level bureaucratic structures that gradually came to control the licensing of teachers and the guidelines within which schools were allowed to operate. This is not to say that a bureaucratic organization was necessarily evil or the only option available. In fact, Michael Katz has pointed out that four models of school organization competed for supremacy in the first half of the nineteenth century. These models included paternalistic voluntarism, corporate voluntarism, democratic localism, and incipient bureaucracy.[4] The central question that emerges from the study of this period is: Why did the bureaucratic model eventually triumph?

As was illustrated in Part Three, Horace Mann, Henry Barnard, and other common-school proponents saw the spread of public education as crucial to the development of a national character. From the standpoint of these educational reformers, however, the central purposes of education could not be left to the chance of voluntarism (paternalistic or corporate) or to the caprice of democratic localism. While the main actors in the common-school movement generally endorsed the social and moral goals of the voluntarists (uplifting of character, inculcation of virtue, cultural homogenization) they felt, in general, that a system left entirely to local control could never grow to the scale required, nor be staffed by professional educators. On the other hand, the ideal of democratic localism stood in direct opposition to the aims of those committed to greater state authority in education.

The conflict between democratic localism and incipient bureaucracy was over the fear of democratic rule, the "unique" demands of urban education, and the desire of educators to increase the authority of the school in the child-rearing process. School reformers were suspicious of the populist notion of democracy, which, they believed, could lead to a majority forcing its educational views on a minority. Such a system could lead, they claimed, to abridging "the liberties of parents by forcing them to choose between submitting their children to alien points of view" or enrolling their children in expensive private schools.[5] Of course, this left unanswered the questions of whether or not democratic localism actually functioned in this manner and whether governance by educational officials at the state or city level would be any less likely to infringe upon the liberties of parents. But it was the beginning of the argument that justified centralizing educational authority.

Urban school reformers argued that the ideal of democratic localism might work in rural areas but could not meet the demands of competing interests in urban areas. (It was one of the ironies of school development in this period that the argument for bureaucratic organizational structures was applied to rural areas shortly after its successful establishment in urban areas). Urban education, with its large and heterogeneous population, had to be centrally organized and the operation of schools removed from petty partisan bickering. Second, given the ethnic diversity of the urban area, it was thought vital that immigrant children be weaned away from the alien cultures of their parents. As we saw in Part Three, the values necessary for success in a developing industrial society were often assumed to be absent in the alien cultures of the urban poor. Thus it was vital to deliver control of the school into the protective sphere of the professional educator and prevent it from falling into the hands of the poor.

The hallmark of bureaucratic reform was centralization. Through the replacement of small district school boards by citywide boards and the establishment of a single central high school in each city, control over schools was gradually assumed by a small cadre of educational professionals. Direct, participatory democracy in education was replaced by a limited system of representation designed to put schools above politics. By the last decade of the nineteenth century the expert advice of professionals began to dictate the educational agenda as school systems expanded to the point where only a full-time professional had the time and knowledge required to manage the increasingly complex social institution called the school.

The basic elements of the American educational bureaucracy were taking shape. Control and supervision were put in centralized offices, and for the first time administrative and teaching roles were separated. The call went out for the professional training of teachers, and the search was on for a pedagogical science that would include objective, standardized, and precise rules for teaching. Power over the educational system was increasingly centralized and decisions were gradually removed from the realm of democratic action. Bureaucratic organization worked to replace political action.

Educational statesmen in the mid-nineteenth century were salesmen for centralization and bureaucracy, and their efforts set the stage for the creation of a common, standardized system of schools. Most important, they established the notion that the state was responsible for the education of the child, and that the teacher operated *in loco parentis*. This concept, which differed from the colonial notion of schools as an extension of families, was a critical precondition for the evolving state and professional control of schools.[6]

RATIONALIZING THE BUREAUCRACY: THE EARLY TWENTIETH CENTURY

It would be a mistake to assume that the entire pattern of school bureaucratization was set by the end of the 1800s. But the preconditions were there for the ascendency of bureaucratic politics and control.[7] During the first third of the twentieth century bureaucratic control was finally rationalized; that is, it was made to seem the only possible way to manage the growing public school system.

Previously we pointed out how the expansion of schooling coincided with the growth of modern manufactures and led to a hidden curriculum highly dependent on the values of modern industrial capitalism. Additionally, a management structure was used that attempted to emulate that of business. Parallel to both of these trends was an attempt to restructure school politics to eliminate participatory decision making. This further shift in education decision making was accompanied by the increasing complexity of urban schools, the growth of the educational profession, and the fear of an increasing immigrant population's effect on democratic institutions.

With the consolidation of both rural and urban school systems, the complexity of schooling increased to the point where a bureaucratic organizational form seemed the only practical possibility:

> As the organization of urban education became more complex, schools were increasingly divorced from the communities they served, and laymen had progressively less power to influence school policy. In turn, schoolmen themselves gained augmented power to run the school as they saw fit, with little or no reference to the actual requirements of the community.[8]

In rural settings "the locus of power over rural schools was transferred from community leaders to administrators, and from amateurs to professionals."[9]

The continued professionalization of teachers and administrators further consolidated the power and control of educators over the system. The tasks of schooling became more specialized, with educators taking on a differentiated array of responsibilities, each seemingly more esoteric than those before. Increasingly there was a call for more carefully trained teachers and administrators. This reflected the organization of work life in general and the emphasis placed on scientific management, scientific measurement, and scientific pedagogy. The first professional degrees in educational administration were offered, and the numbers of "normal schools" for the exclusive purpose of preparing of teachers increased. As educational systems became more complex it was increasingly clear that only professionals could manage them effectively. The final push to rationalize school bureaucracy was thus directed at closing off public participation in educational decision making.

The limits put on democratic participation at the turn of the century were carefully presented in the image of depoliticizing school decisions. School boards were reduced in size. Election to these smaller boards was on a citywide (as opposed to a ward or district) basis. Politics, however, were *not* removed from decisions about schooling. Rather, election by citywide vote diluted ethnic, minority, and working-class input. The funds required to carry on election campaigns were usually only available to economically well-established candidates.

Many reformers felt that it was precisely the personal characteristics displayed by the ethnic, minority, or working-class population that should be eliminated in school. Preventing them from controlling school boards was necessary to this purpose. The "public interest" thus established was a system of school politics created to allow elite social and business groups to control school policy. The result of these political maneuvers was democratic elitism. As Joel Spring argues:

> This notion is a winner-takes-all view that believes the democratic process should be organized to give the majority of voters the right to select those who are best able to represent everyone's interests. Since, it is assumed, other voters don't really know what is in their best interests, elections must be structured so that only the best candidates can present themselves to the voters. This view of democracy was the goal of the campaign to 'keep the schools out of politics.'[10]

The bureaucratization of the early twentieth century had profound and lasting effects on the shape of schooling in the United States. First, it made education seem so complex as to be virtually unalterable or at least untouchable by ordinary citizens:

> Viewed from above such a system seemed a rational model of scientific management; viewed from the teachers' perspective it often seemed hermetic and autocratic; viewed from the outside, it often seemed so complex and opaque as to be hard to influence.[11]

Second, school systems seemed to build up an immunity to innovation and change. A bureaucracy thrives on rule-governed behavior with uniform patterns of action. This may suffice for an institution charged with *implementing* policy, but when such a structure dictates the *making* of policy, spontaneity and originality are often stamped out. Finally, all of these changes worked to close off schools from democratic control—or, as argued above, to depoliticize them. What this actually meant was that schools came under the political power of business and social elites who, along with the educational professionals, defined the schools' political agenda. Thus it was necessary to convince "a whole range of fellow professionals that education should be depoliticized, if by that one means not that educators should always agree, but that lay people should be kept at arms' length. This might be called the politics of lay acquiescence."[12] In short, political control shifted from the lay public to the professional. This was done in the name of depoliticalization.

THE GROWTH OF FEDERAL INVOLVEMENT IN EDUCATION

Continued concern over the weakening of the uniquely American idea that local communities should control the local schools has most recently focused on the perceived federal takeover of education. The claim is that local school districts are overrun with rules and regulations from the federal government that severely limit the range of local decision making. While widely believed, this argument is much too simplistic to explain the way in which local communities do or do not control their schools.

Until the 1950s the federal government played a very small role in educational politics. Federal involvement in education had been confined to the granting of land for state colleges and the allocation of modest sums of money to vocational education. The Constitution had implicitly left education to the states, a prerogative that states closely guarded.[13] Attempts to develop a consensus in Congress for general aid to public education had failed repeatedly since being first introduced in 1870 amid fears of a "federal takeover."

In the 1950s the federal government was virtually forced to intervene in the bitter conflict over school desegregation. The federal response to this crisis was clearly based on the constitutional mandate to protect equality of rights for all citizens; it was not intended to revise the structure of the school bureaucracies. While this and subsequent federal interventions were often in opposition to prevailing local or state beliefs, they seldom challenged the bureaucratic structure of school politics. On the contrary, they depoliticized a variety of very hotly contested issues.

Federal education programs, termed "categorical aid," were targeted to specific categories of students or programs. First generation "categoricals," such as NDEA (the National Defense Education Act), were largely aimed at the general student population. Funds were to be spent, within designated programs, as the local school saw fit. This was to change with federal aid programs in the 1960s and 1970s.

The two flagships of categorical aid in the past twenty years have been aid to educationally disadvantaged children in low-income areas and aid to handicapped students. Criteria for need were established, and schools were given specific instructions as to how to meet such needs. Both programs were prompted by a concern with issues of social justice and equality—the kinds of issues we focused on in Part One. But acceptance of the funds invited more detailed federal intervention in the operation of the local school. The large amounts of money associated with these programs were usually incentive enough to encourage the tolerance, if not the willing acceptance, of federal regulation.

Although federal involvement in public education did not significantly change the general direction of the politics of schooling, some specific directions of educational policy were very significantly changed by the new federal role. Its greatest impact was in the area of discrimination. Between the "carrot" of federal funds and the "stick" of court action, local districts were forced to abandon their most blatant practices of exclusion as applied to racial, ethnic, and language minorities; women; and the handicapped. However, all of this occurred within the confines of accelerated bureaucratization, resulting in the depoliticizing of significant social issues.

Perhaps the clearest example of this pattern is seen in the outcomes of PL 94-142. This legislation came about as a result of intense lobbying by the parents of handicapped children who felt the needs of their children were not being met. Parents did not trust local school officials to change their practices and appealed first to the courts. As we have seen, the PARC decision extended the equal protection clause of the Constitution to handicapped children. PL 94-142 attacked discrimination against handicapped students and led gradually to greater integration of such students with the normal population, because it mandated placement of handicapped students in the least restrictive environment possible. As judicial mandates were translated into legislation, the federal government was lobbied by interest groups that still did not trust either state or local officials. Lawmakers relied heavily on court decisions for objectives and procedures. This produced an extensive body of law and regulation with tightly specified procedures, including an Individualized Educational Plan for *each* child covered within the law. In addition, qualifications for professionals in the field were defined and student classifications were carefully spelled out.

The result, whether by design or accident, was the concentration of power in the hands of a relatively few bureaucrats at federal, state, and local levels who made decisions about how to educate a particular segment of the population. A cadre of professionals having specific qualifications then undertook to follow a carefully delineated set of procedures, objectively and consistently, in meeting student needs. The very individuals (parents) who had worked so diligently to change the way the handicapped were treated were now often prevented by professionals from influencing their children's education. This occurred even with legal safeguards protecting parents' rights to consent to options for treatment offered to children. In this way federal intervention followed the pattern of bureaucratization, sometimes replacing a local bureaucracy with a state or federal one, but more often merely transferring power to another group of local professionals.

It is important to remember that much federal intervention was called for by local groups of parents dissatisfied with the inability of the local school bureaucracies to meet the needs of minorities, women, and the handicapped. It is true that the federal government has altered the way in which local schools are run, and there is no denying that local school officials spend a great deal of time meeting requirements to qualify for federal support. Underlying the surface issues, however, is a more important dynamic. Given the historic evolution of school politics, there is no reason to believe that local schools (particularly urban ones) would have proceeded in any other way if left to their own devices. That is to say, the real issue in local school politics is not external intervention in local school affairs but the bureaucratic local governance structures that violate the ideal of local democratic control.

Opposing Bureaucratic Growth

It would not be fair to say that bureaucratization proceeded apace without conflict. Opposition was especially pronounced in rural areas where local leaders were perceived as "far closer and more responsive to the concerns of rural parents than either the policymakers at the state capitol or the business-oriented urban administrators could ever be."[14] Of course, this is not to say local, decentralized authority was always democratic in nature. Class, ethnic, and racial biases existed in small communities, and power was often held by a small group of local elites. The argument, however, was over who should control the education of a community's children, where power should lie, and how much room there should be for community control.

There were also educators in the Progressive Era who fought against the drive to make schools into factory-style bureaucracies. As would be expected, they were the same individuals who opposed the ethos of scientific management. John Dewey was one of the leaders of the fight against the bureaucratization of schools. Dewey, it will be recalled, believed that the ideological function of the school should be to promote the democratic values of equality and participation. To him the top-down management of a "democratic" school was a contradiction in terms. The very organization of the school should be consistent with its social ends. Schools should operate like a small democracy, argued Dewey, for only then will students genuinely understand what it means to live in a democratic society.[15]

Dewey's ideas about school organizations and politics were put into action by Ella Flagg Young, superintendent of schools in Chicago from 1909 to 1915. She worked to open up Chicago's schools to more localized control. In particular, teachers were given greater authority over the daily decisions made in the school. On her retirement from the superintendency she summed up her vision for schools:

In order that teachers may delight in awakening the spirits of children, they must themselves be awake. We have tried to free the teachers. Some day the system will be such that the child and teacher will go to school with ecstatic joy. At home in the evening the child will talk about the things done during the day and will talk with pride. I want to make the schools the great instrument of democracy.[16]

While Young and Dewey focused on the internal workings of schools, George Counts directed his attention to community politics. Most importantly, his *Social Composition of School Boards* (1917) demonstrated clearly the control of school politics by small elite cliques in most cities. His argument was that political reform in general did not genuinely *remove* politics from school business. Rather, it limited *access* to school politics to the monied and social elite.

Teacher unions also developed as a way to counteract the authority of central control. Led by teachers such as Margaret Haley in Chicago, unions were formed to extend teachers' rights to negotiate their wages and working conditions. Even the NEA, which began as a professional association run by school administrators, turned to collective bargaining in the 1960s as a tool to combat growing bureaucratic control of schools. Teacher unions, however, have developed their own bureaucracies and have at times supported as well as opposed the growing centralization of school control.

Yet these protests did not change the direction of school politics. Scientific management and the narrowing of access to participation in educational decision making were made to seem both inevitable and legitimate. The influence of the movement to professionalize and depoliticize schooling can be traced in large part to the fact that it operated "in concert politically, ideologically, and programmatically with the most powerful forces in America, the economic and political elites that were transforming the ways in which society conducted its business in both public and private."[17] While opposition and protest kept organizational alternatives alive, the dominant form of school politics was bureaucratic and professional. We turn now to the school choice movement, the most recent challenge to the bureaucratization of schools.

SCHOOL CHOICE AND LOCAL CONTROL

Throughout this chapter we have stressed two ways in which local control of schooling has been eroded. Reformers in the early twentieth century were able to narrow greatly the possibilities for public activism by eliminating partisan, ward-based school board elections and reducing the number of board seats. Ellwood Cubberley, writing in 1916, argued for school boards to be reduced in size and portrayed the ideal situation as

[A] body small enough to meet around a single table and discuss matters in a simple, direct and business-like manner, under the guidance of a chairman who knows how to handle public business, and take action as a whole, is very desirable. If the board confines itself to its proper work, an hour a week will transact all of the school business which the board should handle. There is no more need for speeches or oratory in the conduct of a school system than there would be in the conduct of a national bank.[18]

Thus, in the movement for public education we see a narrowing of public control over schools. Schools were to be run by a *particular segment* of the public in a community.

The second way in which local control was abridged was through the drive for the professionalization of education. The growth of school bureaucracies that we have been tracing put decisions in the hands of administrators and curriculum experts rather than parents and teachers. Citizen participation in school affairs is limited by the belief that "professionals operating as technical experts in their public service area make decisions that are value free and apolitical."[19]

Finally, there is the abridgement of local control by what David Cohen has called the "private government: that wide variety of private agencies that carry out public business."[20] Among these are lawyers, testing services, textbook publishers, and educational researchers. At issue here is the amount of control these individuals and corporations exercise over public schooling while being politically accountable to no one. For example, what democratically elected official oversees the production of textbooks to be used in a local school district? Local control of texts is lost to what is rapidly becoming, de facto, a national curriculum. The same can be said of businesses such as the Educational Testing Service (ETS), whose Scholastic Aptitude Test (SAT) is often required of high school students for college admission. ETS may produce tests that have little relation to what a local school district hopes to accomplish with its students, but the district must accede to the dictates of the test makers if its students are to go to college.

The issue is whether or not the primary interest of these businesses (to make a profit) can genuinely reflect and serve popular public interests. If not, how are such corporations to be held in check? Their form of political power—the control over schooling's agenda and the belief in apolitical expertise—has done more to limit local control than federal intervention has.

In response and reaction to these trends and growing concern over the quality of public education (see Part Five), parents and educators have mounted two recent challenges to school politics "as usual." The first is the school choice movement, encompassing a wide variety of plans to empower parents and students to choose their own schools. The second is the movement to decentralize educational decision making, thereby empowering local school people to choose the way their school will be run.

Parental Choice

Since the early 1960s there have been calls to allow parents to choose their children's school. The free market, it was imagined, would regulate student and parent choice. Students would supposedly flock to good schools, and attendance would dwindle at poor ones. A form of "voting with your feet" would replace school politics.

The earliest proposal to organize such choice was in the form of vouchers. Under this system every parent would be provided with an educational voucher equivalent in value to what is spent yearly on his or her child's education. The parent could then use this voucher to pay tuition at any school or approved educational agency.[21]

A similar proposal uses tuition tax credits to enhance parental choice. Under this proposal parents may deduct a percentage of the private school tuition they pay from their federal income tax. The goal here is to subsidize choice for parents who might otherwise be unable to afford it. Recently both the Reagan and Bush administrations have endorsed tuition tax credits and parental choice.

A recent book by John E. Chubb and Terry M. Moe entitled *Politics, Markets, and America's Schools* has captured public attention by issuing a renewed call for parental choice.[22] This work is a direct attack on the bureaucratic nature of schooling. The authors argue that good schools are those which have the fewest administrative restraints. They are places where educators are free to develop flexible approaches to teaching and learning.

Based on James Coleman's study of private versus public schools,[23] Chubb and Moe see the superior results of private schooling as a product of the democracy of client power. The good school, they say, has to avoid becoming entangled in bureaucratic rules and regulations so that it can quickly meet the demands of its clients—parents and students. When clients cannot choose, schools become unresponsive, and bureaucracy rather than demand dictates school policies. Thus, Chubb and Moe propose a modified voucher plan in which every certified school would receive a scholarship or payment for each student enrolled.

Plans for choice similar to this are currently in operation. In Minnesota students can choose to attend any public school. In New York City and Milwaukee all high schools are part of an open-enrollment plan whereby students apply to the public high school and are admitted according to established criteria. However, no system has gone so far as to include private schools in their choice plan.[24]

No matter how they are designed, critics charge, none of these plans for overcoming the bureaucratic control of schools solves the problem of choice and equity. For example, Coleman's findings that private schools do better than public schools in educating children (a study upon which Chubb and Moe base their case) have been widely challenged. If we look more closely at his results we find that private school students come from families with higher socioeconomic status (SES) and educational attainment levels than do students in public schools. In fact, with students of the same SES, public schools do just as well as private schools. Critics of choice thus ask, what will prevent the newly "privatized" schools from merely excluding the hard-to-teach children? Will private schools, free from bureaucratic controls, simply exclude those students who are now protected from discrimination on the basis of race, gender, ethnicity, language, or handicapping condition? In fact, this is precisely what happens in cities with open-enrollment plans. Parents wait in lines for hours to get their child a seat in a prestigious school, while other schools are seen as "dumping grounds" for what is left.[25]

The answer to limiting the bureaucratic control of schools most likely includes some element of choice. If an individual cannot opt out of a system, he or she has no choice but to accept the will of those who administer the system. This is especially true of large bureaucratic systems like public schools where the decision makers (federal and state officials, test and textbook publishers, for example) are not subject to direct, democratic control. Choice without adequate concern for equity can only make a mockery of our public commitment to an equal education for all.

Unlike private schools, public schools have a commitment to serve *all* children. That is, they have the obligation to provide an equal educational opportunity to all. Such a commitment is simply not present in private schools. The impact of vouchers and tuition tax credits would, say their critics, undermine the public school commitment to equal educational opportunity. The reason is simple: Funding for public schools would decline, thus undermining their capability to honor their commitment to *all* children. Public education is made possible only by the commitment of large segments of the population to the ideal that democratic government is best preserved by providing, at public expense, the means to educate the citizenry to govern itself. The means themselves are public funds to support schooling accessible to all children. Public funding, controlled by the public, for public enlightenment, to serve the public interest, has been a time-honored formula for public education.

In response to demands for schools to be more politically responsive on the one hand and to provide a more adequate and equitable education on the other, a new movement for reforming school politics has emerged. We turn now to the resurgence of local control.

Local Control

After two decades of teacher strikes, underfunded schools, and growing public distrust, the people of Chicago were ready for a change. Politics as usual were not providing an excellent or equitable school system. Their frustration, displayed in marches on Springfield, the Illinois state capital, resulted in perhaps the most radical political restructuring of schools to date.

In 1989, in return for increased school funding, the Chicago public school system was divided into nearly 600 separate school districts—each school being its own district. Now, schools are governed by a local school council with elected representatives of teachers, parents, and community members. These councils are empowered to spend the school's budget, write the school curriculum, and hire and fire the school principal. It is the most dramatic example of the push for decentralizing school control and moving toward what is often referred to as site-based management.

A similar plan, tied to changes in the funding of public schools, was passed by the Kentucky state legislature in 1990. Under this plan schools are free to develop their own strategies to meet state educational goals. Each school must have its own site-based management council, made up of teachers and parents with decision-making powers.

Like calls for parental choice, the push toward site-based management arises from a concern for educational reform. Frustrated with the ability of large bureaucracies to respond to the needs of students, many parents, teachers, and administrators see site-based management as a way to circumvent overly restrictive policies and regulations. Local school councils are usually empowered to make all the daily decisions about a school as long as they stay within a district- or state-approved budget and curriculum guidelines.

The push for more local control in some ways complements the calls for parental choice. It is only when schools have the ability to develop their own "personalities," to be different and to excel, that parents actually have a choice. As local-control advocates point out, choosing between several schools that all have the same structure and curriculum is no choice at all.

More importantly, advocates of restructuring the political control of schools see such moves as giving *every* school the tools needed for reform and improvement. Rather than allowing a few good schools to attract the most easily educated students, the argument here is to improve every school. While even the most committed advocates of site-based management do not see it as improving every school, they do argue that it at least gives all schools the chance.

Time and the politics of schooling will tell if these proposals for more local control will work. As educators in Chicago are finding out, the established school bureaucracy is very powerful, and on occasion even teachers' unions oppose such restructuring. As we saw with education at the turn of the century, there is still concern that these local approaches will be very parochial in their treatment of curriculum. There are also evolving issues of power in moving to more localized school control. For example, the Chicago and Kentucky plan differ in their allocation of power to parents and teachers; in Chicago parents hold a majority in school councils, while teachers run them in Kentucky.

Regardless of the outcome of these debates one thing seems clear: The credibility of bureaucratic control of schools is exhausted. Once individuals or local groups have the power to choose and/or run schools, it seems highly unlikely that they will voluntarily relinquish that authority. What we do not know yet is how immovable the existing bureaucratic structure is and what shape the alternatives will take.

SCHOOL POLITICS AND PUBLIC CONFIDENCE

In the discussion of local school governance we have seen how the bureaucratic structure of school administration profoundly affects educational politics. Decisions about who should be educated and how that should occur have been narrowly limited to those with claimed expertise or public prestige and standing. This has been the logical consequence of a long trend to depoliticize educational issues. However, the issues are really as political as ever. They still require decisions that affect, for good or ill, the social fabric of each community's life. Yet the decisions are often made by a small minority who are in only a very limited way subject to public control. There is little, if anything, that might be called democratic about an arrangement in which a closed administrative structure has supplanted open decision making. Under these circumstances, issues of fairness, opportunity, and equality are decided by the ideological parameters within which educational bureaucrats operate.

There have been two consequences of this trend. The first can be seen in the continuing roller-coaster ride that public support for (and criticism of) schools has taken. As we will point out in Part Five, the history of public schooling has been fraught with public dissatisfaction and proposals for change. There are a wide variety of causes for this, and it is important to note that all of our major public and private institutions have gone through similar crises of faith.

One persistent concern of the public, of parents in particular, has been the inaccessibility of the schools. Parents often find schools and educators to be unresponsive to their concerns and demands. When children then perform in an unacceptable way (for example, when they do not learn to read, write, or compute, or fail to secure employment upon graduation) the schools bear the brunt of the community's wrath.

Additionally, as schools (rural ones in particular) become more removed from local control through consolidation, the level of fiscal support for them decreases. It is easier to vote against a tax levy for a school in the neighboring county than for one down the street. School professionals, by isolating themselves from the general public in order to increase their power, may be, paradoxically, reducing their power. As competition over the public purse becomes more intense, schools will need a wide range of allies. Those allies will not be coming from a public that feels it is called upon only when funds are needed and has little access to decisions about programs.

The second consequence of the trend to depoliticize educational issues has been the failure to represent the interests of children, the consumers. Since children cannot vote, who will protect their interests? G. Norton Grubb and Marvin Lazerson observe:

> Children suffer an obvious liability within democratic politics: they cannot vote, and many of them cannot even speak on their own behalf. Instead others speak for children in public. In fact, despite a wistful view that children's issues should be above politics and that family issues should remain private, there is no dearth of interest groups and professionals speaking for children.[26]

What this has meant is that children's interests are only represented when they match those of another interest group.

The most central failure of the bureaucratization of school politics is the lack of a voice for students. They are assumed to behave as passive consumers of a product they are not allowed to choose. Even indirect influence, through their parents, is often denied to them. The fragmentation and professionalization of schooling has proceeded apace, often with little regard for the needs of children.

The political agenda for schools, while often claimed to be guided by a concern with "what's best for kids," is actually guided by a concern over what's best for powerful interest groups. These include, for example, business, teachers, and various levels and agencies of government. The schools are seen as an instrument to be used in achieving a goal not necessarily linked to the welfare of children. As Grubb and Lazerson so pointedly put it:

> It has become impossible to justify public spending on schools that are challenging, enjoyable places for children; only the demonstration of future benefits—in cognitive skills, in reduced delinquency and crime, above all in earnings differentials—is regarded as a legitimate argument.[27]

As with many of the issues discussed in this book, the bureaucratization and depoliticizing of school politics are products of general cultural trends. Solutions to the problems presented need to be found in the larger public domain. But this does not absolve public schools of their responsibility to address these challenges in their own right. In particular, the question before public education is how an institution supposedly dedicated to the perpetuation of democracy can be so undemocratic in its own organization. Unless this paradox can be resolved, the claims that educators make about preparing young people to be fully participating citizens in our democracy will continue to sound hollow at best, hypocritical at worst.

NOTES

[1] From *The Shorter Oxford English Dictionary*, Vol. 2 (Oxford: Clarendon, 1933).

[2] Carl J. Friedrich, *Constitutional Government and Democracy*, rev. ed. (New York: Blaise, 1950), p. 44.

[3] Stuart A. Rosenfield and Johnathan P. Sher, "The Urbanization of Rural Schools, 1840–1970," in Johnathan P. Sher, *Education in Rural America* (Boulder, Colo.: Westview, 1977), p. 12.

[4] Michael B. Katz, "From Voluntarism to Bureaucracy in American Education," *Sociology of Education* 44 (Summer 1971), pp. 297–332.

[5] Ibid., p. 313.

[6] Rosenfield and Sher, "Urbanization of Rural Schools," p. 19.

[7] Katz, "Voluntarism to Bureaucracy"; David B. Tyack, *The One Best System* (Cambridge, Mass.: Harvard University Press, 1974); Colin Greer, *The Great School Legend: A Revisionist Interpretation of American Public Education* (New York: Basic Books, 1972).

[8] Michael B. Katz, *Class, Bureaucracy, and the School* (New York: Praeger, 1971), p. 103.

[9] Rosenfield and Sher, "Urbanization of Rural Schools," p. 26.

[10] Joel Spring, "The Structure of Power in an Urban School System: A Study of Cincinnati School Politics," *Curriculum Inquiry* 14, no. 4 (1984), p. 403.

[11] David Tyack and Elisabeth Hansot, *Managers of Virtue: Public School Leadership in America, 1820–1980* (New York: Basic Books, 1982), p. 207.

[12] Ibid., p. 205.

[13] Lawrence Iannacone, "Changing Political Patterns and Governmental Relations," in Robert B. Everhart (ed.), *The Public School Monopoly* (Cambridge, Mass.: Ballinger, 1982), p. 301.

[14] Rosenfield and Sher, "Urbanization of Rural Schools," p. 19.

[15] John Dewey, *The School and Society* (Chicago: University of Chicago Press, 1899) and *Democracy and Education* (New York: Macmillan, 1916).

[16] Ella Flagg Young quoted in John T. McManis, *Ella Flagg Young and a Half-Century of the Chicago Public Schools* (Chicago: A. C. McClurg, 1916).

[17] Tyack and Hansot, *Managers of Virtue,* p. 206.

[18] Ellwood P. Cubberley, *Public School Administration* (Boston: Houghton Mifflin, 1961), p. 92.

[19] L. Harmon Zeigler and M. Kent Jennings, with the assistance of G. Wayne Peak, *Governing American Schools* (North Scituate, Mass.: Duxbury, 1974), p. 301.

[20] David K. Cohen, "Reforming School Politics," *Harvard Educational Review* 48, no. 4 (November 1978), p. 431.

[21] Milton Friedman, *Capitalism and Freedom* (Chicago: University of Chicago Press, 1962).

[22] John E. Chubb and Terry M. Moe, *Politics, Markets, and American Schools* (Washington, D.C.: The Brookings Institution, 1990).

[23] James Coleman and Thomas Hoffer, *Public and Private High Schools: The Impact of Communities* (New York: Basic Books, 1987).

[24] As of this writing a plan in Epsom, New Hampshire, is being developed that would allow taxpayers to deduct from their property taxes tuition paid to private high schools.

[25] See Samuel Freedman, *Small Victories* (New York: Harper & Row, 1990) for a description of one nonelite school's struggle to attract good students.

[26] W. Norton Grubb and Marvin Lazerson, *Broken Promises: How Americans Fail Their Children* (New York: Basic Books, 1982), p. 98.

[27] Ibid., p. 55.

9

Readings on the Politics of Schooling: The Centralization of Control

How did the modern, centralized, bureaucratic, and supposedly depoliticized organization of schools come about? What historical forces gave rise to modern school organization? We begin to explore this question with an 1893 piece by Andrew Draper, the superintendent of Cleveland City Schools. In the article we can see all of the themes that were to emerge in the campaign to depoliticize and centralize school government. Draper argues that universal suffrage leads to weak educational leadership and thus requires the narrowing of the power of school boards, the reduction of their numbers, and the election of all board members as members at large rather than by wards to ensure the election of those who are above politics. We can also hear the request for the bureaucratization of school governance in Draper's call for the specific division of functions and a clear-cut chain of command. Draper's work set the stage for school governance reform over the next five decades.

We can see the ideological and political intent of the proponents of school centralization in the second article, by Ellwood Cubberley. A leading advocate of school centralization, Cubberley was instrumental in founding schools of educational administration. In this selection he argues that the control of schools in large cities ought ideally to be put in the hands of small school boards chosen in citywide elections. By this expedient, less desirable elements could be kept from board service and interference in school business. The local elite would dominate board service and would willingly cede control of the schools to educational bureaucrats. The model Cubberley describes here and advocated in a variety of forms became the dominant way of organizing schools.

The last two selections, by Alan Peshkin and Joel Spring, point out the modern-day consequences of the Draper/Cubberley model. Alan Peshkin's careful look at school governance in a small American town describes the nature of school organization in "Mansfield" and explores how the town gets what it wants. Peshkin points out some of the paradoxes faced by schools in towns like Mansfield. His study presents an important example of how, in a relatively homogeneous community, political power is structured around schooling. Further, it makes apparent how the political structure legitimizes a particular ideological role for schools.

The politics of large city schools in Cincinnati, Ohio, is the focus of the next selection, by Joel Spring. Spring traces the history of the Cincinnati School Committee, a private group of businessmen who worked to control the makeup of the city school board. We can see in this process all of the tendencies identified in the writings of Draper and Cubberley. Spring calls the type of school governance found in Cincinnati "democratic centralism"; his term is useful for explaining school politics in other cities also. Indeed, the process of electing a school board to govern the schools is democratic in that it is open to all eligible voters and candidates. However, due to the political structures established at the turn of the century, access to a position on the ballot is, in fact, centrally controlled.

In considering the politics of schooling as displayed in these readings, the reader may find the following questions helpful: What was behind the claim that the professional control of schooling would lead to the depoliticizing of school governance? Who stood to gain from the so-called depoliticizing of schooling? What was the political agenda of those behind school centralization, that is, what was their political intent?

Andrew S. Draper

PLANS OF ORGANIZATION FOR SCHOOL PURPOSES IN LARGE CITIES

Of all the unsolved and troublesome problems in government which present themselves to the minds of thoughtful Americans, the most prominent is that of municipal administration in large cities. The news editors, the magazine writers, the good people in the literary and scientific clubs, the great body of honest voters throughout the country, discuss it perennially, and then vote so ineffectually that the worst elements of society control the governments of the great cities of the republic. It is a suggestive fact that the only real progress in the direction of municipal reform has been made through the imposition of limitations upon the common suffrage, through taking away authority from the representatives of the people, through the centralization of power and responsibility in fewer individuals, and through statutory requirements and prohibitions upon public officers. It will continue to be so. Unintelligent voting is not wholly responsible, nor is intelligent voting the cure, for all maladministration in municipal affairs. If honest voters will vote only for proved men for city officers,

From Andrew S. Draper, "Plans of Organization for School Purposes in Large Cities," *Educational Review* (June 1983), pp. 1–4, 13–16.

if in all that pertains to municipal business they will be guided by business principles rather than by political preferences, the problem of municipal reform will become solvable; but even then the larger the city the greater will be the necessity for statutory plans of organization which centralize responsibility and direct and limit official action.

As cities increase in population, and even out of proportion to the advance in population, the volume of municipal business enlarges, the magnitude of the transactions becomes more and more appalling, the subjects presented more and more involved, the temptations become greater, and dishonesty more and more difficult of detection. As it becomes more and more imperative to have strong men, experienced men, and honest men to manage the business of great cities, it also becomes, for obvious reasons, more and more difficult to secure them upon the basis of an unrestricted suffrage. It is therefore meet that the best thought of the country should be turned, as it is turned, to plans for the government of cities.

And what is true of municipal business in great and growing cities is true in still larger degree of their school business. The proper education of the children is infinitely more important than even the management of the street, fire, and police departments of such cities. And in view of the marked extent to which our people are congregating in cities, it is well for us to remember that if the public school system is to hold the confidence and esteem of the country it must hold the confidence and esteem of the cities, and to do that it must bear fruits worthy of confidence and esteem.

The most important public work of any community is providing and managing the means of popular education. The people may neglect municipal business, and the penalty is the plundering of the city treasury. In time, mismanagement and thievery become intolerable, there is a municipal revolution, the house is cleaned, a boodler or two indicted, the loss struck off, the plan of city government remodeled, and quiet and comparative indifference once more resume their sway. The people may neglect the schools and permit them to be despoiled by thievery or degraded by place hunters, and the penalty is not only a plundered treasury, but a low and almost irredeemable tone of moral and intellectual life. Defective municipal organization and maladministration of municipal business can benefit only a very small number of individuals, while they affect the pockets and arouse the indignation of the multitude. Defective school organization and maladministration in school affairs are not only more far reaching and deadening in their influences but more subtle and insidious in their manifestation. School boards lay larger claims to character, fitness, and disinterestedness than aldermanic boards, and, as a rule, they are far more respectable and responsible. Occasionally they loot the treasury, but more commonly they do what is not technically so criminal, but what is in effect really worse. The circumstances press them hard, the wrongs they do or suffer to be done are not so deep, their friends and not themselves get the benefit, they fail to appreciate, or they deceive themselves about the harm that flows from their acts. The chief element in school expenditures is the wages of the teachers. In the entire country this one item amounts to $88,000,000 annually. Of course the people want to share in the distribution of this fund, and the less competent they are for the service, the more intense is the desire for a share in the fund. Incompetency creeps in, and once in can scarcely be put out. The people do not understand what the incompetency of the teacher means, or how it burdens school work; and, competent or incompetent, the teacher has a large hold upon popular sympathy. The result is deadening and disastrous. Under such circumstances, the standard of popular education becomes low, and the intellectual life of the people of the city lacks purity, virility, and power. Little is demanded of, and not much given by, the schools. There is little strength and no growth. The more intelligent will not patronize them, and the whole structure of public education is weakened and falls into disrepute. Even those who have been in them become indifferent to them. And when the people, the body of the citizenship of the country, high and low, rich and poor alike, are without affection for, or come to lack confidence in, the public schools, the circumstances will be hard and the outlook very much obscured.

So here is the pressing question of the day in public school work, one which goes to the very life of the system. It will be solved, *because* it is one which goes to the life of the system. . . .

In the meantime, it is incumbent on us to understand the general principles upon which the good government of the schools in great cities rests, and to declare the lines upon which reforms must proceed.

In my opinion these are the following:

First. The elimination of politics from the selection of school boards. Dr. Philbrick rightly characterized this point as "the supreme educational problem," but we shall not cease hoping that it may be solved. Special school elections and appointments by public officers do not offer a complete solution, but are certainly in that direction. Much depends upon the state of public sentiment, which should at least demand the complete elimination of politics from school administration, if not from school elections; and no opportunity for asserting the principle should be lost.

Second. Small school boards with members representing the whole city and not wards or districts.

Third. The complete separation of school administration from municipal business. This is imperative. Laws which put the schools at the mercy of a board of aldermen are unsound in principle and deplorable in their operation. Even the determination of the sum to be levied for school purposes should not be left to a common council, which, by legislation and by usage, has come to represent, and has become representative of, interests not in harmony or sympathy with school administration. If there is a finance board or tax commission which receives estimates from all sources and finally determines the amount to be levied, it is not so objectionable that the school estimates should go with the others to this board, for such a board may be assumed to be independent of all special interests and representative of the best sentiment of the whole city. But the only sound rule is that school administration shall be entirely independent of municipal business. The two do not rest upon the same foundation; the power which manages each proceeds from entirely different sources, and the object and purposes of each have nothing in common.

Fourth. The school system of a great city must not only have an autonomy of its own, but its administration must be departmentalized. Material affairs should be entirely separated from the work of instruction. Officers must have ample authority, be properly paid for services of high grade, and held to personal accountability. If there is cause for complaint, there should be a place to make the complaint, and an officer who can neither shift nor shirk responsibility. The Cleveland plan, which creates a salaried officer directly responsible to the people for the proper care of all their school property, and for the proper management of all the business affairs of their school system, is, in that regard at least, very nearly ideal. It is economical and businesslike. It will secure a responsible man, and it will insure the alert and careful administration of business interests. All subordinates and employees are amenable to him and to him alone. The man will not only have responsibility, but he will have independence and self-respect as well. On the other hand, the superintendent of instruction should not be burdened with any of the material interests of a great school system or with keeping records or accounts relating thereto; but he should be chosen with special reference to the work of instruction, and in that department should likewise have full authority, be given ample assistance, and charged with complete responsibility. Such responsibility is well-nigh overwhelming. To secure a teaching force numbering hundreds or thousands of individuals, all of whom are capable and have individuality and teaching power, and so to organize them as to get the best results from each, and then to lead and train them so that there will be harmony, enthusiasm, growth, and continually increasing power, is a great undertaking; but under proper conditions it is not altogether impossible of accomplishment. Where teachers are appointed by school boards or committees or members thereof, or by ward or district trustees, its accomplishment is impossible. If superintendents are only allowed to nominate, and nominations are to be confirmed by a board or committee, other elements than the fitness of the candidate will of necessity be taken into consideration. If a superintendent cannot dismiss teachers, or change them about, as exigencies may require and experience suggest, without being obliged to advise with and secure the approval of boards or members who are looking for votes, or who are anxious to please friends, and who have no appreciation of the importance and delicacy of the questions involved, he will not do it at all. Every teacher knows that this is so, and every teacher knows why it is so. Every teacher knows also that there is no danger of his doing too much in the right direction. This is no reflection upon superintendents. To expect otherwise would be to expect more than that of which human nature is capable. Comparatively few men have all the elements which adapt them to such service, and those who have can accomplish their undertaking only when given a position of such power, responsibility, and dignity, as will give them the undisputed right of leadership, and will command the respect of their associates and subordinates and of the body of the people.

These are the lines, as it seems to me, upon which reforms in the administration of the school systems of great cities must proceed. Such reforms should proceed more easily when we remember that schools do not belong wholly and alone to the communities in which they exist, but are parts of a State system which derives its existence and character from State legislation; and that the whole subject is one which claims the attention of all the reformers and the foremost statesmen of the country: for it is one which goes not alone to the material well-being, but to the intellectual life and the public security of the city, the State, and the republic.

ELLWOOD P. CUBBERLEY

THE ORGANIZATION OF SCHOOL BOARDS

TENDENCIES IN RECENT REORGANIZATIONS

As was pointed out in the previous chapter, the tendency has been, with the evolution of the professional superintendent and the delegation of administrative functions to experts, to reduce the size of the board, to curtail both the number and the work of the board committees, and to eliminate all *ex-officio* members from the board. By this means the board is reduced to a small and businesslike body, and transformed into a real board for school control.

Within recent years many of our city boards of education have been so reduced in size and the number of their standing committees decreased, with a view to securing a better educational organization for the administration of the schools. Sometimes these changes have come as a result of the people of the city asking for an amended charter or a special law. Most of the earlier reorganizations came about in this way. More recently the tendency has been for the State, by means of a general state law, and without waiting for the cities to act voluntarily, to compel a reduction in size and a change in the basis of selection of board members for all cities of the State, doing so in the interests of a more efficient administration of the schools in the city school districts. Some of the changes produced by these recent general laws have been large, and thoroughly fundamental in nature. Some of these recent laws have even limited and specified the number of standing committees which may be created, and, most important of all, have clearly stated that certain executive functions must be delegated to specified executive officers to be appointed by the board.

As a result of the discussion, legislation, and experience of the past two decades in city school organization and administration, it may be said that the best type of board for educational control in our American cities, large or small, now seems to be a small board—five or seven members being the most desirable numbers—with no *ex-officio* members;[1] elected from the city at large, or, perhaps, appointed by the mayor, or commission for the city; elected for relatively long terms, with only a small percentage elected or appointed at any one time, and with not too long continuous service for any one member; few or no standing committees; and with a clear differentiation stated in the law between the

From Ellwood P. Cubberley, "The Organization of School Boards," *Public School Administration* (Boston: Houghton Mifflin, 1916), pp. 87–95.

legislative functions of the board and the executive functions of the experts of the department. The reasons for the impositions of such standards in the organization of boards of school control for city school districts are about as follows:—

SIZE OF SCHOOL BOARDS

The experience of the past half-century, in city school administration in this country, is clearly and unmistakably that a small board is in every way a more effective and a more efficient body than a large one. It of course should not be too small, as very small boards tend too much to become one-man affairs, and the gain that comes from having a number of heads consider and discuss a proposition is lost. On the other hand, a few men can always work more economically and more efficiently than can a large body. The unquestioned experience of our American cities, having large school boards or city councils, has been that the real thinking and planning and executing is usually done by from half a dozen to half a score of men within the group. The inevitable result is cliques, factions, and wheels within wheels in the administration. A board of five or seven is now generally regarded as the most desirable size for all but perhaps the very largest cities, and with from nine to fifteen proposed for such large cities as Chicago and New York. (See Figure 1.)

The small board is far less talkative, and hence handles the public business much more expeditiously; it is less able to shift responsibility for its actions; it cannot so easily divide itself up into small committees, and works more efficiently and intelligently as a committee of the whole; and it cannot and will not apportion out the patronage in the way that a large ward board can and will do. A large board is unwieldy and incoherent; it seldom transacts the public business quietly and quickly, it tends too frequent to become a public debating society, where small or politically inclined men talk loud and long and "play to the galleries" and to the press; while personal and party politics, and sometimes lodge and church politics, not infrequently determine its actions. It is almost always divided into factions, between whom there is continual strife and rivalry, and important matters are usually caucused in advance and "put through" by the majority at that moment in control. A reduction in size to a body small enough to meet around a single table and discuss matters in a simple, direct, and business-like manner, under the guidance of a chairman who knows how to handle public business, and then take action as a whole, is very desirable.[2]

BASIS OF SELECTION; WARDS *VS.* AT LARGE

The election of school-board members from city wards or districts is a survival of the early district system of school control, and the evidence everywhere is against the continuance of this practice. No surer means for perpetuating the personal and political evils in school control can be devised than the continuance of the ward system of representation. In cities where part of the school board has

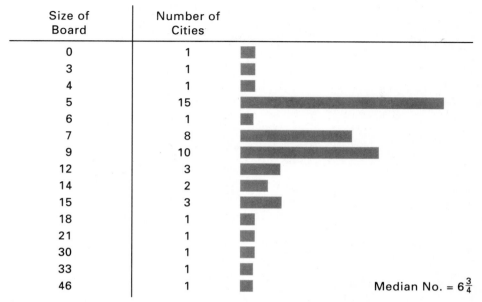

Size of Board	Number of Cities	
0	1	
3	1	
4	1	
5	15	
6	1	
7	8	
9	10	
12	3	
14	2	
15	3	
18	1	
21	1	
30	1	
33	1	
46	1	Median No. $= 6\frac{3}{4}$

FIGURE 1 Frequency of size of school board (as found in the fifty cities in the United States which, in 1910, had a population of over 100,000 inhabitants).

been elected at large and part by wards, those elected at large have almost invariably proved to be the better members. In cities where the complete change from a ward board to a smaller one elected at large has been made, the change has practically always resulted in the production of a better board from among the body of the electorate, and a better handling of the business of public education. The larger the city the more important that the ward system be abandoned.

The tendency of people of the same class or degree of success in life to settle in the same part of the city is [a] matter of common knowledge. The successful and the unsuccessful; the ones who like strong and good government, and the ones who like weak and poor government; the temperate and the intemperate elements; and the business and the laboring classes;—these commonly are found in different parts of a city. Wards come to be known as "the fighting third," "the red-light fourth," "the socialistic ninth," or "the high-brow fifth"; and the characteristics of these wards[3] are frequently evident in the composition of the board of education. The young and ambitious politician not infrequently moves into an "open ward" in the hope of securing an election there, and, when elected, makes the school board a stepping-stone to the council and higher political preferment. Not infrequently the school janitor, appointed in the first place as a reward for political services, becomes the ward boss in turn and dictates the nomination of the school-board members. (See Figure 2.)

One of the important results of the change from ward representation to election from the city at large, in any city of average decency and intelligence, is

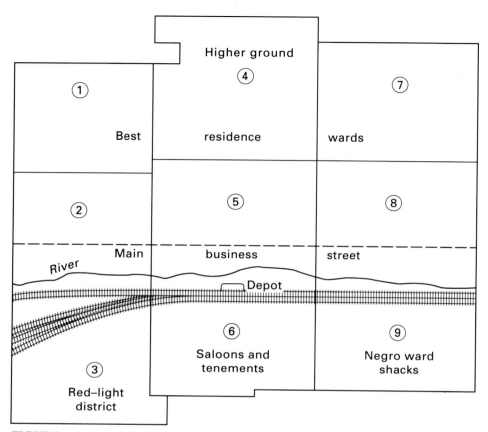

FIGURE 2 A city of nine wards: The three wards south of the river contain the poorer classes of the city. These live in the cheap homes south of the railway tracks. Wards 1, 4, and 7 lie on higher ground, and the better residences of the city are in these three wards and in the upper edge of Wards 2, 5, and 8. The business district of the city parallels the river, and lies in Wards 2, 5, and 8.

Wards 1, 4, and 7 always select good members for the Board of Education, while Wards 3, 6, and 9 practically always select poor members. The fight then hinges around Wards 2, 5, and 8, the better element of the city being compelled to watch these wards carefully, so as to select good men from at least two of these three wards.

that the inevitable representation from these "poor wards" is eliminated, and the board as a whole comes to partake of the best characteristics of the city as a whole. The members represent the city as a whole, instead of wards; they become interested in the school system as a unit, instead of parts of it; and the continual strife in boards caused by men who represent a constituency instead of a cause, and whose efforts are constantly directed toward securing funds, teachers, and janitors for the school or schools "they represent," is largely eliminated.

Under the ward system of representation, too, it is matter of common knowledge that men are nominated and elected from wards who could not be nominated, much less elected, from the city at large. Better men are almost always attracted to the educational service when election from the city at large, and for relatively long terms, is substituted for ward representation. A man of affairs, really competent to handle the educational business of a city, often cannot be induced to accept membership on a large ward board because of the great waste of time and the small results attained. If the management of a school system is political, or personal, or petty, the best men tend to keep off the school board, which in turn accentuates the trouble and brings a constantly poorer quality of men to the service.

NOTES

[1] It used to be a somewhat common practice to include the mayor, *ex officio*, as a member of the board of education, but the plan has almost invariably given poor results, and has been abandoned generally. The temptation to the mayor, who is primarily a political personality, is always strong to play politics at the expense of the schools, and the elimination of this official is a necessary step in the elimination of politics from the administration of public education.

[2] With such a board, long evening meetings are unnecessary. If the board confines itself to its proper work, an hour a week will transact all of the school business which the board should handle. There is no more need for speeches or oratory in the conduct of a school system than there would be in the conduct of a national bank.

[3] The writer once knew a ward board composed of one physician, two business men, one good lawyer, two politician lawyers with few clients, one bookkeeper, one blacksmith, one saloonkeeper, one buyer of hides and tallow, one butcher, one druggist, one worker in a lumber yard, one retired army officer, one man of no occupation except general opposition to any form of organized government, and one woman. The result was a board divided into factions, members from the better wards having but little influence with those from the poorer wards. The constant danger was that the less intelligent and less progressive element would wear out the better element and come to rule the board. Important measures had to be caucused in advance of proposing them to see that a majority was a probability. In appointing the committees, the chairman had to choose between having half the board do all of the important work, or of placing men on committees for which they were wholly unfitted.

ALAN PESHKIN

WHOM SHALL THE SCHOOLS SERVE?

Local control of their schools provides American communities with a substantial measure of freedom to teach what they wish. And who will gainsay the right of

From Alan Peshkin, "Whom Shall the Schools Serve? Some Dilemmas of Local Control in a Rural School District," *Curriculum Inquiry* 6, no. 3 (1977), pp. 181–183, 187–204. Copyright © 1977, John Wiley & Sons, Inc. Reprinted by permission.

local communities to determine how and by whom their children will be educated?

Yet, adherence to the principle of local control can result in controversial educational policy. Through conformity to the will of the local community, schools may teach bigotry in place of tolerance or contempt for learning in place of the love of it. And who then is well served? The community? The students? The nation? Consider the case of Mansfield.[1]

Corn and soybean fields make an island of Mansfield village. Here, in the heart of America's agricultural Midwest, live 1,500 people. Few of them are farmers. Some run stores, other do maintenance for the village, still others teach school. Because there is no local industry, the majority of working villagers commute to the factories of Stanton, twenty-five miles away.

Around the town, in an area of seventy-five square miles, live another 800 people—mostly farmers and their families. In common with the villagers they patronize the stores, attend the churches, and pay their taxes in Mansfield. Some exercise considerable influence, for the farm families of the community are also its residents of longest standing and hold offices in local organizations. Hence they bring their own concerns to bear on the lives of the villagers.

Together the residents of the village and of the countryside make up the Mansfield community. It is a modestly prosperous one; the median family income in 1970 was $9,500, which exceeded somewhat the median for the state as a whole. At the same time, only 5.6 percent of the residents had an annual income of less than $3,000, the poverty level designated for the 1970 census. Mansfield is also a homogeneous community. None of its residents is black, and nearly every one was born in the United States to English-speaking parents.

Like American communities of all sorts, Mansfield supports a school system. There are two schools in the district: an elementary school consisting of kindergarten through sixth grade, and a secondary school—Mansfield High School—consisting of seventh through twelfth grade. In 1973, the system en-rolled 500 students and employed thirty-five teachers.[2]

These were the characteristics of Mansfield and its school that had drawn my interest. Initially I had gone there to investigate the relation between school and community in a rural setting.[3] The study of rural schooling has been relatively neglected in recent decades; and yet, with the continued growth of urban society, small-town life has increasingly become an endangered species. Of late, small towns located near places of work have attracted migrants from the cities, refugees from the discontents of urban life. Because Mansfield has not had the housing to accommodate many urban migrants, it has retained the features of rural life that I had come to study.

For two years, then, and with the help of six research assistants, I directed fieldwork in Mansfield, studying the high school and the community that supports it. We began with the school, interviewing teachers, school board members, and students; attending classes, school-sponsored events, teachers' meetings, school board meetings; reading through school documents of all sorts.[4] From the school we turned to the community, interviewing the mayor and the village board, whose meetings we also attended. We took part in local church and organizational activities. I myself lived in Mansfield during most of the second year of fieldwork. Like any Mansfielder I shopped, paid my bills, maintained a bank account, and frequented the post office there. Yet, though I lived and worked in the community steadily for a year, though I associated daily with Mansfielders, they for their part continued to regard me as a visitor. I remained the professor who had come to conduct research. Perhaps it was because they knew I did not plan to stay, perhaps because I had not brought my family. In any case, I was never viewed as a member of the community, not even as a sometime resident. For Mansfielders maintain a vital and exclusive *sense of community*, and that sense may be crucial to maintaining the community itself.[5] Hence my study, which had started as a general inquiry into the relation between Mansfield and its high school, came to center on the role of the high school in maintaining Mansfield's sense of community and, conversely, on the interest of the community in maintaining Mansfield High School.

• • •

THE SUPERINTENDENT AND THE SCHOOL BOARD

Superintendent Tate welcomed me and my project to Mansfield, promised and delivered his full cooperation, and stipulated only that we do nothing to disturb the routine of the school. This condition on our work embodied a concern of considerable importance to him and to the school board. A substantial part of a teacher's esteem depends on his capacity to maintain order. The school leadership recently was pleased to learn of the resignation of an otherwise good teacher who "couldn't cut the mustard with the kids" (keep them quiet).

At the time my study began, Tate had been at Mansfield High School for twenty-one years, five as coach and industrial arts teacher and sixteen as superintendent. Though not of local origin, nor in fact of rural background, he was most comfortable with country life. He had been content to confine his career to Mansfield despite job offers from larger school systems. In their turn, Mansfielders and the school board were very pleased with him; he became a person of consequence in community life and an accepted agent of community values in his capacity as educational leader. The school board, guardians of the community, trusted him on matters of fact and judgment, secure in the knowledge that he served their interests.

The seven-member board was presided over by a Mansfield-born farmer. Five of the other six members also were native Mansfielders and farmers, notwithstanding that most school district residents work in factories and live in town. In fact, over the twenty years this school board has existed, the president has always been a farmer and at least five of seven members have been Mansfield-born farmers.[6] Because school board elections generally inspire a good turnout—about two hundred of a possible seven hundred eligible voters— the "right" candidates continue to get elected. (The right candidates are those without the kind of "axe to grind" that might disturb the status quo.) The credentials of the newest board member were his status as a native and the well-known fact that he loved Mansfield and had a deep regard for its traditions. He replaced a man of demonstrated skill, a six-year veteran on the board who had lived in Mansfield only ten years.

One year after my study began, Superintendent Tate died. This misfortune required the school board to undertake a task they had long dreaded—selecting a new superintendent. They assembled in special session one hot August week to interview five candidates. Afterward, as they sat together to make a choice, their desiderata emerged.

"Should we talk about Hagedorn to see why we don't want him?"

"Yes, let's get the feeling of the board on him. I believe we have better men. Not quality-wise, though. He could handle the job and the P. R. [Public Relations]. I don't think he's the type we're looking for."

"I hate to say it, but his physical appearance is against him. You need to call a spade a spade."

"He's not stable like some of the others."

"I'm afraid he'd be the butt of behind-the-back jokes."

"He's carrying far too much weight. That's a strain on the heart."

"He was tired. A man that size gets physically tired. We shouldn't kid ourselves. Image is very important. That size is against him."

"The next one is Dargan."

"I was impressed, but I feel he is too big for our town and school. His ideas are for the city, for bigger schools. We're not ready for all that."

"I felt he would probably be anxious to start a lot of things I don't know if we're ready for. He's definitely for a nongraded system. He said he'd start slow but he wanted it pretty bad. Knocking down walls scares you just a bit."

"I was impressed. But then we had more fellows in. We learned more about this nongraded idea. He would be a pusher, I'm sure."

"He had too many ideas to start off with. You need to see what a school has before jumping in."

"I thought he might be a little slow with discipline problems."

"I saw dollar signs clicking around in my head when he talked. He may be too intelligent for this community. He may talk over the heads of the community.

"Another thing. He was emphatic about four weeks' vacation."

Salary-wise he asked for the most."

"Well, this Dargan, he said he wanted to come to a small community. I think he may want to bring too many ideas from the city with him. He may be more than we want."

"What did you like about Morgan? These next three are a hard pick."

"He gave a nice impression here, I believe, of getting along with the public and the kids. This impressed me more than anything."

"To me he talked generalities."

"He had a tremendous speaking voice. He's young."

"His voice got very nasal at the end when he got relaxed."

"He wouldn't stay."

"He's on his way up."

"I believe he'd be a forceful individual."

"Take this other man, Rogers. I had a feeling about him. He said, 'If you hired me and I accepted it . . .' I don't think he's too anxious for the job."

"I can see why he was offered a job selling real estate. He's got the voice. He'd have your name on the line. I'm inclined to believe he'd talk himself out of most situations. Getting down to brass tacks, he spoke in generalities. He admitted he didn't know too much about new things in education. We need more specific answers."

"More or less this leaves us with Reynolds."

"He's the man to put on top."

"I'd hate to pick any one of the top three over the others."

"Both Reynolds and Rogers said that they have no hours. They work by the job. Reynolds worked his way through college."

"He was on ground floor as far as salary goes."

"And he's country."

After rejecting candidates for adverse physical appearance and for holding city and big-school ideas, they selected Reynolds, who worked hard like a farmer, would settle for a "reasonable" salary, and was "country"—a designation that had never before been mentioned as a criterion for selecting their new superintendent, or anything else, for that matter. Perhaps it should have been self-evident that no one could be chosen superintendent of schools in Mansfield who did not appear "country," the board's shorthand description of a suitable candidate for their rural-dominated, traditionally oriented school district.

TEACHERS AND THE SCHOOL EXPERIENCE

The central fact characterizing Mansfield's teachers is their small-town origin. Of the eighteen teachers in the high school, six had fathers who farmed; but ten were born and raised in or around towns of under 2,000, three in towns of under 4,500, four in towns of under 15,000, and only one in a city of 800,000. Indeed, the teachers not only grew up in small towns; they generally studied at the smallest of the state universities, Central State,[7] and after graduation taught in schools very much like the ones they themselves had attended. From all indications they are at home in Mansfield; when asked about their ideal place to live, 75 percent indicated a preference for towns of 4,500 or less.

To get some idea of teacher views about education, we asked what changes they would like to see made. They generally confined their responses to the redress of particular grievances. A few wanted a new building; others, a chance to teach only their special subject, better discipline, more vocational courses, or less money spent on athletic programs. Most frequently they wished to eliminate poor teachers, the "dead weight" who had been in the system for too many years. There were no grand schemes, no innovations proposed by the group, 81.7 percent of whom had agreed that one of the most important things in Mansfield was its good school system.

The apparent comfort of the teachers with the education they provide may be attributed to their own upbringing in communities much like Mansfield and their generally expressed satisfaction with small-town life. The reasons for this satisfaction strikingly accord with those offered by Mansfield's adults and students—the security, absence of anonymity, open doors, friendliness, and uncrowded feeling of living in a slower-paced atmosphere. "We'll be here when we die, I'm sure," said Mrs. Adams, a native Mansfielder, "I can't imagine living anywhere else," concluded Mr. Shirley, an adopted Mansfielder.

Some teachers held modest expectations about what the school could accomplish but acknowledged their hope of reaching at least one or two students in a serious way. None was truly doubtful about his own and his colleagues' opportunity to do something of value. Mr. Thompson, the biology teacher, noted that teachers tended to maintain a close relationship with students and parents. Because of the intimacy of this small, stable community, some teachers admitted to being less than objective in their judgment of students. One suggested that Mansfield teachers are "more lenient because we're more familiar with [students] and their families," meaning by this that the teachers are "not as strict academically as maybe we should be." Yet Mansfield would hardly have it otherwise. "The schools are just about what the people want," observed Mr. Shirley. "They do what they are expected to do." In this Mr. Cahill concurred. "The high school does a better than average job of socializing the students for this community."

On entering high school, the children of Mansfield's farmers and factory workers are given a handbook. Like so many other documents cluttering the drawers of Mansfield and other schools, this one contains a mixture of specific statements to guide the behavior of the students (for example, regulations that relate to the prom, detentions, driving one's car at noon) and more general, usually unread, statements. The handbook's list of "General Behavior Principles for Students" suggests how Mansfield's educational leaders believe students should behave. The attention of students is directed to:

- Regular attendance
- Punctuality in all matters
- Careful preparation and learning of assignments
- Orderly classrooms
- Courtesy
- A relaxed but business-like atmosphere
- Acceptance of the authority of teachers
- Pride and concern for school property
- Personal appearance
- The desire to be a contributing member of society

These are norms that reflect an emphasis on social control. Clearly, the ideal student is one who would make life easy for teachers and administrators.

A further clue to the nature of a school is provided by its objectives. To be sure, statements of objectives often originate in requests from outsiders (the state visiting team, for example) and serve only ceremonial purposes. Teacher and student conduct in class tells more about the academic experience than do statements of objectives, but the latter may be valuable for suggesting not so much what really happens in schools as what ideals undergird the behavior of its educators.

The most recent occasion to prepare objectives was provided in 1972 by the State Office of Instruction's request that each school system prepare a document called "Goals for Tomorrow." Excerpts from the document that was submitted to the state are included below.

A. The Instructional Program.
   Provide for such quality education that should help every student acquire to the fullest extent possible for his mastery of a good basic education and to open further channels of study to him as an adult . . .
B. Suggested Student Goals (Desired Learner Outcomes)
   I. Develop growth in their ability to think rationally, to express their thoughts clearly, and to read and listen with understanding.
   II. Develop salable skills . . .
   III. Develop the ability and desire to understand the rights and duties of a citizen of a democratic society, and to be diligent and competent in their performance of their obligations as members of the community and citizens of the state, the nation, and the world.
   IV. Acquire good health habits . . .
   V. Develop a better understanding of the methods of science and man's environment . . .
   VI. Develop areas of concern that include responsibility, honesty, self-respect, justice, courtesy and kindness, discrimination between right and wrong, respect for individual differences, obedience to parents, and respect for authority and laws. [An earlier version of this goal included "loyalty, patriotism, and nondiscriminatory behavior," but was omitted from the final statement submitted to the state office.]
   VII. Provide opportunities to develop their capacities to appreciate beauty in literature, art, music, and nature.
   VIII. To provide opportunities to learn to use leisure time well and budget it wisely . . .

When we compare Mansfield's "Goals for Tomorrow" with those prepared by other schools from neighboring districts of approximately the same size, we find many similarities. A number of broad categories dominate the goals of all the school districts: (1) basic skills, (2) vocational training, (3) consumerism, (4) leisure time, (5) democratic citizenship, (6) health, (7) the arts, (8) thinking ability, (9) family, and (10) personal qualities. In addition to these shared categories, however, are several which Mansfield omits from its lists, as either oversights or ideas to which Mansfield is not committed. For example, a number of school systems, usually somewhat larger ones, mentioned that they planned to enable each student to: "develop . . . the ability to identify problems and to apply clear, critical, reflective, and creative thinking . . . to reach their solutions"; "develop an awareness of the history, influence, and interrelationships of all cultures"; "be . . . acquainted with his rights and responsibilities . . . as a member of a pluralistic society"; develop intellectual curiosity and eagerness for lifelong learning." My impression is that in Mansfield these latter goals are not so much disapproved as they are unimportant; they do not occupy the foreground of concern.

In contrast, the provision of "a good basic education" is of major concern. It is mentioned under the Instruction Program and voiced frequently by Mansfield's school board members and administrators. It is one of three fundamental points that bear on the academic aspects of the school. The second is the development of "salable skills," listed under Suggested Student Goals, and the third is the provision of courses that will enable students to attend postsecondary institutions.

The emphasis on the "basics" is not readily observable in the classroom. It is used more as a slogan, a conventional way of affirming that the board and administration do not concern themselves with lofty intellectual goals, that they do not have pretensions of sophistication, and that they mean to keep down the costs of schooling—for money spent on the basics is by definition money well spent. Mansfield's investment in the development of "salable skills" is evident in the variety of courses offered in home economics, business education, industrial arts, vocational agriculture, and auto mechanics.

Notwithstanding the curriculum-oriented meetings held in preparation for state and North Central Association visitations, Mansfield teachers neither plan nor coordinate the value orientation of their instruction. To be sure, they attempt cooperative planning when a subject has a sequential basis—English, for example. But there is no party line, no deliberate effort to endorse a particular view of religion, politics, patriotism, or community. Perhaps no such efforts are necessary if the process of selecting teachers and administrators has already ensured their suitability for service in Mansfield. In any case, the classroom behavior of Mansfield's teachers rather consistently displays the value orientation of the school board and the community. But other sorts of aims that go unstated in Mansfield's official documents also go unpursued in its classrooms. There, the discourse, while often provocative, is not distinctly critical or reflective. Examinations tend to focus on recall. And traditional American attitudes toward God, country, and self-reliance are manifest and unchallenged, as we see in many different classes.

U.S. History

For most of the lesson, two students took the part of female slaves, one owned by a cruel master and the other by a kind master. Following this presentation the class discussed blacks in contemporary America, a vocal group taking the position of "ship 'em back to Africa," angered by what they believed to be the especially favorable treatment blacks get in jobs, sports, and education.

STUDENT A: Okay, this is actual fact and I can prove it. There was this basketball player, he was colored, and in high school at Bradlow High. He made a D average and he tried to pass an examination to get into college. He couldn't make it at State so he goes to a school where they've got a lot of blacks and he makes it, makes it all the way through school. He had a D average in high school taking simple courses like how to cook or something. He hooked up with a junior college in Detroit that was all black; then he went to a major college and made it all the way through. Now he's making big money. Now do you think that's fair? Now there might be white kids, but they're not going to get the same opportunity.

TEACHER: Don't you think that a natural-born basketball player that was white wouldn't get the breaks too?

STUDENT A: No.

STUDENT B: I know a few that haven't and are just as good.

STUDENT C: Yeah, you take all the major sports and you see the ratio of white to colored in those. The coloreds outnumber 'em.

STUDENT D: Yeah, they're better.

TEACHER: Okay, this is the idea of the pendulum swinging back and forth that we were talking about yesterday at the end of the hour. Think about this just a little bit. No matter what we're talking about—it could be anything, campus riots or whatever—usually it's like a pendulum. Things are usually far off to one end, then they swing far off to the other end before they eventually get back to the middle. Now I'm not saying that everything is exactly fair that happens to blacks today, but think about the pendulum. One time it was way over here—unfair, today maybe it's over here, being a little bit unfair the other way. Maybe tomorrow it will be back here in the middle.

STUDENT A: I doubt it.

English

This sophomore English class has been discussing "Julius Caesar" for some time. On introducing the play, the teacher had announced that there was much "parallelism" between it and the events of the day, so that it is not surprising that she frequently digressed, holding fast her students' attention in the process.

TEACHER: At the time she [Cleopatra] married Caesar it probably was a political advantageous thing. See, it was at the time of the triumvirate. All right. I think I told you—this is clear off subject—but I told you about being in the audience listening to a talk the other night about this young woman's life in Tunisia. Well, she was telling us about the married situation. The bride and the bridegroom in Tunisia never see each other. They don't even know who it is until the day of the wedding.

STUDENT: Oh.

TEACHER: Don't say "oh." This is a country custom. So how do we know that *this* wasn't a type of prearranged thing for political power, for political solidity, see, in Rome. From where we're talking [pointing to a map] here's Rome. And right down here is Tunisia. We're talking about a country that is not native black. We're not talking about African natives, we're talking about a civilized nation. And it isn't African yet . . .

STUDENT: How come she [Cleopatra] was supposed to marry her brother? It says this brother was the one she was supposed to marry.

TEACHER: To solidify the kingdom so that they wouldn't have any outsiders. We still don't understand. We can't in 1973, in our Christianity, understand how these people could do this. But what did I tell you yesterday? I don't condemn them for their barbaric attitude, for their un-Christian-like acts. I condemn you for not living Christianity when you have a chance to do so. I think it is more dangerous for us, in our nation, than it was for them. . . . Well, let's go on. We're procrastinating. You people can get me off the subject. . . . Until all the facts are in, we are in a very precarious position in this nation right now. They tell me that it will be before the first of the year before Mr. Ford will be confirmed or not confirmed as Vice President of the United States. We are without the Vice President as of the very hour that Spiro Agnew resigned.

STUDENT: Do you think he should have done that?

TEACHER: Oh, I tell you . . . there is one thing that nobody will get me to do. Nobody will ever get me to say that I am guilty of anything unless I am guilty of it. So with the philosophy that I have, I cannot believe that Spiro Agnew is anything but guilty, regardless of what he said.

STUDENT: I think he is, too.

TEACHER: But I'll tell you this. Unless you people start standing up when you are guilty of something—take your quinine medicine, stomach it, and puke it back up—until you learn you are responsible for that which you do, we are going to be in trouble in this nation. We've got to look to you people for the future leaders. You must learn to say, "I made a mistake." And don't look at somebody else for your scapegoat and your savior.

STUDENT: Isn't that what Russians are wanting to happen? For us to destroy ourself?

TEACHER: Why, I think this has to be true. That's right. I honestly believe it. If they can just keep things stirred up, and get us suspicious, and keep using everybody as a scapegoat and a fall guy, then we are just playing into their hands. They are just going to show the world that the capitalistic world cannot rule itself.

Biology

Mr. Thompson opened his lesson by asking what the earth was like at its beginning. His students did not know. So he undertook a long presentation about the conditions on earth that led to the emergence of life. This is a delicate subject in Mansfield, one that Mr. Thompson characteristically approached with caution.

> A few years ago there were some scientists working on this theory that simulated the conditions at the time of the beginning, or what might have been present at the time that life began on earth. They had a bunch of ammonia gas. Any of you ever smelled ammonia? Pretty pungent, right? Methane gas is a type of natural gas, or gas out of swamps or coal mines. They had that. They had a small amount of oxygen and they replicated the other conditions on earth. And you know what? They did discover a new organism that was capable of living under those conditions. But this still doesn't take away the possibility that this was under the guidance of some super-being. Maybe this is the way that life evolved. The thing we don't know is: Was the earth always spinning at the same rate that it is today? Was it always spinning around on its axis every twenty-four hours day and night? Or was there a time when it took, in the beginning of life, or the beginning of the earth, a year or 1,000 years to go around? The Bible talks about the earth being made or the world being made in what? Seven days. What was the length of the days back then in the Bible? I don't know. I don't think the Bible ever says. Supposedly on earth, according to all the things that we can find, there were exceedingly cold periods and warm periods. Fossils indicate that this pattern of rotation and this pattern of planning was not necessarily the same as it is today. Even if we go back to many years before the birth of Christ—this is such a short period of time in comparison with the age of the earth—we have really no way of discovering or judging how or rather under whose directorship life originated. We have fossil remains. Maybe life didn't originate here.

Later in the semester, Mansfield adults expressed disapproval of the statement in "Goals for Tomorrow" that promoted the study of science. They believed it would encourage the teaching of evolution. Judging from Mr. Thompson's performance, their fears were groundless.

Outside School

At Mansfield High School, sports and extracurricular activities more than hold their own in competition with academic matters. Indeed, at times they almost overwhelm academics.[8] Football practice begins before school opens in fall and the final baseball game is not played until May. In between falls an avalanche of athletic events played by varsity and junior varsity teams, male and female, spurred on by the cheerleaders who are backed up by the pep club.

No less overwhelming are the money-raising activities of clubs and classes, which introduce students to American voluntarism through magazine and newspaper subscription drives, bake sales, cake walks, car washes, soup suppers, ad infinitum. Each day students are thus drawn out of their classrooms and the school by a round of events which provide the main school attraction for many students and a major source of recreation for the community. Mansfield

High School's balance of curricular and extracurricular activities appears to serve Mansfielders well. They are not distressed with what could be interpreted by some critics as a disproportionate investment of student and educator time, money, and energy in nonacademic pursuits. From their perspective, Mansfield High School, like a good shoe, fits Mansfield.

PARENT AND STUDENT EXPECTATIONS

In the absence of a formal survey of what Mansfielders want their school to accomplish and whether they believe they get what they want, we must depend on several different indicators of the community adults' agreement with the teachers' assessment of schooling in Mansfield. Data from 239 Mansfield adults, representing perhaps one-third the number of families in the school district, show that 69 percent believe Mansfield has a good school system (7 percent disagreed and 23 percent neither agreed nor disagreed).This fairly high figure,[9] the paucity of complaints presented at school board meetings or to the administrators, the dearth of responses (less than thirty) to the superintendent's invitation to react to the new "Goals for Tomorrow" (sent to every boxholder in the school district), the disbanding of the PTA some years ago—all suggest that the community is essentially satisfied with its school system. These facts do not indicate parental apathy so much as an absence of contentious issues. The parents clearly are interested in education. In 1969 they voted to build a new grade school; in 1975 they voted to increase their education tax levy at a time when that was a rare occurrence; and throughout each year they demonstrate their affection for the high school by attending its many activities—from football games to the Christmas program to the graduation exercises. In two recent years, more than 40 percent of the school district population attended *each* of the football team's five home games.

I conclude, accordingly, that while Mansfield adults might be unhappy with a particular teacher, a losing football season, or some incident, they are basically content with what they perceive the school to be doing to Mansfield's youth, with the shape, though not necessarily with every detail, of their children's education. Thus, when a teacher observed that the school gives the community what it wants, her judgment appeared sound.

Students basically join their parents in affirming their esteem for Mansfield High School and Mansfield. A recent class of graduating seniors was interviewed to explore their views.

Some of the college-bound students entertained thoughts of eventually moving away from the community, though not to towns either too distant from or even much larger than Mansfield.[10] Places like Chicago and St. Louis appeared attractive in the way that a fantasy does. ("You know, having never lived there [Chicago] it's kind of the ideal place right now." This same student, now at college, is homesick and hopes to transfer to a school closer to Mansfield.) Seldom, however, did seniors refer to settling in places much larger than Auburn (approximately 5,000); even Stanton (approximately 100,000) is too large. In fact, as of fall, 1972, more than 50 percent of the seven hundred graduates from the period 1947 to 1972 lived in Mansfield or the surrounding twenty-five-mile region which constitutes the effective home area for all resident Mansfielders—the area where they shop, date, get medical attention, and seek recreation. Those few seniors who perceived Mansfield school and community as providing unduly restricted social and academic opportunity were more than matched by many others who feared the dangers and seeming anonymity of larger places, and even doubted that they could master driving in city traffic. They were reasonably realistic about what Mansfield offered, though less so about urban schools and communities.

In their characterization of Mansfield, the seniors show the impact of having grown up in a small rural setting. Some express a desire to get out ("seems like people who stay in Mansfield don't get anywhere") and others express pleasure at staying home. Wayne reflects the distress of many adults who oppose the possible consolidation of Mansfield High School into one large county school. He shares the sentiments of Elmer, who better than most students conveyed the special quality of life in Mansfield as experienced by those who belong. Elmer felt that "deep down the people of Mansfield care for everybody. I think that it's really a good town . . . that everybody cares for each other and . . . if something big came up . . . everybody would join in and help each other." These views, frequently expressed by community adults, are not shared by all Mansfielders, but they represent a salient characteristic of life in the town.

Teachers, as previously indicated, acknowledged that they were "not as strict academically as we should be." Students also acknowledged this fact but did not seem troubled by it. Both teachers and students implicitly concur in a level of academic expectation they find comfortable. Even capable students fail to perceive value in the more abstract aspects of education, and their speech often reflects a casual style that has its counterpart among the adults. ("You're not supposed to use 'ain't,' but I say it all the time.") With the exception of Maryann, who meant to maximize the academic possibilities of high school and got encouragement to do so from her father, students disdain the need for hard work, even if one hopes to achieve acceptable high grades—that is, to make the B honor roll. Wayne, now a university student, admits he could have worked harder, but, he observes, "Who wants to sit at a book for each class an hour a night? It's no fun. There are too many other things going on." Mike imagines that the people who get As stay at home so much they don't learn to communicate with others, rationalizing his own modest efforts with the thought that "there is more to life besides grades." Marge finished near the top of her class but regrets, as she contemplates her questionable preparedness for college, that she did not try harder. "It wasn't that important to me," she concludes. And students in the National Honor Society are accused of putting on airs. "They act like they're higher than everybody else," says Helen, who preferred fun to study and settled for being on the B honor roll rather than seeming a "real brain."

From the views of these seniors, it seems that the school experience offers more than students without college plans want, but no more than the college bound want to work for. Somewhere between these modest points Mansfield's teachers pitch their intellectual tents, accommodating themselves to a level of aspiration that threatens few.

LOCAL CONTROL AND ITS DILEMMAS

Community control of the schools flourishes in Mansfield. The community's elected school board chooses a superintendent who selects the teachers and supervises the operation of the schools. If the board trusts him, as it trusted Superintendent Tate, then it often rubber-stamps his decisions, confident that he knows what the community wants. Nevertheless, though it defers to his expertise, the board also keeps an eye on his work. And this is the evident, the officially constituted machinery of community control in Mansfield.

Yet, as we have seen, a great deal of the machinery is neither evident nor officially constituted. Such features of Mansfield High School as the level of academic expectation that guides classroom practice and the relative importance of curricular and extracurricular activities are also determined by the local community, though not by deliberate choice. When we asked board members and administrators directly about their criteria for selecting teachers and instructional materials, they did not mention maintaining the community and its values. They said they preferred teachers who had both curricular and extracurricular strengths, liked children, and were good disciplinarians. Not until the school board met to select a superintendent did someone voice a criterion that explicitly reflected the community's ethos. He is "country," they said of Reynolds. Judging from recent appointments to the teaching staff, the board liked to hire local people, though its members did not acknowledge that they gave preference to such persons. After the meeting at which Reynolds was chosen superintendent, one board member regretted that the ideal person for the job could not apply because he lacked the appropriate credentials. This ideal person happened to be a local man, now working elsewhere in the state.

Mansfield's educators do not decide the level of academic discourse in classrooms or the relative importance of academic and nonacademic matters. Rather, the prevalent academic standards are determined by the district's hiring practices and are put into effect as those whom the board has hired interact with one another, the students, and the parents of the community. The result is an academic posture well suited to the concerns of a small rural community.

School policy is not calculated to promote this outcome. To be sure, there are policy statements in several district documents, but they are consulted only in exceptional cases (involving, for example, expulsion) and are couched in typically grand language. One item in the board's *Rules, Precedents, and Procedures* explicitly requires the sort of congruence between school and community that we have been discussing: "The teacher should have a respectful attitude toward the standards and the accepted patterns of behavior of the community in which he is employed." But the fact that teachers actually possess a respectful attitude is attributable not to this regulation but to the process of recruitment and selection. Mansfield's teachers do not need to be taught what behavior is acceptable in Mansfield.

Over the years there has been little active participation by the community-at-large in educational policy making. Nothing has arisen to demand it. The community itself has not changed much. The migration rates during most of this century have been moderate, and many local families have remained in residence from generation to generation. Like-minded people replace one another on the school board, and they comfortably reflect the school district's stability. Hence factional dispute is rare and particular instances of displeasure with the school can be dealt with informally. A telephone call to one of the board members, or a remark in the restaurant or the post office, is sufficient.

Whatever its benefits, the close fit between school and community in Mansfield results in four dilemmas.

Although the school experience of Mansfield students does not preclude occupational and educational success, it is still comparatively limited. In other school districts, parents, students, and teachers place more emphasis on academic achievement and press for more resources to be directed toward intellectual goals. Consequently, there are children in the state and nation who are taught better mathematics and science, and who are better informed about their nation's political and economic complexities. Mansfielders strive to hire, not the best teacher in an intellectual sense, but the teacher who will best serve Mansfield. This is an important distinction. They would dismiss as unsuitable teachers who were "too intelligent for this community" and therefore "more than we want," just as they dismissed the candidacy of Dargan for the superintendency. Thus the first dilemma: If education is thought best when it attempts to maximize the intellectual potential of a child, then Mansfield High School may be faulted; but if under the conditions of places like Mansfield the schools contribute to a sense of personal identity and low alienation,[11] then something of possibly compensating value has been gained. I suggest that Mansfield's children do not have educational opportunities equal to those available in larger cities and their suburbs. They are denied equal opportunity not because of their race, religion, or national origin, but rather because they are being schooled in the prevalent ethos of Mansfield. Yet if different standards were instituted for academic performance, the selection of educators, and the balance between academic and nonacademic activities, Mansfield High School would no longer suit its community. Such standards would have to be imposed from the outside, for they find little support in Mansfield. Indeed, they might threaten the community.

The close fit discussed here promotes generational stability in Mansfield. Neither by learning nor by aspiration are the community's children sharply distinguished from their parents. Their shared feelings about where to live and what to believe suggest a second dilemma: In Mansfield, maximizing intellectual achievement and high intergenerational stability are probably incompatible.

Though Mansfield has no black residents, it sustains anti-black sentiment and thus socializes its children into attitudes that conflict with national ideals.

No school policy supports this sentiment, but the school is a forum for its expression and its reinforcement by peers. This points to a third dilemma: Mansfield's harmonious relation of school and community is maintained at the cost of compromising some national ideals. In this dilemma, *particularism*, in the form of the local community's sense of the good, is pitted against *universalism*, in the form of the nation's sense of the good—both of which inspire essential activity, the former to human dignity and the latter to national unity.[12] Plainly, the interests of any individual community may differ from those of the nation as a whole. It is unpleasant, however, to contemplate a national society so insecure that it cannot believe itself the richer for its subgroup enclaves, each with its own identity. Yet if the outlook of some subgroups became dominant, then social justice and national integration would be threatened.

These dilemmas of local control suggest that there is no good social organization without a boundary to its goodness. That local autonomy has limits was made clear by the 1954 desegregation decision of the U.S. Supreme Court. Thus, at the same time that we see virtue in the intimacy of Mansfield school and community, we must be prepared to appeal to principles of justice and equality and condemn what we have praised if the price exacted by their harmony is judged intolerable. Who is to judge? And when is it to be declared that the cost of goodness for some has become intolerable for others? These are especially complex and controversial questions. For example, F. A. Rodgers (1975) discusses the pre-integration high school in North Carolina. He concludes that, as a result of desegregation, not only did many black educators lose their jobs, but the black community lost a critical factor in the facilitation and development of its political and social activities. Rodgers's doubt about the outcome of the 1954 Supreme Court decision suggests that one may question whether or not local community gains and losses should take priority over national ideals.

Rodgers's conclusions bring us to the final dilemma. To those with roots in Mansfield's past, to those who resonate with their little school's special balance of academic, athletic, and other nonacademic activities, school reorganization is anathema.[13] Yet, reorganization is an increasingly likely solution to the problems of the Mansfields of America, as lower enrollments necessitate the closing of classes and small schools fall victim to declining economies of scale. "Over my dead body" was the response of a Mansfielder to consolidation. He is one of many who react to the proposed loss of their school with a passion comparable to that of people who feel that their cultural survival is in jeopardy when their native language is threatened. The continued existence in Mansfield of a school that can contribute to subgroup maintenance, to the integration of its community, is inversely related to the application of two universalistic principles: fiscal rationality, which argues for school reorganization; and academic excellence, which supports the employment of educators and promotes curricular reform that would not be suitable for Mansfield as presently constituted. These principles are espoused by educational organizations ranging from state teachers' unions to state school board associations.[14] They are therefore strongly supported. Countervailing arguments are just beginning to gather force among diverse groups which urge resistance to the increasing scale of contemporary society.

I have tried to resist the allure of romanticism here. Mansfield is not a paradise either to me or to those of its inhabitants who for different reasons remain outside the charmed circle of acceptability. It is a community in a psychological sense and, like all such communities, somewhat exclusive. While not everyone does feel or can feel he belongs there, I find Mansfield appealing because it is able to embrace, to attach, those who, in a manner of speaking, will submit to it. Believing that such rewards are uncommon, I value places where they are available.

With its particular brand of instruction, its ideological orientation, and its stress on sports and money-raising activities, Mansfield High School is not a school for everyone or everyplace. Given local control, it was not meant to be, nor could it be. But it does belong in Mansfield. As one teacher observed after reflecting on the school's strengths and weaknesses, "I guess it's as good a school as you can expect Mansfield to have." Under circumstances of local control, her comments are essentially accurate. She did not intend to be patronizing. As a native of the area, she knew what kind of school the desires and expectations of Mansfield's adults would support. Given the people, the school is appropriate.

Based on external perspectives, Mansfield High School may be judged more harshly than my comments suggest. But as I assured my Mansfield hosts, I had not come to conduct an evaluation. I planned, rather, to examine the relationship between school and community in a rural setting. I found the relationship to be mutually beneficial. The two are joined in the maintenance of an American subgroup which I do not see as prototypical for all of us, which is flawed, but which is worth treasuring—if the price paid by Mansfield and the nation is not too high.

In 1975, at the height of the resistance to busing in Boston, a journalist reported the bitter observations of a former Bostonian:

> "I'll never forgive them for this. Forcing me out."
> "Why?" I asked. "Most people who have the money *want* to live in the sub-urbs."
> "You could never understand," he said. "I'm a townie. I lived all my life in Charlestown. You know, we got something special here. There's only one Bunker Hill in the whole country." (Klein 1975, p. 82)

And they've got something special in Mansfield, too. Keeping that something special depends upon whom Mansfield High School serves.

NOTES

[1] To preserve the anonymity of my informants, the name of their community has been altered, as have all other names.

[2] Since 1967, enrollment in the school district has declined each year. In 1975, the salary offered a beginning teacher was $8,336 and the maximum teacher salary was $13,144. (For the state as a whole, in 1974, the median salary for a beginning teacher with a B.A. was $8,400 and the median maximum salary $14,350.) On the basis of *effort rank* (which is the correlation between a district's potential wealth, as measured by its assessed valuation per pupil, and the degree to which it draws upon its wealth for the support of

its schools, as measured by its total tax rate), Mansfield is an above-average school system.

[3] In many respects, this study is the tradition of such earlier community studies as West (1945), Vidich and Bensman (1958), Lynd and Lynd (1929), and Hollingshead (1959). The first three focus on the community, and schooling is an essential but subordinate concern of these studies; the fourth centers on the school, but views schooling chiefly through the concept of social class. Though my own fieldwork encompassed the entire community, I intended to center my inquiry on the school, considering its function within the community.

[4] In approaching the school, we moved very slowly to establish ourselves as unthreatening observers who would participate upon request in the life of the school but whose prime interest was in finding out about the school in all its aspects. We believed it important to establish that we had not come to evaluate the quality of instruction or administration. In time our data collection came to include: (1) observing and tape recording lessons; (2) interviewing all of the teachers and school board members, and many of the students; (3) reading student diaries; (4) analyzing documents such as statements of course objectives, teacher-made tests and student homework, school board policy statements and minutes, etc.; (5) administering a questionnaire. We attended all school events, teachers' meetings, and school board meetings. We moved into the community through introductions provided by the superintendent. There we met and interviewed the mayor and his village board. We attended village board meetings, collected all available documents, and became part of community life through participation in local church and organizational activities. Data collection culminated with the administration of a questionnaire, which was followed up by in-depth interviews. These were the formal activities. But since I lived in Mansfield during most of the second year of fieldwork, I was an informal participant as well. Because I did not bring my family, I was unable to learn about the community through their experiences.

[5] MacIver and Page define *sense of community* as "common living with its *awareness* of sharing a way of life as well as the common earth" (1961, p. 10). As a result of "sharing a way of life," a subgroup has developed in Mansfield whose members share "some common quality that makes them distinguishable from other members of a major group to which they belong" (*Webster's Third International*, s.v. "subgroup"). To be sure, the Mansfielder is readily recognized as an American, but the outcomes of growing up in Mansfield and places like it differ from those produced in other social settings in the United States.

[6] The grade and high schools were organized into a unit district about twenty years ago.

[7] This is a neighborhood-type institution which serves, though not exclusively, small-town graduates in the central part of the state.

[8] The investment in sports is substantial, certainly consonant with the level of expenditure made by other schools in Mansfield's athletic conference. One hears grumbling about an overemphasis on sports, but at no time did teachers state that they were deprived of what they needed for instructional purposes. Mansfield considers itself a football town, turns out in large numbers for most athletic events, but by no means neglects the school's musical and dramatic events. The school's laboratory equipment acceptably serves the needs of biology (the only required science), chemistry, and physics, which is occasionally offered depending on enrollment. Mansfield High School has one laboratory for all of its science courses.

[9] According to a 1971 Gallup Poll (1972, p. 17) conducted in communities of 2,500 or less, 64 percent were satisfied with their children's education; 26 percent were not, and 10

percent did not know. Comparable statistics for the nation as a whole were 60, 20, and 12 percent. I cite these figures with diffidence since, unlike the Gallup Poll election outcomes, I am uncertain of their accuracy for the groups they supposedly represent. Moreover, I did not ask if people in Mansfield were pleased with their children's education, but if they thought the school system was one of the most important things in Mansfield.

[10] From 1947 to 1972, approximately 40 percent of all graduates continued their education after graduation. In the 1947–65 period, for which the data are most complete, 46 percent of the graduates in the top half of their class were living in or around Mansfield as of 1972. This group includes most of those who attended college.

[11] These data are not fully persuasive, but they tend to confirm my sense of Mansfielders' low level of alienation, particularly among the mainstream vis-à-vis non-Mansfielders (see Table 1 . . .).

[12] See Fein's (1971) excellent book for further discussion of universalism.

[13] Reorganization, while much discussed, is not necessarily imminent. Many residents fear that their high school will be consolidated with the other county schools to create one large system. Their shrinking enrollments and the disposition of educators to prefer larger systems suggest that Mansfielders' fears have some warrant.

[14] See the *Illinois Education News* (February 1975) section on school reorganization which shows the heads of the Illinois Education Association, Illinois Federation of Teachers, Illinois Association of School Administrators, and Illinois Association of School Boards favoring the universalistic principles that support school reorganization.

TABLE 1   The Alienation of Mansfielders Compared with That of a National Sample[a]

| | | Responses (in Percentages) | | |
Item[b]	Population Sampled	Agree	Neither Agree Nor Disagree	Disagree
1. Nothing is worthwhile	Mansfield adults	15.0	7.9	74.4
anymore.	Mansfield students	8.2	23.5	68.1
	U.S. adults	43.3	—	55.9
2. People can't be	Mansfield adults	17.5	12.5	67.3
trusted.[c]	Mansfield students	25.4	28.6	41.3
	U.S. adults	56.1	4.3	39.5
3. I can count on	Mansfield adults	75.2	9.1	14.2
someone to help me	Mansfield students	64.7	19.7	15.2
when I'm in real	U.S. adults	24.0	—	75.1
trouble.				

[a]For Mansfield adults $N = 239$; for Mansfield students $N = 157$. The national sample N of 1484 is taken from the N.O.R.C. publication, *National Data Program for the Social Sciences*.

[b]Item 1 is from N.O.R.C., July 1974, p. 44; item 2 is from July 1975, p. 75; item 3 is from July 1974, p. 46. The wording for N.O.R.C. and my items is almost identical. I asked additional questions on the alienation dimension but could not find comparative data which would put them in perspective. For example, "I'm satisfied with the respect I get from other people"—87.8 percent of the adults and 71.0 percent of the students agreed; "I feel somewhat apart even when I'm among friends"—59.7 percent of the adults and 57.2 percent of the students disagreed.

[c]This question was asked in the spring of 1974, when the Watergate affair was daily headline news. Students and the national sample may well have been reacting to these events.

REFERENCES

Fein, Leonard J. *The ecology of the public schools: An inquiry into community control.* New York: Pegasus, 1971.

Hollingshead, August de Belmont. *Elmstown's youth: The impact of social classes on adolescents.* New York: John Wiley & Sons, 1959 [1949].

"The issue is: School district reorganization." *Illinois Education News* 4, no. 5 (1975): 2, 14.

Klein, Joe. "The Boston busing crisis." *Rolling Stone* (23 October 1975): 32–82 passim.

Lynd, Robert S. and Lynd, Helen Merrell. *Middletown: A study in American culture.* New York: Harcourt, Brace and World, 1929.

MacIver, Robert Morrison, and Page, Charles H. *Society: An introductory analysis.* New York: Holt, Rinehart & Winston, 1961 [1949].

National Opinion Research Center. *National data program for the social sciences.* Principal investigator, James Davis. Chicago: University of Chicago Press, July 1974; July 1975.

Rodgers, Frederick A. *The black high school and its community.* Lexington, Mass.: Lexington Books, 1975.

"Satisfaction Index—Education." *The Gallup Opinion Index,* report 81, March 1972.

Vidich, Arthur J., and Bensman, Joseph. *Small town in mass society.* Garden City, N.Y.: Doubleday, 1958.

West, James. *Plainville, U.S.A.* New York: Columbia University Press, 1945.

JOEL SPRING

THE STRUCTURE OF POWER IN AN URBAN SCHOOL SYSTEM: A STUDY OF CINCINNATI SCHOOL POLITICS

Various studies in the history of urban schools have explored how the governance of them has come under the political control of elite business and professional groups. In the United States, the dominance of such groups came after and was the consequence of the reform of large school systems during the early part of the twentieth century. Despite the evidence of previous studies, the methods used by these groups to retain their control are not well documented and understood. The Citizens School Committee (CSC) controlled the politics of Cincinnati schools from the early 1920s until the late 1960s and is typical of the organizations that dominated educational politics in many large American cities at that time. Correspondence obtained recently by the Cincinnati Historical Society sheds new light on the working of the Citizens School Committee and upon the variety of methods used by the leaders of the business and professional community to control the politics of a large city school system. The research reported here rests on the documents of the Citizens School Committee and also upon interviews conducted with many of the participants who made the politics of education in Cincinnati schools of that time. These informants participated on the understanding that their comments would be used in this study.

From Joel S. Spring, "The Structure of Power in an Urban School System: A study of Cincinnati School Politics," *Curriculum Inquiry* 14, No. 4 (1948), pp. 401–403, 407–424. Copyright © 1984 by John Wiley & Sons, Inc. Reprinted with permission.

The significance of this research is not limited to Cincinnati, for it provides a model that explicates the techniques of control elite groups use to dominate school boards and their politics. It describes further how these elites control relationships with school administrators and the flow of information between the school system and the public. The power brokers in Cincinnati were, moreover, more than local bosses; they were as well leaders of national and international corporations. One key figure who worked behind the scenes, Neil McElroy, was president of Procter & Gamble and served in the 1950s as chairman of the White House Conference on Education and was Secretary of Defense.

In another perspective, this research reveals the political consequences that flowed from early twentieth century urban school reform in the United States. Most studies of this reform movement agree that changes in school board elections and the rationalization of school administration allowed for professional and business domination of urban schools.[1] There is some disagreement about the issue of class politics. Most studies picture the changes as resulting from an upper-class desire to take power over the school system away from lower and middle classes. A recent study has pictured this reform movement as a struggle between middle-class professionals and traditional business elite. The argument is that autonomous middle-class professionals "may have brought about urban educational reform without any close identification on the part of the reformers with the interests of either business leaders or workers."[2]

With regard to the above debate, my research shows that urban school reforms did allow professionals and business leaders to continue their domination of school politics. What it cannot show is whether the reform movement permitted the upper class to usurp the power of the lower class members and professionals who sought their own places in the power structure. My research does argue that the reform movement enabled the business and professional communities to perpetuate their power over the schools. Of particular importance is the continued control and active participation in urban school politics by heads of major national and international corporations.

The control exerted by these corporate leaders was made possible by a reform movement which was premised on the idea that traditional political processes should be separated from educational systems. The key phrase used over and over again during the early reform era was: "Keep the schools out of politics." In practice this meant keeping political parties and politicians out of school board elections. The elimination of these traditional means of access for citizen participation in government created a vacuum which was filled by supposedly nonpolitical civic organizations. While these business-dominated civic organizations waved the flag called "Keep the schools out of politics," they moved to nominate and finance their own candidates to school boards. Because membership in these civic organizations required individuals to have a background in business, the abandonment of traditional party machinery for nomination and campaigning made it more difficult for non-business and professional types to be elected to school board positions.

In addition, there were changes in the methods of election to urban school boards which made it difficult for the citizen without strong organizational and financial backing to be elected. The changes, as has been shown by other historians, were the reduction of the size of school boards and citywide elections as opposed to election by district. Election by districts made it easier for the average citizen to be elected because campaigning was limited to a small geographic area. Elimination of election by district required the candidate to have the financial and organizational resources to campaign throughout the city.[3]

When the above changes began to take place in urban areas around the country in the early part of the 20th century, the average citizen found it increasingly difficult to gain access to school board membership. Without the possibility of backing from the established political parties, the average citizen found it almost impossible to gain the organizational and financial support required to conduct a successful election campaign covering an entire urban school district.

When elite business and professional groups began to dominate and control school boards they did so in the name of the "public interest." They claimed to know what was in the best interest of the educational system and the education of the child. Their claim to knowledge of the public interest in education was based on the assumption that those in society who had the most education and were successful in life had the most knowledge about educational needs and goals.

In another publication, I have labeled this way of representing the public interest as "democratic elitism."[4] This notion is a winner-takes-all view that believes the democratic process should be organized to give the majority of voters the right to select those who are best able to represent everyone's interests. Since, it is assumed, other voters really don't know what is in their best interests, elections must be structured so that only the best candidates present themselves to the voters. This view of democracy was the goal of the campaign to "Keep the schools out of politics."

Another way of understanding democratic elitism is to compare other concepts of representation in education. For instance, democratic localism in the 19th century and community control in the 20th century were premised on the idea that all members of the community should be directly involved in the decision-making process in education. Rather than have an elected board of education to represent individual interests, it was felt in both of these cases that direct participation and decision-making at open meetings were the best means of representing the individual. Indeed, since the leaders of the community control movement of the '60s and '70s believed that boards of education represented only elite, racist groups, they concluded that the only way to incorporate the viewpoints of racial minority groups in the governing structure of schools would be to change fundamentally the procedure that determined those structures.

Even if one rejects direct community control of schools and accepts school boards composed of elected representatives, one does not have to reject also the notion of community participation. One can structure school board elections for community representation of viewpoints by an elected school board; there does not have to be a rejection of the notion of maximum participation. One can structure school board elections for maximum representation by increasing the size of boards, electing by district, and allowing a full range of political party participation. Here the goal is to present the voters with a full range of candidates so that they can choose the candidate they feel best represents their interests. This, of course, was the model rejected by democratic elitism. And in the case of Cincinnati and other urban centers, the abandonment of this model of democratic representation allowed for elite business and professional interests to control school politics.

• • •

THE METHODS OF CONTROL

The central mechanism of control by the Citizens School Committee was its nominating committee, which made the decisions about who would be sponsored and financed in school board elections. Membership on the nominating committee was limited and carefully selected from leading members of the Cincinnati community. The primary source of evidence for the workings of this group comes from documents made available for the 1950s and 1960s and, consequently, is limited to that time period.

The most important person in selecting members of the nominating committee was Ewart Simpkinson, a local insurance executive, who firmly believed that the key to a good school system was getting the top or best people on the school board. He would later claim to know very little about board educational policy or education "matters" and never considered that knowledge important in regard to his success in school affairs. His philosophy was that all you needed were the top people to take charge of an organization and its success was guaranteed. And by the top people he meant those who were successful in the business and financial communities. It was this type of person Simpkinson wanted on the nominating committee and the school board.[5]

An example of Simpkinson's strategy and civic philosophy can be found in a 1954 letter to Ralph Lazarus, a member and later Chairman of the Board of Directors of Federated Department Stores, inviting Lazarus to be a member of the nominating committee. Federated Department Stores is a major national retail chain composed of 20 divisions including Bloomingdale's, Abraham and Straus, Bullock's, and I. Magnin. Simpkinson wrote Lazarus, "It is important for us to have top quality membership because our job is to select and persuade high-grade citizens for this responsible work in our city." The letter listed the other members of the nominating committee which included executives from important national and local businesses. Listed were Jacob Davis of the Kroger Company, Albert Heekin, Jr. of the Heekin Can Company, Robert Shetterly of Procter & Gamble, Harry Olden of Cincinnati Sheet and Metal Company, and Mrs. George Moyer, representing the P.T.A., the League of Women Voters, and the Women's City Club. In the letter the business affiliation of each member of the nominating committee was clearly specified.[6]

While almost all members of the nominating committee were businessmen, Simpkinson did try to have representation from different constituencies within the city. For instance, in the collection of documents from the Citizens School Committee there is an undated list of 17 possible members of the 7-member nominating committee. Simpkinson had divided the 17 into 7 categories labeled Catholic, Colored, Jewish, Western Hills, Business-Industry, Professors, and Women. These were categories Simpkinson considered important to the Cincinnati community, but they did not all receive representation on the nominating committee. The category Western Hills referred to an area of Cincinnati that was mainly Catholic and considered uninvolved in civic affairs. The categories of Catholic and Colored were special problems for the Citizens School Committee and will be discussed in more detail later in the essay.[7]

The methods used by the nominating committee to select candidates to the school board were explained in a 1949 letter from Simpkinson to Homer Lunken. The letter was stamped confidential and included the following instructions, "Each one of the committee has a similar sheet and we are to rate these candidates in the four columns from one to ten giving first choice ten points." In addition, the letter stated, "It was the unanimous agreement that we would present four candidates and that we would endorse any of the present incumbents who desire to be reelected with the exception of Mr. Becker."[8]

In essence, the rating scale of the nominating committee replaced the democratic process of the ballot box since virtually all candidates of the Citizens School Committee were elected. One major exception was Mr. Becker in Simpkinson's letter to Lunken. Becker had held his position on the Board of Education for twenty-six years from 1934 to 1960 because of support from the large Catholic community in Cincinnati and the Citizens School Committee resented him for it. They felt, however, there was little they could do to remove him because of the possibility of raising the ire of the Catholic community. In a letter that served as a formal report of the Nominating Committee in 1949, Simpkinson wrote, "In the light of Mr. Becker's record on the board, we do not feel that we can recommend his endorsement, but . . . because our opposition to him may involve some religious misunderstanding we do not recommend a campaign for or against him by the Citizens School Committee."[9]

While nominating and financing candidates was one important strategy for controlling board membership, another was the appointment by the Board of Education of a person to fill an unexpired term of a resigning member. This method allowed the Board of Education and the Citizens School Committee to circumvent completely any democratic processes. This was the method the Citizens School Committee hoped to use to get a black candidate on the Board of Education.

By the end of the 1950s, with the national struggle for civil rights it became obvious to the Citizens School Committee that they needed to get a representative of the black community on the Board of Education who would share the values and views of the business leaders of the community. As one member of the Citizens School Committee wrote Simpkinson in 1959, "I think we will be faced with the decision of having to nominate someone from the minority community in this next election. . . ." For this purpose Simpkinson had appointed to the nominating committee a local black physician, Charles Dillard. In 1959 the nominating committee membership included Charles Dillard along with Rueben Hays, chairman of the board of the First National Bank of Cincinnati; Walter Beckjord, chairman of the board of Cincinnati Gas and Electric Company; Kelly Siddall, administrative vice president of Procter & Gamble; Mary Schloss, the wife of the president of Kahn's Meat Company; Edward Wagner, president of Wagner's Sons Co.; and Arthur M. O'Connell, vice president of Thomas E. Wood Co.[10]

No minority candidate was nominated by the Citizens School Committee in 1959, but a beginning was made in the search for the "right" black candidate. In 1961 another attempt was made to nominate a minority candidate. In a letter to Carlton Hill, the president of the Fifth-Third Union Trust Co., Simpkinson wrote, "The public does not yet realize that we are going through a fairly critical period of this phase of the Citizens School Committee activities. Having Dr. Dillard on the nominating committee two years ago was the first time a negro candidate had ever been on this committee." Simpkinson explained the continuation of the search for a minority candidate, "Having the counsel and advise of Dr. Clarke this time made it possible to develope (sic) a good list of prospects from the negro community and it was very significant that your committee was ready to endorse one of these candidates. . . ."[11]

While no minority candidate was nominated in 1961 there was consideration given to using the strategy of appointment as opposed to election. Simpkinson outlined this strategy in another 1961 letter to the head of Fifth-Third Union Trust Company. Simpkinson explained to Carlton Hill, "If we should endorse a colored person we can be reasonably sure that there might be a white candidate run independently and if he were a good one our candidate might well be defeated." The strategy suggested by Simpkinson was, "If a colored person were put on the Board of Education by appointment and then endorsed by us he would have a much better chance of being elected and he would feel more welcome and we might be able to get a more effective person."[12]

The method of appointment did not have to be used when finally in 1964 the nominating committee selected its first black candidate, Calvin Conliffe, for the Board of Education. Conliffe was more representative of the corporate elite in the Citizens School Committee than of the local minority community. When Conliffe was elected in 1964, he was an engineer, inventor, and manager for the General Electric Company.

Probably the most interesting use of appointment as a means of avoiding the democratic process occurred with the death of the board president Fred Heinold in 1959 and the resignation of the vice president Edwin Becker in 1960. These two incidents not only illustrate the methods of control used by the Citizens School Committee, but also the anti-Catholic feeling shared by some of these corporate leaders.

When Fred Heinold, physician and president of the Cincinnati School Board for 19 years, unexpectedly died of a heart attack during a trip to Cleveland in 1959, Ewart Simpkinson, chairman of the Citizens School Committee, quickly wrote the vice president of Procter & Gamble, Kelly Siddall, "This is a [tragedy], but it also gives us a golden opportunity to get someone on the Board of Education without a competitive election." The chairman of the Citizens School Committee emphasized in his letter to the vice president of Procter & Gamble that, "Whomever we advise the Board of Education . . . that name is guaranteed election. This means that we can get the caliber of man who would be possibly unavailable if he had to run under a competitive public election." Siddall, the vice president of Procter & Gamble, was vice chairman of the nominating committee of the Citizens School Committee. The chairman of the committee, Walter Beckjord, the chairman of the board of the Cincinnati Gas and Electric Company, was out of town at the time of Heinold's death and Simpkinson's sense of urgency led him to contact immediately the next person in charge. In a "P.S." at the bottom of the letter, Simpkinson wrote, "Someone from the Procter & Gamble organization would be ideal if you could make the suggestion."[13]

Besides a concern about finding a replacement to serve on the board, a member of the board had to be selected to take over Heinold's job as president. Heinold had kept a tight grip on the board's presidency throughout the 1950s. According to tradition the vice president should be the next in line for the position, but that happened to be the Catholic board member Edwin Becker. Not only should the job have been Becker's by tradition, but also by virtue of his 26 years of service on the board.

But Becker was not elected to the board presidency and he resigned from the board in 1960 charging the other board members with strong anti-Catholic bias. In his letter of resignation he claimed that he had been approached by his fellow board member, Samuel Todd, and was informed that the other board members had met without his presence and had decided that he should not be president. Becker also stated, "When I asked what the reason was, Mr. Todd very frankly stated 'because of your religion.'" Todd then stated that they would allow him to be interim president if he promised not to stand for re-election.[14]

Those most actively opposed to Becker becoming president were Citizens School Committee nominees Stanley McKie and Charles Westheimer. At the time they were serving on the board, Stanley McKie was president of Weil, Roth and Irving, a firm specializing in municipal and corporate bonds, and Charles Westheimer was a partner in the stock brokerage firm of Westheimer & Company. The other board members had selected Stanley McKie to succeed Heinold. In his letter of resignation, Becker stated that, "Mr. McKie and others said that because of the bigotry existing in the community, to have a Catholic as President of the Board of Education would handicap the public schools. . . ." He also stated, "Mr. Westheimer expressed the idea that there was definitely a great deal of prejudice in the community against a Catholic becoming President of the Board of Education."[15]

The public reply by the other board members included the brief reference to Becker's charges. They stated "improper reporting of the confidences of a private conference are not actions of a person who is sincerely interested in the welfare of the schools. Time will, in our opinion, prove that the majority of the Board has made a wise selection."[16] Concern about Becker's religion certainly played a part in some of the public reaction. The school board member who led the delegation to inform Becker that he would not be head of the Board was a friend of both Todd and Simpkinson. His views of the events are seen in his letter to Samuel Todd where he wrote, "Congratulations on your well-deserved election as vice-president of the Cincinnati Board of Education and on your strong stand with reference to Mr. Edwin Becker. . . . I do not believe that we can afford to give purse-string control of public school money to any person or group that is not committed to strict separation of Church and State." The writer viewed the school board drama as a struggle between a Protestant majority and a Catholic minority. He wrote that the event "does give me the opportunity to say something in behalf of the great Protestant majority who are tired of seeing a minority expressing their own bigoted views, and by minority pressure making attempts to thwart the majority-held views of United States citizens." Across the top of the copy of the letter sent to Simpkinson, head of the Citizens School Committee, was penned the note, "And, Sink, (Simpkinson's nickname) the same compliment goes to you—Bob."[17]

In a letter to Joseph Bertotti, Manager, Education Relations and Support, General Electric Company, Simpkinson outlined how the Citizens School Committee exerted control over the events following Heinold's death and Becker's resignation. In Simpkinson's version, Becker's charge of religious bigotry was not correct. Simpkinson wrote Bertotti explaining the sequence of events, "One of our endorsed candidates died in the Fall, just prior to election, and inasmuch as there was no competition to our own slate the five signers of the petition circulating committee were suddenly responsible for replacing Dr. Heinold's name on the ballot with a new candidate." And, Simpkinson stated with a certain air of self-congratulation, "We, fortunately, had a strong Nominating Committee and Board of Directors and came up with an outstanding candidate, who is a young and capable lawyer."[18] The Citizens School Committee's choice to replace Heinold was attorney Louis Schwab, who among other things was a director of Southern Ohio National Bank, Williamson Co., Verkamp Corp., Hawley-Monk Co., Rookwood Oil Terminals, Inc., and Marvin Warner Co. Schwab's ties to education and the Citizens School Committee went back to his grandfather, Dr. Louis Schwab, who also was appointed to the Cincinnati School Board back in 1915 and died while still a member of the board in 1926.[19]

In terms of a replacement for Becker, Simpkinson told Bertotti that Becker had unfortunately brought up the issue of religion but, "However, the School Committee felt that because of the large percentage of Cincinnati's population, also represented by Mr. Becker, that if we could get a capable person to fulfill his place from that group it would be a desirable thing to do. His public statement threw a cloud on the situation and made it embarrassing for someone else from his group."[20] The "capable" Catholic selected by the Citizens School Committee was attorney J. Vincent Aug. The political maneuvers that swirled around the board after Heinold's death illustrate the attempt of the Citizens School Committee to balance their power with the realities of the Cincinnati community. The search for an acceptable Catholic and minority candidate was an attempt to achieve a balanced community representation without threatening the values of the community elite. Representation from the Catholic and black communities was considered necessary to avoid major community conflict which would threaten the power of those in control. But the achievement of this goal meant a manipulation of democratic processes during elections for the Board of Education and for positions within the board structure.

Some of this manipulation occurred behind the scenes with the president of Procter & Gamble, Neil McElroy, as the actor. While the formal and public display of power was through the nomination, financing, and control of school board members, the informal relationships were built on friendship, informal lunches, and meetings. It was in these informal contacts that McElroy played an important role. Simpkinson hinted at the importance of this informal structure in a letter to Richard Peake of the General Electric Company, "I hate to bother you on this School Committee Board member matter but I think this is a perfect spot for a couple of your higher echelon men. We get into politics only indirectly but do get behind the scenes in an interesting way."[21]

In an interview with Roger Crafts, an active member of the Citizens School Committee in the 1950s and the president of the organization in the late 1960s, McElroy was placed at the center of the Cincinnati power structure in the 1950s. "Those were," Craft said, "the Neil McElroy days."[22] Besides McElroy's relationship to the local power structure, he also served as chairman of the White House Conference on Education in 1955 and Secretary of Defense in the Eisenhower administration.

As Crafts describes the period, business leaders would informally gather with Neil McElroy to decide educational and other civic issues. Crafts said, "They would go to lunch and discuss a particular program. If they would decide what to support, Neil McElroy would just point his finger at Zimmer from the Gas & Electric Company, Lazarus from Federated Department Stores—right around the table saying your share is $6,000, your share is $5,000. . . ."[23]

McElroy indirectly described this process in an interview for *U.S. News & World Report* in 1955.[24] The lengthy interview was a result of McElroy's chairmanship of the White House Conference on Education. In response to the question, "Educators are a little busy to be setting standards aren't they?," McElroy responded in terms of Cincinnati. McElroy argued that educators could not set standards without public support. "In our particular community," he said, "thanks to the fact that in Cincinnati there's been no political influence on the school board or the school system in any way—and then, too, partly, I guess, because people in Cincinnati think it's important to have a good school system— they've put up the money when they had to put it up, and a lot had been requested." In contrast to Cincinnati, McElroy argued there were many communities that did not receive public financial support because of the actions of board members or the superintendent.

If one believes that the political process is the most important element of democratic control, one could interpret McElroy's statement in the context of democratic elitism. From this perspective, McElroy's statement meant that elite control of the Board of Education, or "no political influence," resulted in a board and superintendent who could inspire public confidence and move electors to vote for tax levies and bond issues. The further complication of McElroy's statement is that more democratic control of [the] board of education results in conflict between board members and the superintendent. Such conflicts would result in undermining public confidence and making electors unwilling to vote for increased financial support of the schools.

The interviewer for *U.S. News & World Report* also asked why business had begun to take a strong interest in education. In considering McElroy's reply one is tempted to imagine a discussion of the value of education to business at one of McElroy's decision-making businessmen's luncheons in Cincinnati. McElroy told the interviewer, "I believe . . . that unless a good quality of education is offered to the young minds of this country, business itself has a substantial loss to sustain. It has a loss to sustain in the quality of the people that they are training to be their executives." In addition, there was another relationship between business and education. As McElroy stated, "as both the National Association of Manufacturers and the U.S. Chamber of Commerce have shown, the higher the grade of education, the greater the consumption rate of products—which is of obvious interest to business." In other words, education is good for business because it trains workers and consumers.

It would be difficult to measure the degree of influence Neil McElroy exercised over the Citizens School Committee and the educational system. It is apparent that he was a much respected member of the Cincinnati business community. Evidence of that respect is found in Simpkinson's statement that serious consideration was given in the late 1950s to a proposal to use McElroy's face as a model for a statue of Cincinnatus that was to be placed on the riverfront in Cincinnati. The project was never completed, but the thought was important.[25]

The relationship between McElroy and the Citizens School Committee is reflected in correspondence related to another kind of control—the control of information between the schools and the public. This control was to be accomplished by the creation of a private foundation which became the Greater Cincinnati School Foundation. This idea was outlined by Simpkinson in a letter to Neil McElroy in 1954. Simpkinson explained to McElroy that a committee of the Citizens School Committee had argued in a report that the organization had done a "good job in respect to obtaining fine candidates for the Board of Education . . . but the liaison work of informing the public concerning the public schools and their activities left much to be desired." The solution was "to activate the Citizens School Foundation to do the liaison work and the continuing of public education, etc., and that the present Citizens School Committee Board shift over to the Foundation. . . ." Simpkinson went on to argue that a major advantage would be that they could "secure sustaining funds from corporations or individuals on a tax-free basis. . . ."[26]

A letter sent to all members of the Citizens School Committee in 1955 described the relationship between the Foundation and the committee as "really sister organizations and there is a great need for both of them, and the work that both of them do—the Committee in election work, and the Foundation in study and interpretation of education policies." The letter explained how the directors of the Citizens School Committee had decided to develop the foundation because of tax advantages. The letter clearly stated that, "Our Board of Directors as a group is the nucleus of the Citizens School Foundation. . . ." It was urged that all members of the Citizens School Committee become members of the foundation.[27]

The name adopted for the Foundation was the Cincinnati School Foundation and its finest president was Charles Sawyer, who had just returned from Washington where he had served as Secretary of Commerce in President Harry S Truman's administration. The chairman of the fund-raising drive for the foundation was Milton J. Schloss, the president of Kahn's Meats. His wife, Mary Schloss, was recording secretary of the Citizens School Committee and treasurer of the Cincinnati Foundation. In the 1970s Mary Schloss would be elected to the Board of Education.

The plan was for the Citizens School Committee to control elections to the board and for the foundation to influence school policy and communicate policy to the public. The first major task assumed by the foundation was to develop a policy with respect to the teacher shortage of the 1950s. This issue had been a major topic of concern at the White House Conference on Education chaired by Neil McElroy, at Cincinnati School Board meetings since the end of World War II, and by local teacher associations.

The approach of the Cincinnati School Foundation to the teacher shortage problem was in many ways best described as condescending and not reflective of a belief that teachers were real professionals. The plan of the Cincinnati School Foundation was to stage a Teacher Recognition Day which would reward teachers with appreciation and supposedly attract other people to the ranks of teaching. The chairman of the first Teacher Recognition Day in Cincinnati was Charles Sawyer, the president of the Foundation.

The plan embodied in Teacher Recognition Day encouraged citizens of the city to invite a teacher home for dinner. Following the dinner everyone was to attend the Cincinnati Garden, which had been taken over by the foundation for the night, and watch a performance of the Hollywood Ice Revue. In their interviews, Ewart Simpkinson and Roger Crafts said they got a feeling after the event that teachers did not appreciate Teacher Recognition Day. Simpkinson said that teachers felt the plan was condescending toward teachers. Crafts claimed that while the plan had little effect on solving the teacher shortage, it did launch the foundation into the arena of educational policy.[28]

While controlling membership on the Board and determining educational policy through the foundation were important elements in the structure of power, there was also the issue of the actual control of the internal workings of the school system. As heads of major businesses, leaders of the Citizens School Committee and the Board of Education were restricted in the actual amount of time they could devote to school matters. This limitation meant that they had to rely heavily upon educational administrators in the system. This dependence made the selection of the superintendent an act of primary importance in controlling the system. From the standpoint of the community elite, the superintendent had to be strong and reflect the values and views of the elite.

In addition, superintendents relied upon the support of the elite community to assure their control and power. Wendell Pierce, Superintendent of Schools in 1963, wrote a public response to the question, "How do you account for the stability of the Cincinnati Public Schools?" In it, he emphasized the cooperative arrangement between the Citizens School Committee, the school administration, and the Board of Education. Pierce's reply claimed that, "The team operation which has existed for many years between the total staff, the administration, and the Board of Education has been possible because, for the last fifty years, the Citizens School Committee has played a major role in the selection of board members and in implementing a city practice of keeping the school system out of politics."[29]

The relationship between community elites and school administration has to be understood in the context of the relationship between the educational reform movement which made it possible for elite groups to take charge and the professionalization of educational administration. During the early part of the 20th century, as several historians have noted, the development of elite control of urban schools occurred at the same time that school administrators began to model themselves after business managers and assumed more and more control of the internal workings of the educational system.[30] It is difficult to determine whether this shift occurred because business-dominated boards of education tended to select those who acted like themselves or because school administrators consciously or unconsciously used businessmen as a model. After the creation of small boards and the professionalization of educational administration, school boards became less interested and active in curriculum development, teacher selection, student evaluation, and staff management. The results of the reform were thus ironically at odds with its rhetoric that had argued that superintendents were to manage the school system with minimum interference from the board, only after the board of education had established general educational policy.

In Cincinnati there was established a system of mutual support between the Citizens School Committee and the superintendent. In the 1921 school board election, Superintendent Condon actively campaigned for the candidates supported by the Citizens School Committee. When a resolution was introduced at the September 26, 1921, board meeting condemning this action, Condon responded, "I want to repeat . . . that it was my duty . . . to advocate election of the candidates who represented the non-partisan control of education, for, to my mind, there is no greater issue involved in the administration of education than this: Keep the schools out of politics; keep politics out of the schools."[31]

Superintendent Condon also gave expression to the ideal relationship between a board of education and a school administration in a report to the Board of Education in 1923 after a trip across the country inspecting educational systems. In his report he identified those characteristics which made one school system superior to another. He told the board, "the best schools are likely to be found where there is the clearest recognition of what constitutes executive and administrative responsibility, with the Superintendent and his staff in charge of the administration of educational policies clearly and distinctly responsible to the Board of Education . . . but unhampered in the execution of educational plans and policies which have been approved." Condon told the board that where he saw this relationship between the board and superintendent there was "peace, harmony, good understanding . . . and good results. Where this relationship did not exist there was controversy, misunderstanding, and a general level of distrust."[32]

School board proceedings reflected the ideal relationship advocated by Condon. During the 1920s there was very little controversy at school board meetings. In fact, there was very little discussion of educational matters. Board proceedings contained endless pages of the drama of real estate deals and bond issues. School board members began to take on all the characteristics of Sinclair Lewis's Babbitt.

During the 1920s school board members did not function according to the model of board members determining educational policy and administrators administering that policy. What board members primarily discussed and determined were real estate deals, the handling of bond issues and the issuance of building contracts. These were lawyers and businessmen of the 1920s who seemed to measure their success in terms of capital expansion and financial management. Words were not lost in discussions of educational policy, but were concentrated in the realm of fine legal and financial phrases.[33]

What emerged from the 1920s was definition of roles which protected the power of the superintendent and allowed school board members to feel comfortable playing roles which fit their everyday lives. Of course, this division of powers did not mean a complete retreat by board members from educational issues, but it did mean that one of the most important decisions to be made by board members was the selection of the superintendent.

So when I interviewed Ewart Simpkinson, who served as head of the Citizens School Committee during the 1950s, one of the questions that kept haunting me was where the leaders of these large corporations could find the time and energy to participate actively in the control of school affairs. From Simpkinson's perspective the key was the selection of the superintendent. In other words, all that was required was a superintendent who reflected the values of the elite members of the board.[34]

A concern about selection of the superintendent surfaced during the 1955 school board campaign when candidate Homer Toms claimed that a member of the executive board of the Citizens School Committee had told him that the committee's ticket was designed to pack the board to control the selection of the next superintendent. Toms had been a member of the Citizens School Committee for ten years prior to the election. His break with the group during the election led him to seek support of the local Republican Party which was also concerned with the issue of elite domination. George Eyrich, the chairman of the local county Republican Central Committee, charged that the Citizens School Committee was a "self-appointed group" that, because of its "manipulation of candidates," should not be "entrusted with the future composition of the school board."[35]

The involvement of the Republican Party in the campaign caused the Citizens School Committee to wave the banner that said keep politics out of the schools. Hiding behind this banner, the Citizens School Committee never denied the concern about controlling the selection of the superintendent. The Citizens School Committee simply issued a public statement saying, "We particularly recognize the achievements of our superintendent, Dr. Claude V. Courter, and if, as our opponents state, it is necessary that a successor to Dr. Courter be selected in two years, we and our candidates would hope that Dr. Courter's successor carry on with the same policies and in the same manner as Dr. Courter."[36]

The hope that Courter's successor would carry on his policies implied support for the Citizens School Committee. Superintendent Courter claimed in an interview that, "The major contribution of the Citizens School Committee was its steadfast ability to recruit School Board candidates who were not subservient to any political party or boss. . . . Across the years, the Citizens School Committee has so consistently selected well-qualified Cincinnatians as its nominees that they literally pre-empted the field." The interviewer concluded that Superintendent Courter's "personal support of the Citizens School Committee was steadfast during his administration as Superintendent of the Cincinnati Public Schools."[37]

The close relationship between the Citizens School Committee and the superintendent was one important element in the total structure of control of the Cincinnati school system. The elements of that control included the nominating and financing of school board candidates, informal contacts between elite members of the business community, the establishment of a foundation to control the flow of information between the school system and the public, and the appointment and control of school administrators. The key to the success of this control was the limitation of community representation through an election structure based on nonpartisan and at-large school board elections.

In fact, it was the issue of limited representation that eventually caused the demise of the Citizens School Committee. The origin of the issue of representation was the defeat in 1966 of operating levies for the school system. In response to the defeat of these levies a new organization was created, Cincinnatians United for Good Schools, to investigate school and community relationships. The membership of this organization was similar in terms of elite nature to that of the Citizens School Committee. The chairman of Cincinnatians United for Good Schools was John R. Bullock, an attorney with the prestigious law firm of Taft, Stettinius, and Hollister, and the secretary-treasurer was Clint Pace, manager of Community Affairs and Shareholder Relations for Procter & Gamble.[38]

The Cincinnatians United for Good Schools hired both Ronald Campbell, at that time dean of the Graduate School of Education at the University of Chicago, and the Midwest Administration Center of the University of Chicago to conduct a survey of the Cincinnati schools. In their report delivered in 1968 they spoke directly to the issue of the limited representation of the Citizens School Committee. The report stated, "Traditionally, the Citizens School Committee, a nonpartisan organization which has existed since 1914, has been the principal sponsoring group for school board candidates." But, in a recommendation that was obviously critical of the Citizens School Committee, the report argued, "If the Citizens School Committee be retained, its membership should be broadened to include representatives from many other segments and organizations of the city. The purpose of the Citizens School Committee should be to get wide participation in selecting broadly representative, able, and devoted citizens for school board membership."[39]

Besides calling for broader representation within the Citizens School Committee, the survey report recognized that the heart of the problem was the structure of school board elections and the report recommended that, "Cincinnati and other major city districts in Ohio may wish to join in seeking to amend the law to permit 9 to 11 board members, the majority elected at large and the remainder from subdivisions of the city."[40]

While nothing concrete was done about changing Ohio law, there was a move to throw open the doors of the Citizens School Committee to greater community participation. This period of the 1960s was, of course, one in which black communities in most urban areas were making greater demands for participation in the decision-making processes. The Citizens School Committee had, as mentioned earlier, controlled the entry of minority representation on the school board by carefully nominating a black candidate they felt reflected their values.

With demands from the black community and the recommendations of the school survey, the Citizens School Committee in 1969 adopted a new constitution under the leadership of Roger Crafts, a faculty member in the Medical School of the University of Cincinnati. The new constitution created an essentially new organization composed of individual members and delegates from 31 organizations that supposedly represented the major segments of Cincinnati. In a letter to Ewart Simpkinson, the former head of the Citizens School Committee, Crafts explained, "This reorganization was undertaken to permit more complete and representative community participation in the nomination of candidates for the Board of Education; it was undertaken with the conviction that the Board must be able to listen to and be heard by all segments of the community and that this liaison with the community can be insured only through election of a slate nominated by a broadly-representative Citizens School Committee—nominated to represent not a minority, not even a majority, but all of the children and parents in our School District."[41]

The irony of the situation, according to Roger Crafts, was that as the representation within the organization broadened, the business elite withdrew financial support from the organization and at a meeting in the law offices of Taft, Stettinius, and Hollister formed a new organization to nominate school board candidates called the Better Neighborhood School Committee. The name of the organization reflected a more conservative approach to school desegregation than that being expressed by the new, more broadly based Citizens School Committee. Without elite support the Citizens School Committee floundered and the Better Neighborhood School Committee became the new vehicle for elite support.[42]

An important lesson to be learned from the collapse of the Citizens School Committee is that the problem is not with the structure of these organizations but with election laws which allow for continued elite control of school systems. To understand this issue it is important to discuss it in the framework of the more general political science literature dealing with representation and methods of election.

NONPARTISAN AND AT-LARGE ELECTIONS

As we have seen in the above account of Cincinnati, the cry of "Keep the schools out of politics" meant giving control to elite forces within the urban community. One of the important findings in the literature of political science is that nonpartisan elections are really partisan in their results. Willis Hawley argues, in one of the most complete studies of the issue, *Nonpartisan Elections and the Case for Party Politics,* that nonpartisan elections create a partisan bias in favor of Republicans. In Hawley's words, "What is referred to here as the Republican benefit thesis rests in part on the notion that Republicans enjoy a 'natural party organization' outside formal party structures."[43] What this means is that Republicans receive greater support from business and professional groups and that it is easy for these organizations to slip into the role of a political party.

Hawley tested the Republican bias thesis by analyzing elections in 88 cities employing nonpartisan ballots in local elections. He concluded from this analysis that nonpartisan elections did enhance the chances of Republicans being elected. But this situation was not true in every case. The most important factors to differentiate between cities experiencing a partisan bias to nonpartisan elections was size and social class. In terms of city size, Hawley found that cities over 50,000 had a definite partisanship resulting from nonpartisan elections. Hawley wrote with regard to social class and size, "The data presented thus far provide support for the general proposition that nonpartisanship facilitates the election of Republicans in large cities and in those with a relatively high proportion of persons who are unemployed, of low income, of low education, and in low-status occupations."[44]

What the above finding implies is that if one wants greater representation on school boards in large cities, one would want to replace nonpartisan elections with partisan campaigns and give active encouragement to the participation of political parties. Without active involvement of political parties, civic organizations and informal business ties assume the dominant role. As Hawley emphasizes, and as history demonstrates in Cincinnati, participation in community organizations is determined by class, with those of high class making most of the decisions.

I conclude from my study that, if partisan elections were allowed in cities like Cincinnati there would be a broader representation of the local citizenry on boards of education. Experience verifies this conclusion in cases where cities have changed from at-large elections to elections by district. The evidence we have on this issue comes from the several cities that have made such a switch in election procedures during the last decade. Probably the most famous case occurred in Dallas, Texas, where a court order forced broader representation on its city council.[45]

For many years Dallas was governed the way the Cincinnati school system was controlled. With at-large elections a small group of leading business and professional men were able, through an organization similar to that of the Citizens School Committee, to control elections to the city council. They, like Cincinnati, even responded to the civil rights movement of the early 1960s by nominating what they viewed as a safe black candidate. When court action forced abandonment of at-large elections for election by district, the elite group lost its strangle hold on the city's elections and a broader representation of the population in terms of race and socioeconomic class began to be elected. The same phenomenon occurred in San Francisco after voters forced a change to an election by district system.[46]

One can go through a steady review of the political science literature to prove that partisan elections by district give a broader representation of the population than nonpartisan elections at-large. But in the end the real question is whether broad representation is desirable. Historically, those who have demanded elite control have viewed the majority of the population as not having the ability to make "good" decisions regarding education. The same argument is true of those who claim that professionals should control education because they know what is in the best interests of the child.[47]

Both the elite and the professional arguments contain a partial rejection of the democratic process and also a lack of understanding of the importance of democratic control of a government educational system. One of the real dangers of a government-operated school system is that the political and social values taught in the system give primary support to one group over another. In our society it is very important who controls the content of the knowledge that schools distribute.

The history of American education is punctuated by racism and an emphasis upon teaching the values of the business community. This phenomenon is not accidental, but rather is directly related to the traditional lack of minority control and representation in education; it is directly related also to the traditional control that local elite business groups have over education. One of the important effects of federal intervention in the schools in the 1960s and 1970s was that it countered traditional elite control of the schools and forced local recognition of the problems of poor and minority groups. One can almost portray the phenomenon of the 1960s as a struggle between the national liberal elite and the local elite over the control of the schools. With the Reagan era we might be witnessing a greater emphasis on control by the local elite.

The issues go beyond just the consideration of one social group controlling the schools in its own interest. It also involves the actual political content of schooling. There were 19th century concerns that a single political ideology would come to dominate the schools. The hope was that democratic control would assure a representation of all the political values of a community in the educational system. In this manner the schools would not serve a single political interest.

If one of the goals of the educational system is to produce a democratic citizen, then one must certainly criticize a governance system that contradicts the democratic values of community participation and representation. In our current system these values have become part of what I call a managed democracy. Community advisory groups are organized by the school system as part of the plan of educational management. The fact that these advisory groups have to be organized says something very important about the nature of school boards. Since these school boards are not representative of the community, educational managers must find other mechanisms like advisory groups to determine community desires and interests. But, of course, there is an important difference between a citizen's advisory group and an elected board of education, and that important element is formal political power which will allow the exercise of control over the system as opposed to an educational administrator determining what should be done with community input.

I would argue that a school system that is to truly reflect democratic values must be governed in a democratic manner. This is important in terms of the political and social values in the system and in terms of the power of one social group over another. It seems quite clear what must be done to assure greater democratic control of the schools. The issue is not simply local control because this can mean control by a small local elite. This is the danger of the present argument for returning power to the local level. What is required is a change at the local level to assure broader community representation so that local control does not mean control by a small handful of local people.

The key to a more democratic political process in terms of representation in urban areas is the restructuring of school board elections so that they are partisan and by district. In terms of school board size there is another important issue. On the one hand, one could argue for increasing the size of the school board so that the number of districts could be increased and their size reduced. This certainly would broaden representation. On the other hand, increasing the size significantly could make the actual operation of boards of education more cumbersome. The answer to that situation is to begin the dismantling of large urban school districts and to create smaller independent school systems that could be subdivided into smaller districts. The smaller the political unit the easier it is for the individual citizen to participate. In concluding, I argue only that if school systems are to teach and reflect democratic values they must function in the context of democratic control.

This essay does not explore the relationship between political power and the content of education. One can hypothesize that the political structure of education determines the content of education. If this is true, then one can argue that the curriculum becomes a function of the direct and indirect control of local power brokers. One response to this argument could be that curriculum decisions are also made at state and federal levels. In the situation discussed in this essay, the local power brokers are tied directly to state and national power structures. This is particularly true of Procter & Gamble's president, Neil McElroy. Another argument could be that the real curriculum decisions are made by local school administrators. But one needs to realize that the local power structure plays a dominant role in the selection of the superintendent. It is easy to argue that a more democratic control of the schools could mean a more democratic control of the curriculum.

NOTES

[1] A general discussion of the political changes that made this control possible in the 20th century is found in Joseph Cronin's, *The Control of Urban Schools* (New York: Free Press, 1973), pp. 39–123; Joel Spring, *Education and the Rise of the Corporate State* (Boston: Beacon Press, 1972), pp. 85–90, 128–135; and David Tyack, *The One Best System* (Cambridge, MA: Harvard University Press, 1974), pp. 126–167.

[2] David N. Plank and Paul E. Peterson, "Does Urban Reform Imply Class Conflict? The Case of Atlanta's Schools," *History of Education Quarterly* 23, no. 2 (Summer 1983), p. 168.

[3] See references in footnote 1.

[4] Concepts of representation and democratic elitism in education are discussed in Joel Spring's *Educating the Worker-Citizen* (New York: Longman, 1980), pp. 105–135.

[5] Taped interview with Ewart Simpkinson, December 16, 1981.

[6] Ewart Simpkinson to Ralph Lazarus, July 15, 1954, Box 2, CSC, MSS (Manuscripts of the Citizens School Committee).

[7] "Nominating Committee Board of Education," Box 3, Citizens School Committee, Manuscript Collection, Cincinnati Historical Society.

[8] Ewart Simpkinson to Homer Lunken, February 9, 1949, Citizens School Committee, Manuscript Collection, Cincinnati Historical Society.

[9] Ewart Simpkinson to Evans DeCamp, April 5, 1949, Citizens School Committee, Manuscript Collection, Cincinnati Historical Society.

[10] Charles Judd to Ewart Simpkinson, October 9, 1959, Box 3, Citizens School Committee, MSS, and "Committee to Recommend Candidates," January 5, 1959, Box 2, Citizens School Committee, Manuscript Collection, Cincinnati Historical Society.

[11] Ewart Simpkinson to Carlton Hill, undated, Box 4, Citizens School Committee, Manuscript Collection, Cincinnati Historical Society.

[12] Ewart Simpkinson to Carlton Hill, April 17, 1961, Box 3, Citizens School Committee, Manuscript Collection, Cincinnati Historical Society.

[13] Ewart Simpkinson to Kelly Siddall, October 20, 1959, Box 3, Citizens School Committee, Manuscript Collection, Cincinnati Historical Society.

[14] *Cincinnati School Board Proceedings*, January 4, 1960, pp. 3–5.

[15] *Ibid.*, pp. 3–5.

[16] *Ibid.*, p. 6.

[17] Robert Weber to Samuel Todd, January 5, 1960, Box 3, Citizens School Committee, Manuscript Collection, Cincinnati Historical Society.

[18] Ewart Simpkinson to Joseph M. Bertotti, February 19, 1960, Box 3, Citizens School Committee, Manuscript Collection, Cincinnati Historical Society.

[19] Companies headed by Schwab in 1959, who has continued to play an active role in business in the Cincinnati community.

[20] Simpkinson to Bertotti, *op. cit.*

[21] Ewart Simpkinson to Richard Peake, March 11, 1959, Box 3, Citizens School Committee, Manuscript Collection, Cincinnati Historical Society.

[22] Taped interview with Roger Crafts, December 21, 1981.

[23] *Ibid.*

[24] "Interview with Neil McElroy," *U.S. News & World Report*, April 1, 1955, pp. 78–84.

[25] Interview with Ewart Simpkinson, December 16, 1981.

[26] Ewart Simpkinson to Neil McElroy, May 4, 1954, Box 2, Citizens School Committee, MSS.

[27] "Teachers Recognition Day," 1955, p. 2, Box 2, Citizens School Committee, MSS.

[28] Simpkinson and Crafts interviews, *op. cit.*

[29] Wendell Pierce, October 4, 1963, Box 3, Citizens School Committee, MSS.

[30] Raymond Callahan, *Education and the Cult of Efficiency* (Chicago: University of Chicago Press, 1962).

[31] Cincinnati Board of Education Proceedings, September 26, 1921, pp. 5–7.

[32] Cincinnati Board of Education Proceedings, January 8, 1923, pp. 16–19.

[33] The extensive involvement of the Board of Education in the bond market in the 1920s and subsequent debt in the 1930s caused a survey team sponsored by the federal government to recommend that the board not issue any more bonds. *Survey Report of the Cincinnati Public Schools Made by the United States Office of Education at the Request of the Cincinnati Board of Education and the Cincinnati Bureau of Governmental Research* (Cincinnati: The Cincinnati Bureau of Governmental Research, 1935), pp. 456–457.

[34] Simpkinson interview, *op. cit.*

[35] "GOP in School Board Battle; Attacks Citizens' Committee," *Enquirer*, November 8, 1955, p. 18.

[36] "Bahlman Replies to Attack on Citizen Group's Ticket for Seats on School Board," October 13, 1955, p. 3.

[37] Erwin, p. 97.

[38] The Midwest Administration Center, University of Chicago, Report Cincinnati School Survey, August 1968, pp. xii–xiii.

[39] *Ibid.*, pp. 99–101.

[40] *Ibid.*, p. 101.

[41] Roger Crafts to Ewart Simpkinson, October 13, 1969, Citizens School Committee, Manuscript Collection, Cincinnati Historical Society.

[42] Interview with Roger Crafts, *op. cit.*

[43] Willis D. Hawley, *Nonpartisan Elections and the Case for Party Politics* (New York: J. Wiley, 1973), pp. 22–23.

[44] *Ibid.*, p. 84.

[45] A discussion of Dallas and San Francisco in comparison to Cincinnati can be found in Howard Hamilton's *Electing the Cincinnati City Council* (Cincinnati: Stephen Wilder Foundation, 1978), pp. 22–35.

[46] *Ibid.*

[47] See Spring, *Educating the Worker-Citizen*, pp. 105–135.

DISCUSSION QUESTIONS FOR CHAPTER 10

1. What similarities are there in Draper's and Cubberley's plans for depoliticizing school politics? In particular, who did they believe should be in charge of the schools?
2. What are the dilemmas of local school control that Peshkin points out? How do you suggest they might be resolved?
3. In Cincinnati, how did school politics develop along the lines suggested by Cubberley? What groups were excluded from this process and why?
4. How does ideology figure into school politics? What are the ideologies behind the various models of school control discussed in this chapter?

10

Readings on the Politics of Schools: Choice and Change

In Chapter 9 we looked at how the current nature of school politics developed. In particular, we pointed out that bureaucracy is the defining feature of the organization of most school systems. The readings in this section challenge "business as usual" and propose, instead, alternatives that emphasize individual choice.

Denis Doyle's essay on vouchers and tuition tax credits is an overview of the historical and political contexts within which these reforms have been proposed. We are reminded of the ways in which the concepts of equity, freedom, and social utility merge in the movement toward privatization. The essay also reminds us of some aspects of public education—professional insensitivity to public opinion, centralization, and inefficiency—that recently have led to broad public criticism of U.S. schooling. Doyle concludes his essay by reminding us that the tax credit issue is not simply a tax issue. Rather, it is an education issue that "goes to our political and social core." It is, in short, an issue of the extent to which public and private interests are compatible.

R. Freeman Butts's criticism of vouchers reflects his thorough understanding of the historical factors that brought about public education in the United States. Professor Butts asks us to consider whether voucher systems are really in the public interest as it relates to the historic purposes of American democracy. The ideal of citizenship, not the values of the market place, argues Butts, should guide our thinking about educational reform.

The final two pieces in this chapter look at the most recent attempts to alter the politics of schooling by introducing parental choice plans. The first piece is by John Chubb, who is the coauthor of the recent Brookings Foundation report that has put choice plans once again on the public agenda. In his essay he argues that parental choice will force schools to improve as consumers, in effect, vote with their feet.

Deborah Meier, the author of the last piece in this section, is a principal of a school in New York's Harlem neighborhood where school choice is practiced. While she is an advocate of choice, she is anxious to point out its pitfalls and difficulties. Of central concern to Meier is how such plans ensure an equitable education for all students.

This, of course, is one of the key questions to consider when looking at plans to alter public school governance through the introduction of school choice plans. We must ask ourselves whether we are merely seeing attempts to make it possible for a few students to get an outstanding education or whether these plans benefit all of our children.

DENIS P. DOYLE

TUITION TAX CREDITS AND EDUCATION VOUCHERS, PRIVATE INTERESTS AND THE PUBLIC GOOD

Tuition tax credits or tuition vouchers are far removed from most of what educators think about—curriculum, teacher licensing, minimum standards, school finance reform, classroom management, and government regulation. Rather, tax credits and vouchers raise fundamental questions about the relationship of schooling to the larger society: the tension between professional and parent, and the role and place of values in education. Finally, and most important in a democratic republic, they force us to re-examine the tension between equality and liberty. This, of course, is precisely why they are controversial. If vouchers or tax credits were simply a device to administer education differently, there would be discussion but not impassioned debate. To see why this is the case, we must return to the beginning.

Over the past 50 years, the line that distinguished the public sector from the private has been blurred. Health care, housing, food and nutrition programs, Social Security, and unemployment compensation are all infused with large measures of public funding. In the case of schooling, however, there has been a strong historical commitment to universal free education, and public funding for private elementary and secondary education has been off-limits. There are some public subsidies of a minor nature: Gifts to private schools are tax-deductible, and private school property is exempt from real estate tax. While these tax forgivenesses are thought to stimulate philanthropy and reduce school costs, their effects are modest.

The current debate about tuition tax credits or education vouchers renews the old question about how and where the line between the public and private sector should be drawn. And it raises two major issues: The extent to which private schools should receive government aid, if at all, and the extent to which such aid might lead to government control of private schools.

The issues are of special interest to economists and political scientists because there is no *a priori* reason to believe that government must own and

From Denis P. Doyle, "Tuition Tax Credits and Education Vouchers, Private Interests and the Public Good." Reprinted with permission from *The College Board Review*, No. 130 (Winter 1983–84), pp. 7–11. Copyright © 1984 by College Entrance Examination Board, New York.

operate the means of production to provide public goods or services. Government may as easily—or even more easily—provide funds and let the private sector satisfy public program objectives. In this vein, state governments do not build their own highways or public buildings: The lowest bidder does. Similarly, Medicare recipients are not required to "spend" their Medicare funds in public hospitals.

The reason for this is obvious enough. At its most elevated it is what Charles Schultze of the Brookings Institution calls the public use of private interest. At a more prosaic level, it recognizes that different people have different tastes and different preferences. In this formulation, choice is a virtue, one that should be satisfied.

Now, if parental choice in education is to be increased, short of wholesale reconfiguration of the public sector, the most obvious device is government funding of private schools. Three principal options are available—direct aid to institutions, education vouchers for individual students, or "negative" transfer payments through the tax system in the form of tax credits. The court has repeatedly struck down direct funding of private institutions as unconstitutional because the vast majority of them have religious ties. But vouchers might pass constitutional muster, as indeed tax credits have recently done in *Mueller v. Allen.*

As well, there is the possibility of public scholarships and loans, or what Senator Daniel Patrick Moynihan calls "the baby BEOGS" program, in which the eligibility floor for the basic educational opportunity grants would drop to primary and secondary education. The advantages of such a program would be several. Because eligibility is based on income, it would go only to the truly needy. If it were designed properly, public school children could use the program for supplemental or enrichment activities. And perhaps most important from an economic standpoint, because it would reach only a fraction of the children in private schools (unlike tax credits which would reach everyone who pays taxes), tuition would not be driven up in an amount equal to the tax credit. Unfortunately, there seems to be no constituency for such a program: It is clearly odd-man out in any discussion of aid to private schools.

At this juncture it is important to stress that the growing interest in private school aid plans is not because of the Reagan administration, but because of a persistent shift toward private education in the recent past. As the number of school-age children continues to decline, the number of children enrolled in private schools is increasing. By 1986, for example, the National Center for Education Statistics predicts a 12 percent increase in private school enrollments, from 5 million to 5.6 million children. Yet as recently as three years ago, the best available data suggested continued private school decline. Bruce Cooper and his colleagues, in the most recent issue of the *Teachers College Record,* report that their data reveal a trend line that points to 15 percent private school enrollment by 1990.

Indeed, we are witnessing a remarkable historic transformation. For years, as private education grew progressively weaker, the clamor for aid became more shrill. But it fell on deaf ears. As recently as 1977, Senator Moynihan's stirring defense of aid to private schools in *Harper's Magazine* was titled "The Federal

Government and the Ruin of Private Education." His thesis was simple: Without aid, private schools would languish and even disappear. But today, it is clear that the system in danger is not private schools. At risk today is a faltering public system. In fact, one interesting way to frame the question is in traditional public policy terms: The justification for public intervention in a private market is real or threatened market failure. Today we see growing "privatization" of education because of public sector market failure. Public schools fail to satisfy an ever-larger segment of the population.

For the first time in recent history, then, there is a realistic possibility of public aid to private schools, not because they are weak, but because they are strong. Ironically, public support could then be the Achilles Heel of private education, for just as the power to tax is the power to destroy, the power to provide aid is the power to control. And if private schools were to become subject to public control, they would lose their unique character.

It is becoming clear that aid to private schools may become as important a public policy issue in the 1980s as civil rights was in the 1960s, and it is more than a curiosity that these two issues are bracketed by two major studies conducted by James Coleman. In the first Coleman report in 1966, his central finding was that what makes a difference in education is the student body, not the building, curriculum, level of funding, or organization. This finding was used to justify and encourage the end of racial isolation.

The second and most recent Coleman report, however, presents us with striking evidence that certain things do matter, that in fact there are differences between good and bad schools, and the differences make a difference. That this finding should be surprising is in itself a surprise, because discerning teachers, students, and parents have always known that some schools are better than others, and all things being equal, it is better to go to a good school than a bad one. If there are quality differences among schools, it is no longer a matter of indifference as to which school one goes. And someone must choose: a parent, a student, or a bureaucrat. In fact, Coleman finds that in certain circumstances private schools do a better job academically than comparable public schools. Thus, Coleman, who provided arguments on behalf of compulsory busing for 15 years, now provides a rationale for choice.

While vouchers and tax credits are frequently discussed in the same breath, there are some differences worth noting.

In modern times, vouchers were first seriously proposed by Nobel laureate and conservative economist Milton Friedman. (John Stuart Mill, ever the libertarian, supported vouchers most enthusiastically. Afraid that public schools would be used to "standardize" children, he wrote what remains as vouchers' most stirring defense.) In the late 1960s, vouchers were adopted as a war-on-poverty strategy by democratic socialist Christopher Jencks in the closing days of President Lyndon B. Johnson's Great Society. The task of implementation fell to the Nixon administration, but vouchers quietly faded under President Gerald R. Ford, sinking without a trace under President Jimmy Carter. Given President

Ronald Reagan's interest in the subject, however, it now appears that the report of the death of vouchers was premature.

What is it we know about vouchers? Are they so much snake oil, a threat to our system of free public education, or might they trigger revitalization and rejuvenation of a faltering public enterprise?

Although there are no elementary and secondary school voucher systems in this country, the federal government did sponsor voucher research for nearly a decade. After several years of planning, in the spring of 1971 a serious effort was made to launch a series of five multi-year voucher demonstration projects under the aegis of the old Office of Economic Opportunity. But even the idea of a demonstration project was viewed as so radical that only one school district in the nation accepted federal funds to serve as a demonstration site. The project, tried in the Alum Rock Union school district in San Jose, California, was severely limited, making it difficult to form judgments about vouchers in general.

For example, because of California constitutional constraints, no private schools joined the Alum Rock project and no teachers' jobs were at risk, so there is no real information on what might happen in a more "competitive" education market. In addition, poor children received extra-value vouchers to provide the resources to give them enrichment programs and to make them "attractive" to schools. Finally, schools could not charge more tuition than the value of the voucher. Nevertheless, the project was surrounded by intense anxiety and extensive publicity.

Why anxiety and publicity? Because of the explosive word *vouchers*. If Alum Rock had been presented as an open-enrollment experiment, it would enter the annals of forgotten federal projects. But in a "voucher" experiment, emotions ran so high that the local teachers' associations disaffiliated from the statewide association for the first year of the project. For vouchers, taken seriously, represent a measured assault on the status quo. They assert that private decisions are better than public, that parents know as much about the welfare of their children as educators, that choice and diversity are to be preferred to the "common core" of the existing system. Thus, even though the Alum Rock project was an attenuated voucher system, the actors in the project— teachers, parents, administrators, school board members—behaved as though it were a real test of the concept. This intensity of reaction in a carefully controlled demonstration project provides some insight into the emotional and political reactions that discussion of vouchers provokes.

Albert Shanker, president of the American Federation of Teachers, in a moment of prescience observed more than a decade ago that the voucher omelette, once made, cannot be unscrambled. And that is the essence of the issue. This homespun comment on the federal government's attempt to experiment with vouchers was precisely on target. There are two reasons that Shanker's observation was correct and anxiety ran high in Alum Rock—and why no other school district would try vouchers, even with the promise of sizable federal funds. First, education is not a game. It is a serious business. Johnny and Suzie each go around once. The sequence from kindergarten to postgraduate school is not something to be tampered with lightly. The stakes are real, and they are high. Parents know it, and teachers know it.

The second reason is more profound but less obvious: Education is embedded in a political process. Any enterprise that commands more than one-half of most state budgets and is the principal activity of local elected officials is up to its neck in politics. It may not be partisan, it may not be ideological, but it is a central part of the ebb and flow of the political process. And no one is going to be able to "experiment" with a system that requires political actors to relinquish voluntarily their responsibility and control. Imagine asking a teachers' union leader, an elected school board official, an appointed public school superintendent, a mayor or city councilmember to step aside for five years to permit a government agency to pass out vouchers and watch what happens.

Any decision to go forward with vouchers, then, cannot be defended or justified as research and development. If vouchers are tried at all, they will be tried as a serious policy alternative to the way in which schooling is financed in this country, not as an experiment or demonstration program.

What is the prognosis if a voucher system is adopted, and does research offer any guidance? Unfortunately, the only honest answer is, "It all depends." It depends on what kind of voucher system is installed, whose purposes it is designed to serve, and what the longer-term unanticipated consequences turn out to be. This is so because there is no single voucher system: Vouchers may be lightly or closely regulated; they may permit wide latitude for parental choice; and they may permit or discourage out-of-pocket supplemental payments for more than the value of the voucher. To illustrate, return to Alum Rock. Conceived of in the heyday of the War on Poverty, it was a last great power-to-the-people program. Parents would reassert their rightful place, the argument ran. Using vouchers, they would choose from among diverse offerings what was best for their children. Teachers and administrators would assume their proper role as providers of service, not as management and workers in a public monopoly.

What really happened? As the superintendent ruefully described it, "power devolved from the board to the superintendent, bypassed the principals, and stopped with the teachers, never reaching the parents." What had begun as a parent-power program became a teacher-power program. And why not? Teachers have the organizational skills, the occupational opportunity, and the professional incentives to run voucher schools according to their lights. Parents, with other demands on their time, were only too happy to leave school decisions to the professionals.

In the 1980s the question of vouchers cannot be raised without at the same time raising the question of tax credits, but the question of tax credits is even more problematic than vouchers because there is very limited experience with them in the field of education. As a generic concept, economists, liberal as well as conservative, view tax credits as a device to stimulate socially desirable behavior that would otherwise be subject to sluggish demand. Energy tax credits are a case in point. A home-owner taxpayer who weather-strips, insulates, or installs storm windows can reduce his federal tax liability by as much as $300. California taxpayers who install solar heating devices can claim a handsome credit on their state income tax as well. Similarly, working parents of young children can claim a daycare tax credit against their federal tax liability.

In each case the credit is designed to stimulate and reward behavior that serves the public good. In the case of education, however, the subject of tax credits raises second-order issues directly. While supporters and opponents agree that tax credits would stimulate demand for private education, they disagree strongly about the desirability of such an effect. Opponents, for example, see tax credits as an elitist raid on the treasury and a threat to public schools, while supporters see them as a response to a pluralistic society in which private education deserves public assistance.

While it is hard to imagine a simpler or more direct system of government support for elementary and secondary private schooling—the whole transaction takes place on individual tax forms—its potential impact on the relationship between the public and private sector is not as clear. Suppose, for example, a credit of $500 were available for every full-time student, kindergarten through postgraduate degree candidate. A family with two students in private school paying tuition of $500 per year for each child could claim a $1000 credit, and so on, up to the limit of the family's tax liability and the actual expense of schooling.

For many families, education tax credits would significantly reduce their income tax liability, but for the very poor or the very rich who escape taxes—those with no qualifying education expenses and those who send their children to public schools, there would be no benefit. But for the taxpayer with qualifying education expenses, tax credits would represent a boon.

Although tax credits might drive up tuition, they would have no direct effect on the way most private schools are organized and operated. As private, not-for-profit corporations, private schools are already subject to internal revenue service scrutiny, and tax credits should not materially affect the status quo. As it is, in most jurisdictions, private schools are lightly regulated: They may organize as they wish; they may hire, fire, pay their staff as they will (and the market permits); they may select students on their own terms; and they may offer any curriculum, including religious instruction, that they think appropriate.

The principal policy question raised by tax credits is the extent to which they would influence behavior. Would more and different children attend private school if tax credits were enacted? It is difficult to predict. The larger the tax credit, the greater the prospect that large numbers of children would move to private schools. Like the self-fulfilling prophecy of the Laffer Curve, which predicts zero revenue at both zero and 100 percent tax rates, small tax credits would have almost no effect on behavior, while a 100 percent credit would presumably produce a major impact. At what point in the size of the tax credit behavior begins a change no one can forecast with certainty.

A recent study, just concluded by the staff of the National Commission on School Finance, has assembled some extraordinarily interesting data on this question. Based on a household sample, preliminary evidence suggests that fairly substantial movement to private schools would occur even with a small tax credit; and that the movement would be heaviest among low-income, minority families, precisely the audience education reformers are most concerned with.

This, of course, should come as no surprise: Upper-income, majority families have long enjoyed the luxury of choice, and as the poor would emulate the rich in other areas, so would they with education. As well, middle-class minorities, when income is controlled for, are equally or over-represented in private schools. Given the choice, there is every reason to believe that poor minority students would at least consider the option encouraged by vouchers or tax credits.

Adding credence to this view is Gallup Poll data on attitudes toward education. Asked to assign schools a letter grade, two strong trends emerge among respondents for more than a decade. First, residents of towns and villages still give their public schools good marks: To them, at least, small is beautiful. Second, that group of the population that consistently gives public schools their lowest marks are inner-city blacks. Without old-boy networks and family fortunes to inherit, inner-city minorities have more riding on good education than any other members of American society.

The final bit of information from the Gallup Poll is the consequence of a most curious but revealing question: Would you favor a voucher system: In 1983, for the first time in history, more than 50 percent of the respondents reported that they would.

Taken together, then, there is every reason to believe that vouchers or tax credits would have exactly the effect one expects: Private school enrollments would increase and public school enrollments would decrease. There is a fine bit of irony in this because proponents of tax credit and voucher schemes have got themselves in a very difficult tangle: To moderate the opposition (particularly the professional education associations), they have argued that there would be little or no switching to private schools. The public schools would be safe. To argue this way is a course of desperation. First, it doesn't for a minute convince public school supporters: they are in a perfect panic about losing students. Second, it exposes supporters of these public aid schemes to charges that public aid is simply a windfall to those families who already have their children enrolled in private schools.

It is interesting that these research findings should converge with these policy views in 1984, because it is inconceivable that the Congress will support tax credits as they have been presented in this economic environment; no one is willing to vote for even bigger deficits, which is what tax credits represent in their present incarnation.

The argument that would make tax credits financially palatable makes them politically unacceptable: Credits will save money. But they will do so only if some large number of children transfer from public to private school. And so long as the value of the tax credit is less than the cost of keeping the student in public school, there will be savings.

Thus, the argument that could gain supporters worried about spiraling ınd increasing government outlays is the same argument that will give ...ıe education associations apoplexy.

An altogether different policy question is raised by vouchers, and that is the extent to which private schools would come under some measure of public control. Even in the most lightly regulated voucher system, a voucher bureaucracy would be empowered to police it. One of the principal events in the Alum Rock project was the transformation of the existing public school bureaucracy into a voucher bureaucracy to oversee and operate the new system. Tax credits, on the other hand, would leave the status quo intact. Because a tax credit is claimed by checking a box on a form and completing the necessary arithmetic, government's role would be limited to additional tax clerks. In fact, tax credit legislation will be heard by the tax committees rather than education committees of the state legislatures or congress. If enacted, it will be administered by tax rather than education departments.

It is this remarkable simplicity that makes tax credits so attractive to private elementary and secondary school supporters. In contrast to the complexity and intrusiveness of voucher systems, tax credits are straightforward, easy to understand, and easy to use.

While vouchers and tax credits differ in important ways, together they raise profound questions about the role of government in educating elementary and secondary school-age children. As a society we provide substantial public funding for both public and private postsecondary education. The question before us today is whether or not public support should be provided for private elementary and secondary education as well.

The claims and counterclaims about tax credits and vouchers cannot be put to rest by the presentation of objective evidence, because the decision that policymakers will be asked to make goes beyond the purview of social science. It goes to our political and social core: Should private values and private organizational forms be encouraged, or should our social and political energies continue to be directed toward public institutions? Is private virtue consonant with public virtue? The question raised by tax credits and vouchers is at once that simple and that sweeping.

R. FREEMAN BUTTS

EDUCATIONAL VOUCHERS: THE PRIVATE PURSUIT OF THE PUBLIC PURSE

Several months ago John Gardner wrote an article for the *Chronicle of Higher Education* titled, in his felicitous fashion, "The Private Pursuit of Public Purpose."[1] His argument centered on the need for tax policies and freedom from

From R. Freeman Butts, "Educational Vouchers: The Private Pursuit of the Public Purse," *Phi Delta Kappan* 61 (September 1979), pp. 7–10. Reprinted with permission.

centralized government bureaucracies that would promote "private giving for public purposes," so that individuals and voluntary groups will be prompted to contribute as private persons to the "charitable, religious, scientific, and educational activities of their *choice*" (emphasis added). He argued further that this protection for private action represents no sentimental aversion to large-scale organization or national action that are necessary to deal with many of our problems—including a vigorous government. But he is worried about the loss of a sense of local community, which has been badly shattered in recent years:

> In a well-designed government, there should be a wise and fitting allocation of functions between the center and the periphery. Those functions that can best be performed at the highest level of government should be performed there, while those best performed in the private sector—or by local government—should be decentralized.

Gardner is particularly at pains to make the point that government and the *nonprofit* private sector should *not* be viewed as adversaries but as workable partners: "There are no villains. Government is necessary to the nonprofit sector; and a vital, creative nonprofit sector is crucial to the nation's future."

I have long admired John Gardner as president of the Carnegie Corporation, as secretary of the Department of Health, Education, and Welfare, and as guiding light of the Common Cause. And I must agree with much that he says. After all, I was supported for some forty years by a private institution of higher education while I worked on behalf of public education. But I devoutly hope that John Gardner's new enterprise will *not* be taken as an agency or an argument for educational vouchers. I believe that a full-scale voucher scheme will promote *private* purposes rather than *public* purposes.

If I may twist Gardner's phrase a bit, I believe that educational vouchers amount to the "private pursuit of the public *purse.*" You might say, "Why not? That is the American way." Every special interest lobbies in Washington and in the state capitals for governmental policies that will benefit its own particular group—and sometimes self-interest may be clothed in arguments that private benefits promote the public interest. But I would argue that such a view is peculiarly inappropriate and even dangerous when it comes to education. I argue this from a study of history and from an assessment of the present mood of the country.

First, the historical argument—and do not take history lightly, for it not only reveals our traditions and ideals but has embedded public education in our constitutions and governmental institutions. Now, *why* was *that* done? The basic reason why the founders of this Republic turned to the idea of *public* education is that they were trying to build common commitments to their new democratic *political* community.

Let me repeat this point. The prime purpose for a public rather than a private education was *political;* it was to prepare the young for their new role as self-governing citizens rather than as *subjects* bound to an alien sovereign or as *private persons* loyal primarily to their families, their kinfolk, their churches, their localities or neighborhoods, or their ethnic traditions. In its origin, the idea of public education was *not* to give parents more control over education, *not* to promote the individual needs and interests of children, *not* to prepare for a better job, *not* to get into college.

Jefferson said it most eloquently just two hundred years ago this year. In his revision of the laws of Virginia, Jefferson was trying to rid his society in 1779 of the economic and political props that perpetuated aristocratic privileges of status for family, kin, or social class. Jefferson thus proposed the abolition of the economic privileges of primogeniture and entail; *and* he proposed a system of public schools, governed by public officials and supported by public funds, to overcome the political inequalities and privileges inherent in private education:

> . . . [Of] the views of this law none is more important, none more legitimate, than that of rendering the people the safe, as they are the ultimate, guardians of their own liberty. . . . Every government degenerates when trusted to the rulers of the people alone. The people themselves are its only safe depositories. . . . *An amendment of our constitution must here come in aid of the public education.* The influence over government must be shared by all the people. (Emphasis added)

Now, two hundred years later, the people of California are being asked to amend their constitution to come to the aid of *private* education. This is indeed a revolution, and its effect will be to overthrow the civic purpose of education that was the basic reason why public education was incorporated in seven of the first fourteen state constitutions and eventually in all. It was seen by a wide consensus of persons ranging across the political spectrum as a necessary corrective for the several kinds of private schools that dotted the American landscape in the late eighteenth century: charity schools for the poor, tuition schools for the rich, proprietary schools run for profit, religious schools supported by subscription. Then, in the early nineteenth century, many kinds of attempts were made to channel public funds into the charity schools, the denominational schools, the private academies, and the philanthropic societies; and in the emerging public schools "rate bills" were levied upon parents who could afford to pay, while "free" schooling was often reserved for the poor. All in all, the diversity and the use of public funds for private purposes approached the situation to which present-day voucher schemes might very well return us.

If Jefferson had read and agreed with much of the voucher literature that I have read in the past decade, he might have prefaced his educational amendment to the constitution of Virginia in 1779 with the following preamble (with apologies to a certain Preamble that came along ten years later):

We, the people of the state of Virginia, in order to

—form a more perfect *pluralism,*
—establish justice *for parents,*
—provide for the defense of *diversity,*
—promote the *private* welfare,
—insure domestic *control of education,* and
—secure the blessings of *Milton Friedman* to ourselves and our posterity

do amend this constitution on behalf of educational vouchers.

Fortunately, I believe, the founders of the Republic and the successive generations of advocates for public schools responded instead to the value claims of the democratic political community that they were trying to build and that they believed should be held in common by the citizens of the American Republic—the values of freedom, equality, justice, and obligation for the public good.

It can be argued that private schools can just as well, if not better, develop common civic values. This is a possible argument for a society that is homogeneous in religion, language, ethnicity, and cultural tradition—or for one where there is a stable hierarchical class society in which education is a privilege of the few and where there is common agreement as to what the core of education should be (the classics, or Christianity, or Islam, or Judaism). But in a democratic society where education is intended for most of the people (if not all of them) and where there is enormous diversity of culture, of religion, of class, and of educational goals, the private schools are likely to separate and divide along homogeneous lines of one kind or another and are not likely to provide the overall sense of political community needed for a viable public life. This is especially true if the government itself and public funds are used to encourage parents and families to coalesce around other like-minded families.

It was in the hope that public schools would surmount the divisiveness of the many segments in American society, while at the same time honoring pluralistic differences, that the idea of a *common* school took root in the nineteenth century and flourished so widely in the twentieth. It came to be generally accepted that only a public school system common to all segments of society under public control could achieve the ideals of common civic community. We well know the goals of common schooling have not always been achieved in public schools, but now Jack Coons would redefine the meaning of "common schools" in such a way that even the *ideal* would be given up. This, I believe, is the real choice before the people of California—*not* whether parents shall have more control over the education of their children, but whether the *ideal* of a common school system devoted primarily to the task of building civic community among the vast majority of citizens shall be given up in favor of private choice.

I believe that this a particularly dangerous time for a new "experiment on our liberties." I believe the future of the very ideal of a common national purpose is at stake, not solely with regard to public education but with regard to our whole public life. Privatism is in the saddle and galloping in a peculiarly ominous way, and a voucher system might just make the race irreversible.

I need not remind you of the mood of the 1970s stemming from a decade of Vietnam, Watergate, campus unrest, corruption in quiet places, violence and drugs in the schools, and the whole litany of troubles. The signs are all about us: cynicism and skepticism about government; alienation from public institutions, including school administrators, bureaucracy, and militant teachers; a simplistic and self-serving complaint by big business booming with high profits about the extravagance of "big government"; the undignified scramble by politicians to echo "me too"; and now the "tax revolts" and fiscal hysteria. Just when it looked as though we might achieve fundamental school finance reforms in the interests of equity (led by Jack Coons in the *Serrano* case), Proposition 13 cut across the reform movement with its meat-axe approach to cutting property taxes, limiting governmental services, shrinking government, and adding fuel to the movement to private schools.

So we now have the prospect of reduced local control over education; greatly increased state control over school finance; depressed teacher morale; monumental layoffs fought by teachers (as in San Francisco); and prospective cuts in funds that would expand California's School Improvement Program designed to increase exactly the role of parent participation that Coons so devoutly seeks through a voucher system. All of this promises to weaken further that "well-designed government" described by John Gardner as a wise and fitting allocation of functions between the center and the periphery.

Meanwhile, at the federal level Sen. Patrick Moynihan lurks in the wings waiting for another try at tuition tax credits, which were defeated by a national coalition last year, while Sen. Jesse Helms seeks legislation to restore prayers to the public schools and prohibit the Supreme Court from interpreting the First Amendment. And Jerry Brown and Milton Friedman want to assemble a constitutional convention to amend the U.S. Constitution to keep taxes under control and budgets balanced.

In California, the state constitutional amendment fever promises a crowded agenda of initiatives on the ballot in 1980. Paul Gann's proposition would limit the growth of government spending at all levels to the percentage increase in inflation and the rate of population growth. Howard Jarvis's proposition would cut the income tax in half. Combine these two with Proposition 13 and what have we left? And Sen. Alan Robbins has led the California legislature to try to limit court-ordered school busing by legislative initiative. What all of this may do to the ideal of the public good and to the role of public education in promoting it boggles the mind.

And now comes on center stage the proposition to amend the California constitution on behalf of educational vouchers. I believe that this is one more effort to return a proper governmental function achieved over two hundred years to the private markets and entrepreneurs of the eighteenth century, now multiplied many thousandfold. There is no doubt about widespread public malaise concerning public schools; there is no doubt that the fever for private schools is rising. Private secular schools, fundamentalist Christian academies, and all sorts of alternatives beckon parents of an affluent society to desert the public schools. And "cultural pluralism" has become one of the most popular terms in the lexicon of professional educators. In none of these movements do I find a well-formulated conception of the common public good nor of the obligation of schooling to try to promote a sense of civic community. Today, even the *rhetoric* of "good citizenship" as the prime purpose of education is all but missing.

Herein lies the challenge to the education profession. In the discussion over vouchers the profession should not be perceived as taking a purely defensive stance of apology for the Establishment or of protection for special vested professional interests. It should take positive, constructive action to reassert the prime purpose of public education. Vouchers advocates argue for parental control rather than official or professional control of education. The profession must recognize the legitimacy of parental participation, but should argue that such participation can be most effective in the long run when it is undertaken in the open arena of the political process of public institutions rather than in the private contracting and bargaining with school owners and employers. We have increasing evidence that parents and public interest groups *can* work constructively with public officials and education professionals in such cities as Seattle, Minneapolis, Indianapolis, Salt Lake City, and in many communities of California and under the School Improvement Program.

We should not allow the choice facing Californians to be pictured as between the public schools as they now exist, with all of their imperfections, and some ideal vision of publicly funded private schools. The choice that a voucher proposition offers is between weakening the public schools still further by encouraging flight from them and *strengthening* the public schools by recalling them to their historic purpose of promoting the ideals of the democratic civic community. I don't see much hope of framing the discussion this way unless the profession takes the lead. We should argue for more parental participation, yes; for more cooperation with the rapidly mushrooming citizen participation movement of public interest groups, yes; for more innovation and experiment, yes.

But on the latter point I believe state policy should *not* be designed to encourage families to promote any kind of education they may devise. Rather, it should encourage innovation, experimentation, and diversity of approaches to the *common goal* of developing informed, committed, and responsible citizens for a democratic political community. Competition among schools should not be simply the market value of attracting students but competition to develop the best programs of citizenship education—including curriculum, methods, governance of schools, community participation, "hidden curriculum," and all the rest. This is the kind of competition upon which public money should be spent.

The undermining of public education can be achieved at a stroke by a constitutional amendment that will disperse public funds to all sorts of competing, specialized private-interest schools. But the *reform* of education, including public education, cannot be achieved overnight. Let's admit that. But let's covenant with the people of California that if they will defeat the voucher idea in June 1980, and if they will provide adequate funds, we *will* work to reform public education so that it will genuinely serve the highest values of the civic community. We have before us the most appropriate timetable I can think of for the revival of the civic learning.

Our deadline is June 1989—the two-hundredth anniversary of the First Congress elected and assembled under the Constitution framed at Philadelphia in 1787. This will give us a decade to reeducate ourselves as teachers and administrators in the historic meaning and ideals of our political community, to prepare a new generation of teachers along the same lines, to reeducate the public about the civic role of public education, and to demonstrate convincingly that public education *can* be an effective force in bringing to reality the basic values of the American civic community: liberty *and* equality *and* justice *and* personal obligation for the public good.

NOTE

[1] 8 January 1979.

JOHN CHUBB

MAKING SCHOOLS BETTER: CHOICE AND EDUCATIONAL IMPROVEMENT

I'd like to begin this article by providing a broad overview on what I think is wrong with American schools and what I think would make a difference.

Most of you are familiar with the state of American education. Just to give you some basic statistics, for roughly 20 years from the mid-1960s until the mid-1980s, the SAT scores of American students dropped sharply. Although scores have been going up for the last few years, they've recently stalled. Our students still are well behind where they were in 1965.

In addition, the dropout rate in the United States is about 25 percent. That is to say, 25 percent of our students are not finishing high school on time. In many of our large cities only half of the students finish high school on time.

Comparing the United States to countries around the world is even more depressing. In math and science, U.S. students rank dead last in any comparison with students from nations that are our leading competitors. The top five percent of students in the United States achieve at the same level as the middle student in the Japanese system.

There is a bit of good news. For the last five years, Americans, mostly at the state level, have been trying very hard to turn things around. The amount that has been done is remarkable. Five years ago, when reports began to come out suggesting various ways to improve our nation's school systems, a lot of skeptics said we could never find that much money. But in those five years or so we have spent far more money than any of the skeptics thought possible.

Between 1981 and 1986 expenditures per pupil for elementary and secondary education went up 40 percent. In real terms we now spend four times as much per child as we did in 1950. In the first half of the 1980s, teachers enjoyed larger salary increases than any other occupational group in the country. Their average salaries are still arguably too low, $29,000 per year, but they have gone up very quickly. We've also spent a good deal of money to reduce the size of classes.

From John Chubb, "Making Schools Better: Choice and Educational Improvement," *Equity and Choice* (May 1989), pp. 5–10.

There has been a crackdown on teacher incompetence. Teachers are being asked to take more tests, to demonstrate that they are able. There has been a crack-down on student underachievement. Graduation and promotion requirements are being boosted around the country.

This is very heartening because it is unusual for our political system to act so forthrightly. Americans are taking the problem seriously. Unfortunately, the prospects that these reforms will make much of a difference are not very good. This is doubly discouraging because we may be wasting a rare political opportunity to really do something.

Why am I willing to say that what has been taking place is not likely to make much of a difference? The reasons are reflected in the study I did entitled "What Price Democracy?" It is an analysis of the largest, most comprehensive data set ever assembled on American high schools and their students. I would like very briefly to summarize the study, its basic conclusions, and the implications for reform.

This study included 500 randomly selected high schools nationwide, public and private. Within these high schools it included the principals, 12,000 teachers, and 12,000 students. We've never before had, in this country, a data set that puts together such detailed information on both students and the schools that they've attended. Large studies usually concentrate on either schools or students. We've combined the two.

The other thing that is virtually unique about this data set is that the students were examined not once, but twice. They were examined when they began high school as sophomores, and again when they graduated. Thus we were able to study not simply changes in the levels of student achievement over time, but how a particular group of students progressed.

We focused on one major issue, academic achievement. Some will argue that schools are trying to accomplish a lot of other things as well. But the thing that we care about is academic achievement. We used five tests: math, science, reading, writing, and vocabulary, and combined the results into a comprehensive measure of student achievement between sophomore year and graduation.

After determining which students were achieving and which were failing, we sought to uncover the sources of success or failure. First came a bit of bad news: the most important determinant of how students achieve is their aptitude. Bright kids learn more in high school than kids that aren't so bright. There is a certain amount of student achievement that is beyond the reach of school reformers.

But the good news is that the second most important determinant of how well students do is the school they attend. The skeptics of the 1960s and '70s, who doubted that schools could make a difference, were wrong. Schools make a big difference. They are marginally more important than the influence of parents. They are far more important than the influence of peer groups.

The next question naturally is, "What makes the difference between successful and unsuccessful schools?" Let me begin by telling you what doesn't make a difference. Neither expenditures, teacher salaries, class size, graduation requirements, the amount of homework assigned, or any other individual school policy that we looked at matters. There was no correlation between student achievement and any of the variables on which school reformers have been concentrating so much time, effort, and money. That is why there is very little reason to believe that school reform, as it is proceeding, is going to work.

What will work? For any of you who are involved in management, the answer may seem pretty obvious. The thing about schools that really seems to matter is how they're organized. To begin with, good and bad schools have different goals. The schools that are succeeding, whether with poor students or the best students, consciously focus on academic achievement. If you ask personnel in these schools what their goal is, they will say, "academic achievement," or "academic excellence." People in schools that aren't doing so well say things like "the basics," "occupational training," or "citizenship." These goals may well be important. But if you want achievement the school has to focus on achievement.

I should also say that clarity and consensus about goals are as important as what you call the goal. The thing that distinguishes successful schools is that there is a real consensus within those organizations about what they are trying to achieve, whether they say, "the basics," or "academic excellence." We asked a random sample of 30 teachers in each school what were the priorities of the school. In the good schools, they agreed on the priorities. In the unsuccessful schools, there was a great deal of disagreement. Other school researchers have said that successful schools have a mission. That appears to be true. The schools in our survey that were succeeding consciously focused on one purpose.

Another important aspect of organization was leadership. The principals of successful and unsuccessful schools were as different as night and day. Successful schools were led by principals who the teachers said had a vision, knew where they wanted the school to go, and knew how to take the school in that direction. These are standard qualities of strong leadership. Also, the principals in the good schools were educationally oriented and thought of themselves as educational leaders, not administrators.

When we asked principals of unsuccessful schools why they became principals, they would say things like "I prefer administration to teaching." When asked what their long-term goals were, unsuccessful principals were much more likely to say, "I want to get out of the school, move up into the central office and rise in the administrative hierarchy."

In the successful schools, the principals wanted to stay in the schools. When you asked them why they became principals, they were more likely to say, "Because I wanted to take control of the school. I wanted to control personnel, I wanted to control policy." They wanted to lead, not merely to manage.

The other profound organizational difference was that in successful schools the sense of professionalism, independence, and responsibility for one's work was enormously higher. Teachers and principals in the successful schools were true professionals. Those in unsuccessful schools weren't professionals at all. The teachers in successful schools had more independence, they participated more extensively in school decisions, and they had more influence over those decisions.

Within their classrooms they were free to tailor their practices to the needs of the students. Any educator will tell you that this is important because education is not a science but an art. It requires discretion, not prescription. In the successful schools, teachers had discretion. To us, the concept that best summarized the difference between the successful and unsuccessful school organizations was that of a team. In successful schools, the organization was held together by consensus and cooperation, not primarily by rules and regulations. The unsuccessful school looked like a classic bureaucracy, held together primarily by rules and regulations—a hierarchy, not a team at all.

If strong leadership, clear goals, professionalism, and team spirit are what is important, how do you instill these somewhat elusive qualities in a school? Can it be done at all?

Many state legislatures believe that it can be done by sending teachers and principals to classes. There may be some management consultants who believe that it can be done that way. But if you look around the country at successful school organizations, it doesn't appear that formal management training accounts for much.

We took a careful look at what accounts for effective organization. The key determinant, more important than anything else, turns out to be autonomy. Successful schools were relatively independent of external influence by administrators: superintendents, central office bureaucrats, and union officials. A school that was free to chart its own course was much more likely to develop effective organization and thereby breed academic achievement.

Principals who had greater influence over curriculum, instruction, discipline, and especially hiring and firing, put together effective organizations. It doesn't take much insight to figure out why. If you're a principal and you get to determine who teaches in that school and what the school's resources are, you are much more likely to trust the members of the organization, which, after all, you assembled. You are more likely to treat them as members of the team and grant them the autonomy they need to do their jobs. If you don't have control over personnel, you're less likely to treat people as if they're team members. You distrust them. You believe there is going to be conflict and you regulate. Soon you have an organization that is held together not by a common vision but by rules and regulations, that is, a bureaucracy.

If autonomy from external control appears to be the key factor, the final question is where do you find autonomy? How do you get it?

You don't often get it in the public sector. In the public sector, autonomy arises only under exceptional circumstances: usually in schools outside of an urban area, where the students are already performing well and the parents are affluent and involved. In other words, in the public sector you get autonomy and good organization in those places where right now you don't need it because they are doing well.

In the cities, in schools that are failing, autonomy is decreasing. These schools are victims of a vicious cycle in which poor performance leads to demands that politicians do something, and politicians demand that administrators crack down. The politicians and administrators have only a limited number of levers to pull. They begin regulating. That regulatory, bureaucratic attitude seeps into the schools, further undermining performance, leading to more complaints and more regulation. The process is one in which succeeding crises lead to endless layers of regulations and broods of bureaucrats to see that they are carried out. The public sector does not provide autonomy for bad or mediocre schools, and therefore bad public school systems typically get worse.

If you don't find autonomy in public schools except under unusual circumstances, you almost always find it in private schools, including religious schools. Private schools are more autonomous and, all things being equal, have more effective organizations and perform better than public schools.

Why are private schools so autonomous and why do they develop these effective school organizations without anyone teaching them how to do it? The reason is really very simple. Private schools have to attract clients. They have to get parents and students to come to school. One way that you do that and keep parents and students happy, is to ensure that decisions are made at the level of the individual school, which is where the parents and students confront the system. You are forced in the private sector to delegate and to decentralize because that is the surest way to give parents and students access, keeping them happy and helping the schools meet their needs.

In the public sector, the people who run the schools must please not only parents and students who are, at least to some extent, trapped in the system, but also various interest groups: the unions, politicians and so forth. Were the people who run public school systems to delegate and decentralize, and provide real autonomy, they might not be able to satisfy these other groups. So in the public sector they centralize. But the private schools have no captive clients. The competition for clients leads the schools to concentrate on pleasing students and parents, and therefore to decentralize and make decisions at the level of individual schools.

I want to close with an anecdote that really brings this home. It illustrates the difference between organization in the public and private sectors in New York City and other urban areas.

Several months ago I was called by a reporter who wanted to know about our research. In the course of explaining about autonomy, I told him that in New York City they have an enormous central office bureaucracy, staffed by 5,000 people, which is tremendously overbearing and leaves the principals with very little influence over their schools. I contrasted this with the Catholic school system in New York City, which despite the church's reputation for hierarchy has only 50 people in its central office, though the system has almost a quarter of the students the public schools have. He took those numbers down and a month later they sent me the galleys of the article so I could check the quotes. I saw all these numbers and I thought, "5,000 versus 50! I better double check," because those figures had come from other sources.

I called the personnel office of the city school system and said, "I have a simple question: how many people work in the central office of the New York City school system?" The first person I reached had no idea, nor did the second or third, but they all promised to transfer me to someone who did.

Thirty-five minutes and many transfers later, I got to a person who said, "Yes, I do know the number, but if you want to know, you'll have to put your request in writing, send it through proper channels and we'll get the information back to you in a month."

Well, I pleaded and explained the circumstances and finally I was put in touch with someone who had the authority and the number. And he told me it wasn't 5,000, it was 6,000.

Now I needed to find out the number for the Catholic school system. I got someone in that central office and said, "I need some basic facts. I need to know the number of students in your school system." She told me. "I need to know the number of teachers in the school system." She told me. "I need to know the number of schools in the system." She told me. So I said, "The last thing I need to know is how many people work in the central bureaucracy of the Catholic school system in New York City."

And she said, "I'm sorry, we don't keep that kind of data."

"Well," I said, "would you have any idea? Is there any way you could get the number for me?"

And she said: "Just a minute—I'll count them." And she counted. There are 25. Twenty-five people running a school system that's a fifth to a quarter of the size of the public school system.

Public and private education are organized in an enormously different fashion. Those differences in organization account for all of the differences between the performance of public schools and private schools and most of the differences between good public schools and bad public schools.

The message for reformers is very simple. If you want schools to be organized more effectively and to teach more successfully, you must give them autonomy. But as any public school administrator will tell you, you can't just turn over a school to principals and teachers without holding them accountable in some way. You've got to provide autonomy without losing accountability. And once public school administrators begin thinking about accountability, they think about tests and rules and regulations and before you know it the autonomy is gone.

The only way to provide autonomy without losing accountability is to go to a different system of accountability. A top-down system will not work. You must build a system of accountability to parents and students rather than to politicians and administrators.

It works in the private sector. Private schools are held accountable to their constituency through the process of competition and choice. Similarly, the surest way to get autonomy and accountability into the public school system is not through regulation or spending, but through a mechanism of choice. There are many ways in which choice systems can be set up. Vouchers, open enrollments, magnet schools, and others. And one of the best ways to see it in operation is to observe the good works of District 4 of the New York City school system. They made it work despite the 6,000 bureaucrats, the 16 offices and the 22 steps. And, as the song says, if you can make it there, you can make it anywhere.

Deborah W. Meier

CHOICE CAN *SAVE* PUBLIC EDUCATION

Before deciding to go down in history as a war President, George Bush called himself our "education President," announcing ambitious goals to make American schoolchildren first in the world by the year 2000. These goals were applauded by politicians, educators and corporate leaders across the political spectrum. America's future itself, they all declared, is at stake, but, unlike the gulf war, they believe this future can be bought cheaply.

The conservatives have the answer: choice. It's a solution, they note, that doesn't require throwing money at schools. And furthermore it's politically correct. The marketplace, they remind us gloatingly, will cure what a socialistic system of schooling has produced: the miseducation of our young. The most articulate and contentious proponents of marketplace choices in education are John Chubb and Terry Moe, whose articles, speeches and book, *Politics, Markets, and America's Schools,* have sparked widespread debate. But this is not merely a battle of words. A number of localities and several states have initiated systems of choice, often using Chubb and Moe's data to support their programs. While Chubb and Moe contend that they favor public education, what they mean is public funding for education. Public institutions are their enemy. They make no bones about it: Private is good, public is bad. Private equals enterprising, public equals stifling bureaucracy and destructive political influence.

The original right-wing challenge to public education, vouchers for private schools, went down to a resounding defeat. The newest star on the right, choice, is both a more powerful challenger and a more interesting one. Because progressives are on the defensive, their concern with equity leads them to attack choice reflexively as inherently elitist (naturally, it has few friends among educational bureaucrats either). This is, I believe, a grave mistake. The argument over choice, unlike the one about vouchers, offers progressives an opportunity. After all, it wasn't so long ago that progressive educators were enthusiastically supporting schools of choice, usually called "alternative schools." However, those alternatives were always on the fringe, as though the vast majority were doing just fine, thanks. We now have a chance to make such alternatives the mainstream, not just for avant-garde "misfits" and "nerds" or those most "at risk."

Americans have long supported a dual school system. Whether schools are public or private, the social class of the students was and continues to be the single most significant factor in determining a school's intellectual values and how it works. The higher the student body's socioeconomic status, the meatier the curriculum, the more open-ended the discussion, the less rote and rigid the pedagogy, the more respectful the tone, the more rigorous the expectations, the greater the staff autonomy. Numerous studies have confirmed a simple fact: The primary factor in determining the quality of schools (as well as programs within

From Deborah W. Meier, "Choice Can *Save* Public Education," *The Nation* 252, no. 8 (March 4, 1991), pp. 253, 266–271.

schools) is not whether they are public or private but who attends them. Changing this is what education reform is all about. What we need is strategies for giving to everyone what the rich have always valued. After all, the rich have had good public schools as well as good private schools. If we use choice to undermine public education, we will increase the duality of our educational system. If we want to use it to undermine the historic duality of our schools, the kind of plan we adopt is more important than choice advocates like Moe and Chubb acknowledge.

When I first entered teaching, and when my own children began their long trek through urban public schools, I too was an unreconstructed advocate of the strictly zoned neighborhood school. I knew all about choice, a favorite tactic of racists escaping desegregation. There were even moments when I wished we could legally outlaw any selective public or private institutions, although I could readily see the risks—not to mention the political impossibility—of doing so. That's no longer the case. My change of heart has personal overtones: I've spent the past sixteen years in a public school district in East Harlem that has pioneered choice, and I have founded a network of small schools of choice in that community: the Central Park East schools. All of District 4's schools are small, largely self-governing and pedagogically innovative. They are schools with a focus, with staffs brought together around common ideas, free to shape a whole set of school parameters in accord with those ideas.

It would have been impossible to carry out this ambitious agenda without choice. Choice was the prerequisite. It was an enabling strategy for a District Superintendent, Anthony Alvarado, who wanted to get rid of the tradition of zoned, factory-style, bureaucratically controlled schools that has long been synonymous with urban public schooling and replace it with a different image of what "public" could mean. The District 4 way was deceptively simple; it required no vast blueprint, just a new mindset. Within ten years, starting in 1974, District 4 totally changed the way 15,000 mostly poor Latino and African-American youngsters got educated without ever pulling the rug out from under either parents or professionals. The words "restructuring" and "reform" were never used—this was, after all, the late 1970s and early 1980s. The Superintendent sidestepped resistance by building a parallel system of choice, until even its opponents found themselves benefiting from it.

To begin with, Alvarado initiated a few model schools open to parental choice, locating them within existing buildings where space was available. He sought schools that would look excitingly different, that would have a loyal, if small, following among families and would have strong professional leadership. Alvarado and his Alternate Schools director, Sy Fliegel, gave such schools extraordinary support in the form of greater flexibility with regard to staffing, use of resources, organization of time, forms of assessment and on-site advice and counseling. Wherever possible, they also ran interference with Central Board of Education bureaucracy. When people in the "regular" schools complained of favoritism, Alvarado and Fliegel assured them that they'd be favorites too if they had some new ideas they wanted to try. Some even accepted the challenge. Each year, more schools were added. They generally started with a few classes and the largest grew to no more than 300 students. Some stayed as small as fifty. Within half a dozen years most of the students in the middle and junior-high grades were attending alternative schools, and each district building housed several autonomous schools.

Schools were no longer equated with buildings. Where there had been twenty-two schools in twenty-two buildings, in less than ten years fifty-one schools occupied twenty buildings (along with two housed in a nearby high school). Only then did the Superintendent announce Stage Two: Henceforth no junior high would serve a specific geographic area. All families of incoming seventh graders would have to choose. The district provided sixth-grade parents and teachers with lots of information to assist them in their choice, although probably word-of-mouth was the decisive factor (as it is in private schools). Sixteen neighborhood elementary schools remain intact, with space reserved first for those living within the designated zone, but Alvarado promised that parents were free to shop around if space existed. In addition, the district supported the creation of twenty alternative elementary schools, eight of them bilingual. As a result, the neighborhood elementary schools became both smaller and, in effect, also schools of choice. Alvarado even enticed a former independent elementary school to enter the public sector, leaving intact its parental governing board.

A majority of the new schools were fairly traditional, although more focused in terms of their themes (such as music, science or journalism) and more intimate and family-oriented due to their small size. Size also meant that regardless of the formal structure, all the participants were generally informally involved in decisions about school life. Most of the schools were designed by small groups of teachers tired of compromising what they thought were their most promising ideas. As a result there was a level of energy and esprit, a sense of co-ownership that made these schools stand out. They developed, over time, differences in pedagogy, style of leadership, forms of governance, tone and climate. A few schools (such as the three Central Park East schools) used this opening to try radically different forms of teaching and learning, testing and assessment, school/family collaboration and staff self-government. In this one small district, noted only a decade earlier as one of the worst in the city, there was by 1984 dozens of schools with considerable citywide reputations and stature, alongside dozens of others that were decidedly more humane, where kids found it hard to fall through the cracks and teachers were enthusiastic about teaching. A few were mediocre or worse; one or two had serious problems. The consensus from the streams of observers who came to see, and those who studied the data, was that the change was real and lasting. What was even more important, however, was that the stage was set for trying out more innovative educational ideas as professionals had the opportunity to be more directly involved in decision making. It was not a cost-free idea, but the added expense was small compared with many other heralded reform efforts; it was less than the cost of one additional teacher for every newly created school.

If this were the best of all possible worlds, the next ten years would have been used to launch Stage Three. The district would have studied what was and was not happening within these fifty-three small schools, examined more closely issues of equity, tracked their graduates over time, studied the families' reasons for making choices and looked for strategies to prod schools into taking on tougher challenges. The Central Board would have worked out ways to legitimize these "wildcat" schools while also encouraging other districts to follow a similar path. Under the leadership of Alvarado's successor, Carlos Medina, District 4 launched Stage Three. But it was not the best of all worlds, and the district found itself on the defensive for reasons that had nothing to do with education in the fifty-three schools. As a result, Medina's efforts to move ahead were thwarted, and new leadership hostile to choice was installed. Today, in 1991, District 4 stands once again at a crossroads, with new sympathetic leadership both within the district and at the Central Board, although badly hobbled by the threat of draconian budget cuts. That the fifty-three schools have survived the past few years in a system that not only never officially acknowledged their existence but often worked to thwart them is a tribute to the loyalty and ingenuity that choice and co-ownership together engender.

While the District 4 story suggests that choice is fully compatible with public education and an efficient vehicle for setting in motion school reform, it is foolhardy not to acknowledge that in the political climate of the 1990s choice runs the risk of leading to privatization.

However, it's not enough these days to cry out in alarm at the possible demise of public education. If public schools are seen as incapable of responding to the demand for wholesale reform, why should we expect the public to resist privatization? Maybe private schools aren't much better, but if public education has proved so inept at meeting the challenge, if it has had such a poor history of serving equity or excellence, it's easy to see the lure of privatization. Given this history, why not just let the chips fall where they may?

The question is a good one. If we want to preserve public education as the norm for most citizens then we'd better have important and positive reasons for doing so, reasons that are compelling to parents, teachers and the broader voting public. To do so we must make the case that the rationale for improving education goes far beyond the problem employers face in recruiting sufficient number of competent and reliable workers or our chagrin at finding the United States at the bottom in test scores for math and science. At least as important is the role education plays as a tool in reviving and maintaining the fabric of our democratic institutions. While public education may be useful as an industrial policy, it is *essential* to healthy public life in a democracy. The two go together, and never has this been clearer than it is today. If we cannot make a convincing case for this, we will see our public schools dismantled in one way or another, either by a misused choice or by erosion and neglect as funds dry up for public education and private schooling becomes the norm for those who can afford to opt out. The status quo plus cosmetic changes won't save public education, at least not in our major urban areas.

The alternative to privatization is good public education, and choice is an essential tool in the effort to create such education. It is the necessary catalyst for the kind of dramatic restructuring that most agree is needed to produce a far better educated citizenry. Virtually all the major educational task forces, for example, agree that dramatic changes will require removing the stifling regulations that presently keep schools tied to outmoded practices, to doing things in lockstep. They agree that if we want change, we'll have to put up with nonconformity and some messiness. We'll have to allow those most involved (teachers, administrators, parents) to exercise greater on-site power to put their collective wisdom into practice. Once we do all this, however, school X and school Y are going to start doing things differently. How then can we ignore personal "tastes"? Besides, it's a lot easier to undertake difficult innovations successfully if teachers, parents and students are in agreement.

We can't expect the marketplace, public or private, to stimulate this kind of reform magically. Private schools as an example of the market at work aren't very inspiring when it comes to innovation. They may encourage livelier educational practice, but in general they are as convention-bound as public schools. They mostly differ in an invidious way, much like their public school sisters. There's a hierarchy among them, based mostly on how choosy the school can be about whom it accepts. The fact that the choosiest schools attract higher-status families and select only the most promising students insures their success; replication, by definition, is impossible. Their value lies in their scarcity. This kind of marketplace has led not to innovation but to imitation on a steadily watered-down basis, appealing not so much to different "tastes" but to different means and expectations. The dual system has remained alive and well in the private sector. But if the marketplace is not a magical answer, neither, experience suggests, can we expect that forced change from the top down will work. What results from such bureaucratically mandated change is anger and sabotage on the part of unwilling, unready parents and professionals as well as the manipulation of data by ambitious bureaucrats and timid administrators. The end result: a gradual return to the status quo.

To improve education for all children will require more than one simple cure-all. It requires a set of strategies. For starters, federal, state and local initiatives can stimulate districts to adopt one or another variation of the District 4 story: providing incentives to districts to break up their oversized buildings and redesign them into many small schools, easily accessible for families to choose from. Once we think small, we can even imagine locating new schools in other available public and private spaces, near workplaces as well as residences, in places where young people can interact with adults going about their daily business. While no system of rules and regulations can insure equity, public policy can assure that resources are fairly allocated. It can go further by establishing guidelines that promote appropriate social, ethnic, racial and academic diversity.

We'll also need a better quality of information if we want to promote long-range school change. We'll need a public that is not confused by misleading data or quickly discouraged by the absence of dramatically improved statistics. Who knows today what the definition of a high school dropout is or what "reading on grade level" means? We'll need to place less reliance on standardized high-stakes testing systems. Good lay information will encourage the kind of lively, even contentious, dialogue about the nature and purpose of education that is so badly needed. Choice offers no guaranteed solution to these concerns, but the existence of clear and coherent alternatives encourages such debate.

Similarly, greater school-based autonomy goes well with choice. School-based management itself does not trigger innovation, but it offers a much better audience for such innovation. Empowered faculties and families are better able to hear new ideas and less likely to sabotage them. Innovation no longer appears threatening. School-based management combined with the idea of small schools of choice allows both parents and teachers to embrace new ideas even if they cannot convince all their colleagues or all the school's parents. Furthermore, once we set loose those who are already eager to "restructure," it will be easier to encourage successive waves of innovators and risk takers. While R&D in education can't take place in labs separate from real life, as it can in most industries, no one wants to be a guinea pig. Creating a school different from what any of those who work in the system are familiar with, one that runs counter to the experiences of most families, is possible only if teachers, parents and students have time to agree on changes and a choice on whether or not they want to go along with them.

Since school officials, like parents, are naturally conservative and reluctant to change their habits, we don't need to sign them all up at once. What's needed first is a range of models, examples for teachers and the public to scrutinize and learn from. Credibility will require a critical mass of such schools; at this stage it is hard to know how many. But we can go only as fast and as far as those who bear the burden of change can tolerate. Putting more money into schools does not guarantee success but it can accelerate the pace of change. Of course, taking money out slows down the possibilities for change too.

In short, choice is necessary but not sufficient. There's something galling about the idea that you're stuck in a particular school that's not working for you unless you are rich enough to buy yourself out of it. Still, if it worked for most students, we'd put up with it, but it doesn't. What's not necessary is to buy into the rhetoric that too often surrounds choice: about the rigors of the marketplace, the virtues of private schooling and the inherent mediocrity of public places and public spaces. By using choice judiciously, we can have the virtues of the marketplace without some of its vices, and we can have the virtues of the best private schools without undermining public education.

DISCUSSION QUESTIONS FOR CHAPTER 10

1. Discuss the extent to which capitalist free enterprise is compatible with the historic vision of American democracy. Relate this discussion to the purposes of American public education.
2. Contrast the ideas of education as a public good and as a private good to be consumed. Pay particular attention to the purposes of each and how these purposes are related to the source of funding.

3. Whose vision of public school choice do you feel is the most consistent with public education for all Americans, that of Chubb or of Meier? Which do you feel has the most chance of changing the way schools operate?
4. Imagine that Jefferson, Dewey, Cubberley, and Bobbitt were able to read the pieces in this chapter. With which do you think they would agree or disagree? Why?

PART FIVE

Schooling and Social Change

11

Reforming the School: Past to Present

In previous chapters we have talked in some detail about the relationships among the ideology of meritocracy, student classification, equal opportunity, the school bureaucracy, the politics of school control, and the purposes of education in a democracy. We saw that all of these have affected in fundamental ways how students are treated and how they are socialized into the culture of the school as well as the larger culture around them. Three of the major concerns we have stressed in connection with this process of socialization have been those of fairness, equality, and opportunity. Repeatedly, we have seen how the meritocratic ideal embodies certain assumptions about what is fair or just. We have seen, as well, how that ideal functions as an ideology to prescribe certain patterns of behavior that many students and teachers have come to accept uncritically. In this and the succeeding chapters we extend these concerns to recent proposals for reform that have received comprehensive news coverage and created a new reformist climate for the 1980s. As we did in previous chapters, we give an historical overview so that the current proposals may be better understood.

In the history of educational reform in the United States certain recurring themes have dominated the concerns raised by educators and laymen. Educational reformers from the late eighteenth century to the present, for example, have repeatedly examined the role of schooling in the civic and economic welfare of the nation. The civic concern tended to dominate prior to 1850, while the economic concern received increasing attention during the last half of the nineteenth century and has remained a priority in the twentieth.

The efficiency of public schooling has also emerged periodically as an issue. As a general concern efficiency became ascendant in the latter half of the nineteenth century and reached its peak with the "cult of efficiency" in the early twentieth century. The creation of large, bureaucratically run urban school systems helped set the stage for lay critics who accused educator/bureaucrats of mismanagement, inefficiency, and a lack of accountability for public funds. Thus the issue of inefficiency in schooling often became a political issue and remains today part of the larger concern with accountability and whether or not schools are meeting their obligations to students, community, and the nation.

The development of education as a profession over the past 150 years also has been the setting for on-going battles over what knowledge is of most worth. This same professionalization has led to continuous conflict between the lay public and professional educators who control the schools.

Certain key periods, or historical watersheds, in American school reform can give us an historical perspective on the reform movement of the 1970s and 1980s. The period between 1893 and 1918 was the first of these. The third was the decade of the 1950s. Between these two periods—in effect, from the end of World War I to the end of World War II—lay the extensive reform movement called progressivism and the more radical reform proposed by reconstructionists.

This chapter deals only in summary fashion with the widespread reforms of the 1960s and 1970s. This is because these two decades were dealt with extensively in Chapter 1. You may wish to return to that chapter to refresh your memory.

A QUARTER CENTURY OF COMMITTEES, 1893–1918

During the twenty-five years between 1893 and 1918 three major reports appeared that helped to shape the structure and policies of American elementary and secondary schools through World War II. The first of these was issued in 1895 by the so-called Committee of Fifteen, formed in 1893. This report dealt with the "correlation of studies" at the elementary level, teacher qualifications and training, and the organization of city school systems. The second report was published in 1893 by the National Educational Association on the recommendation of the National Council of Education, a unit of NEA. Among its more notable features was the continued prominence of intellectual discipline as the leading idea underlying the unity of secondary school studies. The third report was the published findings of the Commission on the Reorganization of Secondary Education. In this "Cardinal Principles" report of 1918, intellectual discipline took a back seat to preparation for life. The pressures of large numbers of children from immigrant families and the commitment to mass education led the committee to reevaluate the purposes of American education.

A subcommittee of the Committee of Fifteen prepared a report on the "correlation of studies" that emphasized the link between curriculum design and the psychological nature of the child. The report recommended, for example, that each branch of study be arranged to suit the natural progress of the child. Studies were also to be arranged so that the level of study would match the "maturity" of the pupil. The Committee's recommendation that studies be correlated with the "civilization into which the child is born" reflected a common expectation for schools.[1]

The number one priority of language studies in the primary grades was evident in the report. Such studies were advocated for both their general academic utility and their usefulness in mental discipline. The subcommittee also attempted to shift the emphasis from memorization to meaning and language. Grammar retained its place in the curriculum because it was seen as useful for disciplining the mind. The committee pointed out, however, that the formal teaching of grammar left much to be desired. They were unanimous in their belief that grammar was "overstudied."[2]

Teacher training and teacher qualifications took twenty pages of the report. The most critical issue addressed by the report in this regard was the on-going debate about the extent and place of academic studies in the curriculum. The committee argued that liberal arts colleges with teacher preparatory departments were, in effect, engaging in a type of compensatory academic training and were inferior to schools whose entire curriculum was professional. Academic work had its place, but that was in relation to practice and application. The answer to the supposed conflict between academics and pedagogy was to have both, not in the training school itself, but in sequence. Academic qualifications ought to precede pedagogical training, said the committee.[3]

Though the Committee of Fifteen did important work for the cause of better elementary instruction, its task was easy compared to the one that faced the Committee of Ten for Secondary School Studies. Theodore Sizer has pointed out that the confusion over content and duration of secondary school studies at the turn of the century was such that the task faced by the Committee of Ten was to "make order out of the widespread chaos in secondary education. . . "[4] In fact, what the committee was faced with was the problem of *defining* what education should be offered by high schools.

In the mid-nineteenth century two types of schools were the mainstays of secondary-level education in the United States: the Latin grammar school and the academy. The Latin grammar school had long been a major college preparatory institution. The classical languages formed the core of the curriculum. Grammar schools served very few students, however, and academies filled an important gap for those who sought secondary-level education but did not wish to go to college. The academies were both college preparatory and terminal. They often allowed a classical language emphasis in their curricula so that students might be prepared for college entrance; however, modern languages and a variety of practical courses were introduced—commerce, navigation, bookkeeping, and surveying, among others. The report of the Committee of Ten was an attempt to synthesize the curricula of the academy and the Latin grammar school.

The Committee of Ten recommended four tracks of study: classical, Latin-scientific, modern languages, and English. There was, however, great similarity in these tracks, especially through the first two years. One of the committee's reasons—avoiding early specialization—has a very modern ring to it: "The wisest teacher, or the most observant parent, can hardly predict with confidence a boy's gift for a subject which he has never touched."[5]

The committee correctly saw the dilemma posed by the dual purpose of secondary schooling in late nineteenth-century America. Preparing students for college was expected, yet this was not the major purpose of public secondary education. The committee noted explicitly that "the secondary schools of the

United States, taken as a whole, do not exist for the purpose of preparing boys and girls for colleges." Thus a curriculum "for national use" must be able to accommodate those for whom the secondary level was terminal.[6]

In 1981 the *Report of the Commission on the Reorganization of Secondary Education* (the "Cardinal Principles" report) was issued. In the report the idea of citizenship was broadly construed to allow the emergence of a new concept of the mission of secondary public schooling. The committee took note of the rapid economic, social, and demographic changes that characterized American society in the early twentieth century. It observed that "secondary education should be determined by the needs of the society to be served, the character of the individuals to be educated, and the knowledge of educational theory and practice available."

The main objectives of education were defined in terms of a democratic ideal. Individual and society, said the "Cardinal Principles" report, were to "find fulfillment each in the other." To implement the major objectives the committee made recommendations for curriculum reform as well as for the reorganization of the schooling process itself.

Each of the reports summarized in the preceding pages addressed problems that affected fairness, equality, and opportunity in American education. Their recommendations, most of which were eventually implemented, helped to structure school life and the expectations of teachers, parents, and administrators. The scientific study of children became the basis for restructuring curriculum according to axiomatic truths about how children learned, developed, and behaved. Thus the professionalization of curriculum making was accompanied by specialized knowledge that gradually left the layman outside the sphere of decision making. The scientific basis for theorizing about curriculum also placed professional decisions about the curriculum outside the reach of many interested parties external to the school proper.

Both the "grouping" of elementary children and the restructuring of secondary education provided greater differentiation within the curriculum and at the same time helped to manage a culturally diverse student population under one roof. To do this required a more complex, bureaucratic administrative structure. It also required a commitment to an ideal of equal educational opportunity that stressed the necessity of differentiated instruction in providing that opportunity. Thus, by the third decade of the twentieth century schools had created systems of student classification and career guidance that offered students blueprints of their futures.

THE PROGRESSIVES, 1900–1950

Led by John Dewey, George Counts, Harold Rugg, William Heard Kilpatrick, and others, the progressive movement was the center of education debate throughout the first half of the 1900s. As we have seen in earlier chapters, progressives worked to reform both the ideological and organizational structures of the school. While it is impossible to say that all progressives argued for a particular plan of action, it is possible to point to one unifying theme in their work: democracy.

Unlike the business interests that worked to mold the schools on an industrial model, the progressives saw schooling for work as only a secondary mission at best. The school was to concern itself primarily with the task of equipping students with the tools necessary for self-governance. As we saw earlier, the progressive camp was made up of both the liberal progressives and the social reconstructionists. We consider both of these in more detail here.

Perhaps the most distinctive characteristic of progressivism was its child-centeredness. Despite the efforts of some mid-nineteenth-century reformers, children continued to be treated as miniature adults. Many educators did not heed the recommendation made by the Committee of Fifteen that studies should be correlated with child development. Thus, it was still common to teach in a way that assumed children would learn through simple exposure to subject matter.

Many of the progressives' ideas about education were based on developments in child psychology. Through the work of G. Stanley Hall and Arnold Gesell, educators became sensitized to the interrelations between maturation, readiness, and motivation. The argument was that the learning environment was of primary importance and should be molded to meet the needs of the developing child.

The argument was most clearly put by John Dewey in his volume *Experience and Education* (1938). Children learn, said Dewey, as we all do—through experience. The task of the teacher is to order and organize meaningful classroom experiences that draw from the child's environment and utilize information from the academic disciplines. For example, rather than lecture children about mathematics, the subject matter could be taught through a sequence of activities. Cooking, for example, involves not only math but reading (recipes), social studies (where foods come from), and science (the application of heat).

The interrelatedness of the academic disciplines was crucial for the progressives. Harold Rugg argued in his *American Life and the School Curriculum* (1936) that the fragmentation of curriculum worked against any ordered understanding of the world. He produced a curriculum which attempted to combine the disciplines of history, geography, sociology, economics, and political science into a program of studies that would bring students to a greater awareness of events that transformed modern civilization. Rugg and the progressives were of the opinion that the starting point for the curriculum was not the learning of facts in the various subject matters. Rather, students should start with a realistic problem of individual and social life and then grapple directly with the problem using facts as they become relevant.

These methods and curricula were a direct attack on the "traditional" school which relied on direct instruction and recitation. The progressive argument was that such regimented instruction did not motivate children to learn. To stress goals far in the future, such as one's life work or higher education, was too far removed from the child's experience. Rather, drawing from the child's own experience, problems could be presented and raised that would require ordered inquiry and the use of facts for their solution.

Perhaps the most telling of the progressive attacks on traditional schooling was the charge that it did not prepare students for active, democratic citizenship. The progressives suggested that schools modeled on the factory (with bureaucratic, top-down forms of management, a tightly controlled curriculum, and wide-spread testing) yielded passive citizens ill-prepared for democratic life. Having spent so much time in an autocratic institution adults were not ready for self-governance.

True to their belief in learning by and through experience, the progressives tried to organize schools that taught democracy directly. These schools were characterized by experiential learning and interdisciplinary curricula. Students were asked to be active problem solvers, and group work was stressed as a way of teaching cooperation. Classroom rules arose from the whole group as a function of the activity in which students were engaged.

The progressives did not say that children were to proceed with no guidance from adults. The teacher played the part of the senior member of the culture in the classroom. She carefully chose from the variety of student experiences the ones to use in class. She helped guide the decision-making process through unfamiliar waters, and was an available source of information for students. As students became more adept at problem solving, the teacher could be less obtrusive and become primarily a source of expert opinion and advice. In no case was the student abandoned without the protection of the teacher.

Historians of education have had difficulty in estimating the extent to which public school teachers implemented progressive techniques of instruction in their classrooms. Undoubtedly, implementation varied greatly. Yet even the Denver school system, with superintendent Jesse Newlon committed to progressive ideas, devoted only a small proportion of its teachers and classes to progressive practices.

Where the commitment was strong, teachers practiced an interdisciplinary approach to subject matter. They also planned lessons *with* students and took into account the expressed needs of students. Motivation replaced punitive measures. Overall, however, the sobering fact was that at the secondary level most instruction and classroom activities were initiated by the teacher. Thus, the traditional teacher-centered classroom remained intact. At the elementary school level student-centered and teacher-centered instruction were more in balance so that teacher-pupil interaction in the classroom was more of a two-way street.

Even though progressive influence was limited, it is one of the great ironies of educational history that proponents of "basics" or "traditional" education found the progressives to be at the root of all that is wrong with public education. Indeed, perhaps if the progressives had had greater influence, today's concerns over student motivation and achievement might never have arisen. By the 1950s the progressives had come under attack for a system of schooling they attempted to reform.

In some respects the progressives continued the reforms of the late nineteenth and early twentieth centuries. In fact, in their embracing of scientific child study they made every effort to propel the trend forward. Curricular reform itself received added impetus by progressive attempts to create interdisciplinary studies. Yet the progressives were also wary of the excesses of the "cult of efficiency" and worked to avoid the unbridled commitment to social utility as the primary goal of public schooling. They were utilitarian, to be sure, in the sense that they saw the place of vocational studies in the curriculum. Yet they also saw the necessity for restoring cooperative, democratic decision making to school life. They grappled continuously with the problem of restoring a balance between the civic and economic expectations for schooling in America.

In the long run, progressivism failed in American education, not because it lacked conviction or was poorly conceived, but because it failed to heed its own best advice—that decision making, in order to serve democratic purposes, must *be* democratic. Progressivism, like so many reforms, became the prerogative of an elite. Though it successfully challenged traditional methods of instruction and the relevancy of many traditional subjects, progressivism fell victim to a growing bureaucratic structure with which it was not entirely unsympathetic. It failed ultimately to reconcile the demands of efficiency with the demands of democracy. It was torn, as was American society, between the ideal of meeting the legitimate needs of every individual and the goal of securing the national welfare. We struggle with the legacy of progressivism today because the same conflicts have gone unresolved.

"BASICS" AND CONSERVATISM IN THE 1950S

Many of the arguments heard frequently in the reform reports of the late 1970s and 1980s are direct descendants of the educational conservatism of the 1950s. Concerns with quality instruction in the "basics," the place of the liberal arts in the curriculum, the efficient use and development of human capital, and the issue of excellence versus equality were familiar themes that spanned the fifteen-year period following World War II.

Among the many voices calling for educational reform in the 1950s, the most articulate was Arthur Bestor. Bestor's *Educational Wastelands* brought educational conservatism and the liberal arts tradition to the forefront of educational debate. In his attack on anti-intellectualism and "life adjustment" education, Bestor singled out professional educationists as liable for the deterioration of American public schooling. Lack of direction, said Bestor, had produced the "mediocre showing of our public high schools."[7]

Bestor's major contention was that the purpose of schooling is to teach students the "power to think." Intellectual discipline was the foundation for that goal. Educators, argued Bestor, were "professionally obligated to oppose anti-intellectualism, no matter how powerful a majority it may command." In the headlong rush to meet the "needs" of students, he continued, educationists absolved themselves of any responsibility for the intellectual content of schooling.[8]

Educational Wastelands was followed quickly by *The Restoration of Learning.*

Here Bestor continued his attack on anti-intellectualism in American education by castigating the "interlocking directorate of professional educationists." They had failed, he said, to provide an intellectually stimulating environment for would-be teachers, and they abused their power to silence their critics.[9]

Bestor's defense of liberal education and intellectual discipline rested squarely on the grounds of social utility. To a lesser extent, the liberal studies could also be defended for their economic utility. The argument for the latter was simply that the basic core of liberal education was the foundation for future professional or occupationally related studies. The argument for the social utility of the "basics" rested on the commitment of the American republic to a highly literate electorate. This commitment had been built on the generic (basic) studies and inspired by a liberal arts curriculum.[10]

The place of the "basics" in schooling drew the attention of other outspoken critics during the decade of the 1950s. This concern was often expressed in the context of dissatisfaction with professional educationists and their use of power. For some critics, such as Albert Lynd in his *Quackery in the Public Schools,* the concern took the form of a layman's crusade against incompetent bureaucrats.[11]

In a far more deliberative and reflective tone, Clifton Fadiman also spoke of the basics in the public school curriculum. Basic education, argued Fadiman, rests on the assumption that there are certain generic subjects that underlie both more complex subject matters and "self-terminating" subjects such as specific manual or vocational skills. Fadiman spoke of the fruits of his own conventional basic education as follows:

> [It] taught me how to read, write, speak, calculate, and listen. It taught me the elements of reasoning and it put me on to the necessary business of drawing abstract conclusions from particular instances. . . . It provided me with great models by which to judge my own lesser performance. And it gave me the ability to investigate for myself anything that interested me, provided my mind was equal to it.[12]

Cold War politics played an important role in the educational reform reports of the 1950s. The cultivation of the intellectually gifted seemed an urgent matter as the beginnings of the space race took shape. The problem of technological change and obsolescence made increased investment in human capital imperative if the international competitive edge of the United States was to remain sharp. Among the various critical appraisals of public education was that prepared by Admiral H. G. Rickover in 1959 for the House Committee on Appropriations and published subsequently in 1963 as *American Education—A National Failure.* Public schooling, said Rickover, suffered from "no clear-cut educational philosophy with firm objectives. . . ." The major symptom was low scholastic achievement; the course of action to remedy the situation was "some kind of machinery to set national scholastic standards which may serve local communities as a yardstick."[13]

Like other conservative critics of the 1950s, Rickover advocated a renewed emphasis on the liberal arts. Such studies, he thought, would restore a sense of identity with the country and a desire "to be publicly active" that once characterized preindustrial, rural Americans. Rickover's romanticizing of the past was linked to a sobering appraisal of current international tensions. Our "contest with the totalitarians," said Rickover, required us to be informed and free to face our thoughts critically. Public schooling itself, he observed, is "letting us down, at a time when the nation is in great peril."[14]

Amidst calls for greater efficiency in the educating of America's talent, James Conant came to the defense, though not uncritically, of the comprehensive high school. He, too, was concerned with the weaknesses of programs for the academically gifted. His solution, however, lay with the reform of the comprehensive high school.

Conant studied and tabulated inventories for twenty-two schools. Generally what he found were weaknesses in foreign language instruction and special programs for the academically talented. Conant found most high schools successful in promoting a "democratic spirit." As a preface to his twenty-one recommendations for the improvement of secondary education, Conant observed that as a rule the talented student "is not being sufficiently challenged, does not work hard enough, and his program of academic subjects is not of sufficient range." It is not possible to review all of Conant's recommendations here, but the highlights included the elimination of "tracks" (college preparatory, vocational, commercial), the use of ability grouping, a core program of the basic disciplines, greater time spent on English composition, elective programs for the academically talented, required science courses, provision for third- and fourth-year language study, and a course in social studies in the twelfth year. Developmental reading programs and vocational education programs were also recommended.[15]

It has been pointed out that the renewed interest in educational reform, including the identification and efficient use of human resources, was, in part, an outgrowth of the intensely competitive international climate of the 1950s. Educationally, economically, and politically the nation was at war with the Soviet Union. There was anxiety over the capability of the nation to respond to technological changes. In the midst of this difficult period came a report of the Special Studies Project, *The Pursuit of Excellence and the Future of America* (1958). The report acknowledged that the Soviet Union was "not the 'cause' of the crisis." "The cause of the crisis," the report continued, was "our breathtaking movement into a new technological era." Said the report: "The U.S.S.R. has served as a rude stimulus to awaken us to that reality."[16] The thrust of the report was to alert the lay public and public officials to the "constant pressure of an ever more complex society against the total creative capacity of its people."[17]

The search for talent should begin early, said the report. Large-scale testing programs were reviewed approvingly by the Study Project. The Study Project eschewed the use of a single test to assess academic ability, but recommended that "the general academic capacity of students should be at least tentatively identified by the eighth grade as the result of repeated testings and classroom performance in the elementary grades." The report went on to recommend a differentiated curriculum for different levels of talent. To assure that these students—"our most gifted, most talented and most spirited youngsters"—receive the very best, we must acknowledge their gifts and "dedicate ourselves to the cultivation of distinction, and a sense of quality."[18]

The resurgence of interest in the liberal arts and the quality of basic skills taught in the public schools in the 1950s paralleled the generally conservative political environment of the period. Critics of education saw the triumph of the educationists as the abandonment of America's intellectual heritage. But they saw, also, the erosion of lay authority in education. In short, they were extremely critical of the growth of bureaucratically controlled decision making. It is worth a reminder that the most vocal critics of educationism were those in positions of leadership in government and universities. Their resentment of the educationists' control of public education was obvious and probably signaled a concern with their own loss of input into the process. Overall, then, it is important to understand that critics of progressivism were not necessarily representing the lay public. The educational debates of the 1950s were very much debates between two elites, each competing for the allegiance of the public.

It is obvious that one of the most powerful appeals made by critics of the educationists was to the necessity for identifying talent more efficiently. This need was explained in terms of the "cold war" and national security. Overall, the appeal was made in terms of greater social utility and the meritocratic ideal. For the social utilitarian, it will be remembered, meritocracy was simply an efficient way of achieving the best (and most just) distribution of rewards. The reform proposals of the 1950s generally saw the two ideals of meritocracy and social utility as serving the larger national good.

THE CURRENT WAVE OF REFORM

Between the conservative proposals for reform in the 1950s and the 1980s lay the massive social and political reforms of the 1960s and 1970s. It will be remembered from Chapter 1 that these reforms had their source in the ideal of equal opportunity and the right to due process guaranteed by the Fourteenth Amendment to the United States Constitution. During a twenty-five year period, these rights were gradually extended to minority groups. Those who championed the idea of equal opportunity generally accepted intact the concept of meritocracy, even though the concept of equal educational opportunity itself shifted its emphasis from an "input" model to an "output" model that judged equality of opportunity not on the basis of what students were offered—equal facilities, teachers, or curriculum—but the basis of skills and knowledge acquired by students. Rawlsian theory offered a challenge to the prevailing concept of equal opportunity, but its impact was limited. By the mid-1970s equity had replaced equality as the major reform word. This shift was significant because it connoted a movement away from an egalitarian democratic ideal. Issues of equity (such as funding) paralleled closely issues of quality. Thus by the latter 1970s equity and quality were often considered together, particularly in the area of school funding. The question most often asked by courts in this regard was not whether funding was equal, but whether it was equitable. Equitable, as it often turned out, was interpreted as what was necessary (minimal) to give a quality education. The merging of the equity and quality issues helped to set the stage for the reform proposals of the 1980s.

The opening of the 1980s saw the smoldering fires of educational debate rekindled. Fanning the fire of parental and public discontent were a series of reports spotlighting a continuing decline in student academic performance on a variety of measures and calling for a reaffirmation of basic education. These reports were not uniform in their recommendations, nor were they unanimous in their interpretation of what ails public schooling. As we shall see below a series of competing claims have been made about the present and future role of schools.

The Pressure for Change

Many of the reports on educational failure take the crisis in the economy as their starting point. Just as the launching of Sputnik crystalized educational criticism in the 1950s, the decline of the economy in the 1970s gave impetus to many of the most widely circulated reports of the 1980s. For example, President Reagan's National Commission on Excellence in Education opened its report with the following statement:

> Our nation is at risk. Our once unchallenged preeminence in commerce, industry, science, and technological innovation is being overtaken by competitors throughout the world.[19]

Or, as a follow-up report issued by the Educational Commission of the States put it:

> Today . . . our faith in change—and our faith in ourselves as the world's supreme innovators—is being shaken. Japan, West Germany, and other relatively new industrial powers have challenged America's position on the leading edge of change and technological innovation. The possibility that other nations may outstrip us in inventiveness and productivity is suddenly troubling Americans.[20]

Much of the criticism of schooling voiced in the 1980s cited the "liberalization" of the curriculum as causing the general decline in school quality. Mortimer Adler saw the widely curricular alternatives or electives as "side-tracks" that would "always lead a certain number of students to voluntarily downgrade their education."[21] Both John Goodlad and Ernest Boyer found fault with the idea that schools should be all things to all people.[22] The National Commission on Excellence in Education put the problem as follows:

> Secondary school curricula have been homogenized, diluted, and diffused to the point that they no longer have a central purpose. In effect, we have a cafeteria-style curriculum in which the appetizers and deserts can easily be mistaken for the main course.[23]

Public discontent with schooling forces us to ask, What factors of school performance can be associated with this trend in declining public regard for schools? Though we will see below that many agree it is simplistic to blame schools for all academic failures of children, there is substantial evidence to suggest that students achieve less today academically than they did just over a decade ago. Scores on the Scholastic Aptitude Tests (SAT), generally believed to be a measure of the overall academic ability of college-bound seniors in the United States, have declined consistently since 1966, with only a small upturn in 1984 and 1985.

Data from the National Assessment of Educational Progress in 1982 indicated an across-the-board decrease in mathematical knowledge since 1972 and a decrease in reading skills among older students since 1970. Added to this are claims that about 13 percent of American 17-year-olds are functionally illiterate, that science achievement among high school students has decreased, and that nearly all tests of achievement reveal an academic decline over the past ten years.

Back to Basics

The first major response to this education crisis was the "back-to-basics" movement. Like Arthur Bestor and the Council for Basic Education in the 1950s, advocates of this position argue that schools are failing because they do not give rigorous instruction in the generic subjects.

The government's recommendations for responding to this "dismal" state of affairs in public education, spelled out in *A Nation at Risk,* are similar to those offered by Fadiman and Rickover in the 1950s: All curricula should include more focus on the educational basics (the basics now include social studies and computer science, however); grading standards, entrance admissions scores for colleges and universities, and textbook rigor should all be increased; more time should be spent in school as well as on homework; teaching quality should be increased and payment should be based on a merit scheme; and educational leaders at the local, state, and federal level should become more effective leaders for change and reform.

As we have observed throughout this book, schooling is usually seen as a means to a larger social end. Recent reports have continued this tradition by viewing schools as both the cause and cure of economic and international weakness in the 1970s and 1980s. For example, in 1990 the nation's governors and President Bush issued a "summit report" on education which included, among others, the following goals:

- Students will leave grades 4, 8, and 12 having demonstrated competency in challenging subject matter, including English, mathematics, science, history, and geography.
- U.S. students will be first in the world in science and mathematics achievement.

- Every adult American will be literate and possess the knowledge and skills necessary to compete in a global economy and exercise the rights and responsibilities of citizenship.

The rationale for such goals, clearly stated in their report, was to reclaim the U.S. role as an economic world leader. In the 1991 Economic Report of the President, the lament is heard again that "primary and secondary education in the country does an inadequate job of producing [skilled] workers."[24]

However, as David Cohen has argued, perhaps this is much too simple a formula. Referring to what he calls the "Toyota Problem," Cohen points out that "since the 1890s we have thought of schools as the chief means for making America more productive, more efficient, more competitive." He continues:

> This is an idea that becomes increasingly problematic the deeper one digs into the relationship between education and productivity, yet few seem inclined to question the notion that schools are responsible for the many failures of General Motors, or Ford, or Chrysler. It is odd, since schools were never praised for causing earlier successes in that industry.[25]

Despite Cohen's reservations, much of the current reform debate focuses on preparing the young for work. The launching of Sputnik caused national concern about the level of scientific knowledge in American society and prompted increased attention to science education. In the 1970s and 1980s the issue is no longer science but technology. As with the concern over science in the 1950s, the expressed concern over technology is not one of public or democratic control of technology. Rather, the issue is seen as that of the general populace's lack of technological expertise, which, critics say, has led to a decline in our national productive capacities. This problem will only be resolved, it is claimed, when future job-seekers have the technological skills that will make them suitable for the workplace. The issue, say these critics, is not to control technology, but to adapt to it. From the National Science Board, for example, comes the following:

> Already the quality of our manufactured products, the viability of our trade, our leadership in research and development, and our standards of living are strongly challenged. Our children could be stragglers in a world of technology. We must not let this happen; America must not become an industrial dinosaur.[26]

It is valuable to note how similar these claims sound to the near hysteria generated by our Cold War competition with the Soviet Union. What does it mean to say our standards of living are being challenged? Will someone soon be at our doorsteps taking away our televisions, refrigerators, and food processors?

Regardless of whether or not such claims are correct, it is clear that the reforms argued for in these back-to-basics reports are being implemented. Students now spend slightly more hours in high school core courses than they did a decade ago. States have set forth more stringent curriculum guidelines; some states, such as Georgia for example, have gone so far as to mandate the entire K–12 curriculum statewide. Students are taking more tests, with states such as Ohio requiring passing test scores before graduating. In fact, increased testing is perhaps the single largest change in American schools with an average of 2.5 standardized tests administered per student per year!

Whether or not the reforms suggested will bring about the desired results seems to be largely a matter of faith. References are made to our historic commitment to education and the "strength" of the American people. The continuing American belief that schooling can resolve any and all social problems, however, seems to be the basis for the reforms offered. The important question not addressed by these reports is whether or not schools *should* take on the task of improving our national productivity. Is this part of the mission of the school? We turn now to a group of reports that have raised this question anew.

The Purpose of the Schools

The recent works of Mortimer Adler, Ernest Boyer, and John Goodlad have been devoted to challenging some of the assumptions commonly made about the purpose of public schooling. Rather than concern themselves with how schools might more adequately meet the demands of a changing workplace or the nation's military needs, these authors challenge the very notion that schools should prepare students for particular social roles. As Boyer has put it:

> Clearly, education and the security of the nation are interlocked. National interests must be served. But where in all this are the students? Where is the recognition that education is to enrich living individuals? Where is the love of learning and where is the commitment to achieve equality and opportunity for all?[27]

The problem with much recent reform is that it takes for granted the continuation of schooling's current role—the provision of occupational skills. Goodlad points out that reliance on standardized test scores is perhaps "the most serious bar to understanding or improving our schools" as they tell us little about the actual condition of schools. But of course the focus on such scores does make sense if they are seen as part of the ticket to the job market that schools must provide.[28]

Adler's, Boyer's, and Goodlad's critique of schooling raises the issue of whether or not it is possible to have everything for everyone in the schools. It goes beyond this, however. In fact, all three argue that it is not desirable for schools to attempt to do all they have been charged with. The educative function of schools is squeezed out as schools "take over what has traditionally been the responsibility of families, churches, and other institutions charged with the well-being of youth."[29] "Less is more" seems to be the central argument of each of these reports—an impression borne out when we examine their proposals for reform.

Adler, Boyer, and Goodlad all argue for a single, one-track curriculum for schools, though they part company in other respects. Adler's clearly stated goal is equal education for all children, meaning more than the same quantity of schooling. "All children, with no exceptions, are entitled to the same quality of education." Adler's position is based on a commitment to meeting our common needs of earning a living, being a citizen, and leading a good life, in a common fashion. Thus, basic schooling for all is to be general and liberal, not specialized or vocational.[30]

Boyer argues for a similar simplification of the curriculum. In his study of high schools, he has found what he calls an "unwritten, unspoken contract between the teachers and the students: Keep off my back, and I'll keep off yours." Merely more time in school will not in any way alter this arrangement. Boyer argues instead for more substance in the curriculum, focusing on the seemingly self-evident propositions that "what is taught in school determines what is learned."[31]

Boyer proposes, as does Adler, a single program for high school students. The focus of this program is to meet with Boyer believes to be the four essential goals of public schools. These are (1) developing in students the abilities to think critically and communicate effectively, (2) developing in students an understanding of our shared cultural histories, (3) preparing students for work, and (4) helping students fulfill social and civic obligations through community and social service. Boyer believes these goals can only be obtained for all students when "the current three-track system—academic, vocational and general—[is] abolished."[32]

Goodlad goes well beyond the recommendations of both. Adler and Boyer by beginning with the premise that support for the autonomy of individual schools should be the focus of school reform. Given clear and articulate goals from the state and assurance by the school district that all children will be dealt with in an equitable manner, the local school should be left alone to construct the curriculum. This reform effort is to be guided by two general principles:

> First, the provision of general, not specialized, education is the role of primary and secondary education. Consequently, the answers to deficiencies must arise out of questions pertaining to what constitutes a general education for all—not college entrance requirements, on one hand, and job entry requirements, on the other. Good general education is the best preparation for both.[33]

Like Boyer and Adler, Goodlad argues that much of what schools currently do should be relegated back to the community at large. "Education," Goodlad suggests, "is too important and too all encompassing to be left only to schools."[34] Education, all three argue, should be interwoven into the very fabric of the community—the home, church, civic club, and workplace. In order for schooling to reassume a primarily educative function, the community must be willing to shoulder many of the tasks now carried out by schools. The important place given to the community in these proposals has not made them immune to criticism. Adler's position has been attacked for its assumption that there exists a high-status knowledge the mere exposure to which can elevate the quality of social life. And while Boyer and Goodlad argue that more of the school's functions should be taken over by the community, they have been criticized for their seeming reluctance to specify the "what" and "how" of such a proposal.

These very limitations, however, force us to return to the issue of what schools should do—what their purposes are. If our society accepts the idea of equality, should we continue with a multitrack school system? How democratic can a society be that provides unequal education? Where does the allegiance of the school lie: with the individual student, the civic culture, the workplace, or the military?

RESTRUCTURING THE SCHOOL

The most recent school reform movement is that which looks seriously at the purpose of schooling. These reformers explicitly reject the factory model of schooling examined in Part Three and the ideological messages discussed in Part Four. Instead of being places just to prepare students for work, they argue, schools should be primarily concerned with preparing young people to be citizens and community members. To do this, these school reformers have proposed "restructuring" our schools.

There is no clear, widely accepted definition of what it means to restructure a school. Yet there is wide agreement about why we should restructure. The first justification for restructuring schools is simply low student achievement. There is no reason to assume that if students are not achieving now, merely doing more of the same (as back-to-basics advocates argue) will change this pattern. Thus, it is argued that we need to change the very ways we teach if we are going to meet the needs of our students.

The second justification for restructuring has to do with the hidden curriculum of schooling. Organizing schools like factories only makes sense if we believe that the only function of schooling is to sort children for the world of work. If our agenda is to prepare children to become citizens, then we should rethink how we socialize children through the structures of the school.

Finally, school restructuring is also undertaken with an eye toward equity. Perhaps at one time, when schools did not serve all children, our school structures worked. Today, as we try to be more inclusive and to confront the multiple problems of poverty and family disruption that many children face, perhaps we need to find new ways to connect with our students.

Drawing from these and other agendas, advocates of school restructuring attack the three central structures of school organization—time, size, and governance.[35] First, restructuring means allowing students and teachers to spend more time together leading to more student-centered teaching. Here the goal is to have teachers and students take on more projects, engage in cooperative learning, and go deeper into the subject matter. Restructuring time limits the number of things a student can do in a day, but the argument is that to do a few things well is better than covering multiple topics at a shallow level.

Size, both in terms of the whole school and the organization of the school day, is the second piece of the restructuring agenda. Breaking up large schools into smaller schools, organizing schools-within-schools, keeping groups of elementary students together with a teacher over a number of years and grades, and using advisory systems with teacher/advisors working with small groups of children for several years are all intended to make schools smaller. The goal here is to move away from the assembly-line treatment of children and provide for more human contact in the school.

Finally, governance, a topic we discussed in Part Four, is also a central piece of restructuring. The goal here is to turn over to those closest to the educational process the power to make educational decisions.

Many attempts at restructuring are going on across the country.[36] It is too soon to tell how successful they will be or how deeply they will be rooted in the educational landscape. Regardless of their outcome, however, these projects have opened up new ways of thinking about how our organization of schools reflects our beliefs about what schools are for.

NOTES

[1] National Education Association of the United States, *Report of the Committee of Fifteen on Elementary Education* (New York: American Book, 1895), pp. 40–42.

[2] Ibid., pp. 48, 50, 51.

[3] Ibid., p. 22.

[4] Theodore R. Sizer, *Secondary Schools at the Turn of the Century* (New Haven: Yale University Press, 1964), p.xi.

[5] National Education Association, *Report of the Committee of Ten on Secondary School Studies* (New York: American Book, 1894), pp. 43, 47–48.

[6] Ibid., p. 51.

[7] Arthur E. Bestor, *Educational Wastelands, the Retreat from Learning in Our Schools* (Urbana: University of Illinois Press, 1953), pp. 7–8.

[8] Ibid., pp. 33, 43, 46–47.

[9] Arthur E. Bestor, *The Restoration of Learning, A Program for Redeeming the Unfulfilled Promise of American Education* (New York: Knopf, 195), p. 79.

[10] Ibid., pp. 27, 29.

[11] Albert Lynd, *Quackery in the Public Schools* (Boston: Little, Brown, 1950), pp. 14, 19, 57, 281.

[12] Clifton Fadiman, "The Case for Basic Education," in *The Case for Basic Education: A Program of Aims for Public Schools,* ed. James D. Koerner (Boston: Little, Brown, 1959), pp. 6, 10–11.

[13] H. G. Rickover, *American Education—A National Failure: The Problem of Our Schools and What We Can Learn from England* (New York: Dutton, 1963), p. 3.

[14] Ibid., pp. 14, 26, 32.

[15] James B. Conant, *The American High School Today* (New York: McGraw-Hill, 1959), p. 113.

[16] *The Pursuit of Excellence and the Future of America,* Panel Report V of the Special Studies Project (New York: Doubleday, 1958), p. 28.

[17] Ibid., pp. 7, 10–13.

[18] Ibid., pp. 30–31, 33.

[19] National Commission on Excellence in Education, *A Nation at Risk* (Washington, D.C.: U.S. Government Printing Office, 1983), p. 5.

[20] Education Commission of the States, Task Force on Education for Economic Growth, *Action for Excellence* (Washington, D.C.: Education Commission of the States, 1983), p. 13.

[21] Mortimer Adler, *The Paideia Proposal* (New York: Macmillan, 1982), p. 21.

[22] John Goodlad, *A Place Called School* (New York: McGraw-Hill, 1948); Ernest Boyer, *High School: A Report on Secondary Education in America* (New York: Harper and Row, 1983).

[23] National Commission on Excellence in Education, *A Nation at Risk*, p. 18.

[24] George H. Bush, *Economic Report of the President* (Washington, D.C.: U.S. Government Printing Office, 1991), p. 121.

[25] David K. Cohen, ". . . the condition of teachers' work . . ." *Harvard Educational Review* 54, no. 1 (Feb. 1984), p. 12.

[26] National Science Board, *Educating Americans for the 21st Century* (Washington, D.C.: National Science Foundation, 1983), p. v.

[27] Boyer, *High School*, p. 5.

[28] John Goodlad, *A Place Called School* (New York: McGraw-Hill, 1984).

[29] Boyer, *High School*, p. 63.

[30] Mortimer Adler, *The Paideia Proposal* (New York: Macmillan, 1982), p. 4.

[31] Boyer, *High School*, p. 84.

[32] Ibid., p. 282.

[33] Goodlad, *A Place Called School*, p. 292.

[34] Ibid., p. 46.

[35] George H. Wood, *Schools that Work* (New York: Dutton, 1992).

[36] The best known of these is described in Ted Sizer's book *Horace's Compromise* (Boston: Houghton Mifflin, 1984).

12

Readings on Educational Reform: The Official Agenda

We look at educational reform first by looking at official, federal calls for school change. In these we find particular concepts of social justice and national purpose that guide the reform agenda. It is an understanding of these deeper purposes of reform, these intentions to carry out a particular ideology, that is of most importance in any assessment of educational reform.

The first selection is the well-known report from President Reagan's National Commission on Excellence in Education, *A Nation at Risk*. We have included the recommendations from the commission's report as well as the introduction. This document is probably the most widely cited and discussed of all the recent reform literature. As such it is an important starting point in understanding the current debate over public education.

The second selection is President George Bush's most recent updating of this national call for excellence. It comes from his 1991 *Economic Report of the President* and includes within it the educational goals agreed upon by governors in their recent meetings.

Following these documents are three pieces critical of the official reform agenda. We begin with David Cohen's essay on the nature of the teacher's work. What he suggests is that much of the argument over reform is moot. What is more genuinely the problem with society is not schooling but large-scale economic and political problems. By looking solely at the schools we do little or nothing to change these problems, and thus genuine reform does not occur. Cohen goes so far as to suggest that what we often see as a school failure—lack of academic challenge, creativity, and individuality—may actually be school success. That is, if reformers are primarily concerned with how schools fit children into society they may have little to worry about—schools are doing that quite well now.

Walter Karp's essay follows Cohen's both in location and in philosophy. Karp argues that many of the failures of American schooling are by design. By design, schools do not turn out rational, logical, and participating citizens. To the contrary, what is desired are individuals who conform to the status quo. Karp goes so far as to suggest that the failure of American schooling is actually a disguised success by design.

Fittingly, the last selection is by Susan Ohanian, a former elementary school teacher. Her fear is of increased bureaucratization, standardization, and mechanization of teaching and learning. She sees the strength of schooling in the skill and craftsmanship of the teacher and fears a great deal of that is being lost. She, like Dewey and Counts before her, locates the real hope for educational change with the people who are most concerned with children in schools—teachers themselves.

NATIONAL COMMISSION ON EXCELLENCE IN EDUCATION

A NATION AT RISK

Our Nation is at risk. Our once unchallenged preeminence in commerce, industry, science, and technological innovation is being overtaken by competitors throughout the world. This report is concerned with only one of the many causes and dimensions of the problem, but it is the one that undergirds American prosperity, security, and civility. We report to the American people that while we can take justified pride in what our schools and colleges have historically accomplished and contributed to the United States and the well-being of its people, the educational foundations of our society are presently being eroded by a rising tide of mediocrity that threatens our very future as a Nation and a people. What was unimaginable a generation ago has begun to occur—others are matching and surpassing our educational attainments.

If an unfriendly foreign power had attempted to impose on America the mediocre educational performance that exists today, we might well have viewed it as an act of war. As it stands, we have allowed this to happen to ourselves. We have even squandered the gains in student achievement made in the wake of the Sputnik challenge. Moreover, we have dismantled essential support systems which helped make those gains possible. We have, in effect, been committing an act of unthinking, unilateral educational disarmament.

Our society and its educational institutions seem to have lost sight of the basic purposes of schooling, and of the high expectations and disciplined effort needed to attain them. This report, the result of 18 months of study, seeks to generate reform of our educational system in fundamental ways and to review the Nation's commitment to schools and colleges of high quality throughout the length and breadth of our land.

That we have compromised this commitment is, upon reflection, hardly surprising, given the multitude of often conflicting demands we have placed on our Nation's schools and colleges. They are routinely called on to provide solutions to personal, social, and political problems that the home and other

From National Commission on Excellence in Education, *A Nation at Risk* (Washington, D.C.: U.S. Government Printing Office, 1983), pp. 5–6 24–33.

institutions either will not or cannot resolve. We must understand that these demands on our schools and colleges often exact an educational cost as well as a financial one.

On the occasion of the Commission's first meeting, President Reagan noted that the central importance of education in American life when he said: "Certainly there are a few areas of American life as important to our society, to our people, and to our families as our schools and colleges." This report, therefore, is as much an open letter to the American people as it is a report to the Secretary of Education. We are confident that the American people, properly informed, will do what is right for their children and for the generations to come.

● ● ●

RECOMMENDATION A: CONTENT

We recommend *that State and local high school graduation requirements be strengthened and that at a minimum, all students seeking a diploma be required to lay the foundations in the Five New Basics by taking the following curriculum during their 4 years of high school: (a) 4 years of English; (b) 3 years of mathematics; (c) 3 years of science; (d) 3 years of social studies; and (e) one-half year of computer science. For the college-bound, 2 years of foreign language in high school are strongly recommended in addition to those taken earlier.*

Whatever the student's educational or work objectives, knowledge of the New Basics is the foundation of success for the after-school years and, therefore, forms the core of the modern curriculum. A high level of shared education in these Basics, together with work in the fine and performing arts and foreign languages, constitutes the mind and spirit of our culture. The following implementing Recommendations are intended as illustrative descriptions. They are included here to clarify what we mean by the essentials of a strong curriculum.

Implementing Recommendations

1. The teaching of *English* in high school should equip graduates to: (a) comprehend, interpret, evaluate, and use what they read; (b) write well-organized, effective papers; (c) listen effectively and discuss ideas intelligently; and (d) know our literary heritage and how it enhances imagination and ethical understanding, and how it relates to the customs, ideas, and values of today's life and culture.
2. The teaching of *mathematics* in high school should equip graduates to: (a) understand geometric and algebraic concepts; (b) understand elementary probability and statistics; (c) apply mathematics in everyday situations; (d) estimate, approximate, measure, and test the accuracy of their calculations. In addition to the traditional sequence of studies available for college-bound students, new, equally demanding mathematics cur-

ricula need to be developed for those who do not plan to continue their formal education immediately.

3. The teaching of *science* in high school should provide graduates with an introduction to: (a) the concepts, laws, and processes of the physical and biological sciences; (b) the methods of scientific inquiry and reasoning; (c) the application of scientific knowledge to everyday life; and (d) the social and environmental implications of scientific and technological development. Science courses must be revised and updated for both the college-bound and those not intending to go to college. An example of such work is the American Chemical Society's "Chemistry in the Community" program.

4. The teaching of *social studies* in high school should be designed to: (a) enable students to fix their places and possibilities within the larger social and cultural structure; (b) understand the broad sweep of both ancient and contemporary ideas that have shaped our world; and (c) understand the fundamentals of how our economic system works and how our political system functions; and (d) grasp the difference between free and repressive societies. An understanding of each of these areas is requisite to the informed and committed exercise of citizenship in our free society.

5. The teaching of *computer science* in high school should equip graduates to: (a) understand the computer as an information, computation, and communication device; (b) use the computer in the study of other Basics and for personal and work-related purposes; and (c) understand the world of computers, electronics, and related technologies.

In addition to the New Basics, other important curriculum matters must be addressed.

6. Achieving proficiency in a *foreign language* ordinarily requires from 4 to 6 years of study and should, therefore, be started in the elementary grades. We believe it is desirable that students achieve such proficiency because study of a foreign language introduces students to non-English-speaking culture, heightens awareness and comprehension of one's native tongue, and serves the Nation's needs in commerce, diplomacy, defense, and education.

7. The high school curriculum should also provide students with programs requiring rigorous effort in subjects that advance students' personal, educational, and occupational goals, such as the fine and performing arts and vocational education. Those areas complement the New Basics, and they should demand the same level of performance as Basics.

8. The curriculum in the crucial eight grades leading to the high school years should be specifically designed to provide a sound base for study in those and later years in such areas as English language development and writing, computational and problem solving skills, science, social

studies, foreign language, and the arts. These years should foster an enthusiasm for learning and the development of the individual's gifts and talents.
9. We encourage the continuation of efforts by groups such as the American Chemical Society, the American Association for the Advancement of Science, the Modern Language Association, and the National Councils of Teachers of English and Teachers of Mathematics, to revise, update, improve, and make available new and more diverse curricular materials. We applaud the consortia of educators and scientific, industrial, and scholarly societies that cooperate to improve the school curriculum

RECOMMENDATION B: STANDARDS AND EXPECTATIONS

We recommend *that schools, colleges, and universities adopt more rigorous and measurable standards, and higher expectations, for academic performance and student conduct, and that 4-year colleges and universities raise their requirements for admission. This will help students do their best educationally with challenging materials in an environment that supports learning and authentic accomplishment.*

Implementing Recommendations

1. Grades should be indicators of academic achievements so they can be relied on as evidence of a student's readiness for further study.
2. Four-year colleges and universities should raise their admissions requirements and advise all potential applicants of the standards for admission in terms of specific courses required, performance in these areas, and levels of achievement on standardized achievement tests in each of the five Basics and, where applicable, foreign languages.
3. Standardized tests of achievement (not to be confused with aptitude tests) should be administered at major transition points from one level of schooling to another and particularly from high school to college or work. The purposes of these tests would be to: (a) certify the student's credentials; (b) identify the need for remedial intervention; and (c) identify the opportunity for advanced or accelerated work. The tests should be administered as part of a nationwide (but not Federal) system of State and local standardized tests. This system should include other diagnostic procedures that assist teachers and students to evaluate student progress.
4. Textbooks and other tools of learning and teaching should be upgraded and updated to assure more rigorous content. We call upon university scientists, scholars, and members of professional societies, in collaboration with master teachers, to help in this task, as they did in the post-Sputnik era. They should assist willing publishers in developing the

products or publish their own alternatives where there are persistent inadequacies.

5. In considering textbooks for adoption, States and school districts should: (a) evaluate texts and other materials on their ability to present rigorous and challenging material clearly; and (b) require publishers to furnish evaluation data on the material's effectiveness.

6. Because no textbook in any subject can be geared to the needs of all students, funds should be made available to support text development in "thin-market" areas, such as those for disadvantaged students, the learning disabled, and the gifted and talented.

7. To assure quality, all publishers should furnish evidence of the quality and appropriateness of textbooks, based on results from field trials and credible evaluations. In view of the enormous numbers and varieties of texts available, more widespread consumer information services for purchasers are badly needed.

8. New instructional materials should reflect the current applications of technology in appropriate curriculum areas, the best scholarship in each discipline, and research in learning and teaching.

RECOMMENDATION C: TIME

We recommend *that significantly more time be devoted to learning the New Basics. This will require more effective use of the existing school day, a longer school day, or a lengthened school year.*

Implementing Recommendations

1. Students in high schools should be assigned far more homework than is now the case.

2. Instruction in effective study and work skills, which are essential if school and independent time is to be used efficiently, should be introduced in the early grades and continued throughout the student's schooling.

3. School districts and State legislatures should strongly consider 7-hour school days, as well as a 200- and 220-day school year.

4. The time available for learning should be expanded through better classroom management and organization of the school day. If necessary, additional time should be found to meet the special needs of slow learners, the gifted, and others who need more instructional diversity than can be accommodated during a conventional school day or school year.

5. The burden on teachers for maintaining discipline should be reduced through the development of firm and fair codes of student conduct that are enforced consistently, and by considering alternative classrooms,

programs, and schools to meet the needs of continually disruptive students.
6. Attendance policies with clear incentives and sanctions should be used to reduce the amount of time lost through student absenteeism and tardiness.
7. Administrative burdens on the teacher and related intrusions into the school day should be reduced to add time for teaching and learning.
8. Placement and grouping of students, as well as promotion and graduation policies, should be guided by the academic progress of students and their instructional needs, rather than by rigid adherence to age.

RECOMMENDATION D: TEACHING

This recommendation *consists of seven parts. Each is intended to improve the preparation of teachers or to make teaching a more rewarding and respected profession. Each of the seven stands on its own and should not be considered solely as an implementing recommendation.*

1. Persons preparing to teach should be required to meet high educational standards, to demonstrate an aptitude for teaching, and to demonstrate competence in an academic discipline. Colleges and universities offering teacher preparation programs should be judged by how well their graduates meet these criteria.
2. Salaries for the teaching profession should be increased and should be professionally competitive, market-sensitive, and performance-based. Salary, promotion, tenure, and retention decisions should be tied to an effective evaluation system that includes peer review, so that superior teachers can be rewarded, average ones encouraged, and poor ones either improved or terminated.
3. School boards should adopt an 11-month contract for teachers. This would ensure time for curriculum and professional development, programs for students with special needs, and a more adequate level of teacher compensation.
4. School boards, administrators, and teachers should cooperate to develop career ladders for teachers that distinguish among the beginning instructor, the experienced teacher, and the master teacher.
5. Substantial nonschool personnel resources should be employed to help solve the immediate problem of the shortage of mathematics and science teachers. Qualified individuals including recent graduates with mathematics and science degrees, graduate students, and industrial and retired scientists could, with appropriate preparation, immediately begin teaching in these fields. A number of our leading science centers have the capacity to begin educating and retraining teachers immediately. Other areas of critical teacher need, such as English, must also be addressed.

6. Incentives, such as grants and loans, should be made available to attract outstanding students to the teaching profession, particularly in those areas of critical shortage.

7. Master teachers should be involved in designing teacher preparation programs and in supervising teachers during their probationary years.

RECOMMENDATION E: LEADERSHIP AND FISCAL SUPPORT

We recommend *that citizens across the Nation hold educators and elected officials responsible for providing the leadership necessary to achieve these reforms, and that citizens provide the fiscal support and stability required to bring about the reforms we propose.*

Implementing Recommendations

1. Principals and superintendents must play a crucial leadership role in developing school and community support for the reforms we propose, and school boards must provide them with the professional development and other support required to carry out their leadership role effectively. The Commission stresses the distinction between leadership skills involving persuasion, setting goals and developing community consensus behind them, and managerial and supervisory skills. Although the latter are necessary, we believe that school boards must consciously develop leadership skills at the school and district levels if the reforms we propose are to be achieved.

2. State and local officials, including school board members, governors, and legislators, have the primary responsibility for financing and governing the schools, and should incorporate the reforms we propose in their educational policies and fiscal planning.

3. The Federal Government, in cooperation with States and localities, should help meet the needs of key groups of students such as the gifted and talented, the socioeconomically disadvantaged, minority and language minority students, and the handicapped. In combination these groups include both national resources and the Nation's youth who are most at risk.

4. In addition, we believe the Federal Government's role includes several functions of national consequences that States and localities alone are unlikely to be able to meet: protecting constitutional and civil rights for students and school personnel; collecting data, statistics, and information about education generally; supporting curriculum improvement and research on teaching, learning, and the management of schools; supporting teacher training in areas of critical shortage or key national needs; and providing student financial assistance and research and graduate training. We believe the assistance of the Federal Government

should be provided with a minimum of administrative burden and intrusiveness.

5. The Federal Government has the primary responsibility to identify the national interest in education. It should also help fund and support efforts to protect and promote that interest. It must provide the national leadership to ensure that the Nation's public and private resources are marshaled to address the issues discussed in this report.

6. This Commission calls upon educators, parents, and public officials at all levels to assist in bringing about the educational reform proposed in this report. We also call upon citizens to provide the financial support necessary to accomplish these purposes. Excellence costs. But in the long run mediocrity costs far more.

GEORGE H. BUSH

EDUCATION REFORM FOR AN ADAPTABLE WORK FORCE

A key determinant of the flexibility of the economy is the quality of its work force. Education raises skill levels that increase job performance and productivity. Well-educated workers have the basic skills necessary to adapt to the changing demands of a dynamic economy and are able to compete with their peers in other nations.

Unfortunately, primary and secondary education in this country does an inadequate job of producing such workers. Parental involvement and student dedication—especially to homework—is essential to the success of any school system. But greater parental and student effort alone cannot ensure success. Comprehensive reform of American elementary and secondary education is necessary.

The educational system should encourage innovation and promote excellence among teachers and students. It should strive to earn the same high reputation as the U.S. postsecondary educational system, in which there is significant diversity and choice. It should provide the foundation that enables workers to adapt and respond to changing workplace technologies and economic conditions. And it should provide all high school graduates with the backgrounds necessary for advanced study or entering the work force.

Many school districts have outstanding educational systems and achieve these goals. And in every school district in the nation there are talented and dedicated teachers and administrators as well as concerned parents who work hard to improve the educational system. Success requires a commitment to excellence from school administrators, teachers, and parents as well as from

From George H. Bush, *Economic Report of the President*, Washington, D.C. (February 1991), pp. 121–127.

students themselves. However, despite some successes, too many State and local educational systems are notably inflexible and resistant to meaningful and effective change. *Because they need not compete for students and are not held accountable for the quality of the education they provide, many State and local education agencies in this country have become entrenched bureaucracies.* As a result, U.S. students often receive unacceptable poor educations. Parents often find they have little power to ensure that their children receive a sound education, and many choose to send their children to private schools.

The primary fiscal responsibility for public education lies with State and local governments, which determine the institutional framework for the operation of the educational system. Local school boards and State education agencies determine who may teach, what schools students attend, how long students are in class, and even the general instructional methods that are adopted. The Federal Government has traditionally provided only a small fraction of total support for education at the elementary and secondary levels; in 1988 it provided only 6.3 percent of the funds spent on education for kindergarten through grade 12.

As well-intentioned as school boards and education agencies may be, a system that is not required to compete for its students and is not judged by their performance is hard pressed to avoid the mediocrity and resist the insularity that comes with being the only "free" game in town. As a result, although the United States spends more money per pupil than almost any other country in the world (in 1989 U.S. per pupil expenditures were $5,172), the return on this substantial investment is unacceptably low.

THE CURRENT STATE OF EDUCATION

Evidence of the inadequacy of education in the United States can be found in the workplace and in the schools themselves.

Evidence from the Workplace

Today's high school graduate is often ill-prepared for the world of work. The 1990 National Assessment of Educational Progress, which reported the results of a nationwide test of students conducted between 1986 and 1988, found that only 6 percent of 17-year-old students demonstrate the capacity to solve multistep problems and use basic algebra; only 8 percent have the ability to draw conclusions and infer relationships using scientific knowledge; and only 5 percent can synthesize and learn from specialized reading materials.

Firms are finding it increasingly necessary to develop remedial training programs in reading and mathematical skills; they spend an estimated $20 billion annually on such programs. Even institutions of higher learning are adapting their course offerings to reflect the poor preparation of many freshmen; the fraction of colleges offering remedial instruction has increased from 79 percent to more than 90 percent since 1980.

A second-rate educational system cannot support a first-rate, world-class economy. Workers unable to read and grasp complex concepts in mathematics and science cannot hope to adapt to changing technologies in the workplace. Poor training in mathematics and science at the elementary and secondary levels also contributes to declining trends in college enrollment in these areas. This pattern threatens the creative foundation needed to discover and introduce advances in technology.

Previous Reform Efforts

In 1983 a commission appointed by the Secretary of Education issued the report *A Nation at Risk,* which painted a bleak portrait of the quality of education in elementary and secondary schools in the United States. The report struck a responsive chord. Reacting to its recommendations and challenges, State and local educational systems embarked on plans to introduce fundamental changes.

It is nearly a decade later, and not much of consequence has changed. To be sure, many bills were introduced in State legislatures in responses to the report, and many were passed. Forty-five States increased graduation requirements for core courses in subject areas such as mathematics, sciences, humanities, and social sciences. Many States also made teacher certification requirements much stricter and, in an effort to attract higher quality teachers, increased salary levels significantly. Teachers' salaries in public elementary and secondary schools increased by 18 percent in real terms between 1980 and 1990. Expenditures per pupil have also increased 28 percent in real terms since 1982.

Despite the efforts in the 1980s, there has been no noticeable change in the performance of the nation's schools. Though students are taking more mathematics, science, and reading courses, test results show that no performance improvements have been made in these subject areas since the appearance of *A Nation at Risk.* The percentage of students graduating from high school remains unacceptably low, falling from 73 to 72 percent since the report's release.

International Comparisons

U.S. high school students consistently perform far below their foreign counterparts, especially in their knowledge of mathematics and science. In an assessment of learning in six major developed countries in 1988, U.S. students ranked last in mathematics and second to last in science. Even the best U.S. students do not compare favorably with foreign students. The International Assessment of Educational Progress found that a very select group of college-bound American students scored far below a less select group of Canadian students on a standardized test, and no better than an even broader group of Hungarian students.

Other indicators are also very telling. U.S. students spend an average of only 3½ hours a week on homework. That compares poorly with 24 hours a week on average that high school seniors spend watching television. Studies show that European students spend far less time watching television and more time studying.

Finally, American students spend much less time in school than their foreign counterparts. Even though the American system of education is highly decentralized, the 180-day school calendar is nearly national in scope. School calendars ranged from 226 to 240 days in pre-unification West Germany. In Japan, schools are open 243 days on average. Some argue against lengthening the school year on the ground that it is the quality, not the quantity, of instruction that is at issue. Certainly, merely lengthening the school year is not the panacea for the ailing U.S. school system, but it is an issue deserving study with consideration by the States. Evidence suggests that *in countries with longer school years, more material is covered at a much less hurried pace than in American classrooms.* Thus even in U.S. school systems that attain high standards of excellence, the quantity of educational material provided to students is not competitive by world standards.

TOWARD AN EFFECTIVE EDUCATIONAL SYSTEM

The Administration is fully committed to promoting excellence in the U.S. educational system and has undertaken significant initiatives to this end. In September 1989, the President convened a summit of cabinet officials and U.S. Governors to discuss the state of American education. Only the third such summit in American history, it was the first ever on education. As a result of this historic meeting, the President and the Governors agreed upon six clearly defined goals for the American educational system to reach by the year 2000:

- All children in America will start school ready to learn;
- The percentage of students graduating from high school will increase to at least 90 percent;
- Students will leave grades 4, 8, and 12 having demonstrated competency in challenging subject matter, including English, mathematics, science, history, and geography; and every school in America will ensure that all students learn to use their minds well, so they may be prepared for responsible citizenship, further learning, and productive employment in our modern economy
- U.S. students will be first in the world in science and mathematics achievement;
- Every adult American will be literate and possess the knowledge and skills necessary to compete in a global economy and exercise the rights and responsibilities of citizenship; and
- Every school in America will be free of drugs and violence and offer a disciplined environment conducive to learning.

The President outlined these goals in his 1990 State of the Union Address. In July 1990, the President issued *The National Education Goals: A Report to the Nation's Governors,* and the President and the Governors established a National Education Goals Panel that also includes participation of the congressional leadership. The panel will recommend a measurement and assessment system that will provide the Nation with information on the progress being made in reaching these goals.

To help ensure that all American children start school ready to learn, the Administration has significantly expanded the Head Start program. And to ensure that the national education goals are achieved, the Administration will propose a new Educational Excellence Act. Initiatives in this important proposal would stimulate fundamental reform through promoting educational choice and alternative certification for teachers and principals, promote local control and innovation by providing increased flexibility in funding in exchange for greater accountability, reward schools that demonstrate improved achievement among students, and provide incentives for innovative approaches to mathematics and science education.

Programs of Choice

The U.S. public educational system must be opened to the invigorating and challenging forces of market competition by enabling teachers, parents, and students to choose their schools. Over time, the schools that survive will be the most innovative and effective institutions, those capable of responding to the changing educational needs of society.

Schools that must compete for students will work harder to deliver quality education. A school choice program can become the catalyst for greater diversity and help eliminate mediocrity in the educational system. An important step in this direction is the magnet school concept in which schools specialize in particular areas or interests—such as science, mathematics, or the performing arts—and students and their parents choose which school to attend.

The Administration has advocated adoption of choice programs in as many jurisdictions as possible across the country. There is no one "preferred" approach to educational choice. A statewide choice plan exists in Minnesota, while a choice demonstration plan including both public and private schools has been launched in Milwaukee, Wisconsin. In 1990 seven States adopted plans allowing various forms of choice. Before 1990 five other States had enacted interdistrict choice plans. The Administration's new Center for Choice in Education has been established to provide information and assistance to anyone interested in learning about or implementing educational choice.

A key to the success of a choice-based program is granting individual public schools the freedom to innovate. Schools must be freed from the grip of bureaucracies distant from the classroom. One popular version of this self-run school approach is to leave the governance of each school to a team composed of the principal, teachers, and parents. Such an arrangement creates a personal stake in the success of the school, rather than reliance on a central bureaucracy. It also provides parents and teachers an effective voice in determining how a school should change to attract students in an open-choice educational system.

Accountability

Unless teachers, school administrators, and elected or appointed officials are held accountable for the quality of the education they provide, the success of open-choice programs and self-run schools will be limited. Merely adopting new approaches does not ensure success. Schools and teachers must be held accountable for what their students learn.

To this end, *State and local education agencies must work together to develop and publish objective measures of the output of the educational system.* Meaningful performance measures are necessary for the success of school choice programs, allowing parents and students to leave choice programs that are failing. Such performance measures include basic competency tests for graduation from high school; annual tests to determine student progress; changes in high school drop-out rates; and high school transcripts that provide meaningful information on course content and student skills to parents, employers, and colleges.

At the Federal level, the Department of Education is charged by law to "collect, collate, and from time to time, report full and complete statistics on the condition of education in the United States." The National Center for Educational Statistics (NCES) has developed a series of national measures of the output of the educational system. The NCES publishes an annual digest of education statistics and periodically publishes the National Assessment of Educational Programs. The NCES publishes an annual selection of indicators on the condition of education in the United States. The 1990 report confirms the dismal state of public education in this country. Each of these reports provides an ongoing basis for parents to test the success of education reform; they are important tools for increasing accountability.

Alternative Teacher Certification Programs

Each State sets up standards that determine who can teach in public elementary or secondary school systems. Differences in certification requirements across States produce substantial limitations on teachers' job market options. Although many States have formal reciprocity agreements, teachers still encounter significant barriers when they try to cross a State line. Until recently, for example, to win a permanent teaching position in a Rhode Island school system, a person qualified to teach in Massachusetts was required to have a master's degree and 6 years of teaching experience, three of them in Rhode Island. This particular limitation is being eased somewhat, since the six New England States along with New York have agreed to accept the teaching credentials of applicants from other States in the region, providing they complete extra education requirements within 2 years.

Eliminating unnecessary barriers to entry into the teaching profession *within* each State is at least as important as eliminating the barriers between States. Most States currently require that an individual either graduate from a 4-year college as an education major or take a certain number of education courses before being allowed to teach. Talented individuals who decide to switch careers and become teachers find they have to complete either a traditional teacher preparation program or, under fairly recent reforms in some States, complete a graduate degree program in education.

While these requirements discourage many talented professionals seeking a career change from entering the teaching profession, they do not ensure that the school system is getting high-quality teachers. In fact, the poor academic performance of teachers in the subject areas they teach led many States to impose minimum grade requirements for education majors.

The solution to the problem of attracting talented teachers, however, is not to regulate the industry further but to open it up to the competitive process and to reduce certification requirements in ways that do not threaten but instead encourage excellence in teaching. Currently, 28 States have implemented some form of alternative teacher certification program. Mainly small pilot programs, these are based on the general principle that an individual with a bachelor's degree in a specific field of study can be a successful teacher, given some minimum level of training in education. The minimum varies across States, but all programs reflect the belief that the minimum needed to guarantee quality is far less than that currently required by traditional certification routes.

It is important to recognize that removing unnecessary barriers to teaching does not threaten the stature of the profession. First, one already well-defined qualification for entry into the teaching profession, the acquisition of a 4-year college degree, will not change. Second, what helps promote respect for the teaching profession is effective teaching, not unnecessary certification requirements. The experience in Texas and in numerous other programs suggests that lowering the barriers to entering the teaching profession can improve the quality of primary and secondary education.

DAVID K. COHEN

THE CONDITION OF TEACHERS' WORK

When I was in graduate school I picked up the historical habit. I have never been able to shake it. So, as I read the reports in this latest round of school criticism, I kept asking what was new. I made a list.

As befits an historian, I found little new. One thing that may be new is the acknowledgment, in a few of the reports, that social justice for minorities and the poor is a legitimate concern for schools. This perspective was largely absent from the last great paroxysm of worry over the quality of U.S. high schools, during the fifties. I do not say that the concern is great now, but it is at least part of the debate.

Something else that seems pleasantly new, in some responses to the reports, is the worry that, in prescribing remedies for school problems, the critics may confuse quality with quantity—asking for more courses, longer school days

From David K. Cohen, "The Condition of Teachers' Work," *Harvard Educational Review* 54, no. 1 (February 1984), pp. 11–18. Reprinted with permission.

and years, and the like. For most of the twentieth century, American education has been notable for its passionate embrace of the idea that quantity is quality. A little hesitation about this is a novelty, one to be cherished.

My list of what is old is much longer. . . At the end of the sixties, in the middle of the fifties, throughout the forties, during the thirties, and even in the twenties, schools received much free advice. Giving it is a national pastime, and the local tax bill is probably the ticket of admission. Nor is it new that in this latest frenzy about education we try to steer the creature by its tail—by devising national standards, by prescribing new courses and curricula, by declaiming doom and destruction from Washington. Some of that does work, of course, but it is a little discouraging to see Americans once again acting as though they believe that is the answer.

Something else that is not new is the notion that the schools must—and can—solve the Toyota problem. We have not always had Toyotas, but schools have long had the problem of improving productivity, or efficiency, or both—or at least schools have long thought they had that problem. Since the 1890s we have thought of the schools as a chief means for making America more productive, more efficient, more competitive. This is an idea that becomes increasingly problematic the deeper one digs into the relationship between education and productivity, yet few seem inclined to question the notion that schools are responsible for the many failures of General Motors, or Ford, or Chrysler. It is odd, since schools never were praised for causing earlier successes in that industry.

Nor is it new that education is considered essential—especially by its fiercest critics and detractors. These critics oddly assign schools even greater tasks than the ones they attack schools for not achieving. One wonders if the schools, or the country, have the capacity to make good on the promises. Education is always more essential in our arguments than in our appropriations. One regular result has been that schools pay for earlier promises in recriminations launched by later generations of amnesiac critics.

Another old-but-good element in the debate is the argument about quality and equality. For as long as Americans have been trying to construct a public secondary school system we have chewed on this bone. The terms in which we argue it today are not that different from the terms in which we argued it twenty or sixty years ago, though many minorities have managed to claw their way into the system and the argument, and that is new. But we still see education as the place where America has to make that big trade-off; when we worry about quality we want to trade equality away.

Finally, it is not new that we hear so little from people who work in schools. Where are the teachers' voices?[1] Their absence eases the official debate; it subtracts many complications from the argument; it avoids many difficulties that cannot be solved by a new curriculum requirement, another test, or merit pay. But if this makes life easier on the commissions, it has a dreadful simplifying effect on what Americans learn about schools from these reports.

One feature of life in schools that therefore is generally overlooked is the condition of teachers' work.[2] The reports acknowledge that something is wrong with instruction, but they focus on fixes: merit increases (for selective inspiration), better pay (to attract better people), and the elimination of methods courses. Some of these ideas are worth action, or serious discussion, but consider the condition of teachers' work in high school. Teachers must face five classes of twenty-five or thirty kids, each day. And they must face many kids who see no point in studying much, or at all. Teachers must deal with 150, or 180, or 200 kids a day, five days a week—many of them kids who do not want much education.

Now teaching is a trade in which one can only succeed if one's students succeed. It is not like baking bread, where part of the satisfaction lies in turning out a good loaf—even if another part lies in someone else's use of the bread. If one's students do not do well, or do not even want to do well, how can a teacher do well? Or gain much satisfaction, or self-respect? High schools are littered with teachers' answers—their accommodations to these conditions—but we hear little of their dilemmas in the official debate. Teachers' salaries are a scandal, but instead we hear of merit pay; teachers' education should be improved, but instead we hear of stiffening graduation requirements for students; teachers' workloads should be adjusted to include more time for their own learning, preparation, and collaboration, but instead we hear more of adding required courses for students, and thus more courseload for teachers. Stiffer graduation requirements and more courses will multiply teachers' problems, but they will not add to the teachers' resources for solving those problems. There are several fundamental problems with the existing conditions of teachers' work, but most of these reports have neither taught us much about them, nor have they proposed solutions that would help. Indeed, many of the solutions they propose, if implemented, would only further stretch existing resources. In the name of solving problems these proposals would exacerbate them.

Another problem in teachers' work concerns commitment. Learning in classrooms requires a serious commitment, not only by a teacher but also by a student. Actually, more than the commitment of a single student is wanted, because students learn in classrooms, in large groups. Mutual commitment in class groups is a sine qua non of good education. Will is at least as important as wit. Yet one rudimentary fact of life in high schools is the lack of such commitment in many, many classrooms. There one finds flat, arid, wasted hours.[3]

Why?

One reason is that much school attendance is driven by compulsion. Students attend school because the law tells them to; because school staves off unemployment or the thin work often found in what we term the service sector; because keeping kids in school protects many adult workers in a precarious economy; because parents want the child care, and so on. Many attend because everyone else does, because in the absence of much else for kids to do that is valuable, school is the scene, the place to be, the place to see your friends and find a little action. Legal and economic compulsions, and the social pressures that they have generated have helped to turn high schools into social centers for otherwise unoccupied adolescents. It is a great help to parents, to the police, to many adult workers, and to those who make public policy. Kids like it, too.

There is little encouragement for *education* in all this, however. Such reasons for going to school erode the commitment required for thoughtful work. A few teachers who labor in such circumstances persist and succeed. Most give in. For many teachers it is easy—they were educated in circumstances just like this and know nothing else. For others, the accommodation is painful. But one way or another, most teachers and students accommodate to the realities of life in high schools: they entertain each other; they do busywork; they have modest classes organized around a bits-and-pieces approach to learning—a few facts here, a date there, a list of phrases, a splintered dialogue of partial sentences. Many people enter teaching because they like kids, because they want to be helpful. In the face of the astonishing workloads and apathetic audiences they still want to be helpful, to like the kids and be liked by them. Indeed, in one sense, they *must* be helpful. Everyone is there, and has to be; there are few alternatives for many kids, and no reasons for them to work hard. What is more, the schools have made great promises: education will make us all productive and enlightened, harmonious and prosperous. To turn kinds out of school—to flunk or expel them—because they do not work, to fill the streets with those whose interest in school has little to do with education, would be to withdraw those promises, to admit that schools cannot do all they have agreed to do. It would weaken the schools' claims on our attention, and on the public purse, and it would erode whatever sense of professional potency educators have. So something must be done to keep everyone inside and to keep them reasonably happy. High school teachers and students are quite good at this. They can work it out. They accommodate well to the reality of school, making life together mostly decent and sometimes genuinely compassionate—and generally undemanding.

American high schools are thus caught in a trap partly of their own devising. Nearly everyone eligible by age is present, but many have no good educational reason to be there; no jobs await, or no jobs with serious educational requirements; and many institutions calling themselves colleges and universities lie just beyond, available for the mere price of a high school diploma, whatever one's grades. They are in fact increasingly available, as the number of potential students shrinks. Some of the causes of this trap lie beyond the schools' control, but the schools have embraced every assignment. They have promised a usable education for all, productivity, political awakening, social skills, and solid academic preparation. No tasks have been turned down, no demands rejected. Schoolpeople have struggled to devise a curriculum that would have something for everyone. They have tried to find ways to interest the uninterested and spark the uncommitted.

I do not argue that good education is absent. Work in the honors and advanced placement classes is generally good, almost surely better than it was three or four decades ago. Work in some vocational classes is solid, demanding, and bears on real skills. And some special needs classes have been brought out of the closet and turned into places where teachers care and children learn. In each of these cases, though, there are sources of commitment outside the school, reasons to learn that make sense. What about kids without such reasons? Most schools do not succeed in their efforts to find something for them. Learning is not easy, often it is not fun. The curriculum for kids in the middle—neither specially talented nor specially problematic—is a species of desert; it is decent, often friendly, but mentally parched. So it is too, for many kids at the bottom. But there is really no reason to do it differently, neither a strong demand to take the promise of a good education for all seriously, nor the wherewithal to do it. That would require a labor market that works, a popular respect for learning that has no economic reason, and a higher education system hungrier for serious work than for bodies.

There is little in the reports about such things. The commissions chose instead to consider schools. Schools are easier to reform than the economy, easier to hold responsible than great corporations, easier to criticize than the colleges and universities that house many of the critics and staff their report-writing. The commissions speak, therefore, of adding requirements to the curriculum, of giving more tests, of lengthening the school day. The schools suffer from a lack of commitment, but they are doctored with the materials of compulsion.

Why then do we say the schools are a failure? Really they are a great success. Indeed, their failure is their success. Many kids for whom there are no jobs are taken care of for a few years. Many kids for whom work holds no challenge and little promise of productivity can put it off for a few years. Many kids who do not know what to do can find a little something. Many adult workers are protected and parents relieved of responsibilities. Many kids who will go on to undemanding institutions of higher education are gently prepared for the life that awaits them. None of these successes requires good education, and several of them are positively hostile to it. They are the successes of a society which does not need secondary education that is both universal and universally sound—or does not think it needs such education. Until the critics see that the failures they decry are really evidence that the schools are succeeding, they have little hope of doing good, and some potential for mischief.

NOTES

[1] I exempt from this comment the academic studies that happened to be published recently, most notably Philip Cusick's *The American High School and the Egalitarian Ideal;* Sara Lawrence Lightfoot's *The Good High School;* and John Goodlad's *A Place Called School.* They are not commission reports, and while they have much to teach us about schools, they are not part of the official argument.

[2] I draw here on my association with "A Study of High Schools," directed by Theodore Sizer, and on the field research and discussions carried on in that project.

[3] On this point, see Cusick's book, cited above, and Sizer's book, *Horace's Compromise.*

WALTER KARP

WHY JOHNNY CAN'T THINK: THE POLITICS OF BAD SCHOOLING

The following books are discussed in this essay:

> *A Place Called School*, by John I. Goodlad. 396 pages. McGraw-Hill. $9.95
> *The Good High School*, by Sara Lawrence Lightfoot. 399 pages. Basic Books. $19.95.
> *Horace's Compromise: The Dilemma of the American High School*, by Theodore R. Sizer. 241 pages. Houghton Mifflin. $16.95.
> *High School: A Report on Secondary Education in America*, by Ernest L. Boyer and the Carnegie Foundation for the Advancement of Teaching. 363 pages. Harper & Row: $16.95.
> *A Nation at Risk: The Imperative for Educational Reform*, by the National Commission on Excellence in Education. 65 pages. U.S. Government Printing Office. $4.50.
> *The Great School Debate: Which Way for American Education?*, edited by Beatrice and Ronald Gross. 481 pages. Simon & Schuster. $17.45.
> *The Challenge to American Schools*, edited by John Bunzel. 256 pages. Oxford University Press. $19.95.
> *The Troubled Crusade: American Education 1945–1980*, by Diane Ravitch. 384 pages. Basic Books. $19.95.

Until very recently, remarkably little was known about what actually goes on in America's public schools. There were no reliable answers to even the most obvious questions. How many children are taught to read in overcrowded classrooms? How prevalent is rote learning and how common are classroom discussions? Do most schools set off gongs to mark the change of "periods"? Is it a common practice to bark commands over public address systems in the manner of army camps, prisons, and banana republics? Public schooling provides the only intense experience of a public realm that most Americans will ever know. Are school buildings designed with the dignity appropriate to a great republican institution, or are most of them as crummy looking as one's own?

The darkness enveloping America's public schools is truly extraordinary considering that 38.9 million students attend them, that we spend nearly $134 billion a year on them, and that foundations ladle out generous sums for the study of everything about schooling—except what really occurs in the schools. John I. Goodlad's eight-year investigation of a mere thirty-eight of America's 80,000 public schools—the result of which, *A Place Called School*, was published last year—is the most comprehensive such study ever undertaken. Hailed as a

From Walter Karp, "Why Johnny Can't Think: The Politics of Bad Schooling," *Harper's Magazine* vol. 270 (June 1985), pp. 69–73. Copyright © 1985 by *Harper's Magazine*. All rights reserved. Reprinted from the June issue by special permission.

"landmark in American educational research," it was financed with great difficulty. The darkness, it seems, has its guardians.

Happily, the example of Goodlad, a former dean of UCLA's Graduate School of Education, has proven contagious. A flurry of new books sheds considerable light on the practice of public education in America. In *The Good High School,* Sara Lawrence Lightfoot offers vivid "portraits" of six distinctive American secondary schools. In *Horace's Compromise,* Theodore R. Sizer, a former dean of Harvard's Graduate School of Education, reports on his two-year odyssey through public high schools around the country. Even *High School,* a white paper issued by Ernest L. Boyer and the Carnegie Foundation for the Advancement of Teaching, is supported by a close investigation of the institutional life of a number of schools. Of the books under review, only *A Nation at Risk,* the report of the Reagan Administration's National Commission on Excellence in Education, adheres to the established practice of crass special pleading in the dark.

Thanks to Goodlad et al., it is now clear what the great educational darkness has so long concealed: the depth and pervasiveness of political hypocrisy in the common schools of the country. The great ambition professed by public school managers is, of course, education for citizenship and self-government, which harks back to Jefferson's historic call for "general education to enable every man to judge for himself what will secure or endanger his freedom." What the public schools practice with remorseless proficiency, however, is the prevention of citizenship and the stifling of self-government. When 58 percent of the thirteen-year-olds tested by the National Assessment for Educational Progress think it is against the law to start a third party in America, we are dealing not with a sad educational failure but with a remarkably subtle success.

Consider how effectively America's future citizens are trained *not* to judge for themselves about anything. From the first grade to the twelfth, from one coast to the other, instruction in America's classrooms is almost entirely dogmatic. Answers are "right" and answers are "wrong," but mostly answers are short. "At all levels, [teacher-made] tests called almost exclusively for short answers and recall of information," reports Goodlad. In more than 1,000 classrooms visited by his researchers, "only *rarely*" was there "evidence to suggest instruction likely to go much beyond mere possession of information to a level of understanding its implications." Goodlad goes on to note that "the intellectual terrain is laid out by the teacher. The paths for walking through it are largely predetermined by the teacher." The give-and-take of genuine discussion is conspicuously absent. "Not even 1%" of instructional time, he found, was devoted to discussion that "required some kind of open response involving reasoning or perhaps an opinion from students. . . . The extraordinary degree of student passivity stands out."

Sizer's research substantiates Goodlad's. "No more important finding has emerged from the inquiries of our study than that of the American high school student *as student,* is all too often docile, complaint, and without initiative."

There is good reason for this. On the one hand, notes Sizer, "there are too few rewards for being inquisitive." On the other, the heavy emphasis on "the right answer . . . smothers the student's efforts to become an effective intuitive thinker."

Yet smothered minds are looked on with the utmost complacency by the educational establishment—by the Reagan Department of Education, state boards of regents, university education departments, local administrators, and even many so-called educational reformers. Teachers are neither urged to combat the tyranny of the short right answer nor trained to do so. "Most teachers simply do not know how to teach for higher levels of thinking," says Goodlad. Indeed, they are actively discouraged from trying to do so.

The discouragement can be quite subtle. In their orientation talks to new, inexperienced teachers, for example, school administrators often indicate that they do not much care what happens in class so long as no noise can be heard in the hallway. This thinly veiled threat virtually ensures the prevalence of short-answer drills, workbook exercises, and the copying of long extracts from the blackboard. These may smother young minds, but they keep the classroom quiet.

Discouragement even calls itself reform. Consider the current cry for greater use of standardized student tests to judge the "merit" of teachers and raise "academic standards." If this fake reform is foisted on the schools, dogma and docility will become even more prevalent. This point is well made by Linda Darling-Hammond of the Rand Corporation in an essay in *The Great School Debate*. Where "important decisions are based on test scores," she notes, "teachers are more likely to teach to the tests," and less likely to bother with "nontested activities, such as writing, speaking, problem-solving or real reading of real books." The most influential promoter of standardized tests is the "excellence" brigade in the Department of Education; so clearly one important meaning of "educational excellence" is greater proficiency in smothering students' efforts to think for themselves.

Probably the greatest single discouragement to better instruction is the overcrowded classroom. The Carnegie report points out that English teachers cannot teach their students how to write when they must read and criticize the papers of as many as 175 students. As Sizer observes, genuine discussion is possible only in small seminars. In crowded classrooms, teachers have difficulty imparting even the most basic intellectual skills, since they have no time to give students personal attention. The overcrowded classroom inevitably debases instruction, yet it is the rule in America's public schools. In the first three grades of elementary school, Goodlad notes, the average class has twenty-seven students. High school classes range from twenty-five to forty students, according to the Carnegie report.

What makes these conditions appalling is that they are quite unnecessary. The public schools are top-heavy with administrators and rife with sinecures. Large numbers of teachers scarcely ever set foot in a classroom, being occupied instead as grade advisers, career counselors, "coordinators," and supervisors. "Schools, if simply organized," Sizer writes, "can have well-paid faculty and fewer than eighty students per teacher [16 students per class] without increasing current per-pupil expenditure." Yet no serious effort is being made to reduce class size. As Sizer notes, "Reducing teacher load is, when all the negotiating is over, a low agenda item for the unions and school boards." Overcrowded classrooms virtually guarantee smothered minds, yet the subject is not even mentioned in *A Nation at Risk,* for all its well-publicized braying about a "rising tide of mediocrity."

Do the nation's educators really want to teach almost 40 million students how to "think critically," in the Carnegie report's phrase, and "how to judge for themselves," in Jefferson's? The answer is, if you can believe that you will believe anything. The educational establishment is not even content to produce passive minds. It seeks passive spirits as well. One effective agency for producing these is the overly populous school. The larger schools are, the more prison-like they tend to be. In such schools, guards man the stairwells and exits. ID cards and "passes" are examined at checkpoints. Bells set off spasms of anarchy and bells quell the student mob. PA systems interrupt regularly with trivial and frivolous announcements. This "malevolent intruder," in Sizer's apt phrase, is truly ill willed, for the PA system is actually an educational tool. It teaches the huge student mass to respect the authority of disembodied voices and the rule of remote and invisible agencies. Sixty-three percent of all high school students in America attend schools with enrollments of 5,000 or more. The common excuse for these mobbed schools is economy, but in fact they cannot be shown to save taxpayers a penny. Large schools "tend to create passive and compliant students," notes Robert B. Hawkins Jr. in an essay in *The Challenge in American Schools.* That is their chief reason for being.

"How can the relatively passive and docile roles of students prepare them to participate as informed, active and questioning citizens?" asks the Carnegie report, in discussing the "hidden curriculum" of passivity in the schools. The answer is, they were not meant to. Public schools introduce future citizens to the public world, but no introduction could be more disheartening. Architecturally, public school buildings range from drab to repellent. They are often disfigured by demoralizing neglect—"cracked sidewalks, a shabby lawn, and peeling paint on every window sash," to quote the Carnegie report. Many big-city elementary schools have numbers instead of names, making them as coldly dispiriting as possible.

Public schools stamp out republican sentiment by habituating their students to unfairness, inequality, and special privileges. These arise inevitably from the educational establishment's longstanding policy (well described by Diane Ravitch in *The Troubled Crusade*) of maintaining "the correlation between social class and educational achievement." In order to preserve that factitious "correlation," public schooling is rigged to favor middle-class students and to ensure that working-class students do poorly enough to convince them that they fully merit the lowly station that will one day be theirs. "Our goal is to get these kids to be like their parents," one teacher, more candid than most, remarked to a Carnegie researcher. . . .

That describes a malicious intent a trifle too mildly. Reading is the key to everything else in school. Children who struggle with it in the first grade will be "grouped" with the slow readers in the second grade and will fall hopelessly behind in all subjects by the sixth. The schools hasten this process of falling behind, report Goodlad and others, by giving the best students the best teachers and struggling students the worst ones. "It is ironic," observes the Carnegie report, "that those who need the most help get the least." Such students are commonly diagnosed as "culturally deprived" and so are blamed for the failures inflicted on them. Thus, they are taught to despise themselves even as they are inured to their inferior station.

The whole system of unfairness, inequality, and privilege comes to fruition in high school. There, some 15.7 million youngsters are formally divided into the favored few and the ill-favored many by the practice of "tracking." About 35 percent of America's public-secondary-school students are enrolled in academic programs (often subdivided into "gifted" and "non-gifted" tracks); the rest are relegated to some variety of non-academic schooling. Thus the tracking system, as intended, reproduces the divisions of the class system. "The honors programs," notes Sizer, "serve the wealthier youngsters, and the general tracks (whatever their titles) serve the working class. Vocational programs are often a cruel social dumping ground." The bottom-dogs are trained for jobs as auto mechanics, cosmeticians, and institutional cooks, but they rarely get the jobs they are trained for. Pumping gasoline, according to the Carnegie report, is as close as an auto-mechanics major is likely to get to repairing a car. "Vocational education in the schools is virtually irrelevant to job fate," asserts Goodlad. It is merely the final hoax that the school bureaucracy plays on the neediest, one that the federal government has been promoting for seventy years.

The tracking system makes privilege and inequality blatantly visible to everyone. It creates under one roof "two worlds of schooling," to quote Goodlad. Students in academic programs read Shakespeare's plays. The commonality, notes the Carnegie report, are allowed virtually no contact with serious literature. In their English classes they practice filling out job applications. "Gifted" students alone are encouraged to think for themselves. The rest are subjected to sanctimonious wind, chiefly about "work habits" and "career opportunities."

"If you are the child of low-income parents," reports Sizer, "the chances are good that you will receive limited and often careless attention from adults in your high school. If you are the child of upper-middle-income parents, the chances are good that you will receive substantial and careful attention." In Brookline High School in Massachusetts, one of Lightfoot's "good" schools, a few fortunate students enjoy special treatment in their Advanced Placement classes. Meanwhile, students tracked into "career education" learn about "institutional cooking and clean-up" in a four-term Food Service course that requires them to mop up after their betters in the school cafeteria.

This wretched arrangement expresses the true spirit of public education in America and discloses the real aim of its hidden curriculum. A favored few, pampered and smiled upon, are taught to cherish privilege and despise the disfavored. The favorless many, who have majored in failure for years, are taught to think ill of themselves. Youthful spirits are broken to the world and every impulse of citizenship is effectively stifled. John Goodlad's judgment is severe but just: "There is in the gap between our highly idealistic goals for schooling in our society and the differentiated opportunities condoned and supported in schools a monstrous hypocrisy."

The public schools of America have not been corrupted for trivial reasons. Much would be different in a republic composed of citizens who could judge for themselves what secured or endangered their freedom. Every wielder of illicit or undemocratic power, every possessor of undue influence, every beneficiary of corrupt special privilege would find his position and tenure at hazard. Republican education is a menace to powerful, privileged, and influential people, and they in turn are a menace to republican education. That is why the generation that founded the public schools took care to place them under the suffrage of local communities, and that is why the corrupters of public education have virtually destroyed that suffrage. In 1932 there were 127,531 school districts in America. Today there are approximately 15,840 and they are virtually impotent, their proper role having been usurped by state and federal authorities. Curriculum and textbooks, methods of instruction, the procedures of the classroom, the organization of the school day, the cant, the pettifogging, and the corruption are almost uniform from coast to coast. To put down the menace of republican education its shield of local self-government had to be smashed, and smashed it was.

The public schools we have today are what the powerful and the considerable have made of them. They will not be redeemed by trifling reforms. Merit pay, a longer school year, more homework, special schools for the "gifted," and more standardized tests will not even begin to turn our public schools into nurseries of "informed, active and questioning citizens." They are not meant to. When the authors of *A Nation at Risk* call upon the schools to create an "educated work force," they are merely sanctioning the prevailing corruption, which consists precisely in the reduction of citizens to credulous workers. The education of a free people will not come from federal bureaucrats crying up "excellence" for "economic growth," any more than it came from their predecessors who cried up schooling as a means to "get a better job."

Only ordinary citizens can rescue the schools from their stifling corruption, for nobody else wants ordinary children to become questioning citizens at all. If we wait for the mighty to teach America's youth what secures or endangers their freedom, we will wait until the crack of doom.

SUSAN OHANIAN

HUFFING AND PUFFING AND BLOWING SCHOOLS EXCELLENT

The good gray managers of the U.S., the fellows who gave us Wonder Bread, the Pinto, hormone-laden beef wrapped in Styrofoam, and *People* magazine— not to mention acid rain, the Kansas City Hyatt, $495 hammers, and political

From Susan Ohanian, "Huffing and Puffing and Blowing Schools Excellent," *Phi Delta Kappan* 66, no. 5 (January 1958), pp. 316–321. Reprinted with permission.

s—are now loudly screaming that we teachers should mend our ays and get back to excellence. I would invite the corporate leaders, the s, and the professional consultants to climb down from their insular glass towers before casting any more stones of censure at, or even advice about, my lack of excellence in the classroom. Life in the Eighties is complicated. All of us are, in Thomas Hardy's words, "people distressed by events they did not cause." There is no reason for teachers alone to shoulder the blame.

The various commissions and task forces on educational excellence seem to exemplify one of those laws of human nature; you can tell what a community thinks of you by the committees you aren't asked to join. All of this education commission razzle-dazzle is nothing new; it constitutes just one more in a long, histrionic string of repudiations of teacher savvy and sensitivity. When national leaders decide that it's time to find out what's going on in the schools, they convene a panel of auto dealers and their fellow Rotarians. Individually, these folks are undoubtedly witty, astute, and kind to cats. Collectively, they produce a lot of bluster and blunder; their notions of reform are, at best, spongy. They say, in effect, "I'll huff and I'll puff and I'll blow your schoolhouse excellent."

Would that they could. But most schoolhouses are built of brick, and, though the people behind those brick walls may listen to a little corporate whistling in the dark, adding a course in computer literacy here and one in consumer math there, they remain impervious to real change, especially since no real change has been called for. If you want real change, you must talk to teachers, maybe even listen to them. For without teachers, real change will never happen.

I confess to feeling about most committees the way Lord Palmerston felt about delegations: they are "a noun of multitude, signifying many but not much." In line with this description, the multifarious state-of-education groups have employed the popular "ready, fire, aim" approach—relying not on the firsthand observations of teachers and students but on the collated reports of other report writers. I propose a national lottery for education consultants. Instead of listening to pronouncements from every state, county, block party, and gathering of the Moose, why not choose just one? We could then syndicate the banalities of this lone lucky consultant and be done with it.

As things now stand, the U.S. would be better served if these commissions and task forces developed a master plan for getting rid of Astroturf and saving the spotted bat, a species as endangered as the science teacher. The education community is ill-served by their unilateral advice pacts. One can't help but wonder why our corporate brethren don't go off and figure out how to run an airline or a steel mill. Not that we teachers wouldn't welcome them into our classrooms. I'm sure that any teacher in the land would extend an invitation to any member of the many commissions on excellence to come to the classroom and show him or her how to make efficient use of school time on the day before Halloween, during a snowstorm, on the morning after an X-rated movie on cable television, during the first half hour after a child vomits in class, or immediately after the school nurse checks the group for head lice.

I can glean a few crystal moments from my own years in the classroom, but

I suspect that the pestiferous pedagognosticians will have a hard time fitting my treasured moments on their graphs of excellence: watching a scruffy, smelly, foul-mouthed 16-year-old emerge from six months of solitary Scrabble-playing to write a letter to a dictionary publisher; seeing a deaf child understand a knock-knock joke for the first time; sharing gravestone rubbings; judging an ice-cube-melting contest; publishing a 45-page student anthology of cat stories. I can almost claim that I never made a curriculum I didn't like—at some particular time, for some particular child. And that's my problem: all I can offer are particulars. When the one-size fits-all, spray-and-use planners gather together, I run for cover. Any good teachers will tell you that a curriculum or an instructional approach can't be standardized and remain effective, even within a single classroom. There's always that child who needs something different.

In my first year of teaching, one of my ninth-graders refused to read *Silas Marner*. Wishing I had had the guts to refuse to teach that particular novel, I gave him a different book. I figured I had enough troubles without carrying the added weight of failing someone for saying no. In my more optimistic moments, I even hoped that this particular ninth-grader was exercising literary taste.

As I look back on that incident 18 longs years ago, I marvel that I had the good sense to avoid that battle. It is fairly easy to see now that *Silas Marner* was not worth bloodshed or even tears, but I marvel that I sensed it then. The burdens of teaching are heavy; the joys, fleeting. Occasionally, good judgment and even excellence can be recognized in retrospect, but in the classroom you usually just hope that you can get through the day without having to apologize for anything.

We are ill-served by the present hardening of the categories, the separation of academic life into the real subjects and the frills. To hear some people tell it, a herd of basic skills escaped from the schoolhouse a few years back, apparently chased away by frivolous, fuzzy-headed electives. Now, if our economy, national security, and petrochemical lifestyle are to dominate, we need corporate help in corraling the wayward critters once again. Balderdash. All of this basic skills rumble-bumble is a smokescreen; whenever folks bring it up, check to see what they're selling. Mom, apple pie, two cars in every garage, and basic skills. Who could possibly be against such things?

People who talk about basic skills are expressing, of course, not a theory but a mood. Calling for a return to basic skills has the moral imperative of eating turnips; it is akin to the plaintive cry for law and order. Sure, we all want peace and quiet, a chicken in every microwave, and everybody reading at grade level. But these are weasel words, as easy to pin down as a whirling dervish.

Discussing absolute curriculums for high school is about as productive as talking about best diets or sharing theories on how to restrain proliferating zucchini. For all their technological pizzazz, our mandarin advisors don't seem to understand that you simply do not educate children by the same methods employed to build rockets or harvest tomatoes.

I dropped out of high school English teaching (the first time) after just one year. Outside the school, students were terrorizing subway passengers, buying and selling dope, having babies. Inside, we gave departmental exams on

Tennyson. Even when I did manage to figure out ways to supplement the curriculum, I had to sneak in early so that I could steal ditto paper and other supplies. Not to mention staying up until midnight weeping my way through 150 themes and my survival plans for the next day. In the ensuing two decades things have gotten not better, but steadily worse.

I wonder if concerned commission members and community leaders have any notion of just how debilitating it is for teachers, having figured out what to teach and even how to teach it, to then be forced to beg, borrow, and steal—and mostly do without—basic supplies. I wonder if the report writers have ever been in charge of a classroom for which it takes two weeks to secure enough chairs for the students. And even then the teacher has to fight hard to convince the janitor that leftover eighth-grade chairs simply won't do for fourth-graders. I know a lot of teachers who would cheerfully give up their copies of the reports on excellence for a ream of paper, a handful of #2 pencils, or a box of staples that fit the stapler.

As I look back over nearly two decades of teaching, I am rather amazed that my goal has remained constant since my second day: to help students believe not only that they have the skill to read but that they might actually *want* to read one day. My teaching career began midway through someone else's lesson plan, and I still have nightmares about that first day—that gruesome moment when I told the students to open the text to the next selection, "Hiawatha." I was out on the pavement that same afternoon, scouring bookstores for used paperbacks. I sensed that I had to encourage students to read for their own information and pleasure, and I carefully watched their choices so that I could find out where to go next with them. When I could steal enough ditto paper, I typed up selections from some of my own favorites for us to read together. It may surprise those who are convinced that "excellence" must be imposed from above to know that the students' favorite literature was my laboriously typed excerpt from *The Once and Future King.* Interspersed with this rather eclectic curriculum was "real" school—the stuff of departmental exams and blue-ribbon commission recommendations.

Once, while I presented for my supervisors a required lesson on *Julius Caesar,* a belligerent girl (whose attendance had improved dramatically since the appearance of self-chosen books) steadfastly read her novel. My department chairman leaned over and whispered to her, "Don't you think you should put that book away and pay attention to the teacher?" "Who the hell are you?" demanded the girl. "If she wants me to put it away, let her tell me." She went back to her book, and I continued my performance. Later, it was hard to convince my boss that the girl's devotion to that book was an excellent moment for me, much more valid than my gyrations on *Julius Caesar.* Six weeks previously she had claimed that she "hated reading." Wasn't this progress? Do 100% of the students have to play the game? Her very presence in my class was a victory of sorts, and she was not, after all, painting her nails; she was reading.

Ten years later and hundreds of miles away, the students had changed but the official expectations had not. An investigator from the state education department complained because all my students were reading different books. He dismissed the fact that delinquents, dragged into our alternative program by truant officers and probation officers, were reading at least half an hour every day, with the query, "What major work do your sophomores read?" He was uncomfortable with and even hostile toward a classroom filled with Dick Francis, S. E. Hinton, Thomas Thompson, John McPhee, Edward Abbey, James Thurber, fix-it books, almanacs, sports and car magazines, and the *Daily News*. He was not placated by the fact that the *New York Times* was also in the room, as were copies of standard classics of literature. He wanted workbooks that focused on skills and 30 copies of *A Tale of Two Cities* or *Our Town*. We could have gotten away with Paul Zindel, if we'd had 30 copies. Experts on how schools should be run make it easier for teachers to pose clever comprehension questions about different drummers than to respect them.

Stan dropped out of high school the day he turned 16 because he "hated the damn bells, always making you stop what you're doing to go someplace else." Stan found a job as a carpenter's assistant in a Neighborhood Youth Corps program; by all accounts, he was clever, industrious, and dependable. That's what his boss told me, and I certainly found him to be all those things in the GED class the Corps required Stan to attend. He whizzed through all the GED sections except math. Although his common sense made him efficient at estimating, approximating, and making good guesses, Stan refused to learn the finer points of multiplication and long division.

It may be fitting and proper that a student who won't cooperate to the extent of learning long division should be denied any sort of high school seal of approval. But, if that is the way it's going to be, we should stop requiring such bureaucratic seals of approval for carpenters' assistants.

As Stan said when the Corps fired him for refusing to take any more classes in math, "All I ever wanted to do was work." If we are going to require college degrees for jobs that people once handled without an eighth-grade education, let us admit our reason: we are much more concerned with delaying entry into a glutted job market than with striving for excellence in education.

But the writers of reports on school reform don't know about Stan. Theirs is a too-narrow outlook on education—concerned with the dearth of foreign-language proficiency among incoming college freshmen, but not with the increasing numbers of young women who must drop out of school because they are pregnant or with the disaffected youths who neither need nor want a college prep curriculum. I am disappointed that the commissions and task forces did not examine the lives of these students. But then, I'm prejudiced. I think that the needs of children should take precedence over the needs of Harvard and even over the needs of General Motors.

The reports on school reform imply that, if we teachers would just become more efficient and use class time more wisely, our students would score better on standardized tests, measure up to the Japanese in auto production, or whatever. What the writers of these reports fail to acknowledge is that in teaching, as in baseball, all moments are not of equal value. You have to put up with a lot of foul balls in the classroom.

Of *course* we need to evaluate teachers. But the current systems, which approach teacher evaluation with a meat inspector's outlook, are doomed to failure. Evaluating teachers is not like grading eggs or beef. We need to encourage the proliferation of a variety of teaching styles, instead of setting up only two acceptable categories: Grade A and Grade B.

Maybe it is time for a doctoral student or a governor's aide to examine the fact that teachers, by and large, are decidedly unenthusiastic about the idea of merit pay. We aren't scared off by so-called standards; we are distressed by the fact that teachers are once again being told how to do their job by people who have never done it. Merit pay will reward once again the politician and the showman among us. Expertise is too easy to fake. The Duke of Wellington once remarked that he liked the Order of the Garter because there was "no damned nonsense about merit" connected with it. If the state legislators and other politicians are so interested in rewarding merit, let them go first. If all teachers were paid a decent wage, maybe the notion of merit pay could be buried in the nearest landfill, along with all the other deadly sludge.

No one intimately involved in a classroom can appreciate the subtle interplays, the minute changes that take place among people in that setting— and, when things go very well, between a student and a text or an idea. So, when we are told to get ready for the lessons-by-appointment that are arranged every six months and duly noted in our personnel files, we go for the grand slam. Most of us can do this on schedule (and we have contracts stipulating that no one dare try an unscheduled visit), but lessons-by-appointment don't reveal tiddly pom about our real strengths and weaknesses over the 180-day season. It always amazed me that students ham up such lessons as much as their teachers, cooperating in the production of show-and-tell tinsel for the benefit of visiting administrators. For 50 minutes twice a year, we all pretend that school is what everybody outside the classroom claims it should be. No student even asks to go to the bathroom.

After a while I stopped playing this game of gray-flannel excellence. I decided, "They want to evaluate me? Well, let them see me in action"—which is often, to the unknowing eye, very close to inaction.

So my boss—the one who gets to lay down policy, write curriculum guidelines, and consult, no doubt, with important people from education commissions—sat in my classroom while three seventh-graders read joke books to one another, four students read notes I had written to them and wrote replies, two students quizzed each other for a social studies test in some other teacher's class. Charlie (left behind from the previous class) remained asleep, Sharon announced she was in love and got a pass to the library to find some poems honoring the event, Raymond picked up his novel where he had left off the day before, and Jack went through his daily litany about "not doing no friggin' work in this friggin' school." Interestingly, on another occasion, when I did perform a "show" lesson for an administrator, Jack played his role of model student. But since I wasn't faking it this time, neither did he.

A good teacher makes important decisions. Does Charlie need his sleep more than he needs reading? Do certain students need a review of social studies more than they need punctuation? A good teacher savors watching youngsters read joke books, when a few months earlier they refused to believe that books could ever be funny or worth sharing. A good teacher needles the obnoxious to get to work and encourages the light-hearted to view the library as a storehouse of infinite resources.

But after 10 minutes of this, my boss couldn't stand it any longer. She gathered up her agendas and her checklists and announced, "I'll come back when you are teaching." I noted that she'd been sitting across the table from Ron, who had gotten a good start on writing a poem. Three times he had called me over for help. I had nudged him to reexamine the sense of a metaphor, persuaded him to stop going for the easy rhyme, and helped him locate the thesaurus when he decided he needed a big word—one that "nobody else would know." I thought Ron's work nothing short of miraculous, but you won't find any record of these magic moments in my personnel file.

Even for the best of practitioners and observers, the teachable moment is fleeting; if you don't have a good eye, you are likely to miss it. Despite the claims of the mastery-learning crew and others of their ilk, teaching, like truth, is never pure and rarely simple. Too many expert witnesses mistake fluff and flutter for consequence. I figure that the only way to teach is well, and just how you do it is your own damn business. If my style doesn't fit on somebody else's checklist, too bad. We teachers must not be railroaded into pretending that we should be responsible for managing the timing and flow of education as efficiently and regularly as assembly-line workers produce toasters. We don't have to jump every time someone else rings a bell.

The various commission and task force reports released a flood of public sentiment for improving our schools—and a lot of cynicism in the faculty room. We knew what would happen. The flurry of public interest would soon be displaced by the next day's headline, and we teachers would be left with the nasty residue—the slush and slime of still more negative messages about how we do our jobs. The reports were so neat and precise, so self-confident in their delivery. And now here we sit in what has been portrayed as a very sloppy profession, never sure from one moment to the next that we are doing more good than harm. We are ill-served by cheap shots from the corporate and political remittance men and their consulting mercenaries whose words are akin to a nasty swarm of blood-sucking mosquitoes. Their bites may not kill, but they sure don't help us do our job.

I wish that the members of those commissions and task forces could realize how frustrating it is for us teachers to be pursued like horse thieves. There are so many witnesses for the prosecution on how we measure up in the classroom: the bus driver, the newspaper reporter, the mayor, the colleague across the hall. And now the professors and politicians are at it again. Teachers, it seems, are never acquitted. The best we can hope for is a hung jury.

Part of the problem is that we have no special skills, no secret rites all our own. Just about anybody can teach a lesson or two—perhaps even cope for a week or a month or a year. A few might even do it well. But the real test is to stick with teaching 10 years or more and *still* do it well, maybe even get better at it. Teaching, done well, can drive you crazy. I have taught for 18 years, 16 in the public schools, and I don't think I had one single comfortable day in the classroom. There is always that tension that you'll miss something important, fail to respond correctly to a student's unspoken need. Thirty years after the fact, my sister is still pained and even intimidated by an English teacher's red-penciled comment on her theme. I worry about how my students will remember me in 30 years. We don't teach a child for just one year; our message lingers for a lifetime. God knows, the temptation is always there to react badly to innumerable provocations: wacky kids, fetid curriculum guides, maggot-brained bureaucrats, sanctimonious reports on excellence.

I like to write about my crystal moments in teaching. The savoring of these times is, I think, what keeps me going. But the call in the current wave of education reports for greater efficiency in the classroom helped me realize that my exuberant vignettes are misleading. Maybe some folks get the impression that I spent 16 years passing efficiently from one crystal moment to another.

Forget efficiency. Not enough attention is paid to the lag time in schools, the interminable length of some of those days. Thomas Boswell writes that a typical baseball game "is primarily dead time begging to be condensed. Any game that has more than a dozen key moments is one whale of a game." He might have been describing teaching—except that we have even more dead time. Any school *year* that has more than a dozen key moments is one whale of a year. Like baseball, teaching needs to develop a system for rewarding what Boswell describes as "a phlegmatic stability—a capacity to endure long aggravation and ignore many losses and embarrassments." Have any of the good consultants come up with a checklist to assess a teacher's response to embarrassment and aggravation?

There is, of course, an important difference between teaching and baseball: we teachers usually don't know when we've scored a run. Often we realize only months or years later that something we did might have been important, might have made a difference. Too often, we never know.

This fact was brought home to me a few years ago, when I was asked to write an article on discipline. I was singularly unenthusiastic. I don't know anything about discipline and don't care anything about discipline, I told myself. Only my disgust with all the wretched writing on the subject—plus my overweening desire to see my name in print—led me to agree to do the article. And then a fantastic thing began to happen: as I read other people's tomes on discipline, as I began to observe my own classroom routines and recall incidents from past years, fairly clear patterns began to emerge. Not only did I find that I have pretty strong convictions about discipline, but I decided that I had reacted rather well to some difficult circumstances in my own classrooms.

Thus my work as a writer helped me discover my craft as a teacher. But most teachers don't have this luxury. Ordinarily, teachers have neither the time nor the inclination to pause and reflect on what they do day after day, year after year. Maybe they're too tired from dodging missiles launched by the outside hordes. Certainly the system seems to be set up to keep teachers isolated, lonely, and defensive.

My own school district, for example, no longer lets anybody go out of town for professional purposes—not even if they pay their own expenses. No conventions, no seminars, no workshops, no chance to meet other professionals. I can't figure out if the people in charge keep us isolated more because they are scared we will *say* something or scared we will *hear* something. This is not to say that my district is not at the forefront of the excellence movement. Officials bought multiple copies of the report of the National Commission on Excellence in Education and offered them free to any teacher who would write a summary for the board of education. The pity is that we would have learned more about excellence had we been allowed to visit our classrooms right in our own buildings. But no one in charge believes that teachers can learn excellence from other teachers, especially not their own colleagues. Excellence is something that travels 'round the country first-class, on a 747. And if you can't afford first-class excellence, it will eventually be packaged and available by mail. But always, always, words about excellence in your classroom come from somewhere else.

Enough of the phenomenology of excellence. Let's look at specifics. Our august advisors offer us fearful choices: four years of English or ignominy, more science and math or the collapse of the American dream. What the fellows spouting this doom fail to acknowledge is that it matters little if Johnny takes two years of English or six, if his teacher cannot do the job right. If ever an impossible task exists in this land, it is that of the high school English teacher.

To avoid being forced back into a high school English classroom, I fought local administrators, the union, and state certification officials. After 16 years of teaching and 48 graduate credits beyond my M.A. in English, I filled my summer with the dreaded course requirements for primary teachers rather than face "Horace's compromise." It is one thing to dream the impossible dream; it is quite another to be overrun by students and curriculum mandates. Until such time as union leaders or district administrators are willing to recognize and admit that merely mortal English teachers, given responsibility for 100-plus students, can do little more than herd the flock, I will find something else to do.

A lot of pompous words are circulating these days about something called scientific literacy, and something else is snowballing along under the name of computer literacy. Writers of the current wave of reports insist that requiring another year of science, another year of math, and a few months of computers will somehow keep us in the forefront of the technological revolution, insuring a rising GNP, and so on. But does another year of the same old stuff really make sense? Most often, more of the same merely produces more of the same. The prestigious panels seem intent on fostering endurance, not excellence. They count minutes-on-task but ignore crucial questions of content.

Not to mention connections. If those panel members had bothered to talk to students, they would have uncovered a recurring complaint: nothing makes sense. Students don't see how given courses connect, either to their own lives or to other courses. I'm not talking about "relevance"—about teaching biographies of rock stars or cash-register math. I'm talking about showing students that learning can enrich their lives.

A rather rigid sequence of courses makes sense for a student who's headed for Harvard. Surely, however, such phenomena as the complex topics researched by winners of the national science competition and swelling enrollments in Advanced Placement classes attest to the availability of traditional academic challenges for those who are ready to accept them.

But what about the others? Do they really need to sit in more math classes, grinding out more solutions to problems on mortgage interest rates for homes they can no longer afford? Does algebra really teach these students to think? Does the inclined plane hold the secrets of the modern industrial state? I suspect that the number of people whose lives might be enriched by knowing about vectors or studying French is extremely small—smaller by far than the number whose lives might be enriched by listening to Vivaldi. Unfortunately, I did not notice any reports extolling the virtues of Vivaldi in our schools. Art, music, and physical education (as contrasted with brute competition) have traditionally been given short shrift by our educational planners. Maybe this is because what students get out of an art class is less readily available to the scorekeepers. It's hard to know at a glance if national art appreciation is up or down by 1.43% in any given year.

I know that science is important. So are music and art and good books and skilled carpentry. Then what is this nonsense about getting rid of high school electives? Since when do U.S. students forfeit individual freedom when they enter the hallowed halls of high school?

I think of my own high school days, when my counselor kept reminding me that home economics was a requirement for graduation and I kept on signing up for music theory—even after they refused to give me any more "credit" for the course. Just before my senior year, my mother begged me to give in. "All they do in home ec is make white sauce," I complained. She pointed out that I didn't know how to make white sauce, but I took music theory for the fourth time anyway. I was corresponding with professors from across the U.S. on the theoretical necessity for the triple flat, and I could not be bothered with white sauce.

This story has two points. First, despite official requirements, I graduated on schedule. I doubt that most experts on education would have deemed my high school an excellent one, but the people in charge of my school—to their everlasting credit—knew when to look the other way. More important, they allowed me to pursue an interest that had no resale value. Even some of the professors of musicology with whom I was corresponding indicated that they thought it outrageous that a high school curriculum should deal with such esoterica. I didn't bother to explain that my teacher hadn't included triple sharps and triple flats in his lesson plans. In fact, he did not know that they existed. But he introduced me to music theory and honored my desire to travel narrow paths. When he couldn't answer my question about the triple flat, he suggested that I write the letters.

And that is where the important learning took place. I learned that it's okay for a person in charge to admit to not knowing everything; I learned that letters put the wisdom of the world in your mailbox; I learned that experts sometimes disagree. I also learned that the most satisfying learning comes when you do it simply because you want to. The course content doesn't matter. With teacher savvy, student cooperation, and a little luck, such excellence can occur in history class, in biology, in shop—anywhere.

High school should be a time of exploration, of trying on different hats— not a time of cramming oneself into a corporate mold. If Harvard wants its freshmen to have two or three or six years of a foreign language, that's fine. But it's not enough reason to make everyone else take two or three or six years of a foreign language too. The attitudes that students carry away with their diplomas are much more important than their SAT scores. If students can learn how to learn during their first 12 years of school, then anything is possible for them later on, and we teachers can feel that we have done our job. But if all that we give our students is more of the same—discrete facts disconnected from meaning or purpose—then we are in trouble.

We must be ever wary of wasting some youngster's life just because of a dubious notion that a rigorous, regimented curriculum will help restore to the U.S. a better balance of trade. As Nobel-Prize-winning economist, Paul Samuelson once noted, man does not live by the GNP alone. At best, the recommendations of the commissions and task forces on school reform are hallucinatory; at worst, they are soul-destroying. Let us teachers not succumb to the temptation of asking what we can do for General Motors; let us continue to ask only what we can do for the children.

DISCUSSION QUESTIONS FOR CHAPTER 12

1. Discuss why both Cohen and Karp see current educational reform efforts as having a limited chance for success. What is it they believe has been left out of the discussion?
2. Karp raises again the question of ideology. What does he believe is the main ideological function of schooling?
3. Why does Ohanian view current educational reform efforts as suspect? How does she see genuine educational reform as taking place?
4. With which conception of school politics and ideology would you say Karp, Cohen, and Ohanian are most sympathetic—that of Cubberley, Draper, and Bobbit or that of Dewey, Counts, and Haley?

13

Readings on Educational Reform: Restructuring the School

In our concluding chapter we return to the themes of justice and ideology. More particularly, we have selected four pieces that raise the question, What is the mission of the public schools?

The first selection is John Dewey's "Democracy in Education." Dewey, as we have seen, was a leading advocate for schools that promoted democracy. In this piece he sets forth the beginnings of his educational thought, which continues to shape our debate over schooling today.

The second piece in this chapter is by John Goodlad. It summarizes some of the recommendations of his more extensive work *A Place Called School* (1984). Goodlad's work is important because he and his colleagues draw on broad-based research into what is actually happening in schools. Given that research, it should come as no surprise that most of the reforms suggested focus on improving the environment of the school. Goodlad argues for changes in school size, abandoning tracking, and giving individual schools and teachers more freedom to do their job. His is a plea for making the school, above all, a positive experience for every child.

Next is George Wood's survey of schools and teachers that are restructuring the way they deal with students. In "Teaching for Democracy" Wood explores how educators attempt to make schools more like communities, make schoolwork more purposeful, and link student work with the world outside the school walls.

The final selection is by Dennis Littky. Like Debbie Meire, Littky is the principal of a school involved with Theodore Sizer's Coalition of Essential Schools, perhaps the largest school restructuring effort in the United States today.

Some questions about school reform may come to mind as you read these pieces. How do these modern calls for reform reflect the efforts of previous generations? What is the conception of social and individual justice that runs through each reform, and how is it reflected in the proposals made? What is the potential of any of these reforms for altering the pattern of schooling in the United States?

JOHN DEWEY
DEMOCRACY IN EDUCATION

Modern life means democracy, democracy means freeing intelligence for independent effectiveness—the emancipation of mind as an individual organ to do its own work. We naturally associate democracy, to be sure, with freedom of action, but freedom of action without freed capacity of thought behind it is only chaos. If external authority in action is given up, it must be because internal authority of truth, discovered and known to reason, is substituted.

How does the school stand with reference to this matter? Does the school as an accredited representative exhibit this trait of democracy as a spiritual force? Does it lead and direct the movement? Does it lag behind and work at cross-purpose? I find the fundamental need of the school today dependent upon its limited recognition of the principle of freedom of intelligence. This limitation appears to me to affect both of the elements of school life: teacher and pupil. As to both, the school has lagged behind the general contemporary social movement; and much that is unsatisfactory, much of conflict and of defeat, comes from the discrepancy between the relatively undemocratic organization of the school, as it affects the mind of both teacher and pupil, and the growth and extension of the democratic principle in life beyond school doors.

The effort of the last two-thirds of a century has been successful in building up the machinery of a democracy of mind. It has provided the ways and means for housing and equipping intelligence. What remains is that the thought-activity of the individual, whether teacher or student, be permitted and encouraged to take working possession of this machinery: to substitute its rightful lordship for an inherited servility. In truth, our public-school system is but two-thirds of a century old. It dates, so far as such matters can be dated at all, from 1837, the year that Horace Mann became secretary of the state board of Massachusetts; and from 1843, when Henry Barnard began a similar work in Connecticut. At this time began that growing and finally successful warfare against all the influences, social and sectarian, which would prevent or mitigate the sway of public influence over private ecclesiastical and class interests. Between 1837 and 1850 grew up all the most characteristic features of the American public-school system: from this time date state normal schools, city training schools, county and state institutes, teachers' associations, teachers' journals, the institution of city superintendencies, supervisory officers, and the development of state universities as the crown of the public-school system of the commonwealth.

From John Dewey, "Democracy in Education," *The Elementary School Teacher* 4, no. 4 (December 1903), pp. 193–204.

From this time date the striving for better schoolhouses and grounds, improved text-books, adequate material equipment in maps, globes, scientific apparatus, etc. As an outcome of the forces thus set in motion, democracy has in principle, subject to relative local restrictions, developed an organized machinery of public education. But when we turn to the aim and method which this magnificent institution serves, we find that our democracy is not yet conscious of the ethical principal upon which it rests—the responsibility and freedom of mind in discovery and proof—and consequently we find confusion where there should be order, darkness where there should be light. The teacher has not the power of initiation and constructive endeavor which is necessary to the fulfillment of the function of teaching. The learner finds conditions antagonistic (or at least lacking) to the development of individual mental power and to adequate responsibility for its use.

1. *As to the teacher.*—If there is a single public-school system in the United States where there is official and constitutional provision made for submitting questions of methods of discipline and teaching, and the questions of the curriculum, text-books, etc., to the discussion and decision of those actually engaged in the work of teaching, that fact has escaped my notice. Indeed, the opposite situation is so common that it seems, as a rule, to be absolutely taken for granted as the normal and final condition of affairs. The number of persons to whom any other course has occurred as desirable, or even possible—to say nothing of necessary—is apparently very limited. But until the public-school system is organized in such a way that every teacher has some regular and representative way in which he or she can exercise judgment upon matters of educational importance, with the assurance that this judgment will somehow affect the school system, the assertion that the present system is not, from the internal standpoint, democratic seems to be justified. Either we come here upon some fixed and inherent limitation of the democratic principle, or else we find in this fact an obvious discrepancy between the conduct of the school and the conduct of social life—a discrepancy so great as to demand immediate and persistent effort at reform.

The more enlightened portions of the public have, indeed, become aware of one aspect of this discrepancy. Many reformers are contending against the conditions which place the direction of school affairs, including the selection of text-books, etc., in the hands of a body of men who are outside the school system itself, who have not necessarily any expert knowledge of education and who are moved by non-educational motives. Unfortunately, those who have noted this undemocratic condition of affairs, and who have striven to change it, have, as a rule, conceived of but one remedy, namely, the transfer of authority to the school superintendent. In their zeal to place the center of gravity inside the school system, in their zeal to decrease the prerogatives of a non-expert school board, and to lessen the opportunities for corruption and private pull which go with that, they have tried to remedy one of the evils of democracy by adopting the principle of autocracy. For no matter how wise, expert, or benevolent the head of the school system, the one-man principle is autocracy.

The logic of the argument goes farther, very much farther, than the reformer of this type sees. The logic which commits him to the idea that the management of the school system must be in the hands of an expert commits him also to the idea that every member of the school system, from the first-grade teacher to the principal of the high school, must have some share in the exercise of educational power. The remedy is not to have one expert dictating educational methods and subject-matter to a body of passive, recipient teachers, but the adoption of intellectual initiative, discussion, and decision throughout the entire school corps. The remedy of the partial evils of democracy, the implication of the school system in municipal politics, is in appeal to a more thoroughgoing democracy.

The dictation, in theory at least, of the subject-matter to be taught, to the teacher who is to engage in the actual work of instruction, and frequently, under the name of close supervision, the attempt to determine the methods which are to be used in teaching, mean nothing more or less than the deliberate restriction of intelligence, the imprisoning of the spirit. Every well graded system of schools in this country rejoices in a course of study. It is no uncommon thing to find methods of teaching such subjects as reading, writing, spelling, and arithmetic officially laid down; outline topics in history and geography are provided ready-made for the teacher; gems of literature are fitted to the successive ages of boys and girls. Even the domain of art, songs and methods of singing, subject-matter and technique of drawing and painting, come within the region on which an outside authority lays its sacrilegious hands.

I have stated the theory, which is also true of the practice to a certain extent and in certain places. We may thank our heavens, however, that the practice is rarely as bad as the theory would require. Superintendents and principals often encourage individuality and thoughtfulness in the invention and adoption of methods of teaching; and they wink at departures from the printed manual of study. It remains true, however, that this great advance is personal and informal. It depends upon the wisdom and tact of the individual supervisory official; he may withdraw his concession at any moment; or it may be ruthlessly thrown aside by his successor who has formed a high ideal of "system."

I know it will be said that this state of things, while an evil, is a necessary one; that without it confusion and chaos would reign; that such regulations are the inevitable accompaniments of any graded system. It is said that the average teacher is incompetent to take any part in laying out the course of study or in initiating methods of instruction or discipline. Is not this type of argument which has been used from time immemorial, and in every department of life, against the advance of democracy? What does democracy mean save that the individual is to have a share in determining the conditions and the aims of his own work; and that, upon the whole, through the free and mutual harmonizing of different individuals, the work of the world is better done than when planned, arranged, and directed by a few, no matter how wise or of how good intent that few? How can we justify our belief in the democratic principle elsewhere, and then go back entirely upon it when we come to education?

Moreover, the argument proves too much. The more it is asserted that the existing corps of teachers is unfit to have voice in the settlement of important educational matters, and their unfitness to exercise intellectual initiative and to assume the responsibility for constructive work is emphasized, the more their unfitness to attempt the much more difficult and delicate task of guiding souls appears. If this body is so unfit, how can it be trusted to carry out the recommendations or the dictations of the wisest body of experts? If teachers are incapable of the intellectual responsibility which goes with the determination of the methods they are to use in teaching, how can they employ methods when dictated by others, in other than a mechanical, capricious, and clumsy manner? The argument, I say, proves too much.

Moreover, if the teaching force is as inept and unintelligent and irresponsible as the argument assumes, surely the primary problem is that of their improvement. Only by sharing in some responsible task does there come a fitness to share in it. The argument that we must wait until men and women are fully ready to assume intellectual and social responsibilities would have defeated every step in the democratic direction that has ever been taken. The prevalence of methods of authority and of external dictation and direction tends automatically to perpetuate the very conditions of inefficiency, lack of interest, inability to assume positions of self-determination, which constitute the reasons that are depended upon to justify the régime of authority.

The system which makes no great demands upon originality, upon invention, upon the continuous expression of individuality, works automatically to put and to keep the more incompetent teachers in the school. It puts them there because, by a natural law of spiritual gravitation, the best minds are drawn to the places where they can work most effectively. The best minds are not especially likely to be drawn where there is danger that they may have to submit to conditions which no self-respecting intelligence likes to put up with; and where their time and energy are likely to be so occupied with details of external conformity that they have no opportunity for free and full play of their own vigor.

I have dwelt at length upon the problem of the recognition of the intellectual and spiritual individuality of the teacher. I have but one excuse. All other reforms are conditioned upon reform in the quality and character of those who engage in the teaching profession. The doctrine of the man behind the gun has become familiar enough, in recent discussion, in every sphere of life. Just because education is the most personal, the most intimate, of all human affairs, there more than anywhere else the sole ultimate reliance and final source of power are in the training, character, and intelligence of the individual. If any scheme could be devised which would draw to the calling of teaching persons of force of character, of sympathy with children, and consequent interest in the problems of teaching and of scholarship, no one need be troubled for a moment about other educational reforms, or the solution of other educational problems. But as long as a school organization which is undemocratic in principle tends to repel from all but the higher portions of the school system those of independent force, of intellectual initiative, and of inventive ability, or tends to hamper them in their work after they find their way into the schoolroom, so long all other reforms are compromised at their source and postponed indefinitely for fruition.

2. *As to the learner.*—The undemocratic suppression of the individuality of the teacher goes naturally with the improper restriction of the intelligence of the mind of the child. The mind, to be sure, is that of a child, and yet, after all, it is mind. To subject mind to an outside and ready-made material is a denial of the ideal of democracy, which roots itself ultimately in the principle of moral, self-directing individuality. Misunderstanding regarding the nature of the freedom that is demanded for the child is so common that it may be necessary to emphasize the fact that it is primarily intellectual freedom, free play of mental attitude, and operation which are sought. If individuality were simply a matter of feelings, impulses, and outward acts independent of intelligence, it would be more than a dubious matter to urge a greater degree of freedom for the child in the school. In that case much, and almost exclusive, force would attach to the objections that the principle of individuality is realized in the more exaggerated parts of Rousseau's doctrines: sentimental idealization of the child's immaturity, irrational denial of superior worth in the knowledge and mature experience of the adult, deliberate denial of the worth of the ends and instruments embodied in social organization. Deification of childish whim, unripened fancy, and arbitrary emotion is certainly a piece of pure romanticism. The would-be reformers who emphasize out of due proportion and perspective these aspects of the principle of individualism betray their own cause. But the heart of the matter lies not there. Reform of education in the direction of greater play for the individuality of the child means the securing of conditions which will give outlet, and hence direction, to a growing intelligence. It is true that this freed power of mind with reference to its own further growth cannot be obtained without a certain leeway, a certain flexibility, in the expression of even immature feelings and fancies. But it is equally true that it is not a riotous loosening of these traits which is needed, but just that kind and degree of freedom from repression which are found to be necessary to secure the full operation of intelligence.

Now, no one need doubt as to what mental activity or the freed expression of intelligence means. No one need doubt as to the conditions which are conducive to it. We do not have to fall back upon what some regard as the uncertain, distracting, and even distressing voice of psychology. Scientific methods, the methods pursued by the scientific inquirer, give us an exact and concrete exhibition of the path which intelligence takes when working most efficiently, under most favorable conditions.

What is primarily required for that direct inquiry which constitutes the essence of science is first-hand experience; an active and vital participation through the medium of all the bodily organs with the means and materials of building up first-hand experience. Contrast this first and most fundamental of all the demands for an effective use of mind with what we find in so many of our elementary and high schools. There first-hand experience is at a discount; in its stead are summaries and formulas of the results of other people. Only very recently has any positive provision been made within the schoolroom for any of the modes of activity and for any of the equipment and arrangement which permit and require the extension of original experiences on the part of the child.

The school has literally been dressed out with hand-me-down garments—with intellectual suits which other people have worn.

Secondly, in that freed activity of mind which we term "science" there is always a certain problem which focusses effort, which controls the collecting of facts that bear upon the question, the use of observation to get further data, the employing of memory to supply relevant facts, the calling into play of imagination, to yield fertile suggestion and construct possible solutions of the difficulty.

Turning to the school, we find too largely no counterpart to this mental activity. Just because a second-hand material has been supplied wholesale and retail; but anyway ready-made, the tendency is to reduce the activity of mind to a docile or passive taking in of the material presented—in short, to memorizing, with simply incidental use of judgment and of active research. As is frequently stated, acquiring takes the place of inquiring. It is hardly an exaggeration to say that the sort of mind-activity which is encouraged in the school is a survival from the days in which science had not made much headway; when education was mainly concerned with learning, that is to say, the preservation and handing down of the acquisitions of the past. It is true that more and more appeal is made every day in schools to judgment, reasoning, personal efficiency, and the calling up of personal, as distinct from merely book, experiences. But we have not yet got to the point of reversing the total method. The burden and the stress still fall upon learning in the sense of becoming possessed of the second-hand and ready-made material referred to. As Mrs. Young has recently said, the prevailing ideal is a perfect recitation, an exhibition without mistake, of a lesson learned. Until the emphasis changes to the conditions which make it necessary for the child to take an active share in the personal building up of his own problems and to participate in methods of solving them (even at the expense of experimentation and error), mind is not really freed.

In our schools we have freed individuality in many modes of outer expression without freeing intelligence, which is the vital spring and guarantee of all of these expressions. Consequently we give opportunity to the unconverted to point the finger of scorn, and to clamor for a return to the good old days when the teacher, the representative of social and moral authority, was securely seated in the high places of the school. But the remedy here, as in other phases of our social democracy, is not to turn back, but to go farther—to carry the evolution of the school to a point where it becomes a place for getting and testing experience, as real and adequate to the child upon his existing level as all the resources of laboratory and library afford to the scientific man upon his level. What is needed is not any radical revolution, but rather an organization of agencies already found in the schools. It is hardly too much to say that not a single subject of instrumentality is required which is not already found in many schools of the country. All that is required is to gather these materials and forces together and unify their operation. Too often they are used for a multitude of diverse and often conflicting aims. If a single purpose is provided, that of freeing the processes of mental growth, these agencies will at once fall into their proper classes and reinforce each other.

A catalogue of the agencies already available would include at least all of the following: Taking the child out of doors, widening and organizing his experience with reference to the world in which he lives; nature study when pursued as a vital observation of forces working under their natural conditions, plants and animals growing in their own homes, instead of mere discussion of dead specimens. We have also school gardens, the introduction of elementary agriculture, and more especially of horticulture—a movement that is already making great headway in many of the western states. We have also means for the sake of studying physiographic conditions, such as may be found by rivers, ponds or lakes, beaches, quarries, gulleys, hills, etc.

As similar agencies within the school walls, we find a very great variety of instruments for constructive work, or, as it is frequently, but somewhat unfortu-nately termed, "manual training." Under this head come cooking, which can be begun in its simpler form in the kindergarten; sewing, and what is of even greater educational value, weaving, including designing and the construction of simple apparatus for carrying on various processes of spinning, etc. Then there are also the various forms of tool-work directed upon cardboard, wood, and iron; in addition there are clay-modeling and a variety of ways of manipulating plastic material to gain power and larger experience.

Such matters pass readily over into the simpler forms of scientific experi-mentation. Every schoolroom from the lowest primary grade up should be supplied with gas, water, certain chemical substances and reagents. To experi-ment in the sense of trying things or to see what will happen is the most natural business of the child; it is, indeed, his chief concern. It is one which the school has largely either ignored or actually suppressed, so that is has been forced to find outlet in mischief or even in actually destructive ways. This tendency could find outlet in the construction of simple apparatus and the making of simple tests, leading constantly into more and more controlled experimentation, with greater insistence upon definiteness of intellectual result and control of logical process.

Add to these typical modes of active experimenting, various forms of art expression, beginning with music, clay-modeling, and story-telling as founda-tion elements, and passing on to drawing, painting, designing in various mediums, we have a range of forces and materials which connect at every point with the child's natural needs and powers, and which supply the requisites for building up his experience upon all sides. As fast as these various agencies find their way into the schools, the center of gravity shifts, the régime changes from one of subjection of mind to an external and ready-made material, into the activity of mind directed upon the control of the subject-matter and thereby its own upbuilding.

Politically we have found that this country could not endure half free and half slave. We shall find equally great difficulty in encouraging freedom, independence, and initiative in every sphere of social life, while perpetuating in the school dependence upon external authority. The forces of social life are already encroaching upon the school institutions which we have inherited from the past, so that many of its main stays are crumbling. Unless the outcome is to be chaotic, we must take hold of the organic, positive principle involved in democracy, and put that in entire possession of the spirit and work of the school.

In education meet the three most powerful motives of human activity. Here are found sympathy and affection, the going out of the emotions to the most appealing and the most rewarding object of love—a little child. Here is found also the flowering of the social and institutional motive, interest in the welfare of society and in its progress and reform by the surest and shortest means. Here, too, is found the intellectual and scientific motive, the interest in knowledge, in scholarship, in truth for its own sake, unhampered and unmixed with any alien ideal. Copartnership of these three motives—of affection, of social growth, and of scientific inquiry—must prove as nearly irresistible as anything human when they are once united. And, above all else, recognition of the spiritual basis of democracy, the efficacy and responsibility of freed intelligence, is necessary to secure this union.

JOHN J. GOODLAD

A STUDY OF SCHOOLING: SOME IMPLICATIONS FOR SCHOOL IMPROVEMENT

In the March *Kappan* I briefly summarized the purposes, sample, methodology, and some of the findings regarding two major themes of *A Study of Schooling*.[1] These closely related themes were "how some teachers teach" and "what some students are and are not taught." The cumulative repetitiveness of the data in these two areas was such that successive additions merely strengthened our preliminary conclusions.

At all levels of schooling, a very few teaching procedures—explaining or lecturing, monitoring seatwork, and quizzing—accounted for most of those we observed overall in our sample of 1,016 classrooms. Teachers varied in the quality of their lecturing, for example, but "teacher talk" was by far the dominant classroom activity. Teachers rarely encouraged student-to-student dialog or provided opportunities for students to work collaboratively in small groups or to plan, set goals, determine alternative ways of achieving these goals, and the like.

At all levels of schooling (but somewhat less in the primary grades), curricular sameness characterized the topical organization, factual orientation, textbook content, and the things tested. The emphasis was on recall, not on problem solving or inquiry. The structure of knowledge, for instance, was sacrificed to activities that became the ends rather than the means. And, again, students worked primarily alone in large-group settings—rarely collaborating on tasks requiring a division of labor, integration of effort, and shared rewards for accomplishment.

In effect, the "how" and "what" of teaching and learning fit together in a kind of bland sameness. The accompanying affective tone can be best described as neutral. These generalizations obtained whether the school was large or small,

From John I. Goodlad, "A Study of Schooling: Some Implications for School Improvement," *Phi Delta Kappan* 64, no. 8 (April 1983), pp. 552–558. Reprinted with permission.

urban or rural, or served affluent or poor families. Markedly different procedures—which we found only occasionally—were as likely to show up in one
type of school as in another. Regarding how teachers teach and what students
learn, if the schools we studied are reasonably representative, it is fair to say that
a school is a school is a school.

Regarding other categories of schooling, however, our data lead to quite
different conclusions. These categories include school climate, classroom
climate, principal/teacher relations and teacher/teacher relations, self-renewing capability, and school/community relations. School-to-school differences were substantial at all three levels. Moreover, our data revealed sharp
differences in the degree to which students, teachers, and parents were satisfied
with their schools. The satisfaction index we employed was a rigorous one
derived from such factors as grading of the school (A, B, C, D, or F) by all three
groups, the degree of congruence between the goal preferred (among four) and
the goal perceived to be emphasized by the school, and the number and intensity
of problems perceived to be present in each school. These data enabled us to
divide the schools at each level into the most satisfying (top quartile) and the
least satisfying (bottom quartile).

Consistently, the schools in the top quartile for satisfaction were also in the
top quartile for self-renewing capability, school climate, classroom climate, and
the rest. With equal consistency, schools in the bottom quartile for satisfaction
were in the bottom quartile for the other characteristics. In other words, the most
and least satisfying schools were *consistently* so—except in regard to two categories of across-the-board similarity: how the teachers taught and what was
emphasized or neglected in expectations and provisions for students' learning.
In these two areas, schools could not be differentiated; there was little variability.[2]

Detailed examination of each successive school added to this picture of
considerable variability among schools on nearly all characteristics. The differences were in what Michael Rutter described as the "ethos" of schools:[3]
pervasive values in the school climate, principals' treatment and views of
teachers, teachers' perceptions of their principals, qualitative elements in the
teacher/student and teacher/teacher interactions, parents' contacts with teachers and their knowledge of the school, the ability of a school staff to manage
school problems, and so on. These qualitative elements in the culture of the
schools varied around a hard core of similarity in the central business of
schooling: namely, formal teaching and learning.

I have repeated this conclusion because it bears so heavily on what follows.
An easy but misleading interpretation is that how teachers teach and what
students are taught have no bearing now or *potentially* on teachers', students', or
parents' satisfaction with their schools. As long as these factors remain more or
less constant *and there are no expectations for anything else*—that is, no desirable
alternatives are envisioned—the bases for satisfaction must be somewhere else.
They could (and, from our data, presumably do) reside for students in such
teacher attributes as warmth, enthusiasm, and demonstrations of caring about

students' learning—areas in which we found class-to-class and school-to-school differences.

The question I sought to answer in the March *Kappan* is why some factors most central to the educative process remain so much the same, not just from class to class and school to school but, it appears, over time as well. I advanced several explanatory hypotheses. The questions I raise now are: 1) Do we want the longstanding instructional and curricular norms to change and, if so, in degree or in kind? 2) How might we effect the necessary changes? My earlier hypotheses enter into my responses to these questions.

WHAT DO WE WANT OF SCHOOLS?

It is difficult to mount a convincing argument for the proposition that Americans want for teaching and the curriculum anything other than what we found in classrooms, partly because so few alternatives are evident in practice. Traditions surrounding the teacher's role, most of the circumstances of teaching, and the surrounding culture reinforce what we observed. Even much of the research regarding time on instruction and time on task tends to reinforce the "frontal" teaching and didactics that most of the teachers in our sample were using most of the time.

However, I would anticipate that any reform effort growing out of alarm over students' performance on standardized achievement tests would focus on teaching behaviors thought to be closely associated with what these tests measure. Further, given our particular interest in improving the academic performance of low-income children, it is to be expected that we would encourage the use of whatever techniques appear to boost their achievement. In effect, then, the most significant educational civil rights movement of the past quarter-century is closely linked to the more general concern for school improvement in the academic realm. Ronald Edmonds, a leading exponent of effective schools, recognizes that there are other important outcomes of schooling than those measured by standardized tests of achievement. However, he notes that "improved academic achievement undergirds and advances pupil prospects for gain in the more exalted purposes of education. The ultimate purpose of education is to teach citizenship, civility, and creativity, but those are topics for another paper."[4]

Although I agree with Edmonds' basic premise, two questions concern me. The first is whether improvements in standardized achievement test scores indicate improved academic quality. The answer, of course, depends on one's definition of academic quality. Edmonds defines it as "independent thinking, more sophisticated comprehension, and other intangible measures of intellectual gain."[5] My summary of the academic expectations for schools supplied by all 50 states included not only mastery of basic skills and fundamental processes but also an array of more complex intellectual abilities such as problem-solving skills; the applications of principles of logic; use of different modes of inquiry; critical, independent thinking that enables one to make judgments and decisions in a wide variety of roles; and so on.[6] Existing standardized tests measure little more than the first of these academic goals. The dominant instructional practices we observed in more than 1,000 classrooms (and which most staff development programs emphasize) appear to provide few opportunities for students to engage in the behaviors implied by the more exalted academic purpose of education, to say nothing of those other goals of citizenship, civility, and creativity to which state documents claim commitment.

My second query is whether the present interest in school improvement will fade as test scores rise. I have no doubt that the long decline in scores on the Scholastic Aptitude Test will be replaced by a slow but steady rise. But as the test scores—the thermometer we use to measure school health—rise above the zone of alarm, it is likely that once more we will be lulled into complacency. Little in the conduct of schools will have changed, however, unless we have paid attention to matters of another kind. Let me suggest several arguments for heeding these other concerns.

First, U.S. society has a deep and longstanding commitment to schools that foster the whole of intellectual, social, and personal development.[7] These beliefs can be traced through Aristotle, Cicero, Erasmus, Rousseau, and Pestalozzi to Whitehead, Dewey, deGarmo, and some contemporary thinkers. Because these beliefs are not easily reduced to specific, quantifiable components, they are frequently dismissed as soft, fuzzy-headed, and impractical. But they do not go away.

Second, analysis of documents regarding goals for U.S. schools reveals a steady evolution from narrow academic skills to a far wider array of concerns— and to citizenship, vocational, and personal goals as well. All 50 states endorse them, as did most of the 8,600 parents surveyed in *A Study of Schooling*. Are we to brush these aside as impractical idealism simply because, for the most part, they elude our ability to measure them?

Third, our data on 1,350 teachers show that their professional values lean strongly toward practices that appear to reflect these broader expectations. In practice, however, these teachers cling to conventional teaching practices because of the circumstances of their classrooms, the models with which they are most familiar, and the messages they hear. Why should they make the difficult (and perhaps even dangerous) effort to deviate? A growing body of evidence suggests, however, that teachers often respond eagerly to alternative methods of teaching that relate to many of their deeper professional values, when they are given support, encouragement, and protection.[8]

Fourth, recent analyses of contemporary society reveal a relentless restructuring taking place that is changing our lives and that demands a fundamental restructuring of schools.[9] We simply cannot afford to be content, for example, merely with providing low-income children access to what more affluent children encounter in schools and with postponing attention to all the goals we espouse for education in schools. Just as the launching of Sputnik in 1957 moved us quickly beyond the narrow focus on the basics of the early Fifties, we must now move beyond narrowly conceived procedures and unimaginative curricula in seeking to create schools responsive to the larger forces that are transforming our lives.

Left alone, things tend to stagnate and disintegrate. We cannot afford to shift attention from the condition of our schools, even if test scores improve. But it will take enormous expenditures of energy to make our schools vital places of learning.

AN ECOLOGICAL PERSPECTIVE ON SCHOOLS

The energy necessary to school *renewal*—not merely to some modest gains in students' achievement—is primarily located in and very close to schools. This is, apparently, a very difficult lesson for us to learn. We readily admit the general ineffectiveness of mandated, top-down efforts to change schools when we read about them in the growing literature on such approaches.[10] But to such approaches we commonly turn, nonetheless. Presumably, persons in federal, state, and local education offices are there to do something. Not having schools to run, their attention tends to turn to giving directions to those who do. Consequently, the energy always present in schools is often directed into channels that are not beneficial to the health of the institution.

Our data give us ample evidence of vital energy being consumed by interests and activities seemingly unrelated to the central business of schooling, or simply not being used. Take students' energy, for instance. In our visits to schools we received an overwhelming impression of students' passivity. Furthermore, they apparently rather enjoyed the dominant activity of listening, which demands so little of them. In the March *Kappan* I referred to students' initiating about seven minutes of the 150 minutes of talk (the rest of it carried on by teachers) in an average senior high school day. Talking requires the organization of thought and can be an important avenue to learning. Teachers, then, were doing most of the learning. Writing even short essays is also conducive to the organization of thought and to learning. Students were not doing much of this, either. The energies of these young people simply were not being adequately absorbed in the business of educating themselves—something their teachers can only guide, not do for them.

Being a spectator not only deprives one of participation but also leaves one's mind free for unrelated activity. If academic learning does not engage students, something else will. Our data and those of other researchers[11] reveal adolescents in particular to be preoccupied at school with one another and with athletics. Overwhelmingly, the junior and senior high school students in our sample chose attractive students and athletes as the most popular; games, sports, and "my friends" as the "one best thing" about their schools; and drugs, alcohol, and student behavior as the worst problems. The numbers of students choosing these alternatives were so large that very few remained to make such choices as smart students, classes and teachers, and instruction or curriculum in answering our questions. As Philip Cusick points out, with other sources of satisfaction effectively denied them (such as a genuine role in planning and pursuing their academic programs), students turn elsewhere—in their thoughts while in the classroom and in their interactions in the hallways and on the playgrounds.[12]

Ironically, the conduct of teaching and learning appeared virtually to direct students toward the social rather than the intellectual function of schools. Students' personal concerns were subjugated to teachers' roles and intents. Paralleling these findings were those showing teachers' powerful need to be in charge and to control the class, a need expressed somewhat more strongly by junior high teachers than by counterparts at other levels.

Composite profiles of the schools we studied revealed differences in the degree to which entire schools were tipped toward or away from an academic ambience. As I mentioned earlier, students' interests dominated throughout, but smart students, classes, and teachers fared much better in the popularity polls in some schools than in others. These schools were always perceived as most satisfying by teachers, students, and parents—and these were the schools in which students more often saw their peers as interested in learning and their school as one that provided a good education. In some of the least satisfying schools, however, nonacademic elements had virtually taken over. The academic and intellectual functions of these schools were in serious jeopardy, and segments of all groups concerned seemed to know it.

Other clusters of data suggested the frequent siphoning off of teachers' and principals' energies in ways that did not appear to enhance the schools' attention to business. In the schools perceived to be least satisfying, principals consistently viewed teachers as part of the school's problem.[13] Teachers more frequently expressed frustrations with the administration and viewed the principal as not supporting them. Conversely, no principal in the most satisfying schools identified the teachers as a problem, and the teachers viewed the principal as supportive and as treating them as the professionals they perceived themselves to be.

It is clear that in some schools the principal and the teachers did not unite in addressing schoolwide problems. Serious problems and issues affecting the general health of the school persisted for lack of attention. We found evidence to show that the principal, teachers, students, and parents were often concerned with the same problems but were unaware of the concern of the other groups. The problems were left to fester. Paul Heckman identified an interesting difference between schools he characterized as more and less renewing: those in the former group had staff members who tended to take care of the school's business.[14]

I have used the adjectives "healthy," "satisfying," and "renewing" to describe schools in our sample that pay more than average attention to the quality of interactions among those inhabiting the school and to the physical and social context in which those interactions occur. Such schools are more able, it appears, to sustain an ambience that favors education than are schools in which the quality of interactions and the physical setting have been neglected and are deteriorating to the point of disintegration. Such schools have little chance of devoting sustained attention to anything, especially the development of sound, engaging educational programs.

Our data showed that even the more satisfying and renewing schools in our sample were characterized by the same instructional and curricular limitations I described earlier. The school-to-school variations were substantially less than the variations in the other characteristics.[15] Schools differed in their ability to create an academic ambience, but the differences appear to be more related to school and classroom climate factors than to methods of teaching per se.[16] What students encountered in the way of pedagogical presentation, seatwork, and curricular organization remained consistent from school to school.

In the March *Kappan* I suggested some hypotheses regarding why some things remain the same in schools. Our own data on teachers in the sample and other studies of schools and teachers[17] led to the conclusion that little in the environment and circumstances of teaching reinforces deviation from common practices. New ideas in education travel rather randomly through the system, from school to school and person to person; they tend to be pursued individually, if at all—not in concert. Teachers are relatively isolated from one another and tend not to receive the peer support necessary to overcome the social pressure to conform to conventional methods of instruction. The culture of the school must operate in such a way as to encourage and give legitimacy to alternative ideas, if such ideas are to take root and grow.

Kenneth Tye's analysis of a portion of our data revealed that staff development activities tended to pull teachers out of the school setting and to offer little substance and depth that might be likely to change existing behavior in significant ways. The evidence does not suggest that teachers come together in their schools to discuss instructional and curricular changes. Rather, "teachers tend to be isolated in their own classrooms, in control of what goes on there and satisfied with the situation as it is. They feel impotent to effect schoolwide decisions, they do not wish to call upon resource people, they individually select their own inservice or post-credential college coursework. . . ."[18]

Moreover, teachers in our sample valued highly the autonomy in their classrooms that most perceived themselves as having. The degree to which the principal also valued and supported this autonomy was a significant factor in teacher satisfaction. It also appeared, however, that, even in those most satisfying schools where the teachers perceived themselves as having virtually all the autonomy they needed to make their own classroom decisions, they did not use this autonomy to engage in alternative teaching techniques or to involve students in ways of learning and knowing beyond those described for our sample of classrooms as a whole. Yet these were also the schools that Heckman found to be, in general, most self-renewing and that I found, almost uniformly, to be the most satisfying not only for teachers but also for principals, students, and parents.

In summary, even the most successful schools appeared not to place the supposedly central business of educating at the top of the school improvement agenda. The failure of schools to do so appeared to become a matter for concern only when virtually everything else in the ecosystem of a school had fallen into disarray. Then students came to see their school as not providing a good education, and large percentages of teachers and parents perceived it as not adequately performing its academic or intellectual function.

Redressing this situation will not be easy. Indeed, it will be extraordinarily difficult—even in our best schools. It will be done not by discarding the schools we have, but by redesigning them piece by piece.[19] Although the culture of the school must be open to ideas from outside the system, renewal must take place from within.

RECOMMENDATIONS

I find myself rather reluctant to make recommendations, lest they become part of the arsenal of those outside agents who would thrust reforms on the schools. Nonetheless, the risk must be taken. The following recommendations are not a laundry list of "musts" to be checked off and implemented; they are designed to create a more supportive infrastructure within which local school renewal becomes feasible, to increase the prospect of schools' having access to powerful ideas, and to augment the chances of those ideas' finding a secure place in the ecosystem of individual schools. My goal is not to exhort innovation but to suggest ways to increase the capability of those in and close to schools to engage in processes of improvement. In what follows, I have screened findings from *A Study of Schooling*—incompletely and sparsely presented in this and my March article—through my own value system. Readers with differing orientations to schooling may certainly draw other conclusions and formulate alternative recommendations.

First, states should articulate clearly the full range of goals for schooling that have emerged over time and on which there now appears to be substantial agreement. Currently, such goals are usually merged inconspicuously with other directives in state documents. The charge to schools is not at all clear. School districts should be expected to assure the presence in each school of a comprehensive curriculum encompassing academic, citizenship, vocational, and personal goals equally accessible to all students.[20]

There should be extensive dialog at the district and building levels regarding the meaning of these goals, the relative emphases to be placed on each in the light of local conditions, and the means of fulfilling them. This dialog should create an awareness of the need for an attention to teaching procedures and learning activities frequently neglected in classrooms. The faculty of the English department in a high school, for example, should discuss how to achieve student competency not only in writing but also in areas of personal and social development. Unless each department considers the whole range of goals of schooling, only those goals within the narrow subject-matter specialization will be promoted in its program—and the same will be true of every department of an entire school. There is much more to schools than preparation for and performance on achievement tests.

Each state should set for school districts a full range of educational expectations for individual schools. But the charge for meeting them is conveyed by the state to district offices, not from the state to individual schools. The district then holds its schools responsible and accountable for providing an appropriately comprehensive, balanced curriculum for each student. With this responsibility must go the requisite authority.

Next, I recommend that each school be expected to fulfill this responsibility by laying out long-term (three- to five-year) plans of development. Bruce Joyce has provided useful guidelines for the work and structure of "responsible parties" conducting the planning process.[21] The expectation for these long-range plans comes from the district office, but the board and superintendent do not impose a uniform set of priorities on each school. Rather, plans come back through the principal of each school for annual or semiannual review.

Clearly implied in this process is a substantial amount of leadership by each principal—much more than instructional leadership. Few principals have had either the necessary experience or the formal preparation required to assume such leadership. I recommend that each district continually search its schools for promising leaders and provide selected individuals with paid leaves of absence for securing the requisite training. States could do much to improve the quality of schools by providing districts with funds for such purposes.

Good planning requires relevant data; few schools have such a data base. My colleagues and I have recommended what we call "contextual assessment," by which we mean both ongoing and periodic gathering of data regarding such factors as time use, instructional methods being employed, curricular records of students, satisfactions and dissatisfactions of those connected with each school, and like matters.[22] School district offices and educational service centers should assist schools in securing the kinds of data necessary to determine priorities for improvement.

The intent of the foregoing recommendations is to set in motion in each school a continuing planning process focused first on the conditions enhancing and inhibiting the healthy functioning of the school's ecosystem, and then to create a sense of responsibility and capability on the part of the faculty, students, and parents regarding school renewal. The concept of vesting autonomy at the local level parallels precisely the practices of successful businesses. But this is *not* a process of substituting decentralization for centralization and then holding the individual units accountable. Such decentralization risks losing touch with outside ideas and also runs the danger of causing unnecessary tension between local and district leadership. There must be strong two-way ties between the district office and the individual school, with the former contributing the resources for effectively developing and executing plans. Staff development for middle management is essential to this relationship.

Thus school improvement shifts from the district level to the school site. Ideally, the staff, students, and parents of each school will gain in ability and confidence in managing the school's affairs. As the principal and teachers become increasingly comfortable with one another, they will include on their agenda for dialog and action those most sensitive and central matters of teaching and curriculum that appear to be so resistant to change. For most school faculties, the discrepancy between ongoing practices and those implied in state goals should become increasingly clear. District officials can create constructive pressures for such dialog by raising questions about overall attention to these goals during annual or semiannual reviews of each school's long-term plans.

Obviously, however, it is very difficult to break free of instructional and curricular rigidity—or surely the most satisfying and renewing schools in our sample would have done so. Dorothy Lloyd studied teaching and student achievement in two settings in which teachers had been exposed intensively to some of the most able consultants on instructional improvement in the field. These teachers rarely used what they had been taught, although they were able to reproduce the pedagogical procedures on demand.[23] (Ironically, the use of the procedures in a controlled situation over a period of time did not result in the students achieving more than did those in the control groups.) The fact is that the set of instructional conditions previously described maintains conventional practices; merely performing somewhat better does not guarantee significant effects.

I believe that we must build into each school a continuing attention to instruction and the curriculum. This does not occur when teachers are drawn out of schools as individuals to engage willy-nilly in workshops and courses and are then returned to the isolation of their classroom and a school culture where how and what one teaches are not matters for peer-group analysis, discussion, and improvement. Teaching must be taken out of its cloak of privacy and autonomy to become the business of the entire school and its staff.

How is this to be done? As yet, we do not know—but we know enough to make some educated guesses. My experience with our League of Schools project (1966–72) convinces me that, with support and encouragement, school staffs will begin to address the sensitive problems of their own teaching when they become both comfortable with one another and confident in their ability to affect the quality of life in their own schools.[24] These conditions emerge out of the processes of dialog, decision making, action, and evaluation to which I referred earlier. Initiating and nurturing such processes will do more in the long run to improve the quality of the educational program than will a direct attack on teaching, especially in schools where the ecosystem is already malfunctioning. Of course, the principal must constantly reinforce the importance of moving on from less threatening matters of students' playground behavior, lack of materials, tardiness, and the like. Richard Turner's studies illustrate the potential power of the principal to turn teachers' attention to students' learning processes.[25]

Even if the staff members and the principal should begin to work together to solve schoolwide problems, the structure of the school serves as a powerful force to maintain the status quo in classrooms. Teachers work alone within the confines of grade standards and expectations set by test scores converted to grade-level equivalents. They are not collaborators in any meaningful sense with teachers of the grades below and above them. For them to become part of a team responsible for the progress of a group of students over a number of years would be to create a structure likely to force attention to instructional and curricular matters. These matters are moved from the relatively sanitized abstractness of total faculty discourse—easily ignored on entering the classroom—to the bread-and-butter concreteness of shared daily business.

I envision schools organized into four-year units of not more than 100 students each at the elementary level and not more than 160 students each at the secondary level. A team of adults (the numbers based on an affordable ratio of teachers to students) guides the learning of this group over the four-year period, getting to know one another very well in the process. In *A Place Called School*, I have described the structure and functioning of such groups in considerable detail.

An elementary school of 400 pupils might be divided into four such units, and a secondary school of 800 students into five.[26] Each unit would be self-sufficient for most learning activities but would share such facilities as the main library, gymnasium, shops, playgrounds, etc. Schools would have considerable autonomy to distribute full-time teacher equivalents (FTEs) as they saw fit, such arrangements to be included as part of the planning documents shared periodically with the superintendent. Consequently, four teaching FTEs might be divided in a primary unit among a head teacher, two career teachers, an aide, and an intern.

Creating the position of head teacher addresses several problems. First, it takes the career flatness out of teaching, providing a position demanding high qualifications and commanding a significantly higher salary. The requirement is a doctorate in teaching that would equip the primary-level head teacher, for example, with the requisite knowledge and skills both for diagnosing children's progress in all goal areas and for planning—cooperatively with the rest of the team—intervention and evaluation strategies. Career teachers are essentially those who now staff our schools. Head teaching positions would not be open to career teachers on the basis of seniority, but opportunities to take leaves of absence for advanced studies and internships would be made available on the basis of merit. The proportion of the team that would be made up of aides, interns, and residents would be left up to each unit, in consultation with the principal.

Critics may argue that existing doctoral programs do not assure the requisite competences in head teachers, and they are probably right. But only a few years ago a doctorate in medicine did not assure much, either. The concept that only M.D.s could be licensed to practice medicine prevailed, however, and the quality of graduates improved with the accompanying advancement of research. A profession can be no better than the knowledge base on which it rests. We will not achieve the requisite knowledge base that will enable teaching to be considered a major profession until we create the demand.[27]

A significant component of my recommendations pertains to the roles of students. As I stated earlier, students are relegated to a passive stance in the vital business of their own school-based learning; classes and teachers are not, to them, the most important part of the school culture. In the classroom, they learn alone in groups. My intent is to mobilize the energies of these groups to the advantage of all. The British infant schools that many of us visited in the Sixties demonstrated extensive peer teaching among children in "family" groups of 5-,

6-, and 7-year-olds. Visitors commonly observed a good reader working cooperatively with a mediocre and a poor reader for the benefit of all three. Benjamin Bloom's studies of highly talented individuals reveal the powerful reinforcing effect of association with talented peers.[28] Why do we not only neglect but virtually eliminate the possibility of such peer teaching in schools?

The multi-aged grouping created by the vertical unit structure directs attention to the possibilities for peer teaching among students. Those of us who once taught in one-room schools found in upper-grade students the teaching resources needed to assure additional practice and, ultimately, mastery learning for other students—and those students doing the teaching enhanced their own mastery of the subjects that they taught. The effective use of students as allies in the teaching process requires that teachers embrace a new perspective on the teaching process. They must promote a classroom ethos in which students are responsible not only for their own learning but also for that of their classmates. Under such circumstances, cheating becomes almost impossible.

My recommendations in this article represent only a few of those required for the necessary reconstruction of schooling. They stem from a heuristic theory of schooling and school improvement that is quite different from the linear model that dominates much current thought, policy, and practice. Consequently, the approaches stemming from this ecological theory are likely to create puzzlement and frustration for those well-meaning reformers who are impatient with schools and don't quite trust the "mindless" people who run them. And these approaches will be turned aside by those who seek quick fixes and who see my suggestions as demanding the expenditure of much human energy.

Surely, however, we now know enough about the minimal impact of top-down linear efforts and the folly of quick fixes. The imperviousness of conventional teaching methods—despite the continued assaults that seek to improve them—stands as mute evidence in favor of alternative perspectives and processes. Those of us who have worked with teachers long enough to gain their trust know that the idea of spending precious time and energy on matters central to their daily lives does not deter them. But they have become, virtually by necessity, extraordinarily facile in nullifying the intent of reforms spawned elsewhere and imposed "in their best interests." Those far removed from the classroom are more skeptical about unleashing the energies of principals, teachers, students, and parents for school improvement than are those whose energy is to be called upon. Fortunately, teachers—on whom school improvement primarily depends—can be motivated to do the job. It behooves those in positions of authority to provide the trust, support, and resources—unless we are content with the schools we have.

NOTES

[1] For a comprehensive treatment, see John I. Goodlad, *A Place Called School* (New York: McGraw-Hill, 1984).

[2] It should be noted, however, that there was within-school variability in content, teachers' expectations, and the like among tracked classes at the secondary school level. See Jeannie Oakes, *A Question of Access: Tracking and Curriculum Differentiation in a National Sample of English and Mathematics Classes*, Technical Report No. 24, A Study of Schooling (Los Angeles: Laboratory in School and Community Education, Graduate School of Education, University of California, 1981).

[3] Michael Rutter et al., *Fifteen Thousand Hours* (Cambridge, Mass.: Harvard University Press, 1979).

[4] Ronald R. Edmonds, "Programs of School Improvement: An Overview," prepared under contract with the National Institute of Education for presentation at the conference "The Implications of Research for Practice," Airlie House, Va., February 1982, p. 3.

[5] Ibid., p. 2.

[6] Goodlad, Ch. Two. Recognition is due to Patricia Bauch of our research staff for her superb work in collecting the information regarding goals in the documents provided by the nation's chief state school of officers.

[7] For a succinct historical analysis, see Val D. Rust, "Humanistic Roots of Alternatives in Education," in John I. Goodlad et al., *The Conventional and the Alternatives in Education* (Berkeley, Calif.: McCutchan, 1975), pp. 77–98.

[8] See, for example, Mary M. Bentzen and Associates, *Changing Schools: The Magic Feather Principle* (New York: McGraw-Hill, 1974).

[9] For one perspective on these trends, see John Naisbitt, *Megatrends* (New York: Warner Books, 1982). For a perspective on the thinking processes schools should cultivate, see Seymour Papert, *Mindstorms* (New York: Basic Books, 1980).

[10] See, for example, Raymond E. Callahan, *Education and the Cult of Efficiency* (Chicago: University of Chicago Press, 1962); Ernest R. House, *The Politics of Educational Innovation* (Berkeley, Calif.: McCutchan, 1974); Arthur E. Wise, *Legislated Learning* (Berkeley University of California Press, 1970); and Seymour B. Sarason, *The Culture of the School and the Problem of Change,* 2nd ed. (Boston: Allyn & Bacon, 1982).

[11] See, for example, C. Wayne Gordon, *The High School as a Social System* (Glencoe, Ill.: Free Press, 1957); and James S. Coleman, *The Adolescent Society* (Glencoe, Ill.: Free Press, 1961).

[12] Philip A. Cusick, *Inside High Schools: The Student's World* (New York: Holt, Rinehart & Winston, 1973).

[13] Monica B. Morris. *The Public School as Workplace: The Principal as a Key Element in Teacher Satisfaction,* Technical Report No. 32, A Study of Schooling (Los Angeles: Laboratory in School and Community Education, Graduate School of Education, University of California, 1981).

[14] Paul E. Heckman, *Exploring the Concept of School Renewal: Cultural Differences and Similarities Between More and Less Rewarding Schools,* Technical Report No. 33, A Study of Schooling (Los Angeles: Laboratory in School and Community Education, Graduate School of Education, University of California, 1982).

[15] For readers concerned that teaching and the curriculum are classroom matters and, therefore, that using the school as the unit of selection and analysis is likely to be misleading, let me point out that using the classroom as the unit produced a similar pattern of sameness. *A Study of Schooling* required careful attention to the importance of deciding among individuals, classes, or schools as the most relevant unit of analysis. See Kenneth A. Sirotnik, *Psychometric Implications of the Unit-of-Analysis "Problem" (with Examples from the Measurement of Organizational Climate),* Technical Report No. 3. A

Study of Schooling (Los Angeles: Laboratory in School and Community Education, Graduate School of Education, University of California, 1979).

[16] For readers who may object to this apparent separation of the climate factors from the more mechanical aspects of teaching, let me say that both the techniques we used to secure students' perceptions and of observing in the classroom facilitated a useful degree of separation. For a description of the methods in general, see Bette C. Overman, *A Study of Schooling: Methodology,* Technical Report No. 2, A Study of Schooling (Los Angeles: Laboratory in School and Community Education, Graduate School of Education, University of California, 1970). Regarding observational methodology, see Kenneth A. Sirotnik, *What You See Is What You Get: A Summary of Observations in Over 1,000 Elementary and Secondary Classrooms,* Technical Report No. 29, A Study of Schooling (Los Angeles: Laboratory in School and Community Education, Graduate School of Education, University of California, 1981).

[17] For example, see Everett Rogers, *Diffusion of Innovation* (New York: Free Press, 1962); and Dan C. Lortie, *Schoolteacher* (Chicago: University of Chicago Press, 1975).

[18] Kenneth A. Tye, *Changing Our Schools: The Realities,* Technical Report No. 30, A Study of Schooling (Los Angeles: Laboratory in School and Community Education, Graduate School of Education, University of California, 1981), p. 52.

[19] For a glimpse into the nature of such redesigned schools, see Diane Ravitch, "On Thinking About the Future," *Phi Delta Kappan,* January 1983, pp. 317–20.

[20] Space limitations have prevented me from presenting data regarding serious school-to-school differences in curricular balance and within-school practices causing inequities regarding access to knowledge, which discriminate particularly against poor and minority children.

[21] Bruce Joyce, *The Structure of Educational Change* (New York: Longman, 1983).

[22] For more information, see Kenneth A. Sirotnik and Jeannie Oakes, "A Contextual Appraisal System for Schools: Medicine or Madness?," *Educational Leadership,* December 1981, pp. 164–73.

[23] Dorothy M. Lloyd, "The Effects of a Staff Development Inservice Program on Teacher Performance and Student Achievement" (Doctoral dissertation, University of California, Los Angeles, 1973).

[24] John I. Goodlad, *The Dynamics of Educational Change* (New York: McGraw-Hill, 1975).

[25] Richard L. Turner and Richard Kroc, "Is There an Ecology of Teaching Talent?," mimeographed.

[26] Regarding the diminishing effects of increased school size, see John Ainley et al., *Resources Allocation in the Government Schools of Australia and New Zealand* (Melbourne, Australia: Australian Educational Council, forthcoming); and Roger G. Barker and Paul V. Gump, *Big School, Small School* (Stanford, Calif.: Stanford University Press, 1964). Regarding our own data, the largest schools almost always were in the least satisfying group and the smallest in the most satisfying.

[27] See Donna H. Kerr, "Teaching Competence and Teacher Education in the United States," *Teacher College Record,* in press.

[28] Benjamin S. Bloom and Laura A. Sosniak, "Talent Development vs. Schooling," *Educational Leadership,* November 1981, pp. 86–94.

GEORGE H. WOOD

TEACHING FOR DEMOCRACY

What does it mean to educate for democracy? What do schools look like when they focus on students as citizens and neighbors rather than as test-takers and employees? To find out, I have spent the past three years in the classrooms of teachers who see their task first and foremost as nurturing the skills, attitudes, and values necessary for democratic life. These visits have taken me to schools in rural Georgia, New Hampshire, and Ohio; to the cities of New York and Milwaukee; and to the suburbs of Chicago. In every case, these schools are guided by a sense of the democratic mission of public education.

This mission manifests itself in a variety of ways. It can be seen in how adults and young people are treated, how the physical environment is utilized, and how instruction is organized, for example. While there are differences among schools, each and every teacher and school exhibited several common characteristics that can guide us as we work to teach for democracy.

SCHOOLS AND CLASSROOMS AS COMMUNITIES

We take for granted that our schools are communities, when, in fact, they are merely institutions that can become communities only when we work at it. But, with proper attention to all the individuals within the school, we can create an experience for students that demonstrates what it means to be a compassionate, involved citizen. For it is only within a community, not an institution, that we learn how to hold fast to such principles as working for the common good, empathy, equity, and self-respect.

I investigated techniques of community building in each school I visited. At Harlem's Central Park East Secondary School, every student is attached to an advisor. Fifteen students are assigned to a teacher/advisor for two years. These advisors become the point of contact for students and parents with the school. Each group of students meets in advisory for more than three hours a week to discuss academics and personal problems, plan social gatherings (each advisory takes a yearly trip to a college outside of the city), write in their journals, and sometimes just study. Each advisor looks after his or her students for two years, filling out progress reports, meeting with parents, and just being there when a youngster needs a shoulder to cry on.

Thayer Junior/Senior High School in Winchester, New Hampshire, has a similar advisory system. Each teacher (including the principal) meets with seven to ten students at the start of each school day, just to check in. Then, once a month, individual meetings of an hour or longer are scheduled to discuss school and personal issues. Throughout their Thayer careers, students will have only two

From George H. Wood, "Teaching for Democracy," *Educational Leadership* (November 1990), pp. 32–37.

advisors in six years—one for the two years of junior high, one for the four years of high school. The purpose of advisory at Thayer is the same as Central Park East's: to connect every young person with the school.

At Chauncey Elementary in Ohio, students develop a sense of community through their Primary Forum. Every Monday morning the 1st and 2nd grade students and teachers gather in the multipurpose room just to celebrate being together. The session begins with a presentation—maybe someone's grandparent has been on a trip, or a visitor has biked around the country, or a student has made a discovery. Teachers take the time to deal with students' concerns and needs: how to solve shoving on the slide, how to get more paper towels for the restroom, or how to find a new best friend for someone whose neighbor moved away. Before they depart, all participants sing a rousing *Happy Birthday* for all who have birthdays that week, and other triumphs are duly noted and cheered. Then out the door go 70 or so smiling children, hand in hand, ready to face the world with their friends.

Children at Chauncey also spend two years with the same teacher, to make sure that every child has the time to connect with the classroom, feel a part of all that goes on, and have the time it takes to succeed in school. Hubbard Woods School in Winnetka, Illinois, uses similar strategies. There, multi-aged classrooms, teachers staying with kids for several years, and the pairing of older children with younger members of the school community for support and guidance—these are the norm, not the exception. Further, at both schools (and at Central Park East and Thayer) there is no ability grouping or tracking. Children learn in mixed, cooperative groups.

In their efforts to create a genuine community, each of these schools makes the time and space for every child to find a meaningful role in the classroom and school. To build community among young people and adults of differing personal histories, these schools discover ways to create a common history for them in the school—Central Park East's and Thayer's advisories, Chauncey's Primary Forum, and the multi-aged and heterogeneous groups in Hubbard Woods. And, as one student at Central Park East put it, it works: "Our school, we think of it as our community. We know we need to work together. Even if we don't like one another we get over that because we want to work together."

PURPOSEFUL SCHOOL WORK

The moment you step into these schools, you know something special is going on. The first clues are visual. It might be that the halls are full of student projects and art work. Or the absence of posted rules carefully spelling out what one can or cannot do. Or brightly painted murals where one would usually see drab, industrial-strength-green cinder block. Then there are the materials—*not* textbooks—that spill out of every corner of the building. Primary classrooms are brimming with children's books, blocks, string, cardboard scraps, plants, animals, rocks, paints, and assorted theater props. For older children, there is hands-on equipment—tape recorders, cameras, science apparatus, good novels, charts and graphs, and objects of art.

Walk down the hall and notice the physical set-up of these rooms. It's hard to find one with the desks all lined up in straight rows, presided over by a lectern and a chalkboard full of notes. Instead, desks, or just as likely tables, are arranged in small groups throughout the room. Teachers and students have created work spaces for different tasks: an easy chair or two for reading, a table with materials for writing, a darkroom built in a spare corner, or just plain open space for gathering as a group.

Then notice the kids. Moments after you enter the school, they want you to know this is a special place. One child takes you by the hand to show you her painting on the wall. Another offers to read to you from his journal. A high school boy, decked out in a T-shirt proclaiming his favorite heavy-metal band, shares with you an interview he's just finished with an 80-year-old bluegrass musician. First graders offer to reach you a book, and they bring their favorite, the one they just wrote and illustrated. A shy 16-year-old explains her science project which involves an inventory of plant and animal species in the forest next to the school. Her not-so-shy friend then proceeds to whisk you out the door so you can see for yourself the rare specimen they found the day before.

Observe the work going on. Seldom is it quiet, and it's not often teacher-centered either. Children are doing things, not just watching someone else. Learning is not a spectator sport in these schools. You will find class meetings going on, with kids planning the next class project or working out class rules. They are more likely to be working in groups than alone, collaborating to solve a difficult math problem or gathering historical information for a presentation. They are busy writing as they produce their own books, newsletters and newspapers, or videotapes. Or they are very carefully putting the finishing touches on a display of what they have learned about houses, trees, the solar system, Steinbeck, geometric equations, or the Constitution.

The best-known example of this type of work goes on in Eliot Wigginton's high school classroom in Rabun Gap, Georgia. It is here that for nearly 25 years students have turned out the *Foxfire* books and magazines. These books (and now videos, radio programs, and musical recordings) are more than a collection of interviews with Appalachian elders. They are ways of helping students acquire a wide variety of academic skills doing something that really matters—creating a product that will entertain and enlighten thousands of people. "What we do has to be good," asserts one of Wig's students, "because people count on us to get it right."

This ethos of excellence also permeates Bill Elasky's 6th grade classroom in Amesville, Ohio. Three years ago a chemical spill in a local creek launched Bill's kids into becoming experts in water quality testing. Seizing on the moment, Bill and his students met with environmental experts, researched and purchased a chemical testing kit, and sampled all the tributaries to the local watershed. Their classroom became one of the more trusted sources of tests for private wells, and they began producing radio public service announcements on how to maintain safe water supplies. Not to be outdone, students in subsequent years produced a book on the way people use math in their daily lives (complete with interviews, charts, tables, and photographs all done by kids) and built a nature study area for use by all students in the district. These projects cover subject matter in a much more powerful way than any textbook ever has.

Rather than just cover material, these projects help kids see that what they do does matter. For example, the students in Richard Cargill's English class at Willow Brook High School in Villa Park, Illinois, built on the environmental issues raised in his class by convincing local grocery stores to go back to using paper bags rather than the new plastic variety. They also exposed the illegal draining of a nearby wetland and persuaded the school to build a nature area rather than drain land for another athletic field. As Bill Elasky says, "I want kids to see that they can make a difference now, not just in some far off future." Can there be any doubt that this is where the tools of democratic citizenship are developed?

CONNECTIONS TO THE OUTSIDE

Schools with a civic mission open their doors to the world around them. This is how they keep the school community from closing in on itself and how they show their young people the needs and possibilities that will confront them when they leave school.

At Fratney Elementary in Milwaukee, to organize the curriculum, teachers use schoolwide themes that connect the school to its neighborhood. For example, the school year opened with a study of the school's "Riverwest Neighborhood." Students conducted scientific studies of the river, studied the arts from various community museums and artisans, interviewed local residents, and read books from the local library about the area. Throughout the year, students' thematic work was based on the experiences of the residents of this integrated neighborhood of African-, Hispanic-, and Oriental-Americans.

Marcia Burchby, who teaches with Bill Elasky in rural Amesville, Ohio, finds the source of much of her 1st grade curriculum in the world around her school. Stop by the school any Thursday and her room will be empty. You'll find Marcia and her 6-year-olds wandering through town surveying housing types, hunting dinosaur bones, or following a creek to its origin while making an inventory of local wildflowers. Starting from these local origins the curriculum reaches out to the world beyond Amesville, but it is always grounded in the daily experience of the students.

Beyond using the world outside the school as a curricular resource, students at Central Park East provide services to that world: every student spends one morning a week in a community service project. You'll find these young people writing for community newspapers, conducting tours of local museums, assisting in daycare centers, and attending to patients in hospitals or residents of nursing homes. The point of these experiences is not to provide job skills but, as one of the community service coordinators puts it, to "show our kids that they can contribute now. And they are all capable of understanding the difference they can make."

In both learning from and working in their own communities, young people take the first step toward productive, engaged democratic citizenship. When their work begins in a genuine and secure community, when the skills they gain empower them to make a difference, the final and logical step is to make sure the walls of the school are porous enough to allow for a genuine engagement with the world in which our children live. To be a site of democratic education is to be a school where the community genuinely is the classroom.

RECLAIMING THE DEMOCRATIC VISION

These are just a few examples of what the best of our schools are doing to nurture and develop the attributes of democratic citizenship in our future neighbors. These schools are laboratories where democracy is experienced, not museums where it is just observed. I am happy to report that these kids do just fine on standardized tests of achievement. But more important, the young people in these schools will leave knowing what it takes to be an engaged, democratic citizen. They will have the ability to use academic skills to make a difference in the world; a sense of the importance and value of their contribution to their community; a commitment to fundamental democratic values such as equity, justice, and cooperation; and the self-confidence tempered with empathy that it takes to act on behalf of the common good.

The schools I have described are public schools in ordinary circumstances. They suffer from the same funding and political problems every American school has. However, what they do have that makes them extraordinary is a vision—a vision that is clear in everyone's mind and that guides virtually everything that goes on in the school, a vision of students as citizens. It is a vision we need to reclaim and proclaim if we are ever to teach for and reach democracy.

DENNIS LITTKY

CARING AND RESPECT: KEY FACTORS IN RESTRUCTURING A SCHOOL

Here's the situation: I'd just been named principal of a 300-student, rural junior-senior high school and was taking a tour of the building. The school was old and run down and in appalling physical condition. My first impression as I walked along the drab, institutional corridors was that if I were a student I wouldn't be there unless I had to be—unless the law required it.

Everywhere paint was peeling; the windows were cracked and broken.

From Dennis Littky, "Caring and Respect: Key Factors in Restructuring a School," *Democracy and Education* 4, no. 4 (Summer 1990), pp. 3–14.

Every surface was dirty and broken: the floor, the walls, the ceilings. The cafeteria was in the worst condition: gaping holes in the tabletops, some of them measuring 2 feet in diameter; broken chairs; stained or missing ceiling tiles; graffiti on the walls and scratched into the tabletops by bored hands; layers of floor wax over years of accumulated dirt. Even the main office and the principal's office were no exceptions with their torn carpeting, peeling paint, and cracked windows. The impression was the same: drab and uninviting.

I sat down at my desk and was contemplating how to tackle this problem when a 17-year-old boy walked in and said he wanted to talk to me. He told me he was there only because his mother had made him come. He had dropped out of school that year and was drinking. He was down on everything, particularly school and himself. We talked for a while, and I learned he was a self-taught artist. So I asked, "If I could get you a job painting a mural in the school, would you take it?" He said yes.

I called the regional vocational rehabilitation coordinator and asked her if there was any money available to pay this boy to paint the school. She said there was. The next day the boy was back at school surveying the cafeteria wall he had been given to paint, choosing the colors, planning out the design. The subject he settled on was a huge white Pegasus, with flowing mane, ready to take flight. He showed me the design, and I told him I thought it was great. The work began. Every day that summer he painted. When the Pegasus was done, and it was magnificent, he started on the rest of the cafeteria walls, cleaning, repainting, then finishing them with bright geometric graphics. Meanwhile, a crew of students and the new custodian were replacing all the ceiling tiles, making new plywood tabletops, painting the lockers, repairing the windows and, in general, scrubbing and polishing the place.

Throughout the summer people gathered at the cafeteria windows to watch progress on the mural. Bets were made, even among school board members, that the painting wouldn't survive the first day of school. Not only did it survive that first day, but it's still there today, unblemished, nine years later.

The boy returned to school that fall buoyed by daily accolades from his classmates and teachers. As part of his coursework, he painted two more murals—one at the entrance and another in the gymnasium. The following year, he attended Greenfield Community College, majoring in art. His work has served as a model for other students and every year since, at least one mural has been designed and painted by a student.

This example illustrates what I believe is one of the most important elements of an effective school: a solid structure aimed at caring and respect. Such a combination, however, might suggest an anomaly under the conventional definitions of the words "structure" and "caring." There is a tension between them. Structure conjures up images of institutions: solidity, uniformity, discipline, the rigorous application of procedures, rules, standards. Caring suggests sympathetic attention to the individual: subjectivity, malleability, warmth.

A STRUCTURE WHICH INSTITUTIONALIZES CARING

At first blush, the notions of caring and structure may seem at odds with each other. In many respects, I suppose it's fair to say they are, which may underline the complexity (though not the impossibility) of restructuring a school into a caring, responsive, alive place. Often when we consider how best to restructure secondary schools, we crave large-scale solutions: a re-vamped curriculum, a re-designed school day, re-defined roles for faculty and so forth. The notion of caring is taken for granted: of course good teachers care about their students; good students care about getting an education; a good principal cares about the well-being of the school community. Why do we need to structure or institution-alize caring?

Making caring an active, on-going and consistent part of any school requires work and diligence. To be effective, such a process must penetrate all levels—administration, school board, teachers, students and community. Ev-eryone must participate. Often that means restructuring attitudes. For example, how do you deal with a superintendent who swears up and down that he re-spects teachers, but who consistently fails to ask them for their input on matters that directly affect them? How do you deal with a teacher who complains about how unresponsive his students are and takes it out on them by issuing punish-ments, like doubling their homework load, popping surprise tests, or holding them for detention? Both cases are ironic. The superintendent probably genu-inely believes he respects his teachers, but his behavior says he doesn't. The teacher probably genuinely cares about his students and wants them to be responsive, but his behavior says he doesn't.

In both cases, it seems easy enough just to say, "Hey, if you want to show your teachers that you respect them, give them some control," or, "If your students are unresponsive in your classroom, maybe it's the way you're teach-ing. Maybe you're not doing enough to engage them in the learning process; maybe you're spending too much time lecturing and not enough time coaching." On paper, the remedy is simple—in reality, it is very difficult. To change the structure, all (or most) of the players in the structure have to be able and willing to change themselves; to change attitudes, a solid new structure must be in place. It's the old chicken and egg conundrum. So, what's the secret? What's the key to implementing change effectively? For the remainder of this paper, I will draw upon my personal experiences at Thayer Junior and Senior High School to demonstrate some of the steps we have taken to restructure the school, always with the goal of heightening the level of caring and respect exercised at all levels.

That brings me back to the anecdote at the beginning of the paper and how that ties in with efforts to structure caring and respect. Here's a boy who was down on himself, down on life and all of a sudden somebody in a position of authority told him the school needed him and gave him a wall, a 7-by-30-foot school wall, to do with as he wanted. It was his responsibility; he knew that whatever he painted would be on display for everyone—his family, his class-mates, his teachers—to see. He knew that if he succeeded, he would do it himself. He would have ownership in the school and pride. Indeed, through the efforts of one boy, the school was a cleaner, brighter, more inviting place to be. The endeavor went a long way toward helping build that young man's self-esteem and also made a very important statement to anyone passing through the halls. When school reopened in September, student and teachers entered a different building and a different school. The physical changes plainly showed that somebody cared enough about the school to clean it up. That physical evidence helped clear a path for the more important message: that the school system cared about its people.

The physical condition of the building, however, was not the most significant problem facing Thayer High School in 1981; it was just one of the most visible. The dismal school building was symptomatic of deeper, more serious problems lurking in the school. The most important task was to pinpoint the source of those problems and to work to remedy them quickly. The changes had to be in place for the start of school; they had to be dramatic and very visible. Students had to know unequivocally that things were different, that school was not a place to avoid or a system to beat, but a place that played a crucial role in their future.

I met with anyone associated with the school—parents, students, administrators and teachers. I did a lot of talking and a lot of listening. The image of the school was deplorable. It was a common joke around the region that if you couldn't spell you must have attended Thayer. Tension was everywhere: between students and teachers, parents and school, administration and teachers, and on and on. It wasn't as if the teachers had not been working hard the year before; they had been. The problem was with the big structures, the hapless leadership, and the lack of a unified aim or plan. Though many staff members toiled diligently and had good ideas, their energy was scattered as it didn't fit into any kind of masterplan. The teachers had the energy and the desire, but without an organization to support and use that energy, the school foundered.

The condition of the school, its reputation and the tension all had to be remedied within the constraints that came with being a poor, rural school. Winchester's welfare rate was the highest in the county, and the unemployment rate double that of the state as a whole. Because there were few industries in the community and because state aid to education in New Hampshire was the lowest in the country, the local taxes needed to support the schools were disproportionately higher for Winchester's residential property owners. Ironically, a community that was the least able to afford it had some of the highest taxes in the state. Whatever programs or resources were sought had to be culled from somewhere other than the local taxpayers' pocketbooks. The task was to learn how best to use ourselves, the community and others—how to beg, borrow and inspire help and enthusiasm for the school.

I made a public statement to the community that Thayer would be the best junior-senior high school in New Hampshire. It would never have the most kids going to college or the highest SATs, but it would be the most appropriate school around. Appropriate meant that we would provide an education meeting the needs of the rural Winchester students and get the school and the students out of the trap of "just getting by." At that point, most of the students and staff had settled into a pattern of just muddling through. Individual attention to students' needs, abilities, desires, and goals was practically non-existent. There was no concerted effort to try to help students know their own strengths or an effort to build on them. Exceptions to this rule were rare and couldn't be handled well in the *laissez faire* system that existed. . . .

TRACKING DOWN THE PROBLEMS

Throughout that first summer, I . . . met individually with all the teachers. I asked all of them what worked and what didn't work, and what were their personal strengths and weaknesses, their goals, ambitions, and dreams. I asked everyone what they would change in the school.

Ideally, it would have been best to meet as a group with the teachers to work out the changes together, but unfortunately, the short time between my hiring and the start of school made that difficult. So I put together a laundry list of problems that needed tackling, based on all those interviews and meetings, and then built a schedule. This was the list of problems:

- Students' disrespect for teachers and each other.
- Students only taking the minimum number of courses required by the state.
- Conflicts caused from 12-year-olds mingling with 18-year-olds, and by high school teachers being required to teach at the junior high level.
- Poor condition of the building.
- High rate of absenteeism.
- Large numbers of dropouts.
- Students hanging out on Main Street during school hours.
- Students lacking future plans.
- Not enough college-bound graduates.
- Students and teachers fearing for their safety at school.
- Poor image in the community.

These problems could be traced to two fundamental issues: a poorly structured school day and a lack of respect. Changing the schedule, by far the easier of the two tasks to accomplish, had far-reaching implications that helped lay the groundwork to build respect. Under the old structure, students had unruly, aimless schedules that often left them with too much time on their hands. That contributed to the overall apathy which took the form of absenteeism, dropouts, discipline problems and vandalism. While it might be relatively easy to change the schedule and get students on a purposive educational track, apathy would continue to flourish if something weren't done to heighten respect. That required changing something much more elusive: people's attitudes.

All fingers couldn't be pointed at the students either. If students believed the administration and teachers don't value them as individuals and don't treat them with respect, how can the administration and staff expect respect from the students? If the community has little regard for the school, how can the students be expected to respect it? Students need to know it's their school, too, that they have ownership in it, that they can make a difference. The murals by the 17-year-old were a demonstration of that attitude of mutual respect. The school respected the youth enough to call upon him to undertake an important project and the youth took the project seriously enough to do a good job. That, in turn, improved the appearance of the building as well as the attitudes of those who spent time in it. It also helped set the tone for the changes in how classes were chosen, scheduled and taught. Without that restructuring, the problems might have been eased, but they could never have been eliminated. A poorly structured school day guaranteed certain problems would continue.

The schedule is one of the most important structures in the school. It determines when a student goes to class, what classes are available, the possibility of setting up alternative programs, combined classes, and scheduling student conferences and staff meetings. If the schedule supports and facilitates the school's goals, the task of teaching relevant, engaging and meaningful courses is greatly eased. Scheduling and class content should be a main focus of discussion for everybody. It is the basis for everything that is going on in the school. Often, though, the schedule is something that many principals take for granted, and toss out to a guidance counselor to draw up.

The problem at Thayer was very simply that the majority of students had too much time on their hands. Students had little incentive to load up their days with classes if they could get by with only taking two or three and fill the rest of the day with study halls. Study halls provided students excuses not to do anything academically and all the freedom they wanted to act up. If a student dropped a class, there was always a study hall to take its place. Teachers dreaded supervising study halls, and those students who wanted to use the time productively had to do it in the midst of mayhem.

So, study halls were eliminated. I called the New Hampshire Department of Education to find out the minimum number of hours a school had to be in session daily, and was told 5 1/2. I shortened the day to that exact time, my theory being that at present we weren't doing school very well for 6 1/2 hours, so we'd be better off spending less time, but doing it well. Individual class time was extended from 45 minutes to an hour, and the number of periods were cut from 8 to 5. Because of the fewer class periods, all teachers agreed to teach all five periods. The school day lasted from 8:50 a.m. until 2:40 p.m., freeing up enough time before and after school to hold teachers' meetings and student conferences. Teachers were able to spend more time concentrating on improving class content and helping individual students and less time playing the role of custodian or policeman.

The minimum state graduation requirement was 16 credits: four in English, two in social studies, one in math, one in science, one in gym and the remainder in electives. I increased the graduation requirement at Thayer to include additional math and science credits. Although I don't think that just adding courses guarantees anything, in this case it was the simplest way to get students involved in the curriculum.

The bell system was also eliminated, except to signal the start and end of the school day. This had many positive effects, such as eliminating the chance of a bell rudely interrupting a good classroom discussion at precisely the wrong moment. It also eased the crunch of students and chaos at class change, because all 300 students did not flood the hallways at exactly the same moment. The junior high classes (which are housed in the same building as the high school) were organized on a different time schedule from the high school, thus easing traffic flow. Teachers were also able to dismiss students when they were finished with their business (within a 5-minute period), rather than be abruptly interrupted at an inopportune moment. The absence of bells also acknowledged that people knew how to tell time and didn't need to be reminded every hour.

NEW STRUCTURES FOR STUDENTS

That first summer, I also met with all the high school students for at least 30 minutes each. The overt reason for the conferences was to become acquainted with the students and to set up their schedules. The less obvious reason was to learn from them what their needs were. As administrators, we can sit around and think about what children need to know to equip themselves for life after graduation. Sometimes we might hit it right; at other times, though, we might completely overlook something very important.

One thing that became clear to me is that high school is especially important for non-college bound students because it is their last connection with formal education; it is our last chance to help a student be a self-learner for life. If a student is not going to college, then we must look at the high school curriculum in a different manner. The curriculum must prove itself useful for life, not for what we think colleges want. We want to prepare students to achieve, to produce, to reason, to be happy, to be responsible, to communicate. We want to develop the desire for continuous learning in all of our students. We want all of our students to choose a place in life, not be forced into one because they lack the skills or energy.

Schools must be sensitive to the tremendous physical, emotional, and intellectual upheaval adolescents face; a school's structural composition must reflect that sensitivity and be responsive to those needs. Again, we're talking about the structure of respect and the structure of caring interaction. Students need to feel that school is a safe place, a place where they won't be punished indiscriminately, where the rules are clearly stated, as are the consequences of violating them. Rules of discipline at Thayer were few: No smoking, drinking, drugs, or physical violence. If there was a violation, parents were notified, and the students might be suspended from school for a period of time. Often, parents and child were asked to come to school for a conference to discuss the behavior problem and to work together to solve it. That solution might be in the form of a contract with the parents, the student and the school: "I agree to control my temper and not lash out at others. If I violate this, I will be suspended for five days." The effort was always to make it clear to the student that what he or she did was wrong, not that he or she as a person was wrong. Again, the intent is to say to the student, "I respect you as person, but I won't tolerate this misbehavior."

Students need to feel that school is a place where their strengths and energies are nurtured and applauded, where they matter as human beings, where they have control of themselves and their successes. Beyond the traditional academic curriculum, several structures were put into place to try to meet the wide variety of needs the students had. Here's a sample of some of the major programmatic and structural additions.

Advisory System

Terri, a Thayer High junior, entered my office at 7:20 one morning. "Doc," she said quietly, "I have to tell you something." I knew by the tone of her voice it was something very serious. "I'm pregnant," she said. I gripped the edge of my chair. Terri was one of my advisees. We had been working together and talking since she was a freshman and had developed a mutual respect and friendship for each other.

I didn't express my approval or disapproval. My job was to support Terri in any way I could and help her to continue to get an education. We talked and talked and talked and eventually worked out a plan that would make that possible. "I don't think I would have stayed in school if it wasn't for him," Terri says now, " 'cause I just felt like everyone was going to alienate me and make it weird, and he told me they would look at me as a person. He just stood behind me and pushed me." When her daughter, Elizabeth, was born, Terri was the president of the junior class and an honor roll student for the first time. As a senior, she was again class president, was accepted at a paralegal school, and plans to become a lawyer.

Adolescents need consistency and stability in their communications with adults. Often, schools whisk students through the day in a series of 45-minute periods, rarely allowing students and staff much of a chance to get to know one another. Rarely is there anything built into the program to allow children to look at the total picture of what is happening to them and to have guidance and support in the process. The advisory system provides such a touchstone. Every teacher is designated as an academic advisor to a small group of students, a person who will help those students develop a planned program of study over the years, a person who provides consistency, support, and advocacy for the child.

Each morning, advisors meet with their groups for about 10 minutes, much like a homeroom system. The time is used to make announcements, discuss school issues, share things that have been happening to members of the group, plan group functions, take attendance, discuss current events, and, in general, provide a pleasant, calm beginning to the day.

The half hour before school starts in the morning is often used for individual meetings between advisor and advisee. The private meetings, about 10 for each student a year, are used to help plan the students' schedule, to talk about classroom progress, personal problems, or whatever else might come up. Advisors are friends, counselors, and advocates for students in all school situations. They provide the main link between parents and the school; they act as sounding boards for the students' ideas or as ombudsmen in helping the child work out a problem with a teacher, parent, or peer. As one student put it, "My advisor is not just my advisor; he's my friend." The advisor is responsible for knowing enough about his or her advisees to make proper recommendations to parents and teachers about the child. If a crisis emerges, the advisor is there to speak out on the student's behalf and to try to provide a more complete perspective of the child.

The structure is also there so the student can talk seriously and openly to an adult. The structure doesn't make any demands on the student to develop a deep interpersonal relationship with an advisor; it simply gives the student assurance that there is an adult who will listen. The point is that without this structure, communication is limited and so, therefore, are understanding and trust. In a crisis, two people cannot suddenly develop trust. It must be built beforehand. The advisory system helps make that possible.

The advisor also serves as a friend and link to parents. The advisor is the one who reviews the quarterly progress reports that are sent home. Teachers send all grades and comments about a student to that child's advisor and also meet frequently with advisors to talk about an individual student's progress. The advisor then collates and reviews the information, and passes it along to the parents. The bi-annual parent conferences also give parents, advisors and students an opportunity to develop the best educational experience possible for the child. The fact that each advisor is there to help his advisees succeed in school leads to real individualized instruction. Consider a situation in which a classroom teacher was working successfully with a majority of his class. In most cases, one would say he was a successful teacher. However, what about the minority of students who aren't involved? Those students can take their frustrations to their advisor and, together they can work out a solution to the problem. The advisor, in turn, makes the teacher aware of that student, focusing the teacher to constantly work to make the class appropriate for all students. Whether the solution to the problem is a tutor, an alternative program, or just a modification of the existing structure, the advisor, teacher and student work together toward a solution.

Some advisors plan activities outside of school. One advisor, for example, has taken his group skiing, out to eat at a fancy restaurant, and to a symphony. Having the advisory system as a part of the school structure helps students understand that there is a system available for them to work out problems, to plan, and to be understood. This, in itself, is a good exercise in developing problem solving skills.

For example, during an incident involving the theft of some granola bars from the school, three students were sent to my office as suspects. I knew there were more than three students involved, but I didn't know who. The three in my office refused to tell. I asked again, and one student said, "I want to see my advisor," sounding much like an arrested man demanding to see his lawyer. The advisor was notified and he and the student talked together in another room. When the two returned, the advisor told me the names of the others involved in the theft. The student felt comfortable telling his advisor and the advisor served as an advocate for the student.

Getting the teachers to accept the added responsibility of an advisory system might seem problematical at first. But if teachers truly care about students and understand the merits of the system, they will quickly find that their time with students is made more meaningful and productive as a result of the system. From the beginning, I involved teachers in working out the specifics of the advisor program. That gave them ownership in the process and a solid share in its success. Of course there will always be teachers who buck the idea and resist participation. Those teachers are tactfully told that they must fulfill the minimum requirements of the program, or they won't be teaching at Thayer.

Life after Thayer

One of the most important things I learned from those first meetings with students was that very few Thayer students knew what they were going to do upon graduation and many hadn't even thought about it. Enter a new course: Life After Thayer.

The once-a-week class, taught by several teachers, was mandatory for seniors and was graded on a pass or fail basis. Its basic function was to expose seniors to careers in and out of town, to study relevant social issues they might encounter as adults, and to teach them practical life skills, such as apartment hunting, handling budgets, bank accounts and interviews. But beyond that, and in some ways more importantly, it created a safe environment for students to talk about serious, pressing or personal concerns. The classes were small, about 8 to 10 students each, and were organized by gender. Over the years, students have come to expect that LAT is a class in which they can talk about nearly anything they want and not feel threatened that the information will leave the room or that they'll be graded on it. If students attend class, they receive passing grades.

The LAT class I teach has less instruction from me than from the students. I try to sit back and let the students decide what the topic will be that day and then let them go with it. If they want to know something practical, I can help them. If they want to talk about careers, sex, or relationships, they can. Each week we have topics we want to discuss that help students think about their lives now and after Thayer. Here are some of the questions students have asked that served as the basis for classroom discussions:

"If we can dream it, why can't it happen in real life?" "I need to talk about the marines. Should I go or not? I'm confused." "Can we talk about Bobby? You know he won't be graduating with us now that he put himself in a drug and alcohol rehab center."

Last year, James, one of the boys in my LAT class, came in exasperated by a junior high school boy he was tutoring. "I can't believe how hard it is to teach. I hope I wasn't as bad as that when I was Richard's age. Was I?" He was. Like Richard, when James was in 8th grade he had drinking and behavioral problems and wasn't doing well in school. We talked about those old times and how far he had come. "What happens over the years?" James asked. "Why couldn't I know then what I know now? How come it took me so long?"

I responded, "You should be thankful you are beginning to understand yourself now and be happy it's happening when you are 18, not when you're 28 or 38."

Apprenticeship Program

The more I talked to students, the clearer it became that all the students' needs could not be met within the existing school. Thayer lacked the staff, the materials, and the money to provide the broad range of courses and experiences the students needed. The traditional curriculum just didn't inspire every student to get excited about school, nor did it meet the expectations of some of the highly motivated to gifted students. So the teachers and I began looking outside the school and into the community for help. That triggered the apprenticeship program.

The nursery school in town was called: "How many students can you take?" The elementary school and the retirement center were contacted, and a junior high tutorial program was set up. More and more students signed up and before long we had 65 high school students out of 225 working at apprentice sites. As the word spread, people stopped me in the street or called the school asking, "What are these apprentices? Could I have one?" The list grew—the beauty shop got involved, as did the gas station, the insurance company, the bank, the power equipment store, the local newspaper.

Even with all this enthusiasm, however, such experience-based programs may risk being miseducative. To try to prevent that from happening, the school (with help from a grant) employed a full-time director to oversee all the apprenticeships. The director was in constant contact with the site supervisors to make sure the students were performing satisfactorily and to work with the supervisors in making the student's apprenticeship a productive learning experience. The director made frequent visits to the various sites and required that students keep a weekly journal of their activities and what they had learned from them. In a few situations, the school determined that a particular apprenticeship was not a healthy learning environment and those apprenticeships were terminated.

The structure of the apprenticeship program had many of the virtues of a work/study program, but few of the drawbacks. It put students in a different learning environment where they could get a true taste of the work-a-day world and all that means. For example, it meant writing a resume and interviewing for the position; it meant learning the value of punctuality, following a dress code (if the business had one), working, and meeting a schedule. Although students weren't paid, they still had to perform to the employer's expectation or risk being fired. But the apprenticeship program did much more than that.

The program allowed students to explore careers they were interested in, to see those careers from the inside out and to roll up their own sleeves and give it a try. Students who were thinking about enrolling in nursing school, education, or secretarial school could spend an hour every day for a semester finding out exactly what it would mean. In some cases, it sealed a student's desire; in other cases, it told students this was not what they wanted to pursue. The students had to keep daily journals of their experiences which were checked by English teachers for grammar, content, and creativity. Students were also required to prepare a semester project utilizing their knowledge and skills (which could take the form of an in-depth paper, public presentation, or other demonstration).

Each student in the apprentice program worked with a site supervisor, someone in a career who agreed to work with the student, monitor the student's performance, and be in close contact with the school. Many site supervisors owned businesses; some were highly educated, some highly skilled, but all had expertise and something to teach.

Over the years, the program has been highly successful in appealing to a broad range of students and answering a broad range of needs. For example, we hooked one student, who was a computer whiz who quickly mastered everything we had to offer at school, up with the math and computer department at a local college, where he could also receive college credit. Another student was really foundering in school. His grades were bad, and so was his attitude about school. He and his advisor met to discuss the problem and try to work out a curriculum that would keep him in school. When his advisor learned he was interested in autobody work, he suggested the student contact the owner of the autobody shop in Winchester and see if he could organize an apprenticeship. Excited, the boy immediately called the body shop.

The site supervisor let the student watch all phases of the business and then gave him small jobs to do. Eventually, he loaded him with books and pamphlets about autobody work, which the boy devoured, and sent him to an out-of-town workshop. One day a car was brought in that had been severely damaged in an accident. The owner told the boy to take a section of the car and do the repair work. And he did. Another time, the owner of the body shop said he was swamped with work and was getting farther and farther behind and desperately needed help. So he asked the student to do a couple of major repair jobs on his own, figuring that even if they had to be done over again he would still be further ahead. Much to his delight, the jobs were completed perfectly. That semester, the student made the honor roll for the first time.

There are dozens and dozens of stories like these: students on the brink of dropping out or bored by school who were turned on and turned around by an apprenticeship. Of course not all apprenticeships are wildly successful; sometimes students are fired (itself a good learning experience), and sometimes the experience just adds another dimension to a student's curriculum, but doesn't cause any bells or whistles to go off.

INTEGRATING THE CURRICULUM

The Dovetail program, the two-week exploratory, and team teaching were all efforts to integrate the curriculum and open up the learning process for students. One of the unfortunate messages communicated to students through the traditional 50-minute classroom structure is a sense of disconnectedness. Math has no connection to English, history has no connection to science, and so on. Instead, each class is packaged neatly into the 50-minute structure, and, at the sound of the bell, gears must be shifted for another neatly packaged 50-minute course that has nothing to do with anything else. Since that's not how life actually operates, schools should be places where connections are made and where children are taught to constantly think in those terms.

The Dovetail program was an effort to take a holistic approach to the entire curriculum. Four teachers ran the program—three full time and one part time— and about 50 students were admitted with their parents' permission. Dovetail became a school within-a-school, where the entire school day was dedicated to learning not by subject, but by project, with each project incorporating as many aspects of learning as possible. The teaching team was made up of a math, science, and English teacher and a versatile aide. Those teachers worked together constantly to develop forums for learning. One of the first projects was to build a post and beam house in the style of the early Winchester settlers. The project incorporated math, architecture, science and history and required extensive research of the building techniques and architecture of the 18th and 19th centuries. In addition, students had to keep daily journals about their activities. The journals were graded for content, grammar, spelling, punctuation, and creativity. When the building project was finished, the house became their classroom.

Another project involved exploration of a nearby cemetery. Students, under the guidance of a teacher-historian, researched the names of the deceased to find out what roles these people played in the development of the region. The project involved trips to the library, the archives, and the registrar of deeds. The students took rubbings of the stones, analyzed the artwork and the religious and poetic embellishments, and later conducted an archeological dig of an historic area close to the cemetery.

Students spent hours sifting through the information at the registrar of deeds office, and developed a genuine fascination for the history of the area. One of the unforeseen consequences of the experience was the creation of a new bond with a teacher, who before was viewed as hardnosed and boring by the students. Instead of the straightbacked lecturer clad in skirt, jacket and wearing a bun on her head, they saw her in action, wearing blue jeans, walking happily through mud to point out a bit of history and working side-by-side with them. They discovered she had a wealth of knowledge on the history of the area, and the more excited they became about the project, the more they learned from her, and the more they respected her.

The Two-week Exploratory was a major work in the regular curriculum. The idea of working together in integrated teams came from a teacher and was embraced by the rest of the staff, which worked for a half day on planning in randomly organized teams. That spawned new ideas and more enthusiasm for the endeavor, which eventually turned into the "Two Week Project." For two weeks, all regular classes were suspended, and students and teachers became intensely involved in one of 11 cooperatively-designed two-week courses devised and taught by teams of teachers.

The Exploratory was intended to give teachers an opportunity to team teach, work at integrating the curriculum and break down the barriers of a six-period day. Each team was made up of three teachers from three different disciplines. Each team then devised a course that would draw on the expertise of each member, and give the students necessary work in such basic skills as reading, writing, computing, and critical thinking. Breaking down the barriers of the six-period day became structurally simple—each team was responsible for its students all day.

Course options ran the gamut: a re-enactment of the original settlers' journey into Winchester, a health education course of adolescent girls, a course that studied the interrelatedness of art, architecture and nature.

Teaching basic and essential skills became the focus of the program: emphasizing reading, writing, speaking and problem solving through a variety of themes and projects. Whether students were creating inventions or studying the poetry of Emily Dickinson, the endeavor required students to speak and write clearly and to think logically through a problem. Students were evaluated on their exhibition of these basic skills in a number of forms—public speeches, personal journals, or demonstrations.

"Who Art Thou?" the course on nature, architecture and fine arts, allowed 7th and 8th graders to explore the Clark Art Institute and the Boston Fine Arts Museum, take those impressions back to Winchester with them to study the local architecture. Then students translated those observations into their own oil painting, wax sculpture, or post-and-beam model. One student wrote, "In regular class they tell us and tell us, but here *we* discovered it."

Because of that project, teachers began incorporating team teaching in the regular classrooms. Teachers working together tend to improve their classroom planning, preparation and success. And by looking at one course from the perspective of teachers in two different disciplines, the students are constantly making connections they might have missed under the traditional structure. Several years ago we started formally organizing ourselves for team teaching in all grades. Next year we will be teaming at all grades.

SOME FINAL THOUGHTS

The most important resource a school has is its teachers. All the creativity, energy, and good ideas possible will get a school nowhere if there isn't cooperation among the staff members and between the staff and the administration. The school as a whole must embody energy, creativity, and productivity, and in the end, the school's sum will be far greater than its parts.

Cooperation takes hours and hours of working together. Innovations can't be forced from high up in the administrative hierarchy if a project is to succeed. The ideas have to come from the teachers. People will work harder if their ideas are the ones they're trying to carry out. An administrator telling the teachers what they're going to do is only communicating how little respect he or she has for the staff. Besides, no administrator alone will ever come up with as many good ideas, plans, and procedures as a group of hardworking, highly respected teachers.

We constantly have to ask: How can we better share our resources? Where can we go for more? What kind of new curriculum is possible? Are we doing what we're doing well, and, if so, how can we make it better? Finding answers to these questions gives a school life, and with constant self-questioning, it will grow.

It starts with strong leadership. Without it, little or no restructuring will take place. The leader, typically the principal, prepares the climate for change. He or she looks at the big picture and then works with the staff, students, administration, community and school board to develop a common vision. But by no means does s/he call all the shots or impose her or his will on everyone else. Restructuring is a process that involves everyone. The more people involved in coming up with creative solutions to problems, the more good ideas there will be to work with. The more responsibility is given out, the more responsibility is assumed. When everyone has a stake in the process, everyone wants to see it through. That's the theory, anyway. The reality is not nearly as slick as all that—less like a supercharged locomotive and more like an ornery mule. The process requires incredible patience, persistence, stamina and hard work. It also takes guts and a good sense of humor.

DISCUSSION QUESTIONS FOR CHAPTER 13

1. Discuss the major points Dewey makes about the relationship between school organization and democracy. How do these points effect his theory of pedagogy?
2. Compare Goodlad's "ecological" model for schooling with Dewey's vision of education in the early twentieth century.
3. In what ways do the schools Wood refers to and the work of Littky in New Hampshire reflect both Dewey and Goodlad's ideals?
4. Which model of school reform—that of Dewey, Goodlad, and Littky, or that proposed by President Bush and Reagan—will actually change the ways schools are organized and run?

Index

Index

Accountability, 320
Achievement, 304
  of blacks, 10–11, 31–32
  tests, 31
Adler, Mortimer, 299, 302–304
Affirmative Action, 41, 43, 44
African-Americans, 9–13, 41–50, 60,
  90–92
Alger, Horatio, 115
Alternative teacher certification,
  320–321
American-Indian, 61
American Spelling Book, 114
Anderson, Margaret, 76
Anyon, Jean, 157–172
Apple, Michael, 157
Aptitude tests, 45, 102
Aristotle, 3–4, 73
Ashbrook, John, 16
Autonomy of schools, 276–279

Bank Street College of Education,
  70
Barnard, Henry, 115
Basic skills, 295–296, 309–311
Beecher, Catherine, 69, 70
Bell, Terrell H., 36–41
Bernstein, Basil, 157
Bestor, Arthur, 295–296, 300
Bilingual education, 15–16, 99

Bilingual Education Act (1968)
  (1974), 15
Bill for the More General Diffusion
  of Knowledge (1779), 113
Binet, Alfred, 55
Black:
  English, 61
  flight, 13
Block grants, 48
Bobbitt, John Franklin, 120–121,
  136–145
Bourdieu, Pierre, 157
Bowles, Samuel (and Gintis,
  Herbert), 64, 157
Boyer, Ernest, 299, 302–304,
  326–331
Brown v. Board of Education of
  Topeka (1954), 6, 10, 11, 13,
  27–29, 41, 60, 124
Bureaucracy , 195–201
  opposition to, 203–204, 209
Bush, George, 280, 300
Busing, 12–13, 33, 43–44
Butts, R. Freeman, 268

Capitalism, 6, 117
  critique of, 148–152
Cardinal Principles of Secondary
  Education (1918 report),
  290–292